SO-AGR-169

"Immanuel Ness has added another book to his excellent series for understanding the survival strategies of the politically most profound, yet most deprived, section of the citizens during the last almost five centuries. I expect this book to stimulate fresh debate on what depoliticization of the working class amounts to. Besides, after reading the chapters in this work, the question that haunts the liberal minds is why is this unprecedented intolerance of capitalism occurring at a mature stage of its development? Autonomist restoration is born of the spectacle of irrationality. Its impulse is to demand order in the midst of chaos; it protests, it demands, it insists that the outrage be brought to an end. These essays are most likely to throw challenges to the conventional economics of collective bargaining."
—Debdas Banerjee, professor of economics, Institute of Development Studies, Kolkata, India, and author of *Labour, Globalization and the State*

"Manny Ness has brought together essays that illuminate the most important questions of our time: not only can the labor movement rise again, but can the democratic and transformative currents which sometimes inspired the movement in the past reemerge today. These essays explore these questions over time, and across the globe, making a real contribution to labor's rebirth." —Frances Fox Piven, distinguished professor, City University Graduate Center, author of *Challenging Authority* and *Poor People's Movements*

"By organizing a strike or going out on the street to protest with demands against the bastions of capital, labor activists rarely think about the historical significance of what they are doing. This collection of vivid chapters of major labor struggles reveals the essential nature of the labor movement in the last quarter century. Here in Russia, this book will be very useful as we need to learn the international experience of workers' struggles."
—Vadim Bolshakov, trade unionist, labor movement activist, historian of the Russian workers' movement, and author of several hundred publications

"All those who are fighting for the overthrow of capitalism must be grateful to Immanuel Ness and his team for this new book, which continues the worldwide exploration of new forms of organization and conflict of workers against the rule of capital on humans, environment, and nature." —Piero Bernocchi, national spokesman, COBAS (Cobas Federation) and author of *Benicomunism: Fuori dal capitalismo e dal "comunismo" del Novecento*

"This book is a crucial analytical and tactical handbook for workers protesting against management. In most cases, protests, strikes, and insurgencies are only measured through government data. *New Forms of Worker Organization* provides independent information on workers' protest, their reasons, and the nature in which they are realized—essential for understanding the true shape of the workers' movements in countries throughout the world. This research should be used by workers and labor unions as a tool to reach their objectives and to protect and advance workers' rights." —Vadim Borisov, representative of IndustriALL Global Union, CIS Region, sociologist, and author of over one hundred publications on workers' movements in Russia

"*New Forms of Worker Organization* offers abundant insights on labor struggle in an era when familiar unions seem exhausted or at least too weak and tired to make a concerted effort with concrete examples of workers forming independent unions throughout the world. Get this book and think afresh!" —Paul Buhle, coeditor of *It Started in Wisconsin* and author of numerous works on syndicalism

"This remarkable international collection shows working-class power being built from the ground up by rank-and-file workers self-organizing to create new forms of autonomous, democratic organizations. Grounded in a reclamation of histories from earlier struggles, a strong critique of bureaucratic unionism, and an unapologetically anti-capitalist framework, it offers fresh, compelling analyses, vital conceptual tools—and hope—for the local and global fight for freedom from exploitation, today and tomorrow." —Aziz Choudry, coeditor of *Organize! Building from the Local for Global Justice*, and assistant professor, Department of Integrated Studies in Education, McGill University

"The pseudo-dilemma set to all working people, 'work or starve,' echoes louder today in Europe, Asia, the Americas, and worldwide, where unemployment and poverty are increasing as social provisions are collapsing. Under these circumstances the formation of autonomist workers' organizations and the detailed labor struggles explored in *New Forms of Workers Organization* is necessary for the counterstrike, and towards a long-term political general strike." —Dimitris Dalakoglou, University of Sussex

"Analytically brilliant and empirically sound, a must read for all to grasp the power of workers' self-organization. A superb portrait of the trajectory of independent workers' struggle, a *porteur d'espoir* for the future of class struggles." —Sushovan Dhar, author and independent trade union activist, Indian National Trade Union Initiative

"As the U.S. labor movement conducts its latest, frantic search for 'new ideas,' there is no better source of radical thinking on improved modes of union functioning than the diverse contributors to this timely collection. *New Forms of Worker Organization* vividly describes what workers in Africa, Asia, South America, and Europe have done to make their unions more effective. Let's hope that these compelling case studies of rank-and-file struggle and bottom-up change lead to more of the same where it's needed the most, among those of us 'born in the USA!'" —Steve Early, former organizer for the Communications Workers of America and author of *Save Our Unions: Dispatches from a Movement in Distress*

"*New Forms of Worker Organization* is a significant contribution to understanding the forces propelling the assault against worker organizations as capitalist-driven imperialism extends throughout the world. The book examines how foreign direct investment in the Global South and beyond expropriates the labor of workers and extracts natural wealth in the ineluctable search for profits. Given the contemporary assault against traditional unions formed in the twentieth century, this book provides dramatic contemporary case studies of worker resistance to corporate exploitation and state violence against unionization in chapters with examples drawn from Africa, the Americas, Asia, and Europe through the formation of militant organizations in factories and within their communities." —Bill Fletcher Jr., activist and author of *"They're Bankrupting Us!" and Twenty Other Myths about Unions*

"A dynamic, exciting book! It provides an answer to *Nickel and Dimed*. Alongside the revolt of some of Barbara Ehrenreich's 'Walmartians,' the book chronicles other finely calibrated campaigns from around the globe designed to put power back into the hands of the workers. These green shoots—or 'seeds'—provide inspiring road maps for direct action organizing based on cooperation, imagination—and the resourcefulness of the human spirit." —Jane Latour, author of *Sisters in the Brotherhoods: Working Women Organizing for Equality in New York City*

"A welcome, provocative, and necessary book! While the inarguable truth of this collection's premise—that *in the United States, as elsewhere throughout the world, unions have continued to decline and the wages and conditions of unorganized workers have worsened dramatically*'—could leave one feeling as hollowed out as the labor movement itself, the opposite proves true. Manny Ness and the contributing authors have built a sturdy platform for readers to observe and assess case studies of autonomous, militant, worker-driven, struggles from all points of the globe. Their forms and strategies are divergent, honestly evaluated, and not readily reduced to formulaic categorizations (thank goodness). There is an essential and vital need for this exploration, because bidding goodbye to our post–New Deal labor institutions can feel hopeless; this book shows us it is not." —Ellen David Friedman, visiting scholar, International Center for Joint labor Research, Sun Yat-sen University, Guangzhou, China, and Labor Notes Policy Committee

"Working people everywhere are feeling the pressure in a world where corporations increasingly dominate our economic, political, and social lives. In country after country, traditional unionism, advocacy, and policy reform have been proven unfit for the task of restoring the dignity and financial security of working families. The critical stories of cutting-edge organizing found in *New Forms of Worker Organization* demonstrate that workers themselves hold the key to creating a world where work is honored and freedom of association is absolute. I feel deeply grateful to benefit from this hard-won insight and creative thinking on how to change the world and I know you will too." —Daniel Gross, executive director, Brandworkers, and cofounder, IWW Starbucks Workers Union

"This book, like none other that I know, will move the dialogue about new forms of worker organization into the arena of serious political and social thought. *New Forms of Worker Organization* is simply the best global survey in English of new union formations of what has been called solidarity unionism." —Andrej Grubačić, author of *Don't Mourn, Balkanize!*, coauthor of *Wobblies and Zapatistas*, and professor and department chair of Anthropology and Social Change, California Institute of Integral Studies

"This book is exactly what we need—the experience of workers all over the world inventing new ways to organize from the bottom up! You must get this book now—it is the roadmap to our future." —Frank McMurray, Inlandboatmen's Union, the Marine Division of the International Longshore and Warehouse Union

"*New Forms of Worker Organization* tells us how democratic forms of worker organization can overcome the limitations of conventional labor unions and challenge capitalist exploitation. While internet mobilization has captured a lot of attention in recent years, the case studies remind us of the revolutionary potential of the working class movement. A stimulating book which should interest students, activists, and academics committed to building a world without oppression." —Lee Chun Wing, Hong Kong Polytechnic University

"This exciting collection provides substantial evidence that collective action by workers themselves is indispensable to advancing a strong labor movement. The book's global scope demonstrates that workers in the U.S. and beyond can learn much from the tactics, strategies, and the historical struggles in other countries. Its broad historical and geographic sweep firmly conceptualizes labor as a world phenomenon." —Kim Scipes, author of *AFL-CIO's Secret War against Developing Country Workers: Solidarity or Sabotage?*

"Ness and the contributors to this volume do an excellent job of calling our attention to a form of union organizing that has the potential to save the labor movement and to reignite the struggle for a better world beyond capitalism. This book is essential reading for anyone who wants to understand the past and present of class struggle unionism around the world, which class-compromise unionism had eclipsed for a long time, but which is now poised for a well-deserved comeback." —Gregory Wilpert, author of *Changing Venezuela by Taking Power*

"Conventional unionism's decline over recent decades and now capitalism's worst global crisis since the 1930s are enabling and provoking unconventional forms of workers' struggles. Some are new and others are new versions of old forms with urgently renewed relevance today. Received concepts and theories of class, class struggle, economic democracy, workers' power, socialism and communism are being reexamined and changed to meet the practical needs and conditions of anti-capitalist struggle now. Immanuel Ness's new volume documents some dramatic new projects of self-conscious class struggle around the world." —Richard D. Wolff, Democracyatwork.info and the New School University, New York

"We are living in a stage of capitalism where capital's onslaught on labor has been more intensive but at the same time the effectiveness of traditional labor organizations in defending workers' interests has also been called into question. In China where the union mainly serves the interests of the state and capital, it should not surprise us if workers develop new forms of organization to defend their rights and interests. This book provides a wide range of case studies of experiments and experiences on alternative organizing for workers all over the world who see collective autonomous workers' power as the key to end exploitation."
—May Wong, executive director, Globalization Monitor, Hong Kong

"We need more collections of intrepid essays like *New Forms of Worker Organization*, which reminds readers about how the inventiveness and courage of ordinary people shape history. The remarkable diversity of cases—from India to Italy, from South Africa to Sweden—makes this anthology a 'must read' for those who are troubled by modern capitalism and wonder where alternatives to neoliberalism might come from. A gem of a book." —Cyrus Ernesto Zirakzadeh, professor of political science, University of Connecticut

New Forms of Worker Organization:
The Syndicalist and Autonomist
Restoration of Class-Struggle Unionism

Immanuel Ness

New Forms of Worker Organization: The Syndicalist and Autonomist Restoration of Class-Struggle Unionism
Immanuel Ness
© 2014 the individual contributors. This edition © 2014 PM Press.

All rights reserved. No part of this book may be transmitted by any means without permission in writing from the publisher.

ISBN: 978-1-60486-956-9
Library of Congress Control Number: 2013956926

Cover by John Yates / www.stealworks.com
Interior design by briandesign

10 9 8 7 6 5 4 3 2 1

PM Press
PO Box 23912
Oakland, CA 94623
www.pmpress.org

Printed in the USA by the Employee Owners of Thomson-Shore in Dexter, Michigan.
www.thomsonshore.com

Contents

FOREWORD   Staughton Lynd   **v**

INTRODUCTION   New Forms of Worker Organization   **1**
Immanuel Ness

I. Autonomist Unions in Europe and Asia

CHAPTER 1   *Operaismo* Revisited: Italy's State-Capitalist Assault
on Workers and the Rise of COBAs   **20**
Steven Manicastri

CHAPTER 2   Autonomous Workers' Struggles in
Contemporary China   **39**
Au Loong Yu and Bai Ruixue

CHAPTER 3   Collective Labor Protest in Contemporary Russia   **62**
Piotr Bizyukov and Irina Olimpieva

II. Organizing Autonomy and Radical Unionism in the Global South

CHAPTER 4   The Struggle for Independent Unions in India's
Industrial Belts: Domination, Resistance, and the
Maruti Suzuki Autoworkers   **84**
Arup Kumar Sen

CHAPTER 5   Exploding Anger: Workers' Struggles and Self-
Organization in South Africa's Mining Industry   **97**
Shawn Hattingh

CHAPTER 6   Neoliberal Conservation and Worker-Peasant
             Autonomism in Madagascar   115
             Genese Marie Sodikoff

CHAPTER 7   Sintracarbón: On the Path to Revolutionary Labor
             Unionism and Politics in Colombia   131
             Aviva Chomsky

CHAPTER 8   The Formation of a New Independent Democratic
             Union in Argentina: The Subte Transport Workers
             Union   147
             Darío Bursztyn

III. Organizing Autonomy and Radical Unionism in the Global North

CHAPTER 9   Syndicalism in Sweden: A Hundred Years of
             the SAC   168
             Gabriel Kuhn

CHAPTER 10   Doing without the Boss: Workers' Control
             Experiments in Australia in the 1970s   184
             Verity Burgmann, Ray Jureidini, and Meredith Burgmann

CHAPTER 11   Revolt in Fast Food Nation: The Wobblies
             Take on Jimmy John's   205
             Erik Forman

CHAPTER 12   The IWW Cleaners Branch Union in the
             United Kingdom   233
             Jack Kirkpatrick

CHAPTER 13   Against Bureaucratic Unions: U.S. Working-Class
             Insurgency and Capital's Counteroffensive   258
             Immanuel Ness

             EDITOR AND CONTRIBUTORS   279

             NOTES   285

             INDEX   309

Foreword

Staughton Lynd

Almost before we knew it, an "alternative unionism" is on every radical's agenda.

And this is true not just in one or two countries but, as this important book demonstrates, all over the world.

In the United States, the existing mainstream unionism has the following features among others:

1. Unions compete to become the "exclusive" bargaining representative of a so-called appropriate bargaining unit. The employer has no legal obligation to negotiate with a union made up of a minority of its employees.

2. When a given union has been "recognized," the employer becomes the dues collector for the union. Every employee has union dues deducted from his or her paycheck automatically.

3. The union concedes to the employer as a "management prerogative" the right to make unilateral investment decisions, such as shutting down a particular plant or workplace.

4. The union deprives its members of the opportunity to contest such decisions by agreeing that there will be no strikes or slowdowns during the duration of the collective bargaining agreement. Nothing in United States labor law requires this fatal concession.

This was the pattern that John L. Lewis sought to establish in the United Mine Workers and to impose on incipient CIO unions. Roger Baldwin of the American Civil Liberties Union, who was familiar with the aspirations of the breakaway Progressive Miners of America in Illinois, opposed the National Labor Relations or Wagner Act for this reason.

As editor Ness sets out in his Introduction and chapter, the Communist Party of the United States (and, it seems, elsewhere) accepted these restrictions on self-activity for a political reason. After projecting a strategy of ultraleftism from 1929 to 1935, the international communist movement adopted in 1935 (the same year that the NLRA was enacted) the Popular Front strategy of uniting all progressive social forces in opposition to Nazi expansion and an attack on the Soviet Union. At least at the national headquarters level, this strategy entailed coalescing with Lewis in the CIO and with the national Democratic Party. We are still picking up the pieces from these exaggerated, top-down strategic reversals.

Meantime, as these chapters so richly report, a qualitatively different practice is evolving everywhere. It is horizontal rather than vertical. It relies not on paid union staff but on the workers themselves. (If these chapters have a weakness, it is that only one of the authors, Erik Forman, appears to qualify as such an inside agitator.)

I am reminded of a dream I had more than fifty years ago. While living in a "utopian" community in northeast Georgia, my wife and I along with our neighbors spent a long Sunday afternoon fighting a forest fire that had ignited from a family's picnic campsite. Suddenly, in the dream, I realized that I could stop my incessant activity, something else had taken over. Slowly it came to me. It had begun to rain.

So it is today, at this living moment, as all over our globe workers reach out hands, first to their workmates, then to other workers everywhere. "In our hands there is a power / Greater than their hoarded gold / Greater than the might of armies / Magnified a thousand-fold / We can bring to birth a new world / From the ashes of the old / For our union makes us strong."

Staughton Lynd

New Forms of Worker Organization

Immanuel Ness

This book examines workers' responses to the relentless efforts of contemporary capitalism to transform the workplace as institutionalized labor unions have declined as the dominant model of worker representation worldwide. Existing labor unions have proved incapable of mobilizing mass rank-and-file militancy to resist the ongoing deterioration in workplace conditions and the systematic erosion of workers' power. As capitalism pushes ever harder to reverse the labor gains established in the early to mid-twentieth century, workers are developing new forms of antibureaucratic and anticapitalist forms of syndicalist, council communist, and autonomist worker representation, rooted in the self-activity and democratic impulses of members and committed to developing egalitarian organizations in place of traditional union bureaucracies. In turn, these new forms of representation, which are gaining currency throughout the world, are expanding the democratic capacity of workers to advance their own economic, political, and social interests without external intermediaries.

We critically examine the rise of contemporary forms of worker representation, drawing from examples throughout the world. The case studies in this book challenge the widespread perspective among progressives and leftists that a reinvigorated but conventional unionism is the best institutional means to counter neoliberalism and financialization. We maintain that the alternative means workers are pursuing to advance their own interests through self-organization are more relevant to today's workers than institutional and bureaucratic compromises with the capitalist class and state. These case studies demonstrate that the new workers' organizations are descendants of the socialist and anarchist labor formations of the late nineteenth and early twentieth centuries.

The global decline in organized labor from the 1970s to the 2010s and the ascendance of neoliberal economic policies have led to the erosion and declining relevance of traditional unions. This book examines new configurations of workers' organization that have rejected collective bargaining and corporatist models in favor of direct action and autonomous organization. As unions decline, this collection provides evidence that workers are rejecting traditional labor-management-state bargaining structures that have collapsed around the world.

The book reveals that workers' movements are forming through militant self-activity, autonomous action, and relentless opposition to the status quo. The 2010s resound with echoes of the 1930s, when a militant working class challenged the hegemony of capital in the United States, and after passage of labor reforms during the depths of the depression, engaged in general strikes, and occupied mass production industries in 1937 and 1938. The AFL and the CIO recognized the intensity of worker rebellion, and both federations strove to mobilize and consolidate a militant industrial workers' movement struggling for recognition of its existence and control over the conditions of labor-management relations.[1]

The new forms of worker organization under examination are typically rooted in the class solidarity that emerges in the workplace and community. They seek to counter the growth of precarious labor and reformist labor relations by cultivating democratic structures at the point of production, and they envision a society free of capitalism.[2] In this collection, some of the new forms establish a prefigurative politics of worker organization, setting the basis for the transformation of the entire economy. As workers engage in sit-down strikes, they contemplate the necessity of actual alternatives to capitalism through worker control and self-management. The collection focuses on country studies and specific case studies in the global North and South and demonstrates that syndicalist and autonomist formations are growing worldwide and forging new forms of authentic workers' organizations. While no single example embodies an ideal type of syndicalism, autonomism, or other form, each chapter reveals that through a variety of tactics and strategies, workers themselves are forming independent and democratic unions fundamentally opposed to bureaucratic domination, class compromise, and concessions with employers—the *sine qua non* of traditional unions the world over.

From Rank and File to New Forms of Union Representation

This book draws attention to this vital yet neglected sphere of new democratic labor movements and organizations in a field in which attention has been overwhelmingly and unduly focused on revitalizing and expanding membership in existing labor unions, often without the direct involvement of the workers themselves. In some instances, union leaders negotiate agreements with employers that exclude members from the right to organize and form unions in other geographical locations. No wonder workers are losing confidence in traditional unions. Syndicalist labor unions that originated in the late nineteenth century were motivated by sabotage, direct action, and strikes—forms of militancy that traditional unions ceded to capital and the state after their consolidation of power in the 1930s to 1960s. Viewed as the denizen of direct action, by the 1980s, labor unions, with representatives as intermediaries between workers and capital, transformed the organizations into powerless victims seeking to protect "their" long-suffering members. In the absence of the capacity to strike, union leaders and advocates appealed to the importance of creating a benevolent society. David Graeber asserts: "All this makes it easy to see why the question of 'direct action' has been so often at the center of political debate. During the first half of the twentieth century, for example, there were endless arguments about the role of direct action in the labor movement. Today, it is easy to forget that, when labor unions first appeared, they were seen as extremely radical organizations."[3]

These days, conventional membership in a union is frequently not even improving conditions for those who have depended on strong and powerful leaders to negotiate wage increases in exchange for increased productivity. Today's labor unions are typified by cautious and stodgy leadership, lack of participation by membership, and political strategies aimed at lobbying liberal and social democratic politicians for modest gains. Traditional unions and their allies, once-powerful organizations that gained through legislative and parliamentary action following the mass struggles by workers in the early twentieth century, are now reduced to appealing, mostly without success, to the ethical principles of the liberals in the electoral arena.

Certainly, the desolate state of what many call "the Left" deserves a book unto itself. The contributors to this collection consider the necessity of worker self-activity to be paramount to the formation of workers' organizations and are skeptical of the capacity of traditional union efforts to improve conditions for disengaged workers who have little or no say in organizing, bargaining over wages, benefits, and conditions, or even the right to defend themselves against employer attacks in the current era of neoliberal capitalism. While the state and capital always seek to erode worker power, since the 1930s, union leaders have been eager to offer concessions to management to secure labor peace, undermining the power that workers have through their own self-activity. Perhaps the most patent example of declining worker power is the ubiquitous union agreement to trade away the right to strike. Staughton Lynd and Daniel Gross assert that workers are typically excluded from negotiating with management and are often unaware that the right to strike, their most lethal weapon, is lost given that "the ordinary worker has very little control over what goes into his or her contract. It is pure fiction to say that the ordinary union member has knowingly and voluntarily given up, or 'waived,' the right to strike."[4]

In the last twenty years, labor historians, social scientists, and union organizers have written countless pages prescribing remedies for rebuilding established unions to the perceived grandeur of the past through devoting greater resources to organizing, making contributions to union-friendly politicians, hiring young organizers from elite universities, and implementing variations of social-movement unionism directed at building alliances between communities and labor organizations. The abject failure of the efforts by traditional unions to apply these formulations for rebuilding labor has rendered these books less pertinent, to say the least, and should caution workers against relying on such prescriptions. Union advocates have argued that labor laws have diminished their capacity to organize new members. Some have sought to evade the strictures that prevent unionizations,[5] while others have pursued efforts to convince legislators to mitigate the restraints on unionization and collective bargaining.[6] In the United States, as elsewhere throughout the world, unions have continued to decline and the wages and conditions of unorganized workers have worsened dramatically. In the global North, traditional union leaders have turned their attention to organizing service-sector workers as more workers enter these labor markets. However, most organizing efforts have failed due to fierce employer resistance and the exclusion of workers from campaigns. In the 1990s, organized labor relied on professional bureaucrats and the formation of organizing centers to create what they viewed as an effective and reliable cadre of altruistic, loyal, educated, and professional staff. Today, as in the past, bureaucratic unions have repeatedly revealed a fear of worker self-activity that could potentially challenge the dominance of staff-controlled organizations.

New Forms of Worker Organization:
Syndicalism, Council Communism, and Autonomism Syndicalism

The origins of what we can call "new forms of worker organization" can be traced to the historical experiences of syndicalist movements that started in Europe around 1895 and expanded through North America, Europe, Africa, Australia, and beyond in the ensuing years. Rooted in a revolutionary opposition to capitalism, the primary characteristic distinguishing syndicalist labor organizations from other labor organizations was the centrality of workers rather than designated union leaders or delegates acting as representatives or supportive intermediaries with employers. Emma Goldman defined syndicalism as those organizations that advocated a "revolutionary philosophy of labor conceived and born in the actual struggle and experience of the workers themselves."[7]

This book documents the formation of new models of worker self-activity and rank-and-file participation, a principal foundation of class-struggle unionism prevalent in the early twentieth century, as expressed through the Industrial Workers of the World (IWW) in the United States and related syndicalist formations worldwide that opposed collaboration with management. As employers avoid recognition of traditional labor unions, new syndicalist formations are expanding dramatically with the same outlook and objective: employers are untrustworthy and workers must organize to defend themselves and to improve wages and conditions without the traditional intermediaries that seek compromise that ultimately undermines the power of members.

Direct action is a set of tactics rooted in worker self-activity and dedicated to defending the power of workers against bosses through escalating collective efforts that build solidarity and power. These tactics prevailed among the IWW (Wobbly) unions of the early twentieth century.[8] Syndicalism's principles of direct action and sabotage include the following:

- All forms of action are advanced by workers themselves, not by union officials or bureaucrats, who are often aligned with management.
- Opposition to all forms of collaboration with management.
- Independence from all electoral political parties that can reliably act on behalf of employers to constrain workers' direct action.
- A culture of worker solidarity on the job and in local communities and neighborhoods through cultural expressions that build class

consciousness, as was customary among Wobbly unions, including disseminating literature on worker unity.

- At work, workers exhibit unwavering unity through wearing buttons or hats displaying allegiance to an independent union that is an expression of their own aspirations for democratic control over the enterprise.
- The strike is the principal strategy to achieve concessions and gains from management. Withholding labor and interfering with management's efforts to extract productivity from workers to achieve immediate advantages over employers at the time—on the job—when workers' actions are most effective.
- The greater goal of achieving a general strike among workers in a given location, motivated by broader class solidarity and featuring militant activity—including seizing control over production.
- Opposition to the collective bargaining agreement (CBA) that circumscribes the capacity of workers to engage in direct action. The CBA may bring orderly benefits but has limited guarantees for workers and distorts the innate contestation for power in the workplace every day by making job actions illegal during the course of the contract.

In the early twentieth century the IWW reflected the organizational aspirations of dispossessed exploited workers, mass production workers who recognized their power to exercise control over industry and represented a tangible means of seizing control over capital through militant and self-directed representative unions. Buhle and Schulman argue: "By joining an industrial union, workers prepared themselves to take over society directly. Working people who understood their own power had the capacity to act upon their fundamental right to expropriate and share with other workers across the world everything that they collectively produced; an objective that remains to this day."[9]

Literature on anarchism and syndicalism is almost entirely historical, drawn from the late nineteenth to early twentieth centuries. The vast majority of research on rank-and-file, syndicalist forms of unionization consists of important historical contributions circumscribed and limited by country and region.[10] These contributions significantly inform studies of the primarily early twentieth-century workers' and peasant movements.[11]

Council Communism as a Labor Formation

Council communism is a historical form of worker representation rooted in a Marxist analysis locating class struggle at the point of production. As such, authentic unions must account for the dialectical social relationship between worker and owner that takes the form of an unremitting struggle for power over all aspects of the enterprise. The objective of a council communist union is to create the conditions for forging a proletarian revolution that would lead to the emancipation of the working class directly by workers.

The council communist workers' organization is a labor union that sustains a prefigurative objective to establish the democratic practices and procedures of union organization that are anticipated following a successful workers' revolution.[12] While maintaining the features of a future revolutionary union, the council communists also engage in political struggle to attain a democratic society derived from rank-and-file and community participation. The archetype of council communism is represented by the workers' committees organized by German shop stewards beginning in 1914, culminating in the 1918 German Revolution. These formations are found when bureaucratic unions become detached from the day-to-day lives of workers who seek to operate independent of the constraints of traditional unions. I call contemporary council communist unions "parallel unions" existing within the interstices of traditional unions; these parallel unions engage in direct struggle and resistance against the dictates of the managers on the shop floor or in the enterprise. Through direct struggle, parallel unions develop workers' class consciousness in opposition to capital and reinforce democratic practices that challenge union bureaucracies, corporate domination, and the liberal and left approach of seeking compromise through legal remedies. The practice of democratic worker representation is not unitary and exists within many unions where traditional leaders are discredited and new forms of struggle emerge outside the legal norms of class compromise. As we shall see in the chapters to follow, rank-and-file movements that are often embedded in traditional unions in the United States, Europe, South Africa, India, China, and beyond are resisting concessions and defending their own rights through unauthorized work-to-rule campaigns, direct action, and sabotage. Traditional unions ignore such conditions at their own peril:

- Unions that represent only a portion of workers.
- Unions in which the leadership has nebulous ties to members, or conditions are such that the union as a force is absent and workers may not even have awareness of an actual union.
- Union formations that are not officially recognized by state labor law, legal authorities, or established unions. Frequently, management is

more responsive to the demands of internal parallel formations or organic demands of the workers than to those of organized unions, as a consequence of traditional unions' failure to offer a viable, tactical strategy for workers to build power.

Autonomist Labor Unions

Autonomous Marxists maintain that under traditional union structures workers are reduced to marginal third parties who have no power to defend their interests through class struggle against capitalist domination. As such, autonomist labor unions are distinct from council communist unions that mobilize workers through shop stewards in parallel formations within traditional unions or in secrecy against employers who refuse to acknowledge their presence. In contrast, autonomists seek to mobilize workers and build power as independent unions within enterprises and firms openly and, in most instances, without the support of traditional unions.

In Europe in the late 1960s, autonomism was the primary successor to syndicalism and council communism and posed a major alternative to traditional unionism. Expressed in a multiplicity of regions worldwide, autonomism emphasizes direct worker opposition to capitalist domination and rejects the political compromises adopted by leftist movements in the early to mid-twentieth century in the developed countries of Europe and the Americas.

Autonomism emerged in Italy during the "Hot Autumn" of 1969 and involved syndicalist tactics of sabotage, strikes, occupations, and collective action. The autonomist formation—*operaismo* in Italian—developed at a time of rank-and-file workers' resistance to traditional unions in Germany, the Netherlands, Switzerland, Sweden, and North America, continuing throughout the 1970s, in response to the decline of worker power on the shop floor and the institution of post-Fordist production methods that reduced the capacity of trade unions to confront management, undermining wages and living conditions.[13] In Italy, operaismo took the form of direct action in the workplace and in the community through the refusal to pay rent, and bills for electricity, and other necessary services—without the support of the official trade unions forged by socialists and communists a half-century earlier. In doing so, autonomist workers and community associations were engaged in a tactic, rather than wantonly jeopardizing the lives of workers and their families. When necessary, autonomist unions will negotiate with the state and capital to achieve interim solutions but not the class compromises of traditional unions. In Italy, autonomist unions faced massive state repression through Operation Gladio (as part of the Strategy of Tension), which sought to eliminate all vestiges of opposition to the state. Although operaismo's power declined afterward, the movements have found new life in the formation of Cobas (Confederazione dei Comitati di Base; see chapter 2).

Autonomists reject the capitalist state as impartial arbiter and seek to form independent unions unbound by labor laws, which are viewed as inadequate and ineffective in representing their interests. Autonomist unions have assumed a litany of forms since the 1970s; they do not consider traditional trade unions as legitimate representatives of most workers, but rather as defenders of privileged, elite members with ties to union leadership and the employer. In their place autonomist unions have developed democratic worker-controlled structures that are held directly accountable to members.

As we will see in the chapters that follow, autonomist labor unions have a wide range of ideological perspectives that often depend on the political economic conditions and historical legacies and traditions that characterize each society. On a global scale, the heterodoxy of autonomism spans an ecumenical range of antiauthoritarian ideological positions rooted in the Marxist tradition, distinct from syndicalist formations but still allied in their opposition to hierarchy.[14] They are analogous to syndicalist and council communist forms in their opposition to hierarchy, yet they recognize that to survive they must remain flexible and occasionally compromise with capital and the state to defend their material interests and ensure the survival of their members. Autonomist labor unions engage in a politics of tactics: they are capable of maintaining a commitment to class struggle while rejecting rigid ideological positions that undermine the reproductive material survival of their members.

Whether they be syndicalist, council communist, or autonomist, this book endeavors to examine an array of new forms of union organization that are crucial to understanding labor and the working class today. Its major contribution is the range of contemporary and global cases of labor organizations from which we can learn relevant lessons for application by workers today. Building on important regional studies focused on new unions in Africa, Latin America, and the United States,[15] the examples of rank-and-file unionism in this work add a global and local perspective, incorporating a political dimension of autonomist and syndicalist practices that offer a significant and prescient analysis to many workers.

Background

Most observers of labor, management, and union activity since the 1960s have concluded that working-class power has been diminished by the changing structure of capitalist production, and that growing job insecurity has undermined, rather than generated, class consciousness and militancy. The essays herein suggest, on the contrary, that worker organization is taking new forms, including new models of unionism, emerging in a growing range of previously unexplored contexts, and centering less on a return to traditional bargaining models than on innovative demands, methods, and organizing approaches. Worker militancy is not exclusively propagated within traditional trade unions or left political parties; nor, the case studies show, is it confined to mass industrial sectors. Rather, rank-and-file unionism is expanding beyond, into the complex, transforming nexus of community and workplace.[16]

Labor relations from the 1920s through the 1960s were increasingly managed by states through a combination of repression and institutionalized bargaining, wherein workers' gains were powerfully conditioned by the fortunes of relatively closed national economies. However, an important feature of the contemporary neoliberal phase of capitalism is the replacement, in the global North, of mass workplaces by flexible and smaller establishments, as wage and benefit costs come under pressure. Consequently, patterns of bargaining resting on secure jobs and mass production have declined, with corporatist social dialogue systems either marginalized or rendered impotent as the conditions for sustained class compromise disintegrate in the face of economic crisis and changing labor markets. In the global South, precariousness proliferates alongside the growth of manufacturing industry, and corporatist structures, rather than enabling social democratic outcomes as in an earlier period of analogous manufacturing growth in Europe, facilitate rather than challenge neoliberal restructuring.

A substantial literature on contemporary labor movements claims that these problems can be addressed with a combination of union pressure, adroit policy interventions, and alliances with friendly political parties. There is, however, little in the record of nominally Left governments, North or South, over the last three decades to support such hopes. Most newly elected governments, whether nationalist, socialist, or democratic, have embraced the neoliberal orthodoxy; others have flirted with an authoritarian populism that leaves little space for workers' autonomy. Yet, as traditional unions contract, their leaders are more inclined to cooperate with management than to unleash the self-activity of their members.

As traditional unionism, resting on institutionalized class compromises and peak-level bargaining, struggles to adapt to the new era, vibrant new forms of worker organization, North and South, have demonstrated a remarkable capacity for innovation. Mass unionism in semi-industrialized countries in the imperialist world of the South has partly sidestepped the bureaucratization and centralism of classical Northern unionism to develop powerful subsections with an explicitly revolutionary agenda. Matching this has been an upsurge in workers' movements, North and South, which are consciously inspired by syndicalist and Marxist ideals and opposed to both contemporary capitalist hegemony and the capitalist state.

These rank-and-file, antibureaucratic labor movements inform the focus of this collection on new forms of worker organization. While not all the examples take a *sui generis* anarchist shape, they represent a range of new working-class organizations rooted in workers' self-activity. Similarly, we define the new syndicalist and neosyndicalist movements that have formed in the past twenty years as characterized by the use of democratic organization and militant direct action to humanize work and wages, with a long-term commitment to a self-managed, socialist, and stateless future. These should be distinguished from the other autonomous workers' formations under examination, which share much of their anticapitalist and radically democratic sentiment but display a more eclectic and contested outlook. This collection covers a range of cases, spanning six continents, and represents the first effort to document these forms of militant unionism in the contemporary era.

Changing Shape of Worker Organization: Global South and North

This book is devoted to historical and comparative case studies and assessments of new working-class organizations that have emerged in the global South and North to address the transformation of the workplace following the decline of the Keynesian welfare state. In the advanced capitalist countries, the radical and insurgent impulses of impoverished working classes were constrained and restricted through a range of social policies from the 1930s to the 1970s; in the past decades, these programs unraveled through the introduction of neoclassical national policies aimed at reducing costs by outsourcing production to low-wage regions of the world. As these neoliberal policies undermined welfare-state benefits and eroded union contracts that provided satis-factory wages, labor unions have circled the wagons and negotiated con-cessionary agreements that provide job security for a fraction of their members while most workers lack fundamental protections: job secu-rity, living wages, health benefits, and pensions. Labor unions will rep-resent only privileged workers, resembling the labor aristocracies that preceded mass production, leaving large numbers of workers deprived of the benefits expected by previous generations.

In contrast, workers in the global South are subjected to low-wage industrial jobs with intensified work rules, dangerous conditions, and no job security. As existing unions in old industries seek to protect a shrinking share of new production, most new workers are employed as subcontractors in the "informal" sector, producing goods for major multinational corporations at wages that do not provide for basic needs. Working under dangerous conditions, they are vulnerable to severe forms of exploitation and are frequently unable to defend themselves.

The chapters in this collection all seek to provide case examples illustrating the failures of traditional union models and examine how each struggle unfolded within the political economy:

- What political, economic, and social forces contribute to the found-ing of a new, democratic form of labor unionism?
- Details on the unfolding of events that helped shape the develop-ment of a new labor union, and on the particular as well as universal experiences that are driven by unique social and economic forces and social relations in each country and case.
- Outcomes of the worker-organizing drives and an appraisal of the larger political-economic and individual factors that brought about the specific results.

Each chapter will show how ideological currents within the politi-cal landscape affect organized labor movements and trade unions, the majority of which were established following the implementation of national laws defending workers' rights in the early twentieth century. The growth of bureaucratic labor union structures expanded workers' representation through the support of the state during World War II and thereafter. However, following the consolidation of trade union power in the 1950s, in most countries of the global North, membership declined in response to employer opposition and, in the 1980s, to the emergence of neoclassical economics as the sacred dogma of the state and capital. On the Left, ideological movements in developed countries and the Soviet bloc unraveled as market mechanisms were enforced in the liberal democratic capitalist regions as well as in nominally socialist countries that had broader working-class protections.

As of 2010, even as economic crisis spread throughout the world, all countries had been forced to embrace the neoliberal dogma of financialization by opening trade and undermining workers' rights. Traditional labor unions had lost efforts to facilitate expanded worker organization as governments, irrespective of ideology, severely reduced social protections and restricted the ability of workers to defend against the disappearance of their rights. Today it is clear to most of the organized and unorganized working class that challenging the dictum of neoliberalism will require mass movements. A central question for the Left is whether the remnants of the old economic order could be salvaged—or were even worth salvaging. Young workers have no stake in a system that offered low wages, limited democratic rights, and few options for the future. Increasingly, workers of all age groups are beginning to recognize that the economic crisis is a permanent fixture of the current capitalist world and the need to join in solidarity to build a meaningful workers' movement. These studies will provide comparative and historical background for analyzing the current predicament and offer possibilities for advancing workers' rights in the future.

Structure of the Book

The book is divided into three parts. Part I is a historical examination of country studies from Europe and Asia that provide a framework for comprehending the contemporary crisis of workers' organizations and the origins of the capital-labor compromises that were institutionalized by states. The case studies demonstrate that rank-and-file labor unions have been successful in advancing working-class militancy and, as a result, states and capitalists have endeavored to help established bureaucratic trade unions to restrain the power of workers. These chapters demonstrate that the failure of working-class organizations is embedded in the constitution of the modern bourgeois state and the function of existing labor unions as allies and intermediaries of capital. In Italy during the 1960s and 1970s autonomous union organizations formed during an economic crisis that initiated a state and capitalist offensive against traditional workers' organizations.

The failure of traditional unions prompted the rise of working-class militancy and of local rank-and-file associations known as Cobas (Confederazione dei Comitati di Base). The autonomist Cobas have become a model adopted by workers organizations to various degrees throughout the world as an alternative to traditional trade unionism.

In China, where capitalist enterprises operate under the dominance of the Chinese Communist Party and the All-China Federation of Trade Unions (ACFTU), new struggles of autonomous workers in China for a democratic independent unionism attest to the unvanquished power of a revived workers' movement. In post-Soviet Russia, new insurgencies and protests are forming unions that are challenging the dominant, Soviet-legacy organizational forms of labor representation. The distinctive features of collective labor protest are contesting the system of labor-capital relations, expanding the potential for syndicalist forms in the vacuum created by the decomposition of traditional organizational forms without power to represent the working class. Labor protests contest the new "social partnership" model, demonstrating opposition to both bureaucratic statist unions and the European "social partnership dialogue" within the oligarchic capitalist system.

Part II examines the rise of new forms of union organizations in opposition to new and rapacious forms of capitalist industrialization in the global South. Two chapters examine the rise of police and state repression against independent unions in India and in South Africa. The first charts the rise of independent unions in India's new industrial belts, which employ workers who are denied the right to establish independent organizations even as traditional unions become less effective. Dominated by new rules of foreign direct investment, the Indian government has undermined the ability of traditional trade unions to maintain safe and humane working conditions. While the trade unions had achieved gains for a fraction of the Indian working class, the rise of neoliberal capitalism has undermined conditions even further and helped initiate the formation of a new workers' movement in the rapidly growing industrial sectors of the economy. Independent unions are forming outside of the parliamentary framework and are challenging the domination of the capitalist Indian state, foreign direct investment, and the weak and compliant trade unions.

Next, we examine the rise of independent unionism among mineworkers in post-apartheid South Africa. In both the Indian and South African cases, the states have responded to workers' militancy with direct state repression, including arrests, incarceration, and armed raids. In both states, police and state militias are joining with private security forces to injure and kill workers, most infamously in the minefields of South Africa. However, as the traditional unions fail to represent their members' interests, wages and working conditions erode substantially, as does workers' confidence in traditional forms of labor representation. By 2014, mass strike waves have shifted the focus toward opposing the new economic apartheid in South Africa.

The next chapter examines the development of a worker-peasant autonomist union in Madagascar that is dedicated to biodiversity and ecological preservation. Rejecting the model of conservation and development established by the state, the autonomist workers' unions in rural Madagascar are challenging the institutionalized neoliberal concept of conservation and development promoted by international capital, the state, and NGOs, while advancing a rank-and-file workers' movement committed to knowledge and preservation of the ecology of protected regions through a new discourse of autonomist conservational unionism. The autonomist union that maintains the right to survive in an ecologically sustainable condition is suggestive of the more widely known Zapatista peasant struggle in Mexico's state of Chiapas in opposition to the neoliberal doctrine imposed by the North American Free Trade Agreement.

The next two chapters examine the rise of international solidarity organizations in Colombia and the formation of a new union representing subway workers in Argentina. In Colombia, we examine the unprecedented revolutionary struggle of Sintracarbón (the National Union of Workers in the Coal Industry) to expose the deleterious environmental consequences of the mine on the impoverished surrounding indigenous and Afro-Colombian communities. Sintracarbón workers gained the support of international human rights organizations to expose the environmentally hazardous practices at the Cerrejón coal mine and the company's attempt to break the workers' union in response to demands that the mine negotiate compensation for displaced residents who were forced to move from the surrounding community. The fifteen-year struggle has unified workers and community members against a multinational that exports coal to the United States, Canada, and Europe. In Buenos Aires, subway workers organized a rank-and-file movement to form a new democratic union through decertifying from the bureaucratic transportation union and mobilizing and achieving a cooperative model of representation through the formation of the Cuerpo de Delegados del Subte. Known as the Subte Union, the new workers' union encourages democratic participation and represents the interests of the working-class members and surrounding community.

Part III examines three case studies of syndicalist and autonomist organization in the global North that are rooted in tactics and strategies of solidarity and direct action.

Chapter 9 examines the Central Organization of Swedish Workers (SAC), founded in 1910, a syndicalist union that remains active and represents a counterforce to the dominant Swedish Trade Union Confederation (LO). SAC remains dedicated to radical rank-and-file unionism in the tradition of the IWW in the United States and the Confédération Générale du Travail in France. For more than a century, SAC has maintained its opposition to capitalism and commitment to workers' control and self-activity in determining wages and working conditions and belief that direct action is more effective in gaining concessions than negotiations with management. In the early twenty-first century, as the LO has failed to recognize and respond to the changes in the Swedish labor market, the SAC has gained prominence for supporting worker organization among immigrants and other precarious workers in low-wage sectors of Sweden's economy, including night clubs, restaurants, and other service sectors employing undocumented and temporary migrants at low wages and under poor conditions.

Chapter 10 examines Australian rank-and-file struggles in the 1970s that provide a foundation for new syndicalist and autonomist worker movements within unions. In "Doing without the Boss: Workers' Control Experiments in Australia in the 1970s" the authors examine the rich modern history of workers' movements that shaped a militant culture in their unions that challenged traditional business unionism and stimulated worker occupation and control among construction, mining, and industrial workers. The sit-downs and worker occupations demonstrate the compelling aspirations among workers to challenge capital even before the imposition of neoliberal reforms from the 1980s to the early 2000s. While most labor historians have waxed nostalgic for the past, the Australian workers' movement provides resounding testimony that if the labor movement is to revive, workers must reject unions and leaders that rely on outmoded statutes which contribute to unremitting compromises and concessions with management and challenge business and capital through autonomous direct action.

Next, chapter 11 examines the contemporary resurgence of the IWW in the United States has expanded widely through the formation of active branches. Founded in 1905, the Wobblies were at their peak from 1910 to 1918 through a tactical organizing strategy of industrial unionism, direct action, and rank-and-file organizing. As the mainstream American Federation of Labor (AFL) and Congress of Industrial Organizations (CIO) adopted similar strategies, the IWW waned, although it remained relevant through the twentieth century. In 2005 the IWW celebrated its centenary in Chicago. Even while at a nadir, the union's commitment to syndicalism and direct action remained strong, and in recent years the organization has gained currency among the working classes employed in highly exploitative industries, with successful campaigns including the Chicago Couriers Union, the IWW Starbucks Workers, Focus on the Food Chain (Brandworkers International) and the Jimmy John's Workers Union (JJWU) that formed and expanded in the sandwich shop chain in Minnesota. This chapter examines the range of insurgent organizing tactics adopted by the JJWU, its success in organizing among workers, and the obstacles confronted by accepting the contours of U.S. law. While the IWW campaigns in the United States remain inchoate, workers have gained clear victories through primarily organizing outside of the established labor law.

We examine the rise of IWW workers organization in the UK, especially among low-waged and migrant workers that have been ignored by existing unions. These workers embrace the effort of crafting a union on their own that organizes workers in every industry, irrespective of race, gender, immigration status, or craft. In the UK, the IWW Cleaners Branch embraced a general union that rejects class compromise and reflects the self-activity of workers, sabotage, strikes, and democratic participation long precluded by traditional unions. As capital demonstrates its ineluctable search for profit at any cost and the state remains subservient to the interests of business, the choice for the working class is between maintaining the dominant political economic system or fighting back in search for new democratic forms of representation.

Finally we explore the United States as an archetype of how bureaucracy contributes to the weakening of working-class insurgency and the decline of direct action and strike activity. The class compromise of the 1930s established institutional mechanisms granting labor unions official recognition while curbing a militant workers' movement that was founded in the syndicalist tactics of the IWW. As the labor accords are removed through bipartisan opposition, new forms of worker organizations are arising that augur a return to the militant forms of class-struggle unionism and tactics of direct action that were dominant in the early twentieth century.

I.
AUTONOMIST UNIONS
IN EUROPE AND ASIA

CHAPTER 1

Operaismo Revisited: Italy's State-Capitalist Assault on Workers and the Rise of COBAs

Steven Manicastri

Historically, the defeats of workers' movements vastly outnumber their victories. The proletariat, nonetheless, has repeatedly stood up to the overwhelming forces of capital and reinitiated its struggle to create an alternative to capitalism. In a time when political institutions and parties are continuously used to repress both proletarian class consciousness and the possibilities for emancipation, the phrase "voting for the lesser of two evils" is regularly invoked throughout the world and now considered the form of liberal democratic politics in the early twenty-first century.[1] While it is not my intention to demonize the social democratic and liberal parties, it is important to note that the ineffectiveness of reformist parties provided the inspiration for the founding of the workers' movement called *operaismo*. In a world shrouded by a politics of opportunism and cynicism, the Italian history of operaismo has become a viable alternative for an inspirited politics for workers' movements across the globe.

Operaismo, known variously also as autonomist Marxism or workerism, began in Italy during the 1960s as a theoretical and political offshoot of Marxism, formulated by a group of intellectuals seeking a new approach to social action.[2] The movement seemed completely defeated by the 1980s, largely because, in the words of novelist Valerio Evangelisti, the majority of the militants and theorists were either in jail or in exile due to state repression.[3] Despite the movement's defeat, the idea of operaism—of an autonomous workers' movement unaffiliated with a political party or a union—managed to retain a sizable following. This enabled the creation in the late 1980s of the Comitati di Base, now Confederazione dei Comitati di Base—COBAs (subsequently referred to as Cobas), a rank-and-file workers' institution that has fought for workers excluded from, or otherwise unaffiliated with, the mainstream Italian unions: the left-wing Confederazione Generale Italiana del Lavoro (CGIL), the Catholic-influenced Confederazione Italiana dei Sindacati dei Lavoratori (CISL), and the socialist Unione Italiana del Lavoro (UIL).

In recent years the Cobas have proved very capable at organizing mass movements among workers and students, for example, in protesting Prime Minister Mario Monti's labor reforms intended to appease the EU's demands to rein in Italy's debt. The Cobas pride themselves on being independent of institutions and political parties, as they view a position in government, whether regional or federal, or with a union as incompatible with being solely dedicated to the "betterment of living and working conditions of all workers, from the public sector to the weakest and most marginalized social groups."[4] This independence has often led to criticism from the mainstream political parties or unions that Cobas are taking away constituents or disrupting solidarity among strikes and demonstrations organized by the major unions. These same accusations were made in the years surrounding "Hot Autumn" (1969) by the PCI (Italian Communist Party) and PSI (Italian Socialist Party) against the various workerist groups that sprang up in that period of intense protest activity.[5] The independence maintained by the Cobas is admittedly both a liability and a strength, but much more so the latter; workers' movements in bourgeois democracies where traditional unions are in decline would do well to consider adapting this model in order to create a much-needed labor party as an alternative to the "lesser of two evils."

Autonomia in Italy

To examine the recent activity of the Cobas, it is first necessary to trace the roots of the organization as well as to delve into the rich history of the Italian operaist movements of the 1960s and '70s, which rivaled their counterparts in France and Germany. The political climate of the time was described as follows: "The social revolution... posed a fundamental challenge to the Italian political class. The country was richer than ever before, but in the wake of the 'miracle'... came a series of major social problems which demanded immediate political response."[6] The "miracle" refers to the economic boom after World War II, which positioned Italy as one of the leading capitalist countries of the world. Politically, the country was led by a parliamentary majority of centrist parties—the Democrazia Cristiana (DC) and a handful of satellite parties, including Partito Liberale, Partito Repubblicano, and Partito Socialdemocratico. A government crisis erupted in 1960, when the MSI, a neofascist party, decided to hold its congress in Genoa, a city praised for its participation in the Resistance against fascism.[7] This provoked a revolt among the Genoan population, to which Prime Minister Fernando Tambroni responded by permitting the police to shoot insurrectionists in "emergency situations," and the police were eager to oblige. Although the DC did not openly support the MSI, it did have covert connections to the neofascists, which may have informed Tambroni's decision. Consequently, the CGIL declared a general strike and Italy was thrust into chaos, forcing the DC to remove Tambroni from office.[8]

This event prompted the DC to realize it needed to "open the door to the left," as the DC leaders Amintore Fanfani and Aldo Moro were fond of saying.[9] It is at this crucial moment that the history of operaismo truly begins. Despite some ideological affinity between the MSI and the DC, the DC realized it could not govern with an openly fascist party. Moro's plan to include the PSI in a center-left alliance served to integrate the PSI but to isolate the PCI. U.S. president John F. Kennedy's special assistant, Arthur Schlesinger,[10] encouraged Kennedy to show support for such an alliance with the aim of taming the PSI while also of robbing the PCI of its most valuable allies.[11] Not all Socialists were in favor of this alliance, but they could not stop it, and the PSI entered the coalition government in 1963. The PSI's moderate section, led by Pietro Nenni, had major support for forming the alliance with the DC. Naively, Nenni thought that the PSI could keep itself independent of pressure from the DC and that, unlike its German Socialist Party counterpart the SPD, it would not forsake Marxism for social democracy. Along with what his ally Riccardo Lombardi called "revolutionary reformism," Nenni believed the structure of capitalism could be transformed from within to create a socialist society.[12] The disappointed radical members of the PSI split off to form the Italian Socialist Party of Proletarian Unity (PSIUP), a smaller, autonomous socialist party.

The PCI did not fare any better despite the fact it was the largest communist party functioning in a Western country during the Cold War.[13] It was viewed ominously by conservatives for its success, yet it was by no means as radical an institution as the descriptor "communist" implied. "The longer the party remained becalmed in the alternatively placid waters of the Republic, the more likely it was to be slowly transformed by the experience rather than itself initiate a process of socialist transformation."[14] This was, in fact, the major divide within the

PCI, as its right wing, led by Giorgio Amendola and Giorgio Napolitano, was more than willing to use reforms as a means to achieve Togliatti's "Italian road to socialism." (It should be noted that Napolitano is, as of this writing, serving as president of the Republic.) Amendola and Napolitano viewed the "opening to the left" as a failure, not because they sought for the PCI to structurally move toward a socialist economy, but because they believed they would achieve more reforms if they united with the PSI to form one party. On the left wing of the PCI, Pietro Ingrao assessed the first center-left government as a complete failure, not because corrective reforms were not passed but because he justly feared that the working class would be integrated into the system "by means of progressive neo-capitalist policies,"[15] in a similar fashion to the argument made in Marcuse's *One-Dimensional Man.*[16] Ingrao's judgment would prove correct as the PCI often undermined workers' movements when they needed its support most, in the interest of becoming a "respectable" political party.

Not everyone in the PCI was willing to view the party as a lost cause. Mario Tronti, a PCI member and one of the founders of operaismo, hoped that the PCI could be changed to more effectively represent the working class. Reflecting on operaismo in a speech at the 2006 *Historical Materialism* conference, Tronti described it as "an experience that tried to unite the thinking and practice of politics."[17] In other words, it sought to adhere to Marx's eleventh thesis on Feuerbach, in which he called for political action and not simply philosophical rumination.[18] Operaismo sought to fulfill Gramsci's original conception of the Communist Party, which was to engage in a philosophy of praxis. Operaismo was to become a movement that interacted directly with workers in the factories. The worker "would be the central figure" and "the refusal of work became a lethal weapon against capital."[19]

In 1961 Raniero Panzieri, a left-wing leader of the PSI who was very critical of the party's position on creating a center-left government with the DC, founded a journal called *Quaderni Rossi* (Red Notebooks). It gathered "a group of young intellectuals, workers, and technical employees and started an investigation into the living and labor conditions of the working class in and around Turin."[20] *Quaderni Rossi* would be fundamental in creating the theoretical basis for the workerist movements, bringing together intellectual figures such as the Mario Tronti, Antonio Negri, and other researchers including Romano Alquati and Guido Bianchini. The journal would go onto uncover Marx's lesser-known work, *Grundrisse der Kritik der Politischen Ökonomie (Foundations of the Critique of Political Economy*), and as Adelino Zanini observes, workerism as a movement would base its theoretical approach not on *Capital* but on the *Grundrisse* itself.[21] The main problem with using the *Grundrisse* as the theoretical framework for a movement was that Marx himself, in his later works, corrected his theory regarding the accumulation of wealth, which initially positioned labor as a living subject, rather than as a living object.[22] In the *Grundrisse*, labor's subjectivity does not imply its reification in the manner asserted by Georg Lukács in *History and Class Consciousness*;[23] instead, it implies, somewhat ambiguously, that since labor is a living subject not objectified by the means of production, it has the ability to control those means of production. In *Capital* the worker is turned into an object because that is the only way for capitalism to rationalize his or her existence—by rendering the worker an abstraction—whereas in the *Grundrisse* Marx conceives of labor as subjective, thus implying that the bourgeoisie's control of labor is limited by the desires and actions of the proletariat, who are no longer an objective piece of the equation.

It is apparent why Marx corrected this aspect of his analysis, for if the worker had always wielded such a strong influence upon the bourgeoisie, the proletariat as a class would not be exploited. Yet it was not completely untrue that the worker could influence the rate of production under Fordism. By basing their approach on ways to influence the rate of production, workers found alternative means of resistance in addition to the strike, which still remained the primary means of struggle. What is crucial to this distinction, however, is that by emphasizing their strength as a revolutionary class rather than their powerlessness, workers opened the door for new tactics that were less dramatic than a strike but still just as effective at slowing production down to a crawl. "As it is the only holder of living labour, the working class manifests 'absolute' or separate interest, a unilateral synthesis, the only one which is, historically, thinkable."[24] The possibility of reading Marx in a different light led Negri to create what Jason Read has called a "philosophy of praxis through a new practice of philosophy," meaning that this new approach attempted to close the divide separating politics from economics and metaphysics from politics.[25] It is this duality found in labor that prompted Tronti to view the working-class movement from a completely different perspective: "We too have worked with a concept that puts capitalist development first, and workers second. This is a mistake. And now we have to turn the problem on its head, reverse the polarity, and start again from the beginning: and the beginning is the working class."[26]

With the theoretical groundwork laid in the *Quaderni Rossi* and, upon that journal's disintegration, in other operaist publications such as *Classe Operaia* (Working Class), and *Potere Operaio* (Worker Power), autonomist Marxism proved particularly effective in the years surrounding the Hot Autumn of 1969.

The Hot Autumn (Autunno Caldo) was a tumultuous period for the young Italian republic, during which the working class made considerable gains in the workplace and pushed the center-left government as far as it could go. One of the major, lasting outcomes was the alliance between students and workers—Italian students, unlike their counterparts in Germany, were never dismissive of the working class as "irredeemably integrated."[27] This alliance would be largely dismissed and frowned upon by the political parties but was embraced by the autonomous workers' movement.[28] Tronti would continue his support for the PCI, stating that only through a political party could the working class hope to "consolidate and multiply" its power.[29] His continuing hope was to radicalize the party, but he was unwilling to split the party in order to do so. Negri, on the other hand, viewed the Hot Autumn as "a revolutionary rupture" and focused his attention on the autonomist publication *Potere Operaio*, as well as the movement wing of the same name.[30]

In 1967, in the lead-up to the Hot Autumn, POv-e (Potere Operaio veneto-emiliano), an operaist group in northern Italy, organized a strike in Porto Marghera against the Petrolchimico plant.[31] Workers were frustrated with the regional union's inability to create and implement safeguards against hazardous working conditions. Although the strike only involved five hundred employees out of thirty thousand, the union, CGIL, was forced to act on their behalf. The strike's demographics reflected one of the main characteristics of operaist actions, which tended to include young adults in their twenties to their early thirties at most.[32]

POv-e again forced the CGIL at the Petrolchimico plant to intervene when the time came to negotiate bonuses. The workerists called for a flat 5,000-lire increase, uniting the majority of the factory's workers in action. They used tactics such as numerous stoppages occurring on alternate days for maximum impact, as well as mass picketing to prevent workers who still wanted to work from entering the factory. Their most successful tactic was threatening to reduce the skeleton crew necessary to oversee the plant, which forced a lockout.[33] Even though POv-e gained major support through these actions, in the end it was powerless to stop the CGIL from making a deal with the company to award percentage raises based on job category, rather than the flat increase the workers had demanded.[34] The CGIL's action clearly marked it as an unreliable ally and as an established "tool of capital," thus eliminating any ambiguity as to whether the unions could be used to promote the workerist agenda.[35] By the time of the French uprisings against De Gaulle's government in May–June 1968, operaismo as a movement had become more self-assured as well as more organized in confronting management, the unions, and the political parties. In the meantime the PCI had attempted to integrate the student movement (MS) but, by 1969, whatever radicalism was left within the party had been eliminated, ending the short-lived relationship between the PCI and the MS and uniting the MS with the various operaist movements.[36]

The Comitato Unitario di Base (unitary base committee, CUB) now Confederazione dei Comitati di Base, a precursor to the Cobas, was a rank-and-file organization created in 1968 in Milan. At the Pirelli factory, young, less-skilled workers were tasked with increasing the rate of production despite a lack of staff. The factory-level CUB united the new workers with older, militant unionists who had all but given up on the unions as a means for ameliorating their working conditions.[37] The CUB would successfully introduce the "go slow" tactic, in which workers slowed down production to the minimum required, preventing both management and the unions from forcing them to produce any faster. This tactic spread across Milan, used in actions at the Borletti plant and others, and quietly it would spread throughout Italy.[38] Crucially, the success of the CUB paved the way for a series of workerist strikes at the FIAT Mirafiori plant in Turin.

The strikes at the Mirafiori plant started in 1969 and culminated with the iconic occupation of the plant in 1973. The Mirafiori strikes again united the student movement with the various workerist groups in a national struggle against the exploitation of workers from southern Italy, who were paid less than their counterparts in the north, as well as for an autonomous wage increase not dependent on production, company profits, or the economic situation.[39] The strikes went on despite union negotiation, and within the factory workers used the "hiccup" strike, alternating which parts of the factory would be striking at any given time.[40] The main tactical emphasis was the decentralization of the strike actions, which made it difficult for management to predict where the strikes would begin. Mass picketing outside the factory, aided by students, guaranteed that anyone planning on working would be refused entry. The strike moved out of the factory onto the streets, with workers and students clashing with the police. As the demonstrators marched into the streets, they chanted "Che cosa vogliamo? Tutto!" ("What do we want? Everything!"), sending a "shiver down the collective spine of the Italian business class."[41]

Autonomist movements were not limited to the factory and spread throughout communities. "Mass squatting" became a popular practice, starting in 1969. Squatting and large-scale rent strikes were conducted to gain or retain access to housing. Thousands of people engaged in what was called "self-reduction," refusing to pay full price for their electricity, water, heat, or transportation. These tactics often worked, and judges would normally not prosecute the people who engaged in these actions.

The theoretical emphasis of workerism, focusing on workers' ability to control the rate of production, became the staple of the strikes during and after Hot Autumn, giving workers true political power. The major unions had no choice but to act on behalf of the workers, and this time the unions could not just sell out; they were forced to obtain a national contract, which agreed to the following: flat wage increases were guaranteed to all workers, the forty-hour work week would be established within three years, and student workers and apprentices were given special concessions.[42] For the workerists, however, this meant that the unions had reasserted themselves as the leaders of the working class, and the gains in workers' power proved short-lived. By 1973 the PCI, under the leadership of Enrico Berlinguer, had begun to discuss embracing a "historic compromise" with the DC.

Potere Operaio (PO), the operaist group affiliated with Negri, viewed the Hot Autumn as a failure in the end because of the unions' newfound militancy and their ability to reassert control over workers. PO tried to move the struggle outside the factory, helping the unemployed and disenfranchised groups such as women and migrant workers. Negri condemned "factoryism," the practice of workers defending their positions against the unemployed, and urged that PO fight for a "guaranteed political wage for all."[43] In 1973, PO splintered, with Negri forming a new group called Autonomia Operaia (AO), and the movement as a whole suffered from sectarianism. Moreover, the involvement of former operaist members in the Red Brigades guaranteed that workerism as a movement lost much of the support it once had attained. Former members of PO came under heavy scrutiny from the state as the PCI attempted to distance itself as much as possible from any accusations of being a radical, left-wing party.

The PCI condemned workerist struggles inside and outside the factory, accusing participants of violence and of being connected to the Red Brigades.[44] It was obvious, however, that the DC's intentions were not to change or compromise but to eliminate any opposition to their government, in the same way that they had with the PSI ten years before. Berlinguer had the potential to push forward reform within the PCI without a *transformist* (opportunistic) alliance with the DC, but he was afraid that, given the international hostility toward the party, a situation similar to Chile's overthrow of a democratically elected socialist government might have occurred.[45]

Due to the Red Brigades' increased activity as well as the autonomist movement's radicalism, Negri in particular was erroneously linked with the Red Brigades, and was accused of being the mastermind behind the kidnapping and murder of Aldo Moro in 1978.[46] He was acquitted when the actual leader of the Red Brigades came forward and denied Negri's involvement. Nevertheless, the Italian judicial system made little differentiation between the members of AO or PO and members of the Red Brigades, causing Negri to flee to France in exile; others, such as Luciano Ferrari Bravo, were arrested on the basis of nothing more than being affiliated with "an armed band."[47] It is interesting to note how greatly the PCI had changed since its founding in 1921 by Antonio Gramsci. Whereas it was a pillar of radicalism in Gramsci's time, it had now degenerated to upholding conservative values and distancing itself from "deviant social forces."[48]

The political situation depicting the workerists as terrorists, as well as the lack of direction among the three main, surviving workerist groups—AO, Lotta Continua (LC), and Area Operaia—contributed to a decline in organized action. There was a resurgence of the autonomist movement starting in 1977, which incorporated students, workers, and the unemployed, and was opposed strongly by the official unions. This wave of action culminated with a violent clash over the autonomist occupation of the University of Rome. The resurgence was short-lived, however, when in 1979 FIAT proceeded with the initial "61 politically motivated dismissals." This was followed by a mass dismissal of twenty-three thousand FIAT workers the following year.[49] Whatever workerist members were left staged a thirty-five-day strike, but the unions no longer wielded the same power as they had after the Hot Autumn, and they could not prevent the defeat of the strike.[50]

A New Movement

The disintegration of the workerist movements was a defeat for all workers. As the historic compromise with the DC proved a complete failure, workers no longer had any kind of representation, not even the limited one the PCI could have provided. After the trade unions' major defeat at FIAT and the implementation of neoliberal policies in the 1980s, workers once again looked to the potential of autonomist movements. It was under these circumstances that, in 1987, the Cobas were formed. Learning from the mistakes of the operaist movement, the Cobas remained completely independent from the unions and the political parties. If the Cobas were to become a successful workerist organization, they needed to do so independently and autonomously. Officially founded in Rome, the organization was primarily based in the public sectors, representing teachers and other employees in public schools. They also represented workers employed in "pensions and welfare, fire departments, railways, and bus transportation."[51] In the 1990s they focused much of their activism against the privatization of schools, as well as the increase in job precariousness, a problem that continues to plague Italy today.

The first organization to use the name "Cobas" was the group of teachers subsequently known as the Cobas Scuola. Their model of resistance was emulated and spread out across a striking variety of workers dissatisfied with Italy's autocratic state unions.[52] The idea for an organization like the Cobas germinated in 1985 as a result of a mass revolt in Genoa during the renegotiation of union contracts for teachers, transportation workers, doctors, longshoremen, and food and construction workers.[53] During these renegotiations, the political parties had proposed to abolish the *scala mobile* (literally "escalator," or moving steps). A victory achieved after World War II, the scala mobile served as a way to measure inflation and adjust salaries according to the cost of living.[54] It automatically accounted for 80 percent of the rate of inflation, making it a very effective program to help workers endure increasing costs. The scala mobile had been renegotiated in 1975 to bring it up to the optimal level, but as of a 1985 referendum plans were afoot to abolish it. The strongest of the unions, the CGIL, caved during the renegotiations and accepted the terms that had been rejected by its constituents, and so workers from each of the different unions began setting up rank-and-file organizations in protest. The contestation of the abolition of the scala mobile was a national event, with wildcat strikes occurring in even the most unionized factories.[55] Its abolition, finalized in 1993 and agreed to by the very unions that had helped create it, was a staggering defeat, and would solidify the Cobas as an alternative to the established confederal unions.

In Genoa, for example, the Cobas have completely ousted the three major unions to become the rightful representatives of the workers.[56] The Cobas were not designed to be a single organization, and this is their greatest strength: the organizational capacity to represent a diverse range of workers while at the same time uniting under a single banner of resistance against state capitalism and state syndicalism.[57] Some have accused them of being representatives of highly paid workers for organizing white-collar workers such as bank clerks, but the reality is that the Cobas can represent any worker dissatisfied with Italy's unions and ineffective political parties, drawing on grievances over wages, benefits, and employer misconduct of laborers exploited across skill categories.[58] Listing all the various types of organizations currently using the acronym Cobas would be difficult, as they are very numerous and many have no relation to the original organizations. Cobas Scuola was the initial name, and based on the success of that group, Cobas without the "Scuola" developed and multiplied. The Cobas Scuola still exists and acts as a sister organization to the other Cobas.

In light of the lack of literature on the Cobas in the English language, much of my information on their organizational structure comes from an interview conducted with one of the organization's founders, Piero Bernocchi, who explains that the reason so many organizations use the acronym Cobas is because the original organization in Rome did not copyright its name, nor did the participants wish to do so, in order to enable it to proliferate throughout Italy.[59] This has allowed other groups, such as the Sindicati Lavoratori Autorganizzati Intercategoriale (Slai) Cobas, to use the acronym without having any affiliation with the Cobas organization. In this case the Cobas have benefited from not copyrighting the name, as the Slai Cobas and the Cobas have a good relationship; however, there have been times when the lack of control over the name has placed the Cobas in a precarious situation. The Cobas del Latte, for example, has united small agricultural owners in northern Italy, but as an organization, they have nothing in common with the Cobas—they are associated with the Lega Nord, a xenophobic, reactionary political party.[60] This has caused the Cobas some obvious problems, as they have had to explain that they are not affiliated with that particular group.

The Slai Cobas are specifically involved in transportation, with membership ranging from public transportation workers, such as bus drivers, to airport staff and even car companies such as FIAT and Alfa Romeo. The Slai Cobas organized after the founding of the Cobas Scuola, at the FIAT Pomigliano plant in 1992, and were active against the elimination of the scala mobile.[61] The CUB, as one of the first rank-and-file organizations of Italy, has grown beyond the Pirelli factory, expanding into transportation, textiles, informatics, phones, energy, healthcare, public workers, metal workers, chemical workers, retired workers, and even insurance and housing.[62] However, according to Bernocchi, the CUB differs from the Cobas in the sense that it is still a classical union, with paid representatives and other positions. The major distinction between the CUB and the official unions is that the CUB is more democratic and incorporative in its decision-making. The Cobas have maintained a good relationship with the group, but the CUB has recently split into two groups and, according to Bernocchi, this has made it difficult for the Cobas to coordinate actions with the two CUBs.[63]

Recently, the Cobas have waged an assault on Prime Minister Monti's cuts and against the reforms passed by the former minister of public education, Mariastella Gelmini. The Cobas Scuola on the island of Sardegna was very active during November 2011 protesting Gelmini's reforms, which have led to what an elementary schoolteacher described as "hen-house classes," due to the large number of students in each class.[64] Nicola Giua, national executive of the Cobas, said, "With this government the situation worsens. In seeing Monti's team we are diffident, as it is composed of technocrats and bankers. We're worried about the passing of an increased retirement age and a halt on the ability to bargain contracts and salaries."[65] In the region of Abruzzo, similar protests led by the Cobas were conducted in the cities of Aquila and Pescara, with teachers and university students protesting the lack of education funding (Università: La protesta di migliaia di studenti cortei, sit-in, lezioni sul bus e mobilitazione).[66] On November 17, a national day of action was held by the Cobas to protest against the banks, with slogans taking a cue from Bertolt Brecht, "It is more criminal to found a bank than to rob it."[67]

One of the main issues that the CUBs and the Cobas have pledged to address is the European Union's austerity measures, which Monti's government has been slavishly enforcing on the backs of workers. The CUBs and the Cobas have both stated publicly that the "crisis should be paid by those who caused it," and have signed the pledge together as proof of their cooperation.[68] Since their formation in 1987, the Cobas have been involved in many social protests as well as workplace-specific actions. In addition to the actions against Monti's government, the Cobas protested the G8 Summit in 2009 held in Abruzzo, through demonstrations and marches in Rome and through a paralyzing strike that blocked major roads. The protesters demanded a free Palestine, an end to the lack of steady work contracts, and for the bankers of the world to pay for the economic crisis they have caused.[69] Government response to any manifestation of the Cobas has always been violent. The response of Monti's government to the recent protests and strikes has followed suit, with heavy police repression that in turn led to violence. The level of violence has, however, never reached the heights that occurred during the Hot Autumn.

The similarity of these recent strikes to those of the Hot Autumn clearly links the Cobas to the operaist movement. In addition to the obvious resemblances such as the rank-and-file organization and non-hierarchical structure, the Cobas have also maintained the same distaste for political parties shown by their progenitors. This independence is of paramount importance, as the Cobas have also been very vocal against the state's irresponsible spending of public funds. In an essay titled "Some Interpretations Regarding the Crisis, and on Capitalism and Its Future," Bernocchi argues that the Italian state has become the true enemy of the working class, as it has replaced the bourgeoisie of the private with a bourgeoisie of the state. He observes that the Italian state collects only about 3 percent of the taxes from people with an annual income of more than €100,000, and that the biggest tax evaders are precisely those in control of the state bureaucracy.[70]

The presence of what Bernocchi calls the state bourgeoisie is worse than other scenarios, such as state capitalism, because in the case of the state bourgeoisie, the object of the state is not to coordinate capital but to spend it as if it were privately owned.[71] According to Bernocchi, this is the major problem with the economic crisis in Italy: the enemy is no longer FIAT or another privately owned industry but the state itself, which has subjugated the private to serve its own interests. Silvio Berlusconi was a perfect example, as during his presidency he was the owner of Mediaset, a private media company in which he still wielded considerable power, and he also owned the soccer team AC Milan throughout his term as prime minister. Monti's government is a culmination of the center-right and center-left governments that have ruled Italy since the early 1990s. The policies of both the right and the left governments are completely geared towards an aggressive form of capitalism that has devastated Italy. The idea that Monti's government is in any way neutral is, according to Bernocchi, an excuse for all the major political parties to act without accountability, while blaming a technocratic government that functions with their support.[72]

For Bernocchi, the problem is a Gramscian nightmare of hegemony, in which the state has almost complete control over civil society.[73] This is precisely why it has been so difficult to organize any substantial resistance, because the enemy is the very state that Italians depend on for employment and their public welfare.[74] One of the biggest obstacles preventing an effective, collective response is that Italians, rather than directing their action toward a corrupt state with vested interests in the private sectors, have instead attacked immigrants with what can best be described as a new form of factoryism. For Bernocchi, the solution is to stop investing hope in the state's political parties, be they right, left, or an alliance of both. The actions needed to resolve the crisis involve slashing the salaries of the members of parliament, who are too numerous as well as overpaid in comparison to their counterparts in other European states; taxing financial transactions; levying a progressive income tax between 40 and 50 percent on the wealthiest members of society; placing a ban on all military spending; recovering lost tax revenue from tax evaders; and, finally, instituting a guaranteed living wage for everyone.[75]

Learning from the Cobas

What Bernocchi proposes is impossible to achieve within representative democracy; its function, as Negri argues in *Insurgencies*, is to limit constituent power.[76] The Cobas offer an alternative means of resistance based not on the strict discipline of a Leninist party but on cooperation. Their organizational structure prevents the eventual hierarchies that tend to form within political movements by upholding the principle that the individuals involved are autonomous subjects. It is a difficult model to replicate precisely because it requires so much participation, but it also sets the stage for what true direct democracy would resemble—the cooperation of autonomous subjects able to express their Nietzschean will to power. While the Cobas are a model of resistance in Italy, their model can be used in other countries as well. Germany, for example, has had a history of autonomist movements that emulated the tactics of the older Italian autonomist movements.[77]

It would not be farfetched for organizational structures that take the form of Cobas to arise outside Italy. In many other neoliberal states, workers face similar situations. Austerity measures are especially directed towards unionized workers, but the Cobas are not traditional unions. This would allow workers to be organized without the stigma that the right has attributed to classical unions.

Applying Cobas Transnationally

To bring this full circle to the beginning of the chapter, the Cobas can offer a stark alternative to the political atmosphere in Italy and elsewhere. The situations in advanced capitalist countries are similar, as there is a vested interest to prioritize corporations and other financial institutions over the well-being of workers in the same way that the Italian state has abandoned its own people. This is precisely why it can only benefit workers in the global North and South to familiarize themselves with the autonomist movements that have taken place in Italy in order to create grassroots movements and democratize the political sphere. The rank-and-file organizational method of the Cobas is highly adaptable in contexts beyond Italy. The Cobas' concept of rank-and-file organization can be applied to federal systems where regional and state laws are not governed by national legislation. A local Cobas organization represents specific workers. The intent is not to create an amalgamation of various types of workers under one union, but to have an organization that could cater to their different needs based on each situation. Working at a local level prevents the Cobas from losing touch with workers in the manner that the CGIL and CISL have done over the last fifty years. Thus the constituents of the Cobas can be confident that their organization is truly an extension of their constituent power. Being autonomous, they do not need to appease the government or the unions; instead they can afford to be confrontational when the situation requires. With the decline of traditional unions throughout the world, Cobas provide a forceful alternative.

It has taken the Cobas two decades to establish themselves in Italy as an alternative to the confederal unions, and still they face fierce resistance from both the government and the unions, which have limited their ability to represent a greater number of workers. According to Bernocchi, this is mainly due to the power the unions hold within the government. The unions are an oligarchy that competes with each other for hegemony over the working class, but can present a united front against rank-and-file organizations such as the Cobas.[78] With this in mind, as unions decline in Europe and the United States, an organizational structure like the Cobas has the ability to become much more than a syndicalist movement: it could enter the political realm and challenge traditional political institutions, as long as it is rooted in workers and community demands.

While the Cobas do not endorse political candidates, the political system in Italy is a world apart from the plurality system in other bourgeois democracies. In Italy, numerous political parties form coalition governments in order to win a majority vote. It is obvious why Bernocchi would want to avoid having the Cobas become just another party among the myriad of ineffective Italian political parties. Beyond Italy, in Europe, North America, and beyond, structures like Cobas have the potential as a workplace and political movement and. The Cobas are also viable as potential political organizations because they are not just dedicated to the capital-labor conflict—they also embody many other leftist ideas, from environmental issues to feminism to gay rights to battling xeno-phobia.[79] One of the requirements for joining the Cobas is the adherence to certain progressive principles. Debates on gay marriage or abortion rights do not exist. Upholding such principles may limit the numbers of people within the organization; but it guarantees a united group of activists who will not sacrifice their ideals for political gain that will divide the group the way political parties suffer internal divisions.

To apply the Coba model to the global context, the root of the organization should begin in the workplace and subsequently extend to the larger society. This requires a highly democratic organization in which workers themselves become the elected officials; bureaucracy is limited to that which is necessary. Despite the idealism behind this concept, structurally it is possible. One needs only to look at the constitution of the Slai Cobas in order to see its practice. In Article 8 of their constitution, the Slai Cobas specifically state that there will be no full-time directors as in a typical union. If a full-time director becomes necessary, the Slai Cobas must elect the director and the individual's powers will be restricted. The constitution also states that the Slai Cobas are formed exclusively of workers, retirees, and the unemployed.[80] The original Cobas have not changed this model; in fact, any member who obtains a salary from the group is not allowed to vote. Such members are extremely few, since the organization wants workers to be participants so that their issues can be discussed and resolved.

When writing about the structure of the Cobas, Bernocchi makes it very clear that, unlike the confederal unions, the Cobas function on the principle of direct democracy, which requires the full participation of all its members.[81] In the words of a famous Communist Italian songwriter, Giorgio Gaber, "Libertà è partecipazione," (liberty is participation). This helps prevents the caste system that usually develops within unions by endowing all members with equal responsibility. Another aspect of the organization that Bernocchi speaks to is funding.

In their formative years the Cobas experienced numerous funding challenges because they initially did not require any dues. Their growth over the years has required a minimal amount of bureaucracy, but, as Bernocchi has made clear, the organization still revolves primarily around the voluntary work of its members. The dues are generally renewable on an annual basis and they constitute only 0.5 percent of a member's monthly salary. This has enabled the Cobas to function on both a local and national level. Another form of funding comes through the organization Azimut, a nonprofit organization created by the Cobas, which is involved with international relief efforts as well as with providing additional funding for the Cobas.[82] In Italy a person may donate 0.5 percent of their taxed income to a nonprofit organization of their choice. Members of the Cobas generally select their own organization, as this helps to pay for the rental of offices and transportation for various days of actions or conventions. More importantly, the decision to create even this small layer of bureaucracy was not reached lightly, and the fact that it was consciously discussed and debated proves the worthiness of the Cobas' organizational method.[83]

On a national level the Cobas have monthly committee meetings in which elected members from the various Cobas discuss courses of action, always maintaining the model of direct democracy. The Cobas have no single leader; they are a body of workers and even their national "executive branch" is composed of a committee.[84] Holding a position of leadership does not entitle the elected person to any special privileges or power—he or she will still "paste advertisements on walls or distribute flyers, prepare signs for the protests, and make phone calls to convene at national assemblies."[85] Leaders are elected based on how much work they invest in the organization. Of course, if a member participates more often, he or she will be better known than a member who participates only at a rally or during a vote. Yet, regardless of some members investing more time within the organization, everyone has equal say, and no one is deprived of his or her right to voice an opinion. A question commonly asked of the Cobas is how they manage to function without any traditional leaders, and how they solve internal issues if they do not enforce any kind of discipline. Bernocchi has quipped that the Cobas have become the Zen Buddhists of politics.[86]

On a more serious note, he added that one of the key ways they achieve member support is through dialogue. All decisions are required to have at least a 75 percent vote of agreement, otherwise they are discussed and voted upon again until a consensus is reached. In the eventuality that no consensus is reached, if a particular Cobas group chooses not to follow the guidelines they are simply let go from the main organization, and free to make their own choice. Bernocchi said that not being forceful has proven more effective, and that those who wished to leave have eventually made their way back into the organization. On the rare occasion that they have not returned to the group, the Cobas were not affected as an organization.

Another criticism of the Cobas is what Gall calls "abstentionism," or the Cobas' inability to form a general front with other unions, which can ruin solidarity among workers.[87] At the same time it is difficult to hold this against the Cobas, as their members display a higher level of class consciousness than Italy's confederal union members by viewing critically the system that allows for their exploitation. One way of addressing this problem, which to a degree has already happened, is for the Cobas to participate when the unions have their rallies and to approach those workers in the CGIL and the CISL, creating connections that could bring those workers into a more militant organization. The innate radicalism of the Cobas can be daunting to a regular worker, and alienating that worker is not to the benefit of a growing organization. This does not imply that the Cobas should compromise their autonomy, only that they need to be approachable and embrace new members when the occasion arises. If an organization similar to the Cobas were to be formed in other countries where traditional unions have become less relevant to the wider working class, a similar process would need to occur. Mass support for such an organization would not be immediate, which means that it must acknowledge that its militant members will have to proceed in radicalizing the new incoming members who are not yet comfortable with the idea of autonomy.

The Cobas represent a fresh alternative for the workers where moribund trade unions and their slavish devotion to labor-based political parties have failed to represent their class interests, in Europe, North America, and beyond. There are limitations to the rank-and-file organizations of the workerist movements, the most obvious being difficulty of finding members radical enough to leave the mainstream parties and forms of representation. The biggest issue to overcome is not discipline; rather, it is the elimination of the traditional concept of discipline as necessary for a political organization to function. As Bernocchi argues, a member of the Cobas "feels democratically satisfied," because their voice within the group matters. Will this model be sustainable in the long run? The answer is not yet clear, but the Cobas have proved themselves capable of functioning for more than twenty years on a model of participatory democracy without the rigid discipline of democratic centralism. The fact that a course of action needs the approval of a large majority is a safeguard to promoting cohesiveness within the organization. More importantly, the history in Italy of political parties who enforced strict discipline, such as the Rifondazione Comunista, have had numerous declines in constituents; this has led to the creation of small, inconsequential political parties that are societally useless.

The Cobas have provided the working class the potential for a renewal of the class struggle that has been perennially skewed in favor of the bourgeoisie. Through the Cobas, workers have the chance to prove their autonomous character, with no need to organize themselves around leaders of unions or political parties. The Cobas challenge the conservative notion that any movement needs to have a leader and, more importantly, the conservative notion that representative democracy as it functions today is democracy at all. As Tronti said, "Look. Capitalists are afraid of the history of workers, not the politics of the Left. The first they cast down among the demons of hell, the second they welcomed into the halls of government."[88] It is time for the working class to cease looking for emancipation in the halls of government and to delve into the depths of hell to reclaim and apply its rich history toward a new revolutionary movement.

CHAPTER 2

Autonomous Workers' Struggles in Contemporary China

Au Loong Yu and Bai Ruixue

The Chinese working class has undergone a transformation in the last twenty years on a historically unprecedented scale. From 1995 to 2008 it doubled in size, from about 150 million to about 300 million, as its composition also changed radically after a wave of privatization. The state and collective sector declined from 110 million to 61 million,[1] meaning that by 2012, the Chinese urban workers have little collective class memory of rural life. As mass urbanization expanded dramatically from the mid-1990s, the working class in privatized industry or in state- and collective-run enterprises have failed to defend themselves from capitalist assaults.

Despite its massive numbers, the working class in China might be considered an obsolete class to be pitied rather than a class to be respected or feared. Struggles have been dismissed by scholars as "cellular activism" and "protests of desperation."[2] "A misguided class" is another telling descriptor, alluding to state sector workers' nostalgia for an obsolete "socialist" past.[3] At the other extreme, however, are discourses that argue this sector of workers possesses a "significant degree of socialist consciousness" or "relatively complete class consciousness" and that, in Mao's period, they genuinely were "the leading class" in the country. Although for the present they have failed to resist privatization due to being "politically inexperienced," they are nevertheless destined to "play a leading role in the coming revolutionary struggle."[4]

A more accurate, less polarized account of contemporary Chinese labor struggles will require a historical approach. When considering the lack of strong and coordinated resistance among workers to the wave of privatization among state-owned enterprises (SOEs), for instance, one must take into account the great 1989 Democracy Movement, in which workers heroically played a significant role, and the demoralizing effects of their defeat, which further undermined their ability to resist privatization.

Understanding contemporary workers' struggles also requires a class-relational approach. This is something largely absent, not only from liberal discourses but also from discourses by scholars of the Left. As an example, it is only possible to understand slaves as a class in relation to slave owners; similarly, wage laborers can only be understood in relation to capitalists. In the Soviet bloc and China before the reform period, the absence of a bourgeoisie and a national market makes such an analysis more complicated, but not if we bring the role of the bureaucracy into the picture. The working class since 1949 can only be understood in relation to the bureaucracy that has ruled over it. Certain liberal discourses are keen to point out that there was a division between the rulers and the ruled in "communist" countries, but only when this is used as evidence to support their stance that "communism necessarily fails because it is a utopia," and so this has little analytical value for our study. Of those who wish to rescue the credibility of communism, most fail to identify the bureaucracy as the main force of capitalist restoration and instead are content to look for individual leaders to name and shame as "capitalist roaders." Hence, when they now call for the rolling back of capitalist reform, they are more likely to settle for "good people" among the party leadership rather than calling for institutional change.

The lack of historical and relational approaches in studies of Chinese labor is most often linked to the contemporary trend of depoliticizing the debate on the subject since the collapse of Soviet and Chinese communism. Many have simply accepted without question the mainstream idea of a "transitional economy," thereby serving the purpose of naturalizing capitalism while "denaturalizing" the experiences of Soviet or Chinese socialism. Now, with the economic rise of China, a further retreat is noticeable among certain labor advocates. They argue that a depoliticized labor movement is required, since "in a market economy, labor relations are governed by the laws of supply and demand," and thus labor disputes are just "a civil society matter."[5] This also means that previous calls for independent unions have been quietly dropped, replaced by a call for international trade unions to help the official Chinese union "better serve its members and eventually become a real trade union."[6]

This chapter attempts to weave a historical and relational approach, as well as a call for the politicization of the discourse on the labor movement in China, into a narrative of the struggles of the Chinese working class to illustrate why we should not expect substantial reform for the significant betterment of working people to come from the initiative of the party state. Working people possess the potential to take matters into their own hands, despite their current weakness in developing sufficient class consciousness or forming independent organizations.

The Contradictory and Changing Nature of Working-Class Consciousness, 1949–1989

It was a Chinese peasant army led by the Communist Party that liberated the cities from the Kuomintang regime, and it was Mao's initiative in 1953 to abruptly abandon the New Democracy line, which had fostered the national bourgeoisie. Mao then took a radical turn, beginning a "socialist" transformation that phased out the private sector. This kind of "socialism from above" shaped working-class consciousness in a contradictory way. According to the liberal discourse, the title of "leading class" was pure propaganda, with no real meaning at all except for duping the working class; in this interpretation, the working class was simply "a misguided class."[7] Mao's followers toed the party line and insisted the title did in fact have validity.[8] Neither proposition is entirely accurate.

In terms of direct political meaning, the title "leading class" carried little substance in itself, as workers were not granted any basic political freedoms or democratic rights. Between 1956 and 1979 the working class was neither the class that made political decisions nor was it the "master of the house," even at the enterprise level. In fact, in a political sense, the party cadres took the place of the bourgeoisie as the managerial class. Although official propaganda tried hard to cover up the fact that the bureaucracy was a privileged caste by promoting the theory of "two classes and one stratum," according to which "cadres" were a part of the working class, in reality a deep gulf existed between the ordinary working class and party cadres. There was little upward mobility for the former, except for "activists" who toed the party line in order to climb up the ladder.

There is a grain of truth in the notion that Mao's China was a more egalitarian society than what exists today, but this only holds true for the distribution of economic resources, which was partial at that—the material privileges of cadres in Mao's China were always enormous. This notion of egalitarianism is entirely false where the distribution of political power is concerned. Precisely because the working class was (and is) denied not only political power but also basic civil liberties, the working class had nothing in its hands to stop the capitalist restoration led by Deng and was forced to resist it bare-handed in 1989. The seed of this defeat had already been sown when Mao, despite his rhetoric opposing bureaucratic privileges, institutionally kept the one-party dictatorship intact.

Yet it is also problematic to suggest that after 1956 the title of "leading class" was entirely meaningless. As of the completion of the "socialist" transformation, the title did carry some meaning for workers due to the political and social implications of the absence of a bourgeoisie. It was the working class, rather than a bourgeoisie, which was essential to the modernization of China, and this fact gave workers a source of pride they had not enjoyed before. Furthermore, although the working class was disenfranchised politically, in the socioeconomic arena, which operated according to laws qualitatively different from capitalism, there was no market discipline for the cadres to use to discipline the workers. In place of market discipline, the bureaucracy under Mao used permanent political mobilization, political incentives, and *sixiang gongzuo* ("ideological" work or "persuasion by reason," which very often carried a strong element of coercion) to make workers more productive. But these measures did not carry the mechanism of the constant need to cut the cost of labor.

In a word, the "socialist" transformation opened up the opportunity for job security and social benefits for some workers in a very poor country, an achievement that cannot be denied. Although the bureaucracy ruled over workers in a manner similar to that of other rulers, its expropriation of social surplus did not take the form of extraction of surplus value; it took the form of use value. This placed a limit, in addition to the constraints on private ownership already determined by the revolution, on the extent of its expropriation. The period from 1956 to 1979 can therefore be characterized as "bureaucratic socialism," or "socialism from above," which was relatively successful in its creation of job security and social welfare benefits for the workers. This welfare, which included social security, healthcare provisions, housing, and other benefits, administered on an enterprise basis, formed the foundation of a kind of social contract between workers and the state, whereby the workers largely consented to the system in exchange for the provisions made by the state. It was this social contract that led to workers developing, with some justification, a collective consciousness and a sense of pride in belonging to the working class. This explains in part, along with state suppression of protest action and harsh penalties for dissidents, why labor struggles were comparatively few during this period and why no genuine autonomous workers' movement emerged.

The top-down approach of bureaucratic socialism also explains why class consciousness necessarily assumed a "deformed" character. Rather than the working class itself coming to an awareness of its status and its ability to defend and fight for its interests through collective struggle, the working-class identity of SOE workers was created by the Communist Party in its designating them as the "leading class." Therefore, instead of an awareness of revolutionary popular sovereignty, among SOE workers there was a deep sense of *ganen* (gratitude) toward the party and to Mao. Although it was the party that promoted the ganen mentality among workers, a considerable numbers of workers adopted this attitude due to the real improvement to their material conditions, bestowed from above as a reward not only for their hard work but also for their existence as a class.

What must be addressed, however, is that the working class was also seriously divided and received different levels of wages and benefits. Indeed, many workers did not enjoy the levels of job security and benefits as those granted to SOE workers. In 1960, when the number of urban wage workers reached its height at nearly 60 million, 15.5 percent, or 9.25 million workers, worked in collectively owned enterprises (COEs), and received lower wages and less social welfare than SOE workers. In addition, both SOEs and COEs could hire contract or temporary workers from rural or marginalized urban social groups, who often were not entitled to welfare benefits at all.

Those who favorably view Mao's China suggest that the older generation of SOE workers was the standard-bearer of the socialist ideal, even today representing the "most revolutionary class,"[9] and that those workers developed a "relatively complete class consciousness."[10] In actuality, the collective consciousness of the older generation of SOE workers was always a curious tension between its subject-like mentality in relation to the party and cadres versus its pride in having a higher status than peasants. That is why SOE workers discriminated against rural migrant workers and were unwilling to extend the concept of "working class" to the latter, accepting the party's social apartheid against people with rural household registration. The SOE worker who enjoyed this kind of status differentiation bore more resemblance to a premodern worker than a modern wage worker: in feudal societies, people were ranked according to social strata that accorded them different legal rights and privileges, whereas workers with a modern working-class consciousness recognize their mission is precisely to break down the barriers of privilege between wage workers in order to forge a lasting union among them. This is not surprising, as China was forced to make a revolutionary leap into the modern industrialized world, and therefore often still combines the old with the new. The heavy presence of peasants in the army and the party—a deeply Stalinized party at that—resulted in even more premodern dynamics having influence on both the revolution and working-class thought as well. Although there were no doubt some aspects of a modern working-class consciousness, these were combined with the exclusivity associated with status privileges and servility toward the party, which continued to act as a damper on the development of a full working-class consciousness.

This is not to say that workers' protests did not exist in Mao's China. Incidents of worker unrest and militancy occurred from the beginning and included actions such as strikes, go-slows, refusal of work discipline, and disobeying laws and regulations, as well as attacks on managers or the factory itself. According to Sheehan, "the common picture of Chinese workers as basically supporting the party, and even intervening on its behalf against other groups involved in anti-party protest, is not at all convincing when applied to the whole range of workers in all types of enterprise across the country."[11]

Many of the strikes and labor protests that broke out during the Hundred Flowers campaign of 1956–57 were initiated by temporary and contract workers, apprentices, and others who were not entitled to the same privileges as the SOE workers. Indeed, divisions among workers often resulted in fewer than half of the workers at a given factory participating in a protest action.[12] The unrest and strikes during the Cultural Revolution, in contrast, began among the permanent SOE workers, although this time those involved were often divided into rebel and conservative factions, reflecting the greater splintering into different interest groups that occurred during the Cultural Revolution. Labor associations, making largely economic demands to improve the material conditions of workers, also appeared during this time, but they were quickly condemned by the party and their activities were short-lived.[13]

The 1976 Tiananmen Incident, the first in a new trend of actions among workers, occurred when a million ordinary citizens (which, at the time, meant mostly workers) gathered spontaneously in Beijing to pay tribute to the dead Zhou Enlai, implicitly defying the Gang of Four and Mao. The 1976 incident was different in the sense that it was entirely spontaneous, highly political, and implicitly targeting the top leader,

Mao. It was neither "counterrevolutionary" (as described by the Gang of Four) nor "revolutionary" (as described by Deng's supporters after he returned to power), but it was nevertheless the first time in the history of the republic that a great movement happened entirely independent of Mao and top party leaders, who had no control over it until they finished it off with bloody repression.[14] Workers' widespread disillusionment with Mao had already become obvious toward the end of the Cultural Revolution, but it was not until the 1971 death of Lin Biao, whom Mao had appointed his successor, that workers felt deeply fooled by Mao and the party, responding with widespread go-slows and indifference. This paved the way for the 1976 incident. Although it was an independent political action, the protesters, disgusted by the Gang of Four, this time expressed sympathy with Zhou and, to a lesser degree, with Deng. The incident showed that the workers had now begun to think and act politically for themselves. The most thoughtful contingent of the protesters would later become the main participants in the Peking Spring of 1979. Both incidents acted as a bridge to the next great independent struggle, the 1989 Democracy Movement. Although there was neither organizational nor personnel continuity among the 1976 and 1979 events and the 1989 movement, they all exhibited a continuous development toward greater political independence from the bureaucracy, in inverse proportion to the bureaucracy's diminishing progressiveness and connection to the people. To depict the whole working class as "a misguided class" with no thoughts of its own, as Yu Jianrong does,[15] is simply biased and short-sighted.

1989: A Critical Moment for the Bureaucracy and the Working Class

The beginning of Deng Xiaoping's reform and open policy in 1979 marked a turning point for Chinese workers. It signaled the start of the gradual destruction of the status and job security previously afforded to SOE workers, and also began preparations for a full restoration of capitalism. The 1980s therefore witnessed a series of steps that undermined the position of workers. These included the abolition of the right to strike, in 1982, and enterprise reforms that strengthened the position of managers at the expense of workers and the introduction of fixed-term contract employment in 1986, which made it easier for workers to be dismissed.

Due to the falling living standards that accompanied these so-called reforms, worker discontent increased during this period and a number of wildcat strikes took place across the country. In some instances there were also calls for more independent union organizations. Although workers were not conscious of the imminent restoration of capitalism, they were aware of the cadres' theft of collective property. This led to workers' significant involvement in the 1989 Democracy Movement under the banner of *Dadao guandao* ("Down with officials who use state property to speculate"). This period also saw the establishment of independent Workers' Autonomous Federations (WAFs) and the participation of workers in huge demonstrations in a number of different cities across China. The WAFs were not only active in organizing in the defense of students, but they also held meetings on workers' welfare, human rights, democracy, and freedom as well as demanding wage increases, price stabilization, and publication of the income and possessions of government officials and their families.

Workers' participation in the Democracy Movement—and the challenge that posed to the party's legitimacy to act in the interest of workers—showed that the most advanced section of the working class had reached a new level of consciousness, incarnated in the WAFs, which were politically independent from the two main factions of the party at that time. As for the broader working class in Beijing, it was the first time in the history of the republic that tens of thousands of ordinary workers and their families were determined to defy the top leader of the party and his martial law in order to stop the army and its tanks from entering Beijing. This revolutionized the situation rapidly, severely alarming the Communist Party. It was following the workers' threat of the withdrawal of labor, after talks in preparation for a general strike, that the party-state acted so brutally against the movement on June 4, 1989. The crackdown and the repression that followed have had a devastating, lasting impact on the Chinese working class. Despite a significant increase in the number of worker protests as further economic reforms have been pursued since onset of privatization, no new autonomous workers' movement has emerged in China since 1989.

Ching Kwan Lee describes SOE workers as being "less wretched and less heroic" than many scholars admit.[16] The defeat of the 1989 Democracy Movement must be taken into account when probing the reasons for workers' inability to resist privatization, however.[17] The movement disproves the notion that the old working class lacked heroism, or that workers always lacked the initiative to think or act independently; it highlights the role the working class once played.

The execution of the workers' initiative in 1989, although heroic and highly political, nonetheless still reflected limitations. Precisely because of decades-long repression, the experiences of labor activists across different generations could not consolidate into a coherent and clear program or take any organized form. The more advanced section of workers eventually came to be aware of the importance of democracy to socialism, but their consciousness was still very rudimentary and could in no way fully prepare them to face the upheaval of 1989. That is why we are also skeptical of the notion that Chinese SOE workers ever developed a "relatively complete class consciousness."[18] If this had been the case, then a more coordinated and widespread resistance under a more comprehensive program could have been mounted in 1989 and then again later, against the privatization onslaught. Nevertheless, the 1989 movement was still a landmark for the development of working-class consciousness and it cannot be ignored in any attempt at understanding the Chinese working class.

Indeed, the 1989 movement and its subsequent failure should be seen as a qualitative turning point in the class character of the party-state and its bureaucracy—from fiercely antibourgeois to fiercely anti-worker and absolutely bourgeois. The revolution had come full circle and returned to its starting point, albeit at a new historical and socio-economic level. Only by defeating the working class could the bureaucracy successfully privatize SOEs and COEs. This was followed by the privatization of urban land.

Struggles against Barracks Capitalism

The tragic defeat of the 1989 Democracy Movement demoralized and confused SOE workers such that even when there were sporadic protests against privatization at the turn of the century, they tended to arrive too late. In this rather limited struggle, the actions were mostly confined to single enterprises. The courageous 2002 initiative by the workers of the Liao Yang Alloy enterprise to mobilize workers from other plants into the same struggle was an exception. Precisely because of this, the local government quickly repressed their struggle and sentenced the leaders to prison. Given that the overall balance of forces has never been in the workers' favor, it is not at all surprising that most of the workers' antiprivatization struggles have ended in defeat or, at most, have led to improved redundancy packages.

During the same time period, rural migrant workers found the barracks-like factory regime increasingly unbearable and began to fight back spontaneously. This has played an important role in forcing the government and employers to raise wages and forcing the All-China

Federation of Trade Unions (ACFTU) to become more active in drafting labor laws. In the collective struggles of the first generation of migrant workers, the workers gradually learned a lesson; condensed into a motto, it would be "Small struggles, small gains; big struggles, big gains; no struggle, no gain." Most struggles are not organized, however. In the rare instances that workers have taken the initiative to organize a union, such as the Uniden case in 2004–2005,[19] they have immediately been repressed by the local government or the local ACFTU. It has not just been harsh repression that has stopped rural migrant workers from developing workers' organizations, however. Although they have not experienced the same kind of historic defeat as the SOE workers, neither do they possess any collective class memory prior to their migration to the cities, meaning that their class consciousness is more difficult to develop.

In fact, many migrant workers do not describe themselves as working class, reserving that title for SOE workers and insisting that they are *nongmingong* (peasant workers). Indeed, for the first generation of rural migrant workers the purpose of working in the cities was to save enough money and then go home—hence their worker's identity was temporary, while their peasant's identity was more permanent. And since their expectations were not very high from the start—even if their wages were very low and the work discipline very harsh—as long as the benefits they received were significantly higher than what they earned from tilling their lands, they would endure it provided the bosses did not go too far. This possibility for improving their lives as peasants limited their will to struggle long and hard against discrimination when struggles might result in condemnation and eventual repatriation back to their home villages, if not imprisonment. They also tended to view the overly harsh discipline in the factories as normal, as they had no previous experience of urban or factory life.

What distinguishes China from other parts of the world is that there is coercive institutional control over the class identity of its citizens, meaning that it is very difficult for rural migrant workers to become permanent city-dwellers. The *hukou* (household registration) system denies rural migrant workers permanent residential rights in urban areas, the rights to accessible education, medical care, subsidized housing, and so on. The peasant identity is hereditary, except when one joins the army or enrolls in university. Until 1998 children inherited their rural identity from their mother rather than their father, and, until 2003, there were serious penalties for migrants who violated the hukou system, including being fined, jailed, or sent back home at their own expense. In recent years the household registration system has been relaxed, but the essential character is social apartheid aimed at discriminating against people of rural origin is still largely in place. Under the hukou system, rural migrant laborers find it hard to raise families in cities and establish roots there, and this discourages them from making long-term commitments to organizing or developing a class identity.

Rural migrant workers have fought for their rights, however, when they have been seriously infringed upon or when discrimination has become particularly ugly. Local riots targeting public order teams, which have abused rural migrants while checking their papers, have been common in Guangdong during the past decade. However, these workers have rarely opposed the hukou system itself. Migrant workers might fight against some forms of discrimination, but their consciousness has not been raised to the level of insisting on equal citizenship. Their outlook is still heavily shaped by the party state. The ACFTU, which is supposed to organize workers, did not even recognize rural migrant workers until 2003, when it officially admitted that they are a part of the working class and hence a target group for recruitment. This kind of rhetoric carries little meaning, however, if the essence of the hukou system as a kind of social apartheid remains, and if the ACFTU does not raise a finger to oppose the system.

However, things may slowly be changing for both sections of the working class. Two key struggles in recent years, which are particularly noteworthy and highlight some of the features emerging in contemporary labor struggles, are the antiprivatization struggle by Tonghua steelworkers in 2009 and the strike action taken by Honda workers in summer 2010. While the former is seen as a landmark among SOE workers' struggles, the latter is seen as significant to workers' struggles in the private sector.

The Tonghua Antiprivatization Struggle
In July 2009 an antiprivatization struggle by steelworkers at the Tonghua Steel Mill in Jilin Province, which led to the death of a factory boss, resulted in a victory for the workers as the plans to buy out and privatize the steel mill were dropped. The Tonghua struggle was significant for a number of reasons. First, it illustrated a case of resistance in which Chinese workers were not prepared to sit back passively in the face of privatization. The fact that in this struggle a manager was killed only goes to reflect the growing depth of the anger and desperation of workers whose

livelihoods and means of survival are at stake, while management reaps the rewards and grants themselves even higher salaries. One report claimed, for instance, that while the general manager who was killed, Chen, was paid 3 million yuan in 2008, some of the company retirees were receiving as little as 200 yuan per month.[20] During the enterprise reforms occurring since the late 1980s, it was not uncommon to read in the news that individual workers killed the managers who had sacked them or cut their wages, but this was never before the result of a collective action. Where there were collective actions—mostly demonstrations, camping in front of factories, and so on—they were moderate and disciplined due to fear of retaliation. The Tonghua incident is the first case in which a manager was killed by a large group of workers supported by most of their fellow workers. The workers' violence was also widely supported by Chinese workers. Such a massive outbreak of workers' anger frightened the local government and forced them to make significant concessions to the workers. It remains to be seen whether this represents a singular incident or is a sign that the demoralizing effect of the 1989 defeat is now receding. But future SOE workers' struggles may refer to this example and continue to draw inspiration from it.

At the same time as the Tonghua struggle, workers at the Linzhou Steel Company in Puyang were also fighting against privatization, and the victory at Tonghua greatly encouraged their struggle. At the height of the action the workers locked up an official from the municipal government for ninety hours. They, too, ended their fight with a victory.

Another key contributing factor was that the Chinese steel industry, the world's largest, is one of the industries in which many workers have lost their jobs in large-scale layoffs resulting from privatization. In the ferrous metal industry, from 1996 to 2001, the workforce declined by 40 percent, from 3.37 million to 2.04 million.[21] Although they now represent only one-fifth of the national working class, the Tonghua struggle proves that SOE workers can still be a formidable force. An additional fact is that the most important industries in China are still SOEs, even post-restructuring. This gives more power to these workers than numbers alone might suggest.

Finally, in the cases of Tonghua and Linzhou, all the supposedly pro-labor institutions within the plants—the trade union, the staff and workers' representative congress, and the like—proved ineffective in representing the workers' interests. This was why workers at both plants took actions independent of the official trade union, despite many of the workers being members. One Tonghua employee, speaking to *China*

Daily, commented, "I can't remember the last time we had a conference with our union representative. The union certainly didn't do any good the day Chen was killed."[22]

Struggles such as the one at Tonghua, despite winning important victories and inspiring other struggles, are in a much weaker position to take on the program of economic development embraced by the Chinese state, counter to the interests of the Chinese working class, without an organized labor movement.

The Honda Workers' Strike

In May 2010, in the highest-profile strike actions in China's recent history, Honda workers in Foshan, Guangdong Province took action. They called for higher wages and, perhaps more significantly, for the reorganization of their workplace trade union, triggering a wave of strike actions by workers in other foreign-owned car plants that summer. Unlike the Tonghua struggle, these workers did not take action in the face of potential job losses due to imminent privatization. Working at a privately owned enterprise, they took action in order to actively improve their current situation.

The strike action, which began on May 17, lasted for more than two weeks and ended only after regular workers at the plant had been offered a 35 percent pay increase and interns at the factory had been offered an increase of more than 70 percent. Previously the Honda workers had been receiving wages well below the industry standards. Honda had also been particularly quick to exploit internship programs, since interns were not protected by Chinese labor law and so could be paid wages far below the official minimum wage.

Despite the different circumstances of the actions, one similarity with the Tonghua struggle was the failure of the ACFTU at the Honda plant to protect the interests of the workers. In the course of the strike the local-level trade union showed that its interests did not lie with the workers at all. On May 31, some of the striking workers reported that they had been physically attacked by men wearing union badges. Even after the union issued a vaguely apologetic letter, it was still clear that it was more keen on encouraging the workers to return to work as quickly as possible than ensuring a positive outcome for them. At an enterprise level, the Honda workers recognized that their union was failing them and had already made the reorganization of the workplace-based union a key demand of the strike. In an open letter, workers' representatives condemned the branch trade union, saying, "We are outraged by the trade union's appropriation of the fruits of the workers' struggles. We insist that the branch trade union of the factory shall be elected by the production line workers."[23]

In the end, the workers were unable to realize this demand in their settlement with management. The local trade union soon announced that an election for the workplace union would be held in late August 2010, but despite the rhetoric of party and ACFTU leaders in Guangdong about respecting the workers' right to a democratic election, it turned out that only a by-election was held; only part of the workplace union leadership was open to election. The original chairperson, greatly resented by the striking workers, kept his seat. A full election was eventually held in November 2011, hosted by the local trade union. Yet the outgoing leadership, in accordance to the rules promulgated by the ACFTU, monopolized the nomination procedure for the incoming leadership. In China, managerial-grade employees are not only allowed to stand as delegates to the union congress but also enjoy a disproportionately much higher delegates-to-members ratio than ordinary workers. As a result, members of the company management were elected as members of the union leadership, while the activists who had led the strike in 2010 were pushed out. The full election of the workplace union leadership was followed by the election of the leadership of branches and rank-and-file committees. It was deliberately arranged in a highly complicated manner and the procedure was drawn out so as to allow for manipulation from above.[24] Nevertheless, one positive development reported to have taken place is that the workplace union was able to negotiate a further wage increase in March 2011 as a result of collective bargaining with management.[25]

The fact that many of the workers were young—more than 50 percent of those who took part in the first strike in Foshan were high school students in internship programs—is in itself significant. The Honda strike represents the actions of a new generation of Chinese workers who have no firsthand memory of the defeat of the 1989 Democracy Movement and are prepared to fight to improve conditions at their own workplace. In fact, most of the high school interns probably do not know of the movement at all due to censorship. The older generation of SOE workers generally were not prepared to call for the reelection of workplace unions out of fear of being accused of trying to get rid of the leadership of the party, whereas the young workers in the Foshan private sector, mostly from rural households or small cities, dared to break the taboo. The fact that the Foshan workers held a democratic election for their representatives also shows that they are naturally inclined to run their affairs democratically.

The Honda workers in general demonstrated a much broader vision than their parents' generation. At the height of their struggle they made it clear that they saw their actions as being in the interests of the entire Chinese working class. In the words of the striking workers, "Our struggle to defend our rights is not just about fighting for ourselves, the 1,800 workers of Honda. We are concerned about the rights of all the workers in the whole country. We want to set a good example of workers struggling for their rights."[26] It is unknown how many of the strikers shared this vision, but one thing is certain. Unlike their parents, who often said, "Ershi ding chushan, sishi ding shoushan" ("When we are twenty, we all go to the cities to work, and when we turn forty, we all go back to our home village"), this young generation of rural migrant workers generally has a strong desire to establish roots in the cities, and is more likely to identify with the urban workers than with *nongmingong*. In fact, they rarely till the land and have little intention to live as peasants, having received more secondary education or vocational training than their parents. Even if the case of the Honda struggle remains unique, like the Tonghua case, it will nevertheless stand as an important sign of the development of resistance among young rural migrant workers. What they can accomplish is unknown, but these young workers may surprise us in many ways in the near future.

Meanwhile, the downward mobility of SOE workers on the one hand, and the gradual rise of wages for rural migrant workers on the other, has had an effect in bridging the gap between the two sections of the working class in the longer run. Although the gulf remains deep, both capitalist industrialization and workers' resistance provide aspects of the material conditions necessary for the future unification of these two sectors of workers in common struggles.

The Function of the ACFTU

The lack of any real genuine trade union in China also has crucial implications for workers' struggles. Despite what many have hailed as a more "pro-labor" stance in recent years, the role that the ACFTU has played from its establishment to the present is that of an arm of the party-state rather than an organ that workers can use to fight for and defend their rights and interests. Evidence suggests that in the post-Tiananmen crackdown period, the union bureaucracy has actually become further incorporated into the state structure.[27] While it is true that in more recent years the ACFTU has been involved in drafting seemingly more progressive labor legislation, such as the 2007 Labor Contract Law and, at least in rhetoric, has reached out to better represent grassroots interests, its actions cannot be fully understood outside the context of the party's agenda—a capitalist agenda, one that is fundamentally opposed to the interests of workers but that seeks at the same time to prevent social and political instability and achieve social harmony.

In many cases the reasons behind the ACFTU's increasing attempts to be seen as acting on behalf of workers' interests often have little to do with in the protection of workers' rights. Zhu, Warner, and Feng have suggested that part of the explanation for the ACFTU's intensive unionization drive, beginning in the early 2000s, might be the perceived challenge to the ACFTU's legitimacy posed by the growth, in the late 1990s, of "grassroots workers' protection groups"—a result of the increasing number of labor disputes.[28] This phenomenon represented a potential threat to the ACFTU in that groups outside of party direction and influence were taking over the responsibility for the protection of workers' rights. The subsequent drive by the ACFTU to promote increased unionization is rooted in its keenness to reach out to the grassroots. The ACFTU effort has led to a substantial increase in the number of enterprise-based unions but has meant little for workers in reality. Many of the new enterprise-based unions established in the last decade are little more than "paper unions," existing for the record but not actually functioning in practice. Moreover, the method by which new unions are established in private companies has more often than not been a top-down approach. Rather than seeking to organize workers to form a union, the ACFTU has instead sought the consent of companies to allow the establishment of a union. Such unions immediately fall under management control.[29] It is therefore no surprise that many workers remain unaware of the existence of their enterprise-based union. Despite attempts by the ACFTU to improve and transform its image through direct elections at an enterprise level, the reality is that many such unions remain heavily influenced or controlled by management rather than workers.

Furthermore, when legislation that might be more beneficial to workers has been on the agenda, it has been watered down under pressure from the capitalist business lobby. For instance, the ACFTU helped create the first draft of the 2007 Labor Contract Law, which was subsequently revised after the international business lobby, including the U.S. Chamber of Commerce, threatened that foreign companies would leave China if the original form of the law passed. The revised version weakened some of the provisions for employment security for workers. Likewise, in 2010, under pressure from the domestic business lobby in Guangdong Province and from Hong Kong investors, a clause that might have led to an election of worker representatives for a "collective consultation" was deleted from the draft of Guangdong Province's "Regulations on the Democratic Management of Enterprises." The clause's original reading was hardly revolutionary—the ACFTU would have controlled the nomination of candidates and the word "bargaining" never appeared, as it was considered too confrontational; however, successive revisions rendered the final bill totally meaningless for workers. Huang Qiaoyan, a legal scholar at the Sun Yat Sen University in Guangzhou, described the 2011 revised draft as "reflecting the wish of the people who drafted the bill to continue to control, through different levels of the union, the increasing demands from workers for collective wage consultations. They do not wish to see the rise of a situation where there are spontaneous actions by workers in which the unions cannot intervene, organize and be in control."[30]

The ACFTU's compliance with the government line on protecting business interests was made blatantly apparent when, in November 2008, with the onset of the global economic crisis, the central government demanded a freeze of the minimum wage. Rather than defending workers, the ACFTU simply toed the government line. These examples, and many others, illuminate the inherent contradiction in the ACFTU's alleged role as the protector of workers' rights while it is tied to the Chinese Communist Party, which prioritizes capitalist interests.

Consequently, many workers simply bypass the union and take action by themselves. In some cases, such as the Daqing oilfields protest and Liaoyang labor protests, both in 2002, the ACFTU has actually condemned workers' actions. Even when the local ACFTU chapters have intervened in disputes, their role has been more that of a mediator between workers and employers than that of a union acting on behalf of workers.[31] What has gained attention more recently, due to the high-profile strike action by the Honda workers in the summer of 2010, is the demand by workers for their union to be reorganized so as to better represent them. Rather than calling for an independent trade union altogether, these demands suggest that some workers, despite their experience of the ACFTU's ineffectiveness, have not become disillusioned with the idea of a trade union itself and believe that a more genuinely representative trade union will be beneficial to them.

A troublesome development is the prevailing trend among labor activists to present the apparent "positive change" as a reason for engaging more closely with the ACFTU, overlooking the fact that the ACFTU is still tied to the Communist Party and subsequently carries out the party's agenda at the expense of mobilizing workers in the defense of their rights and interests. Han Dongfang is a long-time critic of the ACFTU and founder of the NGO China Labour Bulletin, which had previously condemned the approach of "constructive engagement" with the ACFTU due to its support of "creeping legitimization."[32]

In his commentary in the *Guardian* in June 2011, Han appears to have changed his stance when he states, "Constructive engagement with the ACFTU at this point in history could produce real benefits—not just for the union itself but for China's workers' movement."[33] The only explanation that Han's commentary seems to offer for this change in position is that the ACFTU has been forced by the increased number of riots and strikes by workers to look at new ways in which it can represent workers' interests, such as by negotiating pay increases.[34] While it is true that increasing pressure from workers' actions may indeed have had some success in recently forcing the ACFTU into portraying itself as the legitimate workers' rights protector, and that therefore workers have won pay raises, this does not mean that the ACFTU itself has significantly changed. Indeed, Han also states that in many cases the ACFTU fails to involve workers and that "other schemes still betray the old bureaucratic habits of trade union officials more concerned with ticking boxes, meeting quotas and making speeches than actually doing anything concrete to help workers."[35] Thus it is difficult to see, even now, any new grounds for constructive engagement with the international labor movement.

Han's stance has been criticized by three Hong Kong–based labor NGOs that all run labor programs in mainland China. They say Han's comments exaggerate "isolated moves of the ACFTU as a huge step forward, while forgetting the much broader picture of the continuous absence of basic rights in China, and in particular, the full right of workers to freely choose and recall their representatives at the workplace without retaliation." Their work on the ground reveals that workers do not feel their interests are represented by unions, and that in cases in which workers have consulted with union officials about how to form a union, they have been met with indifference or discouragement by different levels of the ACFTU.[36]

Engagement with the ACFTU, as in the past, only gives a nod of approval to the status quo and perpetuates a situation in which workers in China are deprived of freedom of association and the right to form and join genuine trade unions. Nevertheless, the trend has been for the international labor movement to work ever more closely with the ACFTU, thereby further legitimizing it. Credibility was again falsely awarded to the ACFTU in June 2011, when it was elected by the International Labour Organization (ILO) workers' group to the ILO governing body. It would appear that there are now only a minority of unions that maintain a position similar to the condemnation outlined by the International Union of Food, Agricultural, Hotel, Restaurant, Catering, Tobacco and Allied Workers' Associations regarding the ACFTU's becoming a member of the ILO governing body: "Meaningfully supporting freedom of association is not a matter of choice for the ACFTU. It is simply impossible for it unless it sets itself in direct confrontation with the political apparatus that set it up and runs it. Given current developments in China today and given its core purpose, it patently cannot do this."[37]

Labor Needs a Political Solution

There have been changes to the ACFTU during the deepening of capitalist reform. The rural township and urban district ACFTU and higher levels of the union are still an arm of the party, but the party (as well as the local government) now takes more of a backseat role in relation to workplace unions. The growth of private enterprises implies that workplace unions, when they exist, are more likely in the hands of the employers, at the expense of the ACFTU. Direct control of workplace unions by individual employers means that the relationship of forces within individual enterprises is now more favorable to workers: whereas in the old SOEs workers were confronted with not only management but also the party, today workers in private companies deal directly with just management. If the workers have developed their own leaders and are organized, it is possible to press for reelection of the workplace union to make it work for the workers—at least some of the time. Hence the support for such calls, such as the Honda workers' call for a reelection of their workplace union, is because they are not only legitimate but also possible and tactically wise.

There is an obvious limit to this tactic, however. Union democracy in one enterprise within a context of absolutism—the absence of civil liberties, the worst kind of collusion between business and government—is not generally sustainable in the long run. To make workplace-union democracy genuine, one needs to have freedom of speech and of assembly, and this goes directly against the party-state. Therefore, either democratic workplace unions must spread to forge an industry-wide union, reaching higher up and gaining power through winning civil liberties, or they will be suffocated under the heavy weight of the absolute state and the employers. Consequently, even the call for the reelection of a workplace union should be seen as a minimum program that will soon exhaust its usefulness when the movement begins to gather momentum and something more radical is needed. In other words, the politicization of the labor movement is, sooner or later, inevitable—even if its initial intention is to defend its newly won democratic rights to control its own workplace unions. Either the labor movement needs to politicize itself by taking a lead in fighting for full civil liberties, distributive justice, democratic rights and, last but not the least, for self-organization, so it can affect the direction society is heading, or it will be continuously subjected to a regime interested only in guaranteeing the accumulation of capital at the expense of labor.

What is objectionable about a 2009 *China Labour Bulletin* (CLB) report is not its calls for the democratic election of grassroots unions, the development of enterprise-based collective bargaining, and the restoration of the constitutional right to strike[38]—rather it is the way it positions what should be a minimum program as its maximum program and places faith in the ACFTU and the party to carry it out. This is in line with Han Dongfang's new position assuring us that "even the party, which in the past only had its own interests to consider, now has to listen to the voice of the workers, and to respond to their increasingly clear and angry calls for change."[39] Even more troubling is the report's ultimate goal, revealed as helping the state to keep social peace by pursuing a strategy of "depoliticization" of the labor movement:

> China is now primarily a market economy where labor relations are governed by the laws of supply and demand and the legal constraints of the state. Disputes emerge because of a divergence of economic interests between workers and management within the enterprise. That is to say, they are a civil society matter. These disputes are the result of a natural dynamic; they do not represent a threat to the state and can in most cases be resolved within the enterprise without recourse to government intervention. In a market economy, the key to stopping labour disputes escalating into social conflict is the establishment of an effective dispute resolution mechanism within the enterprise, namely collective bargaining.[40]

CLB's program, in essence, is to keep workplace union democracy fragmented into tens of thousands of enterprises within a "civil society" of supply and demand. This is even more explicit in its Chinese edition, which calls for "the depoliticization of the contradiction between labor and capital and the depoliticization of the trade union." What follows is not just to appease the ACFTU but also to please the employers. It reassures employers that enterprise-based collective bargaining does not necessarily result in wages rising; it may result in wages being frozen or even in the lowering of wages. It states further that "under the environment of a market economy, wages are ultimately decided by the market.... When the ACFTU depoliticizes its labour protection activities, and returns to the workers and to industrial relations within enterprises... when its workplace union can really enter into collective bargaining with employers, this is the time when the ACFTU can really function in accordance with the market economy, and take a step forward in its self-reform."[41] This position ignores that the purpose of a trade union is precisely to put an end to a situation in which wages are decided solely by market forces or a union has to "function in accordance with the market economy."

In a more "normal" capitalist dynamic, where political power and capital accumulation are separate, it is true that daily labor disputes tend to be confined to enterprises, with an apolitical nature. However, in China—where political and economic power are fused, where the breakneck speed of capital accumulation is underpinned by a police state, where the promotion of local officials depends on how much capital they can attract or how fast the GDP grows—relatively major labor disputes within medium or large enterprises always carry the potential to spread and to become politicized if left uncontrolled. The Honda strike, for instance, spread to one hundred factories in Guangdong alone, and this was in a situation under state control and thus democratic elections of workplace unions had not occurred in other plants.[42] Attempting to support the spread of workplace-union democracy and make it sustainable, while limiting the context to the present structures of the ACFTU, is like trying to fit a large square peg into a small round hole.

Han and the *CLB* have not explained why they have diverged from their previous position of demanding independent trade unions. Nonetheless, the question as to whether we should seek full democratization of the ACFTU from the bottom up or call for the building of an independent union remains a tactical choice, one that will only be seriously raised in a massive upsurge of struggle and will be decided by the concrete relationship of forces at such a time. What matters most at present is whether we remain committed to fighting for at least the three basic labor rights—freedom of association, the right to strike, and the right to collective bargaining—from the workplace level up to the national level. If the answer is yes, then it necessarily follows that we should demand full democratic elections for all levels of the ACFTU rather than being content with the democratization of workplace unions. Thereafter we must consider in which direction we should look for the force of reform. While the *CLB* looks to the ACFTU and the party-state, we argue that we should adhere to the principle of pushing for change through a movement from below. Last, we must remember that the politicization of the labor movement is inevitable if it is faithful to its founding principle; therefore, we should not confine our perspective to demanding democratic trade unions. Either there is no mass upsurge and workers will not be able to force the authorities to respect their basic rights, or, if there is an upsurge of mass struggle that radicalizes the situation rapidly, the labor movement may face a demand to respond with a more comprehensive political program than one limited to just union matters. Instead of assigning the labor movement the minor role of safeguarding the workers' economic interests at the enterprise level, while leaving the political debate to the liberals and the nationalist bureaucracy, we should commit ourselves to a perspective in which the labor movement takes a lead in the fight for political power as well.

For workers to voice this in mainland China remains very risky, but labor activists, at least, should not surrender this basic vision. Only with political rights will labor have some weapons in its hands to defend its economic interests. If the present stage of development of the labor struggle determines that we can only agitate for workplace-union democracy among workers, we should retain our vision of politicizing this lower level of struggle into a more advanced and more political one at the next stage.

Those calling for more accommodation with the party-state often point to its recent pro-labor reforms, called a "New Deal" by some. It is true that the policies as they appear on paper one indicate that a welfare state has largely been installed. A series of labor laws were put in place to protect workers. A social safety net exists, covering pensions, medical care, unemployment benefits, and housing funds, into which employers contribute an amount equivalent to at least 25 percent of all wages paid out. A housing program is about to provide 10 million accessible apartments this year, in addition to the 5.8 million apartments provided last year. The central government has announced plans to raise the share of wages in the national income in coming years.

These kinds of measures tempt some people to look to the party-state for reform. This is misguided optimism. What characterizes the labor law reform is that it is concerned only with economic benefits and welfare, not with empowering workers with any kind of political rights in the workplace. As for the "welfare state," for ordinary workers, much of it exists only on paper because local governments always exempt the local employers from their obligation to contribute to social security funds. It is not our intention to deny the possibility of minor improvements to the livelihoods of common people, but even improvements do not make the need to fight for democracy less urgent.

In the context of the Great Recession since 2008, the terrible human and social cost of capitalism once again raises the question, "Can genuine freedom and democracy for working people materialize under capitalism?" With the spreading of the Occupy Wall Street movement, repeated strike waves in Greece, and more, perhaps it is not too wild to imagine that the debate about capitalism and socialism may be revived within the labor movement in the not too distant future.

Meanwhile a few leftist labor groups and activists in China remain committed to an alternative to capitalism. This is a good sign, indicating that not all people are complacent with the capitalist regime. Certain followers of Mao even argue that because China has long since become capitalist, a revolution is required to return it to the socialist path. Given the long downturn in the labor movement and the tremendous regression in intellectual trends, a revival of the debate on capitalism and socialism in China would surely be a welcome development. But it is also true that a large section of the public in today's China is skeptical of the words "revolution" and "socialism" precisely because of all the negative experiences during Mao's era. Mao's "socialism" had a serious drawback: it was divorced from democracy, and most of the time it was as top-down as any authoritarian regime. This laid the groundwork for the demise of the old working class. The way forward for the twenty-first-century labor movement in China requires us to make a sober reassessment of this period. Any kind of socialism must be wedded to freedom and democracy—a freedom that is more about freedom from exploitation and less about "market freedom," and a democracy that is about placing power in the hands of the working people.

CHAPTER 3

Collective Labor Protest in Contemporary Russia

Piotr Bizyukov and Irina Olimpieva

The neoliberal era in Russia started with Perestroika and the liberal reforms of 1989 into the 1990s. After the privatization of the Russian economy, a distinct model of capitalism emerged that became known as "Kremlin Capitalism," in which the newly created class of uncontrolled capitalists showed little interest in the growth of a healthy and vibrant economy.[1] Economic liberalization took place against a background of weak or absent democratic institutions and a strong anti-Soviet path dependency, including the domination of Soviet-legacy labor unions in the labor sphere and a low level of legal consciousness among the population. As a result, the new capitalists' lack of social responsibility toward workers and a disregard for labor rights have become the dominant norm of labor-capital relations in Russia today.

During the first years of Perestroika, collective labor protests, in particular the mass miners' strikes of 1989–1991, were the most prominent among the social protests nationwide. The miners went far beyond pure economic survival issues, demanding the general reorganization of the economy and changes in the political order of the country. The miners' strikes were among the factors that hastened the demise of the USSR and helped establish the new Russian political order, with Boris Yeltsin as president.[2] Subsequently, deep economic decline and dramatic deterioration in the living conditions of the population, caused by the economic reforms of the early 1990s, resulted in tremendous waves of labor and social protest.[3] Another wave of labor protests emerged at the end of the 1990s as a reaction to the astonishing backlog of wage arrears throughout the country. In the year 1996 alone, Goskomstat, the central state statistical bureau of Russia, registered 8,278 strikes, with 663,900 participants.

And even this tremendous level of protest was considered weak by Western scholars in light of the hardships and desperate living conditions facing the Russian people after the economic reforms.[4] According to a 1998 nationwide survey, 70 percent of Russian workers did not get paid regularly, and in about 60 percent of cases, the delays were longer than a month. Some workers had gone six, nine, or even twelve months or more without pay, and, when they were paid, payments were often made not in cash but in goods produced by the workers' enterprises.[5]

Despite the large number of labor protests, their influence on the economic and political course of the country had declined. The protesters no longer made political demands—nonpayment of salaries was the main reason for more than 95 percent of strikes in the country at that time.[6] As of 1997, most major labor protests were carried out by employees of the budget sector responsible for paying salaries, who made up 70 percent of the strikers (887,300).[7] The lack of reaction from the economic and political establishment led to an escalation to extreme forms of protest, such as hunger strikes (840 cases during the period 1997–2000), suicide (30 cases), blockades of the railways and roads, and more. These actions led that period to be known as the "Railway Wars."

The early 2000s were marked by a considerable decline in labor protest activities that was largely caused by the unprecedented growth of the Russian economy due to higher oil and gas prices in the international market, and a corresponding improvement in the living conditions of the population. Another reason for the decline was the adoption in 2001 of the new Labor Code, which made it almost impossible for unions to organize a legal strike. Since the mid-2000s, however, the estimated number of labor protests has been increasing.[8]

The chapter will begin with a brief overview of the Russian system of labor relations and then provide an analysis of the scope and patterns of labor protests in today's Russia, presenting profiles of the most vivid cases of protest action: the twenty-five-day strike at the Ford plant in Vsevolozhsk in 2007, the 2006 oil protests in the Khanty–Mansi Autonomous Region, the federal highway blockade by citizens of the "mono-city" Pikalevo in 2009, and the 2010 Mezhdurechensk miners' protest. In our conclusion we address the characteristics of the new wave of labor protest and its significance for labor-capital relations in Russia.

Labor Relations in Post-Soviet Russia

Labor relations following the creation of the Russian Federation are generally characterized by the domination of employers in labor relations, an antiunion Labor Code, a divided labor movement, a low level of labor standards, and weak control over their implementation.

Legal Frame of Labor Relations: The New Labor Code

As did many other countries of the post-Soviet bloc, Russia borrowed from the West the ideology of "social partnership" that had been introduced into labor legislation in the early 1990s with enthusiastic support from the International Labour Organization (ILO), the International Confederation of Free Trade Unions (ICFTU), and international financial institutions. Adopted in 2001, Russia's new Labor Code solidified a multilevel system of social partnership, generally resembling the classic European model of social dialogue. However its practical implementation has a number of essential deviations at every level that undermine the core idea of social partnership. These include the continuing dominant role of the state in development of labor policy, the absence and inadequacy of collective representation institutions for the employers at the sector and regional levels, and the weakness of the Soviet-legacy labor unions in the dialogue with employers. With good reason, the new system, as is the case in other Eastern European countries, can be described as "illusory corporatism."[9] Although the new Labor Code was conceived to be different from the Soviet-era labor code, the KZOT (Kodeks Zakonov o Trude), it did not make a "clean break with the past."[10] This is confirmed by empirical evidence demonstrating that the new rhetoric of "social partnership" in fact obscures the considerable continuation of Soviet practices in labor relations, and serves as "a fig leaf on the body of wild capitalism."[11]

According to the opinion of both scholars and practitioners, the new Labor Code as a whole has worsened the position of labor unions in the dialogue with the employer.[12] The most radical change affected the possibility for labor protests: the union lost its right to call for a strike, and now the decision must come from a meeting of the workers' collective of that given enterprise. Solidarity strikes focused on social economic policy were prohibited, the number of sectors in which strikes are outlawed increased, and more obstacles were placed in the way of adopting a decision to start a strike. The new requirements make it almost impossible for unions to organize a strike legally.[13] As in other post-Soviet countries, labor relations in Russia after reforms are characterized by an obvious contradiction between the de jure widening of the labor rights and the de facto weakening of their actual defense.[14] When the level of labor standards is considered, Russia's is the lowest among post-Soviet countries, both de jure and de facto.[15]

Divided Labor Movement

Since the beginning of the 1990s, Russia's labor movement has been split in two continuously warring camps: the "official" trade unions affiliated with the Soviet-era Federation of Independent Trade Unions (FNPR)[16] and the so-called "alternative" or "free" labor unions, which are independent from the FNPR. The FNPR dominates the labor sphere, claiming to represent 26 million employees, which equates to 45 percent of total Russian employees and 9 percent of all unionized workers.[17] Free labor unions differ from the official ones in many respects. While official unions follow the ideology of social partnership, stressing the commonality of interests among employees and employers, and serving as an element of the state system,[18] free labor unions are more oriented toward identifying labor conflict and fighting against the employer. Unlike official unions that usually build their primary organizations from above, free labor unions typically emerge on the wave of some protest action from below, often at enterprises unionized by the official trade unions. In these instances, the newly created unions experience double pressure—from the employer as well as from the official union, which makes it very hard for the new organization to survive. Due to their militant character and protest ideology, free labor union activists are prime targets for tough administrative pressure and even physical assaults. Unlike the official unions, which have access to resources accumulated by their predecessors during the Soviet era, free labor unions must rely almost exclusively on membership fees. The two types of unions also differ in terms of their repertoire of collective actions. Free unions much more frequently use noninstitutional forms of protest, such as unsanctioned strikes, rallies, pickets, and street actions. They actively cooperate with various social movements and protest groups, organizing coalitions and participating in joint protest actions. In general, the official trade unions are closer to a bureaucratic structure while the free unions more resemble a social movement.[19]

The Influence of Globalization

The spread of transnational corporations (TNCs) in recent decades has presented new challenges to the Russian labor unions. For the official unions it has resulted in the emergence of intraregional and even international "corporative" labor unions, for instance, the labor unions of LUKOIL, GAZPROM, SIBUR, and others. For the corporative unions membership fees are not the main or sole source of financing. They work as distributors of social benefits provided by corporations and serve as intermediaries between management and employees rather than as defenders of employees' rights. In transnational companies, unions also help management to overcome cultural barriers and build corporate solidarity.[20] At the same time, transnational corporations have ushered in several of the most militant and organized alternative labor unions in Russia, such as the free labor unions at Ford, GM, RENO, and other foreign enterprises. Therefore, the real struggle for labor rights in today's Russia is taking place in TNCs with foreign capital.[21] There are several reasons for this: First, the free labor unions are formed by the initiative of the workers themselves and work to serve their members' interests. These new labor unions leverage the international status of the TNCs by using the channels of international labor solidarity and support from international trade union organizations. A second reason is anchored in the different business cultures and corporative ethics of Western companies. They are generally more law-abiding than Russian companies and more concerned with maintaining a public image as a socially responsible company; therefore, they try to avoid open labor conflict that would strengthen the position of labor unions. And, last but not least, workers in the TNCs tend to represent a younger generation of employees who are not burdened with the Soviet-era attitude toward labor unions as an integral part of the management system.

The Scale of Labor Protests in Early Twenty-First Century Russia

The issue of labor protests in contemporary Russia is complicated. There is almost no empirical research and data on the subject. Rosstat (the Russian federal state statistics service) registers only legal strikes, which, given the provisions of the new Labor Code, are almost impossible to organize. Thus, according to Rosstat reports, in 2008 there were only four strikes, just one in 2009, and none in 2010. Official statistics do not report spontaneous or illegal strikes, nor do they reflect the other forms of labor protest actions multiplying inside or outside of enterprises.

In order to analyze the real scale and dynamics of labor protests, a special methodology to monitor protest actions was developed in 2008 by the Center for Social-Labor Rights (TsSTP).[22] Monitoring data disproves the official statistics by revealing hundreds of protest actions and strikes, legal and illegal, which have taken place around the country. In the last four years 831 cases of labor protest were included in the monitoring database.

Stop-actions as a specific form of protest action are highlighted in order to demonstrate the dynamics of protest tension, defined as the

TABLE 3.1 The dynamics of labor protests in Russia, 2008–2011

	Overall number of actions	Monthly average number of actions	Overall number of stop-actions	Monthly average number of stop-actions	The share of stop-actions (%)
2008	93	7.75	60	5.0	64.5
2009	272	22.7	106	8.8	38.9
2010	205	17.1	88	7.3	42.9
2011	262	21.8	91	7.6	34.7
Total	832	17.33	345	7.2	42.5

ratio of stop-actions to the overall number of protests. Stop-actions do not always take the form of strikes; they may be a refusal to work by one or several employees (in compliance with the Labor Code) if a salary delay exceeds two weeks, and may not lead to the stoppage of the whole enterprise if management employs strikebreakers.

As can be seen in Table 3.1, the jump in the number of labor protests in 2009 was due to the economic crisis, followed by a decline in the number of protests in 2010 (though it did not fall below the pre-crisis level of 2008). In 2011 the number of protests did not continue to decrease but instead grew by 27 percent, despite the fact that 2011 was an economically successful year for Russia. Thus, the growth of labor protests in 2011 indicates problems in the labor sphere that cannot be attributed merely to the state of the economy.

Geographic dispersion of the protests, calculated as a proportion of the number of regions where protests occurred in relation to the total regions in Russia (eighty-three), indicates that the proliferation of protests across the country increased from 0.48 in 2008 to 0.67 in 2009 and to 0.72 after the economic crisis.

Table 3.2 also shows that the average protest intensity in the "protest regions," calculated as a ratio of the overall number of protests to the number of regions, increased from 2.3 in 2008 to 4.3 in 2011. In 2010, although the dispersion of protests was increasing, the protest intensity declined; whereas in 2011 there was no growth in geographic dispersion but regional protest intensity increased from 3.4 to 4.3.

Looking at the protests by economic sector, 50 percent took place in industrial enterprises. Among the industrial branches, the undisputed leader in protests is machine manufacturing. But in 2011 there was a sharp increase in the number of strikes in the transportation sector. During the first half of 2011, the share of strikes in this sector reached 27 percent.

TABLE 3.2 Geographical distribution and regional intensity of labor protest, 2008–2011

	2008	2009	2010	2011
Dispersion of labor protests	0.48	0.67	0.72	0.72
Regional protest intensity	2.3	4.9	3.4	4.3

It is notable that the number of labor protests increased sharply during the economic crisis yet did not decrease considerably in the years following. The same tendency was seen with the dispersion of protests across the country: the number of protest-free regions diminished and the average number of protests in protest regions increased. This means that the intensity of the labor conflict has remained steady despite the end of the crisis.

Changing Forms of Labor Protest

Russian labor legislation provides workers with only two legally acceptable ways to protest: (1) collective strike within the frame of a collective labor dispute, and (2) work stoppage if the delay of wages exceeds two weeks. In economic sectors such as transportation, healthcare, and many others, workers are deprived of the right to strike and cannot use any other methods that would lead to a work stoppage. However, as can be seen in Figure 3.1, workers in Russia have resorted to many other types of protest.

Raising collective claims is the least aggressive and the most common form of labor protest, in which the workers express their disagreement with a situation and indicate readiness to resort to tougher forms of protest action if necessary. Raising collective claims is often the first phase in a protest and in some cases is enough to improve the situation. In 2011 collective claims were raised in more than half of all protests (52 percent).

The second most common form of protest is the organization of meetings and pickets, which were used in a third of all cases in 2011, as well as in previous years. This is the most demonstrative action, aimed at drawing attention to the conflict, and its popularity is related to the growing interest today in public actions.

Illegal (or spontaneous) stoppage of the enterprise or subdivision is the third most frequent form of protest. Although the ratio of illegal stoppages has declined from 44 percent in 2008 to 28 percent in 2011, stoppage remains a popular form of protest action. Among the total number of illegal stoppages, a complete stoppage of the entire enterprise (a strike) should be specifically highlighted. In 2008 the protesters resorted to this form in almost every third case (32 percent), in 2010 in every fifth case (21 percent), and in 16 percent of cases in 2011.

Appeals to the authorities (local, regional, or federal) and to the law enforcement agencies—including official public letters, petitions, and complaints—are aimed at attracting the attention of external, powerful institutions when it is impossible to solve the problem from within the enterprise. In 2011 appeals to the authorities were undertaken in every fifth case of protest; the popularity of this form in recent years has remained steady and is even growing.

One of the most noteworthy features of Russian labor protest today is the generally low rate of legal protests, as prescribed by the Labor Code. The data demonstrate the continuing decline in using legal stoppages or collective labor disputes (the official legal procedure of solving labor conflicts at an enterprise). In recent years an average of less than

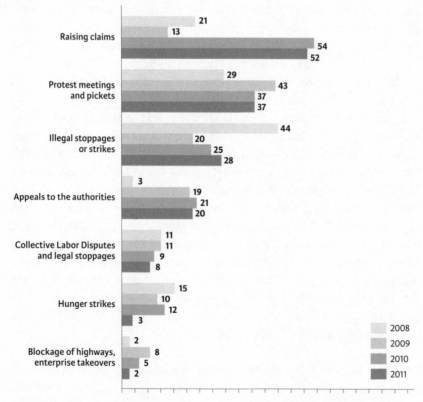

FIGURE 3.1 Forms of Labor Protest, 2008–2011 (percentage of total number of actions)
Note: the overall sum for a given year may exceed 100 percent because one action may use a combination of different forms.

10 percent of protest actions (11 percent in 2008 versus 8 percent in 2011) used these legal forms of protest.

Extreme forms of protest deserve special attention, particularly hunger strikes, enterprise takeovers, and the blockade of roads and highways. In 2008, 17 percent of protests came under this category, 18 percent in 2009, and 17 percent again in 2010. In 2011, however, extreme protest actions dropped to only 5 percent. If radical protest actions are taken to represent reactions to severe violations of labor rights by employers, then the reduction in the number of radical actions in 2011 may indicate that there were fewer such violations.

A protest action can use, simultaneously or consecutively, multiple forms of protest. In 2008, single-protest actions dominated (78 percent), whereas in 2010 they had dropped to 50 percent, and decreased again in 2011 to only 43 percent of all protest actions. In the remaining cases, protest actions were more complicated. Frequently, an action escalates to a more serious protest form due to a lack of response from the employer to initial employee complaints. The growing use of multiple forms of protest suggests that workers today need to resort to increasing force in order to start a dialogue with the employer.

Overall, the forms of labor protest implemented during the last several years are characterized by minimal radical actions and an increase in actions directed outside rather than inside the enterprise. Although the classical strike (a complete stoppage of the enterprise) remains among the dominant forms of labor protest, it is more risky and less effective today due to the strict provisions of the new Labor Code. The growing frequency of street protests can be attributed to workers' lacking the leverage within an enterprise to influence relations with their employer. Today, when Russian employers can legally sidestep the procedures of collective agreements and block labor disputes, protests often spill beyond the gates of the enterprise onto the streets in order to become visible to the authorities, journalists, and public leaders. The shortage of means for resolving labor relations inside enterprises channels labor protest energy into the larger community where it has the chance of enjoining a broader social protest.

Causes of Russian Labor Protest against Capital and Dominant Unions

From 2008 to 2011, nonpayment of salaries or delays in payment was the predominant cause of labor protests in Russia (Figure 3.2). Protests due to other factors were much less frequent. Exceptions were downsizing and firing during the 2009 crisis year, and the reorganization of enterprises the following year, which provoked 21 percent and 22 percent of protest actions, respectively. If other reasons connected to salaries—low salaries, disagreements over changes in wage systems, and so on—are included, it becomes clear that salary-related issues are far and away the main reason for labor protests. Even so, the percentage of protests provoked by salary issues has been declining in recent

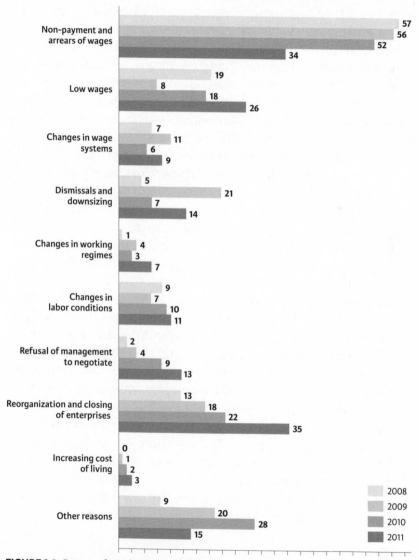

FIGURE 3.2 Reasons for Labor Protests (percentage of total number of actions)
Note: since the same protest can have more than one cause, the sum of the percentage for a given year may exceed 100.

years: 83 percent in 2008, 75 percent in 2009, 76 percent in 2010, and 69 percent in 2011.

More notable are changes in the structure of salary-related reasons. During 2008–2010, more than half the protest cases grew out of wage arrears (57 percent in 2008, 52 percent in 2010); yet such cases represented only 34 percent in 2011. There was also an increase in protests against the changing system of wage calculation adopted during the crisis. Protests against low salaries also increased to reach 26 percent in 2011, advancing over the previous year, when low salaries caused only 18 percent of the disputes. Workers began to strike and protest not only because their salaries were not being paid, but also because their pay was too low. This dynamic reflects a normalization of economic conditions.

Another shift in the focus of the economic battle is also evidenced by the increasing number of protests due to reasons such as reorganization and the closing of enterprises. These reasons are related to managerial decisions, such as the outsourcing of some production subdivisions that results in downsizing, dismissals of personnel, or alteration of workers' employment status (for instance, switching from permanent contracts to temporary). In 2011, 35 percent of labor protests were due, at least in part, to these reasons, up from 22 percent in 2010.

Sometimes protest action is used as a tool to draw an employer into negotiations over issues of salary or working conditions. The number of protests caused by employer refusal to negotiate has grown consistently (increasing from 2 percent in 2008 to 13 percent in 2011), reflecting changes in the pattern of interaction between employees and employers and indicating attempts by workers to overcome the imbalance of power in labor-capital relations. This increase illustrates that the situation in Russia is still far from an actual social partnership, in which an employer is expected to enter a dialogue with employees without requiring additional pressure from the workers.

Overall, the structure of the reasons for labor protests has shifted fundamentally in recent years. The spectrum is widening as salary-related reasons decline, in particular nonpayment or arrears of wages, which were more typical of the crisis period. The structure of protest causes has come to resemble more closely that of a "normal" economic situation than an economy in crisis.

Who Organizes Labor Protests?

The question as to what actors participate in labor protests and what role labor unions play in the organization of protest action—strikes in

TABLE 3.3 Protest organizers (percentage of total number of cases)

	Employees themselves	Primary trade union	Higher-level trade union	Political parties, social movements	Workers' committees	Other
2008	62	33	3	–	–	2
2009	43	42	28	9	–	2
2010	38	44	29	12	6	3
2011	41	48	26	7	2	3

Note: As a given protest could be organized by several actors, the overall sum may exceed 100.

particular—requires an understanding of how the Labor Code provisions work in reality. As can be seen in Table 3.3, in 2008 the majority of protests (62 percent) were spontaneous, organized without any support from either labor unions or other social actors or institutions. In the following years, the role of labor unions has increased. This tendency applies both to the primary labor unions operating at the enterprise level and to the higher-level trade unions—sectoral or territorial trade union organizations. In 2011 almost half the protest actions were organized with the participation of primary labor unions (48 percent) and in more than a quarter of actions, higher-level trade unions were involved as well (26 percent).

It should be mentioned here that official and free labor unions act differently in the organization of the protest actions. While free unions more often initiate the protests themselves by mobilizing workers, official labor unions usually seek to avoid any open form of conflict with employers. When official unions do participate in an action they join when the action is already under way, functioning rather as "coordinators" or "assistants" than as initiators or organizers of the protest. Official unions see their main task as controlling against the expansion of the protest and keeping the protest within a legal framework. If doing so proves impossible, they try to prevent aggressive or destructive actions by the protesters. The fact that official labor unions do not organize protests themselves but join later allows them to avoid punishment from the higher-level trade unions for organizing illegal action, and at the same time to maintain a good reputation in the eyes of union members. The official unions' strategy of controlling rather than initiating labor protests developed during the years of economic crisis, when multiple and deep violations of the employees' labor rights could not be ignored, even by the official unions. Today the position of "mediating organizational support" of the protest at the enterprise level has become standard for primary official unions.

The workers start the action and then the unions join the protest, assisting workers in formulating their demands, organizing and mediating negotiations with employers and authorities if necessary. The higher-level labor unions also play a mediating role by conveying the workers' demands, formulated by the primary union organizations, to regional authorities or top corporate management through channels inaccessible to ordinary employees and primary union organizations. It appears that official unions have become accustomed to their role as "protest assistants" and have no intention of increasing their degree of involvement.

In the 2000s, labor protests began to attract the attention of other social actors, including political parties and groups, primarily leftist youth organizations. Political parties such as the Communist Party of the Russian Federation, the Russian United Democratic Party, or United Russia, join protest actions more rarely, seemingly only when they need to demonstrate support for the protection of workers' rights. In these instances the parties behave much like the official unions, mediating the transfer of the protesters' demands to the upper level of the state hierarchy, imbuing the workers' claims with greater importance. In small towns and villages, labor-related protest actions may also be led by local public activists.

Protest in Action
Ford Factory—Twenty-Five Days of Strike

The Ford plant under discussion, one of the assembling production units of the transnational Ford Motor Company, was built in 2002 in the town of Vsevolozhsk.[23] In 2005 a new labor union formed at the Ford plant as a splinter group from the official primary union organization. Today the Ford labor union has more than 1,200 members (out of 2,900 employees), is the leading member of MPRA (the Interregional Labor Union of the Workers of Automobile Industry),[24] and has become one of the most organized and militant free labor unions in Russia. Upon its inception the labor union began its fight against company management for higher salaries and better working conditions. Trade unionists used a wide spectrum of methods ranging from collective labor disputes and raising claims to temporary plant stoppages and a work-to-rule strike. The culmination of the conflict was a twenty-five-day strike in 2007 with the participation of 1,500 workers. Among the main demands of the workers were a 35 percent wage increase, the indexing of wages to inflation rates, triple overtime, bonuses for duration of service, and other social payments and benefits for workers.

Protest actions started on November 7, 2007, with a warning strike organized after collective negotiations with the employer failed. In compliance with legal requirements, the employer was notified ten days before the strike. This allowed Ford management to file an appeal with the labor court, which declared the strike illegal. The protest action was finished just as it had begun. Organizing a new strike meant going through all the formal procedures again. That required extra time and more organizational efforts; however, the labor union was particularly concerned that everything be done according to the legal provisions of the Labor Code. In order to continue the strike while preserving its legality, the labor union organized several meetings of the workers' collective in advance, each of which resulted in the participants' decision to go on strike. Thus, after each successive court ruling declaring the strike illegal, the labor union immediately submitted to the employer another set of documents announcing a new strike. Only through such a maneuver, balancing on the edge between legislative provisions, did the union manage to continue the strike and keep it legal.

On November 20, work at the plant stopped; however, every morning, hundreds of workers gathered in pickets in front of the plant gates. The confrontation reached its peak on November 27, when the "living fence" of the protesters prevented a bus carrying strikebreakers from entering the enterprise. In the following days, picketing continued despite the onset of winter frost. The strategy changed: now, when strikebreakers tried to enter the enterprise, they had to pass through "corridors of shame" organized by the protesters, who lined the entryway to the plant. Pressure from the employer's side was increasing. Management made hundreds of telephone calls trying to convince workers to come back to work. Although all the strikers received financial support amounting to two-thirds of a worker's basic salary, many families were barely making ends meet. So, after more than three weeks of strike activity, some strikers decided to go back to work. The strike was suspended on December 14 by a decision of the general meeting of strikers.

The protest resulted in a compromise between the labor union and management. Wages were raised 16 percent to 21 percent; overtime would be restricted and became a matter of agreement between management and the labor union, with double overtime payments; and agreements were reached regarding pensions and other social benefits.

The strike's success was facilitated by the support provided by other free labor unions, which made contributions to the strike fund and organized solidarity actions and pickets at their enterprises and in front of Ford dealers. The strike was also supported by the international labor movement. It is especially notable that Ford management's attempts to cover the shortage of vehicles by importing them from a German Ford plant encountered resistance from the German workers. But the key factor allowing for the very possibility of such a long and persistent protest was the democratic character of the free labor union of the Ford plant. All basic questions regarding the strike's organization and maintenance were discussed at the workers' meetings, held by the union in front of the factory gates. The labor union's policies were transparent and decisions were made in full view of all the protesters.

Oil Protests in 2006

In 2006, the Khanty-Mansi Autonomous Okrug (KhMAO), a region in the center of the country that provides nearly 60 percent of Russian oil, was engulfed by a wave of labor protests.[25] In addition to local protest actions in the largest cities of the region, such as Surgut, Megion, Khanty-Mansiysk, and Nizhnevartovsk, pickets were organized by oil drillers in Moscow near the offices of the major oil companies and in front of the building where the annual congress of FNPR, the top level of official labor unions, was held. The protesters demanded wage increases and the end of repression against union activists. It is noteworthy that this protest was directed not only against the employers and local authorities, but also against the policies of FNPR, which the workers accused of suppressing the labor movement.

The main reason for the protests was the growing income inequality between the workers and the oil companies' shareholders. Despite the increasing profits of the oil companies in recent years, workers' wages had remained relatively low. Up to 80 percent of a workers' salary was dependent on incentives and premiums built into the salary structure, which left workers vulnerable and dependent on managers' attitudes. Social tension was also caused by the increasing outsourcing of various services that had been formerly performed by employees of the oil companies. For these workers, this meant losing the essential social benefits and privileges of employees of the oil mining economic sector. Another issue was the expansion of the shift method through low-cost migration; the oil companies filled necessary positions by bringing migrant workers from Central Asia, at low pay and in substandard housing.

The first protests began at Slavneft-Megionneftegaz. The reason given for the action was the company's decision to pay prohibitively high dividends to shareholders. According to the leader of the primary union organization, "The shareholders of the company, who received billions of rubles, were able to allocate only 25 million for housing construction. It turns out that they suck out all the profit from the company, and we are left destitute." Indeed, the housing situation at the majority of the oil companies is catastrophic. Many workers still live in the "beams" (wooden plank huts, covered with slate or coated with clay). After the company's director refused to negotiate, the trade union organized a protest rally followed by a citywide meeting that brought together about seven hundred people. The union demanded a significant increase of labor tariffs and the allocation of 3.5 billion rubles to address social benefits, housing, and other issues.

Protest activity broke out later at one of the enterprises of TNK-BP in Nizhnevartovsk. Despite an ostensibly "worker-friendly" social policy, the enterprise was undergoing reorganization, and in the reorganized structures wages had changed unevenly. The workers of the less profitable enterprises had received a large salary increase due to the organizational merger, while in the more profitable enterprises salaries remained largely the same. The latter group of workers was demanding a wage increase. The *profkom*, or enterprise trade union committee, did not support the protesting workers, which resulted in sixty people withdrawing their membership from the official trade union and creating an alternative.

The wave of labor protest did not bypass even the most profitable of the oil companies, Surgutneftegas, which had the highest wages among the oil companies in the region. In mid-July 2006 in Surgut, a protest rally was organized, with up to five thousand workers of the company participating. In contrast to the protest at Slavneft, where the official trade union led the protest, the union of Surgutneftegas took an anti-worker position: "You get a little, because you work a little"; "We [the company] bought a new field, and we must tighten our belts"; "Rallies are extremism." Thus the Surgut protest was organized by a newly emerged alternative trade union organization, Profsvoboda ("Union freedom"). The administration responded to the formation of the new union with repression. Specifically, the leader of the Profsvoboda was denied all premiums due him and then fired. However, under pressure from the workers, the management of Surgutneftegas was forced to negotiate with the new union and to accept the workers' demands.

Pikalevo: The Blockade of the Highway

The town of Pikalevo is a so-called mono-town, in which the overwhelming majority of the population works at one city-defining enterprise, in this case the aluminum plant that provides jobs for about 3,500 Pikalevo citizens.[26] In 1992 the plant was privatized and two separate production companies were created: ash production (ZAO Metachim) and cement production (Pikalevsky Cement). Reorganization of the enterprise, which began in 2007, was conducted with no concern for its technological or organizational unity, or for its crucial function in supporting the life of the city—for instance, providing citizens with heat and hot water. Price wars between the owners completely destroyed the once-united production complex. The problems began in 2008 with layoffs at the cement plant, where 700 of 1,100 employees were dismissed. Soon the crisis spread to the other production companies and resulted in the closure of all three enterprises. The total sum of wage arrears amounted to 41 million rubles (about US$1.3 million).

Limited work opportunities, typical of a mono-town, and exacerbated by the Soviet-legacy low level of labor mobility, were a critical factor in this social disaster. By spring 2009, the lack of jobs and money had brought hundreds of families to the edge of starvation. None of the legal protest actions, such as meetings organized by the official labor union or citizens' appeals to the authorities, had any effect. The already dire situation was aggravated by the shuttering of the thermoelectric plant serving the enterprises, which also turned off the city's hot water supply. Together these factors impelled the radical protest action. On June 2, 2009, thousands of Pikalevo citizens blockaded the federal highway A-114 Novaya Ladoga-Vologda. The blockade of the highway lasted for several hours; traffic stretched over 438 kilometers. Representatives from the local authorities, top enterprise managers, and labor union leaders arrived on the scene. As a result of negotiations, the employers and the authorities made a commitment to begin a responsible dialogue with the workers, with the labor unions as mediators, to find solutions to the problems. After the agreement was signed by all sides and loudly announced to the protesters, the highway was unblocked.

It is unknown, however, whether these commitments would have been upheld by the employers and authorities if not for the appearance of Prime Minister Vladimir Putin in Pikalevo, two days after the blockade. Putin held a local meeting on Pikalevo's problems with the participation of the three enterprise owners and high-ranking government officials. The result of the meeting was a tripartite agreement, signed by the owners, providing for normalization of the production process at the enterprises and the recommencement of work at the city-sustaining infrastructure. After Putin left Pikalevo, the enterprises and the thermoelectric plant resumed functioning, and the workers were paid all the debts on wages. It is evident that Putin, a consummate self-promoter, took advantage of the protest in Pikalevo to strengthen his image as "the defender of the working people" by solving the problem and openly humiliating the owners of the enterprises, in particular, the unpopular oligarch Oleg Deripaska.[27]

Miners' Protest in Mezhdurechensk

Two explosions during the night of May 2010 killed more than a hundred miners and rescuers at the Raspadkaya mine, the largest coal mine in Russia, located in the town of Mezhdurechensk (Kuzbass, Kemerovo Region).[28] Spontaneous protest arose after the funerals and resulted in a blockade of the railway, which led to the stoppage of twenty trains. Although the tragedy was the catalyst for the protest action, a profound labor conflict had been brewing long before the explosion. The preceding February, the sinkers had announced their readiness to strike. The main reasons were low wages and the high proportion of premiums in the salary structure. But finally, the administration was forced to come down to the shaft and managed to defuse the situation. The miners demonstrated high levels of discontent with Rosugleprof, the official trade union, which they claimed, never supported their demands. During the annual trade union conference, the workers tried to replace the conciliatory union leaders with more militant representatives that reflected their interests. But due to administrative interference, their attempts failed, and many workers resigned from the official union to demonstrate their disapproval.

The funerals of the miners on May 14 transformed into a spontaneous, citywide memorial as nearly 1,500 people—mainly workers, relatives, and community members from the Raspadskaya mine, gathered in the central square. With no particular plan; speakers addressing the crowd expressed grief about the tragedy and reflected on the causes, including ineffective mine security systems and the administration's responsibility for the accident, the lack of reliable information on the scale of the tragedy, and the attempt by the mine's administration and city authorities to cover up the accident, which had occurred on the eve of "Victory Day"—a traditional national celebration of the USSR's victory in World War II. The miners expressed concerns about their employment status, given the lack of information about the administration's future plans for the destroyed mine. Speakers were particularly outraged by the interview the mine's director had given to the media the day before the funerals, commenting about the "high salaries" of the miners, about 60,000 to 80,000 rubles a month ($2,000–$2,500). Passions ran high, and the memorial turned into a protest against the mine's administration and the local authorities. Some of the protesters decided to go to the city hall, and formed an initiative group to attempt to negotiate with the mayor. However, the mayor could not meet the demands of the protesters, as they primarily concerned the competence of the mine's management. After not getting the desired results, some of the most radical protesters made their way to the railroad and blocked the tracks.

Representatives of the railway administration, the police, and the mayor arrived at the site almost immediately. All attempts to persuade the protesters to clear the tracks failed. After midnight, special riot police (OMON) arrived in the town and began the operation to oust the protesters. The first attack failed and the protesters started throwing stones at the police. Only after a third police attack was the railroad unblocked. During the operation, twenty-eight protesters were arrested and seventeen policemen were mildly injured. It was the first post-Soviet-era labor protest to be suppressed by force.

The events in Mezhdurechensk resonated strongly in the region and throughout Russia. The morning after the blockade, Aman Tuleev, governor of Kemerovo, arrived in Mezhdurechensk, promising that all victims of the accident and their families would receive monetary compensation, and that working conditions in the mine would be brought into compliance with legislative safety standards. In the following days a large teleconference was held with Prime Minister Putin and mine owners (including oligarch Roman Abramovich), the mine's administration, and representatives of the federal, regional, and municipal governments. As a result the city received significant funds to support the miners injured in the accident and the needs of Mezhdurechensk residents as well. Significant steps were taken to preserve employment at the Raspadskaya mine; idled workers were guaranteed wages and the preservation of their jobs during the repair period. Had there been no blockade of the railroad, the citizens' demands would not have received the necessary attention, resources, or support from the authorities and the mine owners. Events in Mezhdurechensk triggered a wave of solidarity among workers across the country, including more than forty meetings in support of the miners.

Conclusion

The wide scale and the situational specifics of labor protest in Russia illustrate the limitations of the social partnership model and its inadequacy in contemporary Russian capitalism. A reduction in legal protest actions while illegal forms, such as spontaneous strikes and stoppages, continue to dominate demonstrates that the mechanisms of conflict solutions provided by labor legislation are generally insufficient. The growing emphasis on demonstrative methods, whereby workers prefer to appeal to the authorities and other powerful institutions outside the enterprise rather than engage in direct dialogue with the employer, also shows that the balance of power in this social partnership is disproportionately on the employers' side. The ambiguous role of the official labor unions, which prefer to assist and mediate rather than to initiate or organize labor protests, does not correspond to the role that labor unions are supposed to play according to the social partnership model.

A summation of the practice of labor protest in Russia must include government regulation, which formally permits the organization of the protests, but makes them impossible in practice. Any attempts to organize a legal strike would lead to a guaranteed defeat. Although workers have found some tricks to make a legal strike possible, as in the case of the strike at the Ford plant, in general, legal strikes are possible only in spite of rather than because of legal regulation. It seems that the current Legal Code is designed not to help in resolving labor conflicts but to suppress the protest activity of the workers and their militant trade union organizations at the enterprises. At the federal level, the illusion of Russian tripartism and the generally dependent position of labor in the dialogue with employers and the state reveal that the official labor unions are unable to revise the legislation, while the authoritative bodies stubbornly refuse to simplify the procedures for workers to obtain permits to protest their wages and conditions.

The protest actions described in this chapter represent two distinct patterns of mass labor protest in Russia today—spontaneous defensive resistance and organized offensive strategy. The changes in the forms of, and reasons for, protest actions in recent years have demonstrated a general reorientation of labor protest from issues of survival, which were more typical of the economy of crisis, to a wider range of employment issues. A sustained, high level of protest activity even after the crisis, the continuing proliferation of protest across the country's regions with growing intensity, and the preservation of the strike as one of the dominant forms of protest suggest some essential changes in the general mode of relations between employees and employer. These can be described as a transition from a purely defensive mode of labor protest to a more demanding and even offensive protest strategy.

II.
ORGANIZING AUTONOMY AND RADICAL UNIONISM IN THE GLOBAL SOUTH

CHAPTER 4

The Struggle for Independent Unions in India's Industrial Belts: Domination, Resistance, and the Maruti Suzuki Autoworkers

Arup Kumar Sen

Rendering the workers footloose is a key feature of neoliberal capitalism.[1] It follows that subcontracting and casualization of the workforce are characteristic components of the new capitalism emerging in the Indian automobile industry in this age of neoliberal globalization, further skewing the balance of power in favor of the employers. In this context, we should keep in mind the Gramscian insight that domination never becomes total: the workers make their signature stamp of resistance in diverse forms. This chapter will explore the dynamics of domination and resistance in the Maruti Suzuki plant at Manesar in Gurgaon, located in the state of Haryana in India.[2]

History of Maruti Suzuki India Limited

Maruti Udyog Limited (MUL) was incorporated as a government-owned company in 1981. In 1982, after a global search for prospective partners, it entered into a license and joint-venture agreement with the Suzuki Motor Company of Japan with the purpose of manufacturing a low-cost and fuel-efficient "people's car." Suzuki acquired a 26 percent equity holding in MUL with an option to increase its shareholding in later years. Suzuki's equity stake in MUL increased to 40 percent in 1989, to 50 percent in 1992, and to 54.2 percent in 2002.[3] MUL is credited with bringing about an "automobile revolution" in India. It was renamed Maruti Suzuki India Limited (MSIL) in 2007. Maruti Suzuki emerged as the market leader in India in the passenger vehicle segment in the late 1980s. However, intense competition has eroded its market share in recent years, with Maruti Suzuki's share declining from 82 percent in 1997 to 45 percent in 2008 and dropping to 39 percent by early 2012.[4]

The Social Landscape of Gurgaon and Manesar

Gurgaon, situated in the state of Haryana and adjoining Delhi, was a small city of 12,500 inhabitants in 1989. Today, its ever-growing population—1,500,000 inhabitants, including 300,000 industrial workers—resides on an area of 600 square kilometers. Since 2010 Gurgaon has been linked to Delhi by a metro railway line. Manesar, officially designated as an industrial model township (IMT), is a subdivision of Gurgaon, situated at its extreme southeast, and is around 15 square kilometers in area. It is a new town of 200,000 inhabitants.[5] The construction of auto assembly plants by Maruti Suzuki in Gurgaon in the early 1980s and at Manesar in 2007 transformed their social landscapes. Gurgaon today is home to giant industrial units in several industrial sectors—automobiles (Maruti Suzuki, Honda Hero, and others); electronics and telecommunications (Motorola, Nokia, and others); IT (Microsoft, IBM, and others); food processing; pharmaceutical manufacture; call centers; and more. Gurgaon is portrayed in the mainstream media as a symbol of capitalist success. In reality, stories of wealth and poverty unfold side by side in Gurgaon, among seventeen-story towers for the middle-class professionals, hovels for workers, shopping centers, traditional small shops, and street vendors.[6]

Profile of the Maruti Suzuki Workers

There are several different types of workers at Maruti Suzuki. In general, workers are initially hired as apprentices, then taken on as temporary workers, promoted as trainees, and finally—but not necessarily—they attain the status of permanent workers. Most of the workers do not get past the stages of temporary workers or trainees. Wages differ according to the status of workers.[7] Nonpermanent workers are employed in the factory via another company or via "recruiters." "Recruiters" are the managers of small, nameless companies, who supply workers to the large companies in the region on a day-by-day basis.[8]

The educational qualifications of Maruti Suzuki workers vary across the different categories of work. All the workers in the tool and die shop and the engine and transmission assembly are Industrial Training Institute (ITI) qualified. In the press shop, weld shop, machine shop, paint shop, final assembly, final inspection, quality assurance, and maintenance (mechanical and electrical), there are ITI qualified workers with qualified secondary education. In nonproduction, there are matriculation qualified workers; illiterates are found in the materials division; and BA/MA qualified workers are there in the sales and dispatch section.[9]

More than 125 workers at Maruti Suzuki are land-displaced workers, who have been granted jobs at the plant as compensation for the seizure of their families' land by the company for its factory construction.[10] They are not ITI qualified.

When the automotive assembly plant opened at Manesar in 2007, Maruti Suzuki recruited young, skilled workers from various technical institutes in northern India, most between the ages of eighteen and twenty-five. Originally from the hinterland of Haryana or Uttar Pradesh, they now live in the dormitory villages in and around Manesar and Gurgaon. The temporary workers mostly come from the surrounding countryside—fifty to seventy kilometers away—of Haryana, Punjab, and Rajasthan. Around 1,000 permanent workers, 800 apprentices, 400 trainees, and 1,200 temporary workers make up the staff of Plant A of Maruti Suzuki at Manesar.[11]

Workers' Experiences of Oppression in Daily Life

Gurgaon Workers News conducted field surveys of workers at the Maruti Suzuki plant at Manesar and its suppliers between April and June 2012. The conversations centered on the workers' struggles in 2011. Both permanent workers and the different categories of nonpermanent workers participated in the surveys.

Most permanent workers at Maruti Suzuki own houses and live with their families. There is a company housing complex, Maruti Vihar, where permanent workers have houses built with loans from the company. Field surveys revealed that temporary workers, trainees, and apprentices live together, sharing rooms in rented houses or apartments. For nonpermanent workers, their state of being is split between the "stress of the assembly line" and the "boredom of the dormitory villages."[12] Migrant workers are a main source of income for the local landlords, who also own shops in the workers' neighborhoods. Workers are disciplined by the landlords/shop owners at the behest of the company or labor contractors. If the workers go on strike and stop going to the factory, the landlords may threaten and even beat the workers. The same happens if the workers do not pay rent or spend money at the shops.[13]

Maruti Suzuki workers at Manesar live in Aliyar and other nearby villages. When Maruti Suzuki expanded into the region in 2001, the peasant families of Aliyar were forced to sell their land for "industrial development." With the compensation money, the former peasants built houses on the vacant land surrounding the company, renting out rooms to workers and operating as landlords. They complained that their sons could not get permanent jobs in the local factories. In addition to the landlordism of the locals, we find here other manifestations of social and patriarchal control. In the field studies, some workers alleged that they were not permitted to use the roof of their house. A report described workers' dormitories in Aliyar as huge concrete blocks with holes in the wall and little dark rooms where hundreds of workers are squeezed in. Locals complain about the increase in prostitution in Manesar. But resident workers say, given workers' low wages, that they cannot afford the price for sex.[14]

The oppression of the Maruti workers does not let up at the workplace. Every Maruti Suzuki worker must sign "standing orders" that, among about a hundred other conditions, bar them from slowing down work, singing, gossiping, spreading rumors, or making derogatory statements against the company and management. Some young workers expressed discontent over the workload, which leaves them no time to breathe. The thirty-minute lunch break period is not long enough for them to walk the four hundred meters to the canteen to have their meal and then walk back. The contract workers work on average sixteen hours a day, with perennial compulsory overtime. They bring their own food to the factory or they eat, like hungry dogs, the leftover food of the permanent workers. They face a high incidence of injuries and accidents on the job due to too much pressure and lack of rest. When accidents occur, contractors are told to take away the injured workers and other workers are asked to clean the blood from the machines, which keep running. The workers are required to ask permission from supervisors even to go to the toilet, and disciplinary action is taken against workers who leave for the toilet without permission in an emergency. Not being allowed to go to the toilet has led to renal and urological problems for many workers.[15]

The dehumanizing work schedule is illustrated in this statement of a temporary worker employed in the paint shop of Manesar's Plant A: "On one side are 12 painting robots. On the other are workers carrying 25-kilo head-loads of used screens up two flights of stairs and returning with a 30-kilo load of clean screens.... The lunch break [30 minutes] and tea break [15 minutes] are not counted as part of the working time on the shift."[16]

The experience of working in Maruti Suzuki has shattered the dreams of many workers, as this worker's testimony bears out: "When I first began working for Maruti, assembly lines used to run right through my dreams. These days I suppose I'm so tired that I don't have dreams anymore."[17]

Labor Struggles at Manesar

The Maruti Suzuki *Sustainability Report* 2010–11 stated that the company has a mature and nonaffiliated internal labor union and there had been no "incidence of unrest" in the company during that year. From June 2011 onward the situation changed radically. A major conflict cropped up between Maruti Suzuki management and workers at the Manesar plant when the company tried to sabotage the formation of an independent workers' union by dismissing or suspending the leaders, who had applied for registration of the Maruti Suzuki Employees Union (MSEU). The workers occupied the plant June 4–17 in protest, after which a settlement was reached, granting the MSEU recognition as a "company committee" to represent permanent workers only.

The company imposed huge wage reductions upon the workers for each day of the strike. Between June 17 and August 28, resistance continued in one form or another in response to management's continuous intimidation and harassment of workers. The situation took a turn for the worse on August 28, when the company created conditions for a lockout by forcing the workers to sign a "good conduct bond" as a means of disciplining them. The workers refused to sign. The lockout lasted for thirty-three days and, under the threat of losing their jobs, the workers were forced to sign the "good conduct bond" on September 30. It is worth noting that certain central trade unions advised the Maruti Suzuki workers to sign this agreement.[18]

On October 3, 2011, the first day of work after the lockout, the company refused entry to about 1,200 temporary workers who had participated in protests outside the factory gates during the lockout. In addition, management cracked down on permanent workers by resorting to massive shop-floor reshuffling and suspending the company bus service. In retaliation, the workers occupied the factory on October 7 for a second time. The occupation coincided with the ongoing struggle of the temporary workers outside the factory gates. Inspired by the second factory occupation at Manesar, the workers at Suzuki's other three plants in the region—Suzuki Powertrain, Suzuki Castings, and Suzuki Motorcycles—also went on strike, starting October 7, in solidarity with the Maruti Suzuki workers. The fourteen-day strike ended on October 21 at Maruti Suzuki and the three other Suzuki plants, with management agreeing to reinstate some of the suspended workers and some workers whose contracts had been terminated.[19] The settlement, however, left the fate of the temporary workers in total uncertainty, as management agreed merely to recommend reemployment of the 1,200 temporary workers by their respective contractors. Moreover, instead of recognizing the MSEU as the workers' union, management agreed to set up a "Grievance Redressal Committee" and a "Company Welfare Board" with representation from workers and management. It also agreed to allow the government labor officer to adjudicate between workers and management during the proceedings of the Grievance Redressal Committee in accordance with certain provisions of the Industrial Disputes Act. The workers' struggle ended in defeat and the main leaders of the MSEU quit the company.[20]

The Maruti Suzuki Workers' Union (MSWU) was formed after the founders of the erstwhile MSEU left the firm after reaching a settlement with the company. The new union received its registration from the Haryana Labor Department in February 2012 and management decided to recognize the new union for any future negotiations at the plant.[21] Following the events of October 2011, Maruti Suzuki management adopted various measures to regain control over the workers.

Workers' Resistance, Managerial Repression, and State Violence

The ongoing struggles of the Maruti Suzuki workers at Manesar witnessed collusion between the state government of Haryana and management, enabling repression of the workers and resulting in state violence. Below are details of many such instances in the time period from June 2011 onward.

Eleven representatives of the MSEU, including its secretary, Shiv Kumar, met with officials of the Ministry of Labor of the state of Haryana in the capital of Chandigarh on June 3, 2011, in order to take care of the formalities of registering the union. The same day, the Ministry of Labor informed Maruti Suzuki management of this development and management started the process of making the workers sign blank pieces of paper in favor of the company union, Maruti Udyog Kamgar Union (MUKU), affiliated to one of the major trade union federations, Hind Mazdoor Sabha (HMS), in order to sabotage the formation of the new union.

The next day, June 4, the MSEU representatives tried to get back some of the signed blank papers, and, in retaliation, management sacked the eleven MSEU members who had tried to register the union. In response, the workers occupied the factory. The following day, management sealed off the gates of the factory and stationed security guards in front with the aim of preventing any contact between the workers inside and those outside. The state of Haryana deployed police forces inside and outside the Manesar area on June 6, and they confiscated tents set up by the protesters. On June 10, the strike was declared illegal by the Haryana government and two truckloads of additional police arrived on the scene. The thirteen-day strike was called off following the intervention of the chief minister of Haryana, Bhupinder Singh Hooda, with management agreeing to reinstate the eleven sacked employees. On June 17, when the first occupation ended, Maruti Suzuki management appealed to the Brahma Kumaris, a sect of the Hindu religion, and their representatives were tasked with organizing interactive sessions with the workers. This was an attempt on management's part to gain an understanding of the causes of the strike and to identify the leaders.[22]

On July 16, the company union, MUKU, whose membership consisted largely of workers at the Gurgaon plant, organized an election of delegates for the first time in eleven years. The Manesar workers boycotted the union election. In the words of Shiv Kumar, general secretary of the MSEU: "Three candidates have been put up by the management from the Manesar plant. There are arrangements for the poll but none of our members are taking part in it."[23] The attempts of the MSEU to become a registered union were foiled on July 26, when the labor office of the Haryana state government rejected its application, citing formal reasons—the union had led an "illegal strike" and submitted "faulty" papers. Almost a month later, during the night of August 24, when only a few hundred workers and supervisors were in the factory working overtime, a police force of three to four hundred in riot gear entered the Manesar factory and have subsequently established a permanent station in the plant. The next onslaught followed on August 28, after the workers refused to sign the "good conduct bond." The company began recruiting new temporary workers and started transferring engineers and other skilled workers from its Gurgaon plant to Manesar.[24]

Maruti Suzuki workers also faced managerial and state violence during the lockout period from August 29 to September 30, 2011. Some recruiters and middle-level managers of Maruti Suzuki surrounded 150 workers in the village of Aliyar on September 2. The workers were threatened and some were beaten. The police arrived and arrested the workers, despite the fact they were defending themselves. On September 18, the police arrested three leaders of the MSEU on trumped-up charges as they were leaving negotiations with management and state officials.[25]

Violence against workers continued in October. Immediately before the second occupation, recruiters tried to prevent temporary workers from getting to the factory gates by threatening them with violence. Maruti Suzuki officials announced on October 10 that "they [will] need the police to evict the workers," and "private bouncers," were hired to keep people out of the industrial area of Manesar. (It has become commonplace in the industrial sector for management to use strong-arm tactics such as stationing bouncers in sensitive situations with the purpose of intimidating the workers.) On October 14, one MSEU official was arrested at his home and police raids took place at the homes of other MSEU representatives. At the same time, an estimated 1,500 to 2,500 police officers were stationed inside the Maruti Suzuki factory. They prohibited the workers inside from accessing water, the canteen, and toilets, and the workers were forced to leave the factory late at night to continue the strike outside. In connection with this series of events, after the strikes of 2011 a white wall was constructed surrounding the buildings of Plant A to isolate the workers inside from those staying outside the plant.[26]

Since October 2011, the solidarity of the workers has suffered at Maruti Suzuki at Manesar. The MSWU union leadership failed to nurture the sense of solidarity in its fight against management. Compensating for its structurally weak position, the union resorted to a "tough-guy attitude" and tried to cultivate an image, mainly among permanent workers, of being a group of a thousand "tough guys." In mid-May 2012, the union president, who had generally been viewed as a "softy," slapped a supervisor on the shop floor. The desperation of the union leadership might have contributed to the "showdown" on July 18, 2012. Violence broke out at the Manesar plant around 5:00 or 6:00 p.m. The A-shift workers had finished their shift by 3:30 p.m. and had stayed behind to confront management, while the B-shift workers had already entered. There were more than three thousand workers inside the factory or close to the gates. It has been confirmed by local sources that there were also a substantial number of armed bouncers and *pehelwans* (wrestlers) inside the factory, hired by management. Various sources have reported that there was a strong rumor among workers that a powerful top-level official had warned, a few days previous, that he would clean the Manesar plant of "all the filth very soon." Anxiety, anger, and fear stirred among the workers. In the ensuing conflict, a group of workers and management clashed and an HR manager was killed, with a hundred others injured, including both workers and management. Most Maruti workers fled Manesar after the incident and the company declared a lockout.[27]

In the wake of the July 18, 2012, incident, Maruti Suzuki management and the Congress-led Haryana state government launched a massive witch-hunt against the workers. The labor minister of Haryana backed the company-declared lockout as "appropriate." However, in a communication in September 2012, Paramjeet Singh and Preeti Chauhan of the People's Union for Democratic Rights (PUDR) expressed deep concern over the fact that Maruti Suzuki plans to set up a special security force comprising one hundred ex-servicemen inside the Manesar plant. They further noted that the Haryana government has expressed its intention to deploy five to six hundred Rapid Action Force personnel inside the plant.[28] In a later communication, they alleged that "a large number of the over 145 arrests of workers that have been made in the case are unrelated to the crimes in the FIR [first information report]... the first 93 arrests, for instance, took place at random on July 18–19 and included workers not even present at the factory site."[29] The PUDR further alleged that third-degree torture methods were used by the Gurgaon Criminal Investigation Agency while interrogating Maruti Suzuki workers. In the words of the PUDR press statement: "Workers have confirmed in the MLRs [Medico-legal Reports] that they were stripped naked and beaten, and injured in the groin as their legs were stretched apart on both sides 'beyond capacity' for sustained periods of time. Some were submerged in dirty water for long duration, and rollers run over the thighs of others."[30]

Potential and Limits of India's Independent Trade Union Movement

The workers at Manesar are not a homogeneous community. There is a sharp division between permanent and temporary workers. Maruti Suzuki management encourages this division. Management's sadistic attitude toward the contract workers and apprentices is evident in the following statement, made by a Maruti Suzuki materials manager in an interview from August 2012: "Keep them like that... keep them always hungry, they will do the work for you... they are born to work, and nothing else."[31]

The permanent workers distinguish themselves from the temporaries as "quality workers." They feel that the use of temporaries lowers the quality of production. For their part, temporaries maintain that their work is as good as or even better than that of the permanents. In reality, because of the deskilling of factory jobs, it does not matter whether one is a permanent or a temporary in performing the job itself.[32]

Most of the temporary workers do not get permanent jobs and so carry on as permanent apprentices or permanent contract workers or eternal temporaries on call. The company has a huge inventory of temporary workers, with their addresses and mobile numbers. The permanents see these vulnerable workers as strikebreakers, hate them, and call them *randis* (prostitutes) on demand. The permanents allege that the company is more than willing to run the factory with only these temporaries for a pittance.[33] In a field report from June 2012, a permanent worker reveals the managerial strategy of deepening the divide between the permanents and temporaries:

> There is a clear policy to divide permanents from temporary workers. Supervisors don't put any pressure on permanents, you can do your job, you can walk around. Pressure is solely on temporary workers. These workers obviously complain, but they don't complain in front of the supervisor, they express their anger towards the permanent workers—they in turn tell the temporary workers to shut up and work.[34]

In spite of the divisions, the 2011 struggle of the Maruti Suzuki workers at Manesar is considered a landmark event in the history of the Indian labor movement. It strengthened the labor movement through ripple and solidarity effects in the production chain. Spearheaded by young workers, mostly temporaries at the Manesar plant, the movement drew support from workers in other Suzuki units and supply chain factories.[35] In fact, the move to reoccupy in October 2011 was not so much due to the "political consciousness of unity" of the union leadership but to the enormous pressure of the temporary workers on their permanent workmates.[36] As mentioned above, workers from the different departments of Maruti Suzuki at Manesar and from different supply companies live together in the dormitories and rented rooms. Moreover, most workers have experience from other companies in Manesar or Gurgaon, and everyone has friends in other factories. Since the struggle in 2011, the atmosphere in Manesar has changed and, in some cases, workers have made active use of their connectedness beyond company walls. After the reoccupation, Maruti Suzuki management had to deal with a radical force of three thousand workers in the assembly plant and an extended collectivity of workers in Suzuki Powertrain and other supplier companies.[37] The fact that workers' conditions improved marginally after October 2011 was acknowledged by a temporary worker in the Final Assembly department:

> Now workers can take two holidays within three months—before the dispute, it was only one holiday, which also had to be approved by the supervisor—which hardly happened. The permanent workers

can take four holidays within three months.... Now, as before, in case you are ill you are supposed to take medicine and start working immediately—but at least now the worker can go himself and take medicine; before, the supervisor came and gave it to you.[38]

The hierarchical culture of trade unions is responsible for the defeats of many labor struggles in India. It is also partly responsible for the defeat of the militant movement of the Maruti Suzuki workers at Manesar. The top leaders of the MSEU did not consult the rank-and-file workers regarding the settlement in October 2011, and they did not convene a mass meeting to explain the details of the settlement. On the contrary, the two main leaders of the MSEU, Sonu Gujjar and Shiv Kumar, the president and the secretary, received large cash payments from Maruti Suzuki for resigning from their jobs within days of the October 21 settlement. Gujjar and Kumar were among the thirty MSEU office-holders whom the company refused to take back at the end of the strike. After their resignation, twenty-eight other suspended members also resigned in exchange for severance payments from the company, reportedly on the order of 1.6 million rupees each. The retreat of thirty union militants of the MSEU with sizable "compensation" from management constitutes an act of betrayal from the perspective of fellow workers, who fought resolutely for their basic rights against the company's sweatshop regime.[39]

A similar turn of events took place at Suzuki Powertrain. Three committee members of the Suzuki Powertrain India Employees Union (SPIEU), including the president, were suspended after the October 7–21 strike. The other committee members sided with the Suzuki management.[40]

It is alleged that the trade union federations active in the Gurgaon-Manesar industrial belt played a principal role in strangling the Maruti Suzuki workers' militant struggle, especially the All India Trade Union Congress (AITUC), affiliated to the Communist Party of India (CPI), and the Centre of Indian Trade Unions (CITU), affiliated to the Communist Party of India–Marxist (CPI–M). They joined with other union federations to contain and suppress support for the Manesar workers' struggle, while forcing the MSEU to reach a "compromise" with the company and asking it to keep faith in the Congress-led state government, its labor officials, and courts.[41]

The struggling workers at Maruti Suzuki's Manesar plant did not restrict their protests within legal limits. They occupied the factory and went on strike without giving "adequate" strike notice or resorting to conciliations. They posed a serious threat to employers and the state when they went beyond the charted path of state-regulated industrial action. However, we should not celebrate the militancy of the workers, as noted in the case of strikes at Maruti Suzuki, Suzuki Powertrain, and others, without assessing the bureaucratic functioning of the MSEU and SPIEU and the subsequent impact on the workers' struggle. The leaders of these plant unions completely controlled the delicate negotiation process in order to put an end to rank-and-file workers' struggles once they dared to go beyond institutionalized forms.[42]

State Support for Foreign Corporate Investors

The coercive methods used by the Maruti Suzuki management to discipline workers hark back to modes of labor control in colonial India. Multiple forms of coercion were practiced by the colonial entrepreneurs to discipline workers. They did not hesitate to employ the services of physically imposing men in the industrial neighborhoods as strikebreakers and called upon the coercive arms of the state machinery in moments of crisis.[43] Similarly, the striking workers of Maruti Suzuki received physical threats from local contractors and village leaders during the October 2011 occupation.[44] The blatant use of coercive state machinery in crisis situations by Maruti Suzuki management has already been described above.

The intimidating methods of labor management as practiced by the capitalists in colonial India did not resemble the mode of capitalist labor management conceptualized by Karl Marx. The distinguishing characteristic of Marx's notion of capitalist management is the replacement of coercion by the "rule of law." The development of industrial capitalism in India during the colonial period did not follow the European model of capitalism as formulated by Marx in *Capital*. However, the recent events at the Maruti Suzuki plant at Manesar testify that Marx's concept of "primitive accumulation" is still relevant to understanding the "accumulation by dispossession" taking place in the twenty-first century.[45]

Antonio Gramsci, the Italian Marxist thinker, identified the factory council as the site of workers' democracy and characterized political parties and trade unions as organizations born on the terrain of bourgeois democracy and political liberty. He placed his faith in the factory council, which leads the working class toward the conquest of industrial power through the negation of industrial legality. As the factory council is comprised of workers, its formation coincides with the consciousness of the working class in pursuit of autonomous emancipation from capital. The labor struggles at the Maruti Suzuki plant at Manesar prove, once again, that Gramsci's astute critique of political parties and trade unions continues to be relevant to understanding labor politics in India.[46]

CHAPTER 5

Exploding Anger: Workers' Struggles and Self-Organization in South Africa's Mining Industry

Shawn Hattingh

It is well known that South Africa's mining industry was founded upon the extreme exploitation of Black workers. From its very origins, the industry was steeped in blood and violence. To amass an army of labor to work the mines, millions of Black families were forcibly driven off their land right across the country by the colonial military, beginning in the mid-1800s. Once on the mines, Black workers lived in closed compounds where they were subjected to military-style control and, until the late 1970s, faced prison terms for breaking their work contracts. The notorious apartheid pass system originated in the mining industry, and the ghettos that became known as townships had their forerunners in the infamous mine compound systems.[1] On the back of this exploitation and oppression, mining corporations in South Africa became exporters of huge quantities of minerals, including gold and diamonds.

Even today, racist attitudes permeate the mining institutions. Workers, especially Black workers, are poorly paid. On a daily basis they are still subjected to harsh control, racist slurs, oppression, and humiliation. The mines themselves remain sites of tight security, with workers regularly subjected to body searches and even iris and fingerprint scanning in the name of supposedly reducing theft. Security at the mines is prison-like with barbed wire and electric fences cordoning off sections of the mines, and heavily armed security guards keeping watch over workers' movements.[2] Companies like G4S, which are often contracted by the mining houses to undertake security, boast that they offer trained armed guards and dog units for control of riots or labor "unrest," intelligence-gathering operatives, and the ability to conduct screenings of any employee.[3] The anarchist Bakunin described the situation accurately when he observed that, for an employee in a workplace under capitalism, an "employer will watch over him either directly or by means of an overseers; every day during working hours and under controlled conditions, the employer will be the owner of his actions and movements... when he is told: 'Do this,' the worker is obliged to do it; or when he is told 'Go there,' he must go."[4]

South African mines have some of the worst working conditions and safety records in the world. Each year, hundreds of workers die in accidents underground, while thousands more die of work-related diseases such as silicosis.[5] The mining bosses in South Africa don't particularly seem to care about this because, after all, for them it is only insignificant "others" dying underground. The mining sector in South Africa, however, is merely a reflection of the attitudes and practices of the broader society. The ruling class as a whole in the country treats the majority of people with utter disdain or, at best, with condescending paternalism. For bosses and politicians, workers and the poor in South Africa are simply human fodder for the country's mines, factories, and electoral machine. Understandably, being subjected to such a dehumanizing system has stoked a seething anger among workers and the poor, which has often exploded into struggle and direct action in the form of community protests and wildcat strikes.

During the last few years the anger toward the system and the exploitative ruling class has once again erupted: this time in the form of a series of wildcat strikes and sit-ins at South Africa's mines, with the most well-known at Lonmin's Marikana Mine in the far north of the country. The main grievances have centered on issues with deep historical roots: the racist attitudes of management, unsafe working environments, precarious working conditions, unpaid wages, and inadequate wages.

The struggles at the mines not only reflect the ongoing class warfare in the mining industry but they also bring into the spotlight the cruel exploitation of South African workers in general: they expose the true face of class rule in the country, reveal the many problems within existing unions, lay bare the role of the state in society, and reveal yet again that the Black working class experiences not just exploitation but ongoing national oppression—and accompanying racism—in South Africa. This chapter explores these issues as it tracks the details of the wildcat strikes and sit-ins on South Africa's mines, and discusses the necessity of taking these struggles forward.

Battle Lines Drawn

The battle at South Africa's mines burst vividly into the open in 2009. Up to this point strikes had been common but were mostly channeled through the country's labor laws. In 2009, however, workers went outside of the labor law and over the heads of the bureaucracy of the main mining union, the National Union of Mineworkers (NUM), and began to take the fight to bosses across the mining sector. Between August and December 2012 the sit-ins and wildcat strikes had escalated to the point that workers at most of the mines in the country were out or had recently been out on wildcat strikes, and others were staging sit-ins and occupations or had recently done so.

The origins of these massive wildcat strikes and sit-ins can be traced to the first mine sit-in in recent history, which occurred at the Crocodile River Mine, a platinum mining operation, in July 2009. In order to try to avoid adhering to aspects of South Africa's labor legislation and to lower the costs of employment, the management of Crocodile River Mine hired contract workers through another company, JIC, operating as a labor broker. In fact, a large percentage of the Crocodile River Mine workforce was employed as contract workers, which meant that legally the mine did not have to implement any proper health and safety workplace standards.[6] For the workers this also meant they could be fired more easily than permanent workers, they could be paid less, they could be denied benefits that permanent workers were entitled to, and they could be denied the right to work in a safe environment.[7]

For these reasons the contract workers at Crocodile River Mine engaged in picketing, among other actions, to persuade the bosses to hire them on a permanent basis. Initially, the workers were supported by the NUM, the largest union in the country. The protest actions appeared initially to bring some success, as management promised that all contract workers would be hired on a permanent basis and their grievances addressed.[8] Months passed and this failed to materialize. Frustrated, 560 contract workers decided to occupy the mine on July 9, 2009, in a bid to get management to meet their demands. They shut down the mine's operations and blockaded themselves underground. The mine bosses were caught off guard, as were officials from the NUM. From the start it was clear that the workers were undertaking the action through self-initiative. Upon hearing of the occupation, the NUM sent officials down into the mine to try to persuade the workers to end their sit-in. The workers refused. Soon after, the mine management called in the police and acquired a court interdict against the workers.

Throughout the two days of the sit-in, negotiations continued between the NUM and the bosses until eventually an agreement was reached. The agreement stated that a new round of negotiations would take place between management and the union to consider the possibility of hiring all the contract workers on a permanent basis. Upon hearing the news, the occupying workers decided to surface. Yet as soon as the workers had exited the mine, management once again reneged on its promises and fired all 560 workers involved in the occupation. Adding insult to injury, the police also charged the workers with trespassing and kidnapping. These draconian actions made clear that the state and the Crocodile River Mine were intent on intimidating the workers and preventing the spread of mine occupations.

However, the strategy of trying to terrorize workers into abandoning the idea of staging mine occupations proved a dismal failure, as in the weeks following the Crocodile River Mine action another sit-in occurred, this time at the Aquarius Platinum Kroondal Mine in Rustenburg. The Kroondal Mine sit-in had its roots in a strike that occurred in the platinum mining sector in August 2009. Workers across Rustenburg—at both the Kroondal Mine and mines owned by another company, Impala Platinum—went out on strike for higher wages.[9] Most of the workers were members of the NUM and were demanding at least a 14 percent increase. From the start the strike was marked by a high degree of militancy, which could be seen during the workers' protests.[10] Several days into the strike, the negotiators from the NUM announced they had reached an agreement with the bosses and that as a result workers could expect a 10 percent increase. Workers at both Impala Platinum and the Kroondal Mine were angered by this concession and felt the union bureaucracy and negotiating team had sold them out. Most of the workers continued to strike.

Officials from the NUM then rushed to Rustenburg and tried to intervene to bring the strike to a halt. At Impala Platinum's Rustenburg mine, they received a hostile reception from the workers. When the NUM deputy president insisted that the workers accept the corporations' offer and return to work, some of the workers responded by throwing stones and physically attacking him.[11] Meanwhile, at the Kroondal Mine, the workers remained out on strike and refused to budge. Due to the NUM's acceptance of the wage offer, the continuing strike action lost its protected status and officially became a wildcat strike. The Kroondal Mine's management used this as a pretext to fire the 3,900 workers who had elected to continue the strike.

The workers self-organized protests to demand their reinstatement. During the protests the national police and mine security harassed the workers, opened fire on them on numerous occasions, and set trained dogs on them. It was reported by the Democratic Socialist Movement that, as a result, three strikers were killed, and many went "missing."[12] Under intense pressure from protesting workers themselves the Kroondal Mine managers were eventually forced to reinstate the workers. Yet as soon as the workers returned to work, they discovered that the bosses had erased their employment histories and had terminated some of their benefits. This prompted a second wildcat strike. Once again management fired the workers involved and refused even to issue their Unemployment Insurance Fund (UIF) certificates.[13] At this point, thirty-two of the workers decided to embark on an underground sit-in at the mine.

The workers managed to get through the mine's security systems and gained access to the underground section of the mine, attempting to barricade themselves in. They stated that they would not resurface until they had been issued their UIF certificates so they could claim the unemployment benefits they were due. Management summoned the police. On arriving, police task force members descended into the mine and proceeded to try to arrest the workers and to force them out. In the ensuing altercation, some of the miners and a number of police force members were injured. The police allege that the injuries involved workers setting off explosive booby traps to avoid being arrested.[14]

In the end, all thirty-two of the workers participating in the action were arrested and charged with attempted murder, malicious damage to property, trespassing, and assault.[15] Sadly, NUM officials also turned their backs on the workers. In the aftermath of the occupation the NUM released a statement saying, "We, therefore, call on the law enforcement agencies to ensure that those who are involved in all these irregular activities are arrested and that no one disguises criminal activity as labour matters."[16]

While the Kroondal Mine occupation was being ruthlessly crushed, another mine occupation erupted in Mpumalanga, at the Two Rivers Mine. In October 2009 more than one hundred workers staged a sit-in underground to demand that a racist manager be fired and four of the workers he had dismissed be reinstated. Within hours hundreds of workers had joined in the sit-in and completely shut down production.[17] The bosses clearly felt pressured by the workers' actions, and they agreed to investigate the conduct of the manager and to reinstate the four workers. By early November, however, the four workers had still not been rehired. In response, 1,400 workers decided to once again occupy Two Rivers.[18] They remained underground for more than forty hours until management finally gave in and took concrete steps to reemploy their four colleagues.

With this apparent victory, the occupation was called off. Yet despite the promises of the Two River Mine bosses, there was no investigation into the manager in question and anger among the workers continued to boil beneath the surface. Matters were compounded when management failed to pay workers their year-end bonuses and overtime. As a result, in mid-January 2010, about fifty workers embarked on another wildcat strike and sit-in.[19]

Meanwhile, several hundred kilometers away, more than a hundred workers at the Bokoni Mine also decided to occupy their workplace and refused to leave their shifts. Their demands and reasons were similar to those of the workers at Two Rivers Mine: they wanted the appalling safety standards at the mine addressed, they wanted the bonus system reexamined, and they wanted a racist manager to be fired.[20]

As with the mine sit-ins of the preceding months, the workers involved in these two occupations had undertaken them independently of the unions, the NUM and the Association of Mineworkers Union (AMCU). As such, the workers' actions were based on self-initiative and self-organization. When officials from the unions learned of the mine occupations, rather than supporting the workers, they called for them to end immediately. NUM officials went so far as to accuse the workers involved of kidnapping NUM members and holding them hostage. They also called for the police to intervene and end both occupations.[21]

The owners of the Two Rivers and Bokoni mines, African Rainbow Minerals (ARM) and Impala Platinum, embarked immediately on an intimidation campaign to try to force the workers to surface. Traditional leaders were called in by the mining companies to instruct the workers to end the sit-ins, but workers remained in the mines.[22] When this failed, the two companies obtained court orders to evict the workers.[23] The workers simply ignored the court orders and continued with the sit-ins.

On January 19 a large police contingent was sent down the Bokoni Mine with the intention of forcing the workers out. Under the threat of violence the workers elected to end the occupation.[24] Likewise, when the police presented an interdict to the Two Rivers Mine workers on the same day, they too decided to resurface.[25] While the NUM said they would engage with the workers and management to address the reasons behind the occupations, an NUM spokesman also said the union was pleased that the occupations were over and that production would soon be back to normal.[26] As happened with all preceding occupations, management at the Bokoni Mine also went on the attack in the aftermath and fired the hundred workers involved in the occupation.

Struggles Continue into 2011

In 2011 a number of protected strikes, revolving around formal wage negotiations with the main unions such as the NUM also occurred in the coal and gold mining sectors.[27] Workers were demanding 14 percent increases. Bosses initially offered far less. After several days of strike action, a deal was struck between the NUM and the mining houses. Despite the partial victory, the workers' anger continued to build.

This anger exploded soon after, when subcontracted workers at Platmin, a mine in the North West Province, embarked on a wildcat strike in June 2011 to improve working conditions. This strike occurred outside the formal NUM structures and was marked by a high degree of militancy.[28] Shortly before this, at Lonmin's Karee Mine, nine thousand workers went out on a wildcat strike, in May 2011.[29] One reason for the strike was dissatisfaction with the NUM bureaucracy; some participants were defending a local worker leader in an internal battle with union officials. The Karee Mine strike lasted more than a month and was brought to an end when the owner, Lonmin, with the backing of the NUM bureaucracy, fired all nine thousand workers.[30] In order not to further disrupt production, however, the company rehired many of the fired workers once the action was over. More specifically, they rehired the workers on a selective basis, excluding those seen as having been militant, ringleaders, or "trouble-makers" during the strike action. Of the nine thousand workers initially fired for being involved, only six thousand were rehired, with the most militant being sidelined.[31] What was significant, however, was that even the workers who were rehired left the NUM en masse and joined the rival union, AMCU.

Australia Platinum's mine in the Limpopo Province witnessed a similar story of deception by management. When workers staged a wildcat strike demanding improved working conditions, and the direct hiring of outsourced workers in 2011, management promised to look into their grievances if they returned to work. The workers agreed to this. However, upon their return, disciplinary hearings were subsequently called by management for some of the workers. At the hearings, the workers involved were promptly arrested in an act of blatant intimidation by management and the police.[32] In all these cases it was clear that the police and companies were escalating the existing tensions at the mines through these underhanded and repressive tactics.

The Battle Intensifies

While the period between 2009 and 2011 was punctuated with wildcat strikes and sit-ins, 2012 witnessed a major escalation of the struggles at the mines. Victories were scored by the workers involved, which saw the fires of struggle grow and the strikes assume a form of militancy—and threat—not seen since the massive mine strikes of 1987, 1946, and 1922.

Indeed, 2012 began with a six-week wildcat strike at Impala Platinum, with rock drillers demanding a wage increase from 4,000 rand to 9,500. The demand and subsequent strike arose out of a situation in which the NUM had negotiated wage increases for some higher-paid workers but had left out the rock drillers from the deal. The rock drillers began a process of self-organization, deciding to embark on a strike and demand their own increase.[33] As part of this, they vowed to organize outside of the union and used assemblies and a strike coordinating committee to do so. In solidarity, the rock drillers were joined by other workers, and eventually seventeen thousand workers at the company went out on strike.[34] The strike's approach was militant from the beginning, with workers barricading the road leading in and out of the mine. In a related action, workers also barricaded the road to a nearby informal settlement to prevent anyone from potentially acting as a scab.[35] Businesses in the surrounding areas were also looted as workers took food and other items. The police were deployed in full force and, as a result, the violence escalated. Battles between the police and mineworkers were relatively frequent. The police used rubber bullets, tear gas, armored cars, and helicopters, while workers fought back with rocks and stones.

From the start the NUM was opposed to the strike. Many workers at Impala, therefore, grew increasingly unhappy with the NUM bureaucracy and local NUM officials, who they felt were too close to the bosses, and with the leadership of the parent federation, the Congress of South African Trade Unions (COSATU), which many felt have been too close to the ruling party.[36] Consequently some, but not all, of the striking Impala workers left the union and, of these, many reportedly joined AMCU—the strike committee, too, had given its support to AMCU. It was, however, clear that AMCU was not involved in organizing the strike, which was self-organized by the workers directly. In the end, and due to the militancy of the strike, the workers won their full demand—an increase from a basic salary of 4,000 rand to a guaranteed salary of 9,500 rand per month.[37] The victory scored spurred workers at other mines to also take action.

In the weeks that followed, seventeen thousand workers at Anglo Platinum's and ARM's Modikwa Mine, the largest platinum mine in the world, undertook a protected strike for higher wages. Although initially operating within the labor law and under the auspices of the NUM, the strike quickly escalated. Workers barricaded roads in and out of the mine and clashed with the police.[38] Early August 2012 saw action once again at the Aquarius Platinum Kroondal Mine. Hundreds of mineworkers who had been fired by a subcontractor—Murray and Roberts—for an earlier wildcat strike embarked on a protest to reclaim their jobs. Their attempt to gain access to the mine resulted in clashes with the company's armed security guards and the police, who fired on the workers with shotguns. The workers armed themselves with stones and allegedly even petrol bombs. In the process three of the workers were shot dead by security guards and the police.[39]

August 2012 also saw the infamous events at Marikana. The wildcat strike at Marikana began when rock drillers—low-paid and often out-sourced or contract workers—demanded that their salaries be increased to 12,500 rand from a basic-salary low of 4,500 rand per month in some cases. To organize the strike the workers met in mass assemblies. Tensions also existed at Marikana regarding the NUM, and many of the striking workers felt that the NUM officials were too close to the bosses. Many of those workers were also members of the NUM. On August 11, the striking mineworkers marched to the local NUM offices to put pressure on the union to assist in taking up their issues. The local NUM officials were hostile to this action and attacked the marchers. During this encounter, the local NUM officials opened fire on the strikers. Two of the strikers were shot in the process and were left lying in pools of blood, believed to be dead.[40]

At the time, the police claimed to know nothing of this, which, in the light of evidence that has emerged, was a lie. Through the Farlam Commission, the judicial commission investigating aspects of what took place at Marikana, it was confirmed in February 2013 that the eyewit-ness reports of August 11 were indeed correct: NUM officials had shot at the protesters, who, despite being severely wounded and left for dead, actually survived.[41] In the aftermath of the violence, strikers armed themselves with sticks, knobkerries, and pangas to protect themselves from future attacks. Violence between some NUM officials and some strikers—but by no means all—also escalated, with at least four NUM officials and full-time shop stewards killed in the conflict.[42]

Two days later, on August 13, more violence occurred, again starting out as violence directed at the strikers. On that day, a delegation of striking workers was sent by the strike assembly to cross over to Lonmin's other operation, the Karee Mine, with the aim of convincing workers there also to come out on strike. Discontent had been rife at Karee since the 2011 wildcat strike and subsequent firing by management of thousands of workers. Mine security, however, turned the striking workers' delegation back. On the way back to Marikana the workers' delegation was stopped by a line of heavily armed police. They were told to lay down their knobkerries and other weapons. The delegation refused, saying the weapons they had were necessary for self-defense, as strikers had already been attacked and killed. The police line reportedly parted and initially allowed the workers through, on the face of it appearing to have accepted their explanation. But after the workers were about ten meters away, eyewitnesses have claimed, the police opened fire and some began chasing the workers. With support from a helicopter, the police shot dead two of the workers and severely wounded another. The rest of the workers turned on the police, and in the ensuing clash two policemen were killed. A number of the workers were arrested on the scene and charged with murder, despite having been fired on first.[43]

On August 16, the police publicly declared that it was "D-day" for the strikers.[44] To protect Lonmin by breaking the strike, the police shot dead thirty-four striking workers. Some reports maintain that the workers captured on TV being shot by the police may not have been storming the police, as was claimed, but rather were fleeing Nyala armored cars that were firing tear gas at them. Whatever the case, the police showed little hesitation in gunning down the workers. In fact, many of the police were armed with R5 assault rifles—weapons based on the design of the AK-47. Orders for the police to carry such assault weapons, and for them to be armed with live ammunition, must have come from high within the state.

The workers shot in front of the TV cameras were also reportedly a minority of those killed. It has been reported that other workers fled in the aftermath of the shooting, headed toward the Marikana informal settlement. Some reports indicate that a number of workers may have been run over by Nyala armored cars as they lay flat in the grass, concealing their presence to avoid being shot. Other workers also reportedly tried to flee into a boulder field four hundred meters in the opposite direction from the TV cameras. It has been claimed that they were then pursued into the boulder field on foot or via helicopter by police task force members, and evidence has emerged that some of these workers may have been executed there.[45]

Although the massacre of workers in front of TV cameras may not have been premeditated, the fact that the state announced it was "D-Day" and the fact that some protesters were shot in the back and others were shot at very close range in the boulder field make it clear that the state had intended to break the strike that day one way or another.[46] It is evident that the state and the bosses had decided the strike would end, and the police would handle that, all in the name of protecting private property and the economic interests of the mine owners.

Even after the massacre, the strike continued for six weeks and worker assemblies persisted. The state, however, made it exceptionally difficult to do so by banning all gatherings in the area of more than fifteen people. Police also made regular incursions into the townships surrounding Marikana. In the process, the police subjected these communities to violence, which included firing rubber bullets and tear gas at striking workers and residents venturing out of their houses.[47] Nonetheless, the workers' struggle held firm, and through this pressure, Lonmin—Marikana's owner—agreed to wage increases providing rock drillers up to 11,000 rand a month.[48] In the end, the workers won the battle through a massive campaign of self-organization.

The Wildfire after Marikana

Taking a cue from the workers' actions and victory at Marikana, wildcat strikes spread across South Africa's mines like a raging fire. Self-organized wildcat strikes erupted at most of the operations of the largest mining companies, such as Amplats, Goldfields, Kumba Iron, AngloGoldAshanti, Harmony, and Gold One. In fact, it is estimated that between August and December 2012, well over a hundred thousand workers in the industry went out on wildcat strikes at various times at different mines. In every single case, workers demanded wages of 12,500 rand or higher.

Sit-ins and occupations were also part of these struggles. At Goldfields' Kloof Mine, 5,200 workers staged a sit-in,[49] and at Samancor 400 workers occupied the mine,[50] while in the Northern Cape Province workers occupied diamond and iron mines.[51] At the Sishen Iron Mine, owned by Kumba Resources, workers staged an occupation on the site for several weeks.[52]

These recent wildcat strikes and occupations—post-Marikana—
have met with varying degrees of success. At some mines gains were won,
at others management held out. By January 2013, the wave of strikes
began to ease as workers regrouped. Tensions, however, remain high and
a new round of battles looms—again around higher wages, but also now
retrenchments. In fact, in March 2013 wildcat strikes once again broke
out, this time in the coal mining sector. At one point almost 90 percent
of Exxaro's coal operations workers were in fact out on a wildcat strike.[53]

As part of the wildcat strikes that South Africa has witnessed, mass
workers' assemblies and committees have sprouted up across the mines,
aimed at organizing actions locally. Indeed, there is a relatively long
history of mine workers establishing assemblies and committees to
take their struggles forward.[54] Some attempts have also been made by
the workers to link the workers' assemblies and committees in the aftermath of Marikana. These developments have even led to the establishing of a national strike coordinating committee, which has continued
to function.

The officials from the main unions, the NUM and AMCU, were
largely sidelined by the strikers across the mines, despite some of the
strikers being members of the unions in question. In the case of NUM
officials, they were to a very large degree hostile to the wildcat strikes
and sit-ins as well as the formation of committees. While in a few isolated
cases they provided the strikers with some assistance and placed blame
on the bosses for the problems, NUM officials called for the wildcat
strikes of 2012 and 2013 to end. In fact, the top bureaucrats at the NUM
spent over a million rand in a campaign to end the wildcat strikes and
sit-ins. Along with accusing the strikers of endangering South Africa's
economy, the general secretary of the NUM called on mines not to give
in to the demands of workers. In fact, he said, "You need just one mine
to break this strike."[55]

In part, NUM, due to a reformist political strategy in the trade
union leadership tied to the ruling African National Congress (ANC),
the labor bureaucracy has been hostile to the strikes. In addition, the
leadership is committed to formal central bargaining and social dialogue, which excludes workers and further encourages bureaucratization of the unions. Many of the top union officials' jobs are dependent
on the bureaucracy, including researchers, negotiators, and political
officers. As such they favor stable labor relations within the framework
of the law and oppose open class conflict. Indeed, registered unions
are required to stay within the confines of the labor law and the union

bureaucracies try for the most part to ensure this happens—if they don't, or if they support actions outside of the labor law, they can be fined and even deregistered, meaning their jobs could be put in jeopardy.

Union officials also negotiate long-term agreements with the mines, often spanning years. The unions also have massive investment arms owning shares in many sectors of the economy. These investment arms are capitalist speculators in their own right. The wildcat strikes threaten these agreements, arrangements, social dialogue, and the power held by the union officials tied to them. In short, workers taking actions themselves, going over the heads of the bureaucrats, undermines the authority of top union officials and they don't like it. In addition, union officials have become relatively privileged and have grown distant from the base membership of the unions. The 2012 annual salary of the general secretary of the NUM was a staggering 1.4 million rand.[56] Even full-time paid shop stewards at the platinum mines receive company salaries to do union work full time, and some receive 14,000 rand "bonuses" every month too.[57] Understandably, the companies paying these salaries expect something back from these local officials. For many of the local, regional, and national bureaucrats, therefore, union work is a stepping-stone to a cushy career, and workers' struggles become a secondary issue. This has led to anger among many workers, and it is one of the reasons some local NUM officials were attacked by sections of the strikers at Marikana.[58]

The State and Capital Regroup for Attack on Authentic Workers' Unions
The state and the bosses have been trying to halt the wildcat strikes and undermine the workers' assemblies and committees that have emerged. Post-Marikana these efforts have become more systematic. Across companies there have been meetings about the struggles on the mines and how to deal with them. The state, too, has met with corporations around the issue. This has included drawing in unions to promote collective bargaining.

The state, for its part, has also targeted key activists post-Marikana to try and neutralize the workers' committees that have been formed. Communities that supported the struggles have also been subjected to police action and raids, especially in areas such as Marikana. This has also included shooting at workers with live and rubber bullets, with the consequences being that many strikers have been injured and some others killed,[59] although not on the scale of Marikana.

The mining houses, too, have gone on the offensive recently. Many workers involved in wildcat strikes and occupations, across the industry, have been fired. Notably, the company Harmony Gold has locked out workers from its Kusasalethu mine in retaliation for the wildcat strikes at the company in 2012. As part of this, workers have been denied access to the mine hostels where they lived.[60] Likewise, AngloPlatinum is in the process of retrenching thousands of workers in a barefaced bid to punish those who were involved in wildcat strikes and sit-ins at the company.[61]

The Lessons to Be Drawn from the Struggles at the Mines

Major lessons regarding the nature of the capitalist economy, the role of the state in society, the makeup of the contemporary ruling class in South Africa, and the continued exploitation and racial oppression of the working class can be drawn from the events surrounding the wildcat strikes and sit-ins at South Africa's mines. Today, the wealth of the ruling class still rests mainly on extremely cheap Black labor: it is the reason certain sections of the economy, mining for one, are so profitable. Since 1994 the entire working class has fallen deeper into poverty, including sections of the white working class, as inequality has grown between the ruling class and working class as a whole. However, the Black working class, due to holding mostly the lowest-paid jobs and facing continuing racism, remains subject to both exploitation and national oppression. Until both are ended, along with the capitalist system on which they are based, true freedom and equality for both the Black and white working class will not be achieved in South Africa.

As has been brutally highlighted by Marikana and the other actions at the mines, ending of the national oppression and accompanying racism to which the Black working class is subjected must be central to the struggle to end capitalism. As anarchists have long observed, if a just society is to be achieved, the means and the ends in struggle must be as similar as possible. Hence, if we want a genuinely equal and nonracist society, our struggle to end the national oppression of the Black working class, and the accompanying capitalist and state systems in South Africa, must be based firmly on nonracial ideals.

While it is clear that the Black working class remains nationally oppressed, the situation for the small Black elite, nevertheless, is very different. Some, through their high positions in the state, and consequently having control over the means of coercion and administration, have joined the old white capitalists in the ruling class. They have used their positions in the state to amass wealth and power. Others have also joined the ruling class through the route of Black economic empowerment. This is evidenced by the fact that all the top ANC-linked Black families—the Mandelas, Thambos, Ramaphosas, Zumas, Moosas, and others—have shares in or sit on the boards of mining companies.[62] In fact, Cyril Ramaphosa not only owns shares in and sits on the board of Lonmin, but a number of functions at Marikana are also outsourced to various companies he has interests in, such as Minorex.[63] The wealth and power of this Black section of the ruling class in South Africa rests, too, on the exploitation of the working class as a whole, but mostly and specifically on the exploitation and national oppression of the Black working class. This is why the Black section of the ruling class has been so willing to take action—whether during platinum strikes, Marikana, or strikes in general—against the Black working class.

Mikhail Bakunin foresaw the possibility of such a situation arising in cases in which national liberation was based upon the strategy of capturing state power. Bakunin said that the "statist path" was "entirely ruinous for the great masses of the people" because it did not abolish class power but simply changed the make-up of the ruling class.[64] Due to the centralized nature of states, only a few can rule: a majority of people can never be involved in decision-making under a state system. As a result, Bakunin stated, if the national liberation struggle were carried out with "ambitious intent to set up a powerful state," or if "it is carried out without the people and must therefore depend for success on a privileged class" it would become a "retrogressive, disastrous, counter-revolutionary movement."[65] He also noted that when former liberation heroes enter into the state, because of the top-down structure they become rulers and get used to the privileges their new positions carry, and they come to "no longer represent the people but themselves and their own pretensions to govern the people."[66] History has proven Bakunin's insights correct; former liberation heroes in South Africa rule in their own interests, they wallow in the privileges of their positions, and they exploit and oppress the vast majority of the people in the country.

The blatant state violence during the struggles at the mines, and the very real threat of a reactionary backlash, also lays bare the true nature of the state and the role it plays in protecting the ruling class. It is not an unfortunate coincidence that the state, headed by Black nationalists and neoliberals, has been protecting the mines of huge corporations and has been willing to use violence to do so. Rather, that is one of the main functions of the state (and hence its police): that is what it is designed for. For capitalism to function, and for class rule to be maintained, a state is vital. It is central to protecting and maintaining the very material basis from which the power of the elite is derived. Without a state, which claims a monopoly on violence within a given territory, the elite could not rule, nor could it claim or maintain ownership of wealth and the means of production. In fact, the state as an entity is the "defender of the class system and a centralised body that necessarily concentrates power in the hands of the ruling classes; in both respects, it is the means through which a minority rules a majority."[67] Through its executive, legislative, judiciary, and policing arms the state always protects the minority ownership of property (whether private or state-owned property), and tries to squash, co-opt, or undermine any threat to the continuing exploitation and oppression of the working class. As Marikana and other struggles at South Africa's mines show, that even includes killing those who pose a threat.

What Is to Be Done?

The actions of the workers on wildcat strikes and sit-ins have been for the most part inspiring. Important structures, including workers' assemblies and committees, have been created. Distinctly not inspiring were the actions of most of the union officials involved, which did not just abandon their members but sometimes even actively worked against them. In turn, this led to a minority of workers taking out their frustrations by attacking local union officials in a few cases. The series of occupations revealed once again that workers in South Africa face enemies not only in the form of bosses and politicians, but also sometimes in the form of union officials. As such, if workers are going to emancipate themselves they are going to have to struggle against bosses and politicians as well as a union bureaucracy.

Indeed, what is perhaps really needed in South Africa is for workers to reclaim their unions from a bureaucratic layer and to transform them into self-managed, radically democratic, nonhierarchical, and decentralized unions—in other words, unions controlled from the bottom up by the members themselves and not by officials with centralized power. It is in this struggle that anarchists can make a huge contribution with our knowledge of anarcho-syndicalist unionism and ideas of self-management, self-organization, and opposition to hierarchies. Of course, the challenges in attempting to transform the existing unions into participatory organizations are immense. It has not been unknown for the unions to send officials from their head offices to intervene in, and in some cases even block, meetings to discuss the need for bottom-up, participatory unions. Some union officials have resorted to sidelining and even expelling members who raise difficult questions about the growing centralization within unions. Despite this, the struggle to bring about self-managed, nonhierarchical, revolutionary, and radically democratic unions or organs is vital—whether through transforming existing unions or beginning to organize new ones.

The workers' assemblies and committees that have emerged are highly important developments. They could prove to be a way for the workers to take up struggles outside of the unions and beyond the reach of union bureaucracies. Some weaknesses need to be addressed if the committees and assemblies are to become structures through which workers could take their struggles forward in the long run. It is clear that structures of direct democracy need to be firmly established, consolidated, and built on in these assemblies and committees.

If the committees and assemblies are to go forward, it is also imperative that a healthy, working-class-based counterculture be entrenched and fostered within them. The task, therefore, for the moment is to build the assemblies and committees. The workers have shown no intent so far of fighting to gain control of the unions, and at present any move to do so would be distraction from the vital work needed to maintain the current battles. At a later stage, workers could elect to use the committees and assemblies to mobilize to remove the union bureaucracies and effectively regain full control of their unions. But what is needed now is for the committees and assemblies to become durable. If they don't they will disappear and workers will have to start again.

The strength of the worker assemblies and committees has been that they have united workers across unions, they have drawn in nonunionized workers; some have also included the unemployed and community members. The assemblies and workers' committees have the potential to become a counter power to the multinational mining companies, supported by the South African state. To do so, however, depends on the workers building and sustaining these organs themselves. It is apparent that the state, the ruling party, the South African Communist Party, capital, and most union officials are going to try to prevent this.

What is also clear, however, is that workers in the mines are going to continue struggling in the future. The wildcat strikes, sit-ins, and occupations may go through ups and downs, but they won't disappear. Perhaps one of the biggest challenges in South Africa is how to begin to transform the actions we have seen into a real challenge to the ruling class through a long-term battle by the working class to seize the mines, land, and factories and to fight for worker self-management. Of course, the best process for such a transformation is through struggle itself and the self-education that accompanies it. It is also in this context that anarchists can offer solidarity and support to these workers. This could involve sharing our vision and ideas—without trying to dominate or impose—around a free, nonhierarchical, and self-managed society: in other words, a society that is the antithesis of the oppressive one in which we are currently forced to live.

CHAPTER 6

Neoliberal Conservation and Worker-Peasant Autonomism in Madagascar

Genese Marie Sodikoff

Madagascar is country of great concern to conservationists because of its unique wildlife and the fact that most of its natural habitats are severely threatened by human actions, including industrial logging, fishing, mining, and subsistence-based "slash-and-burn" agriculture (known in Malagasy as *tavy*). The island contains an exceptionally high degree of biological endemism and diversity, positioning Madagascar as one of the world's top twelve "mega diversity" hotspots.[1]

In the mid-1980s, the protection of this natural wealth became a key priority for international donors. Then president of Madagascar, Didier Ratsiraka, who had in 1975 aligned himself with other African leaders and socialized the island's economy, was by the 1980s eager to cultivate ties to Western aid agencies. Madagascar's economy was virtually bankrupt and support from the USSR was drying up. The USSR itself was suffering fiscal crisis. Ratsiraka's turn to the Bretton Woods institutions ushered in neoliberal reforms after a decade of socialist policy that was widely judged a failure.

An emergent model of the preferred donor-funded environmental project—one that combined environmental protection with economic development activities—was being tested at the Mananara-Nord reserve on the northeast coast by 1989. By 1991, a consortium of Western donors and the state had ratified Madagascar's National Environmental Action Plan (NEAP), which made biodiversity protection a key contingency of foreign aid. One of the effects of the NEAP's ratification was the transformation of the national job market. An array of international and domestic environmental NGOs and state agencies devoted to environmental protection and community development projects flourished, as they had elsewhere in the global South.[2] These entities sought Malagasy employees skilled in small-enterprise development, agronomy and agroforestry, forestry, animal husbandry, gender analysis, and participatory rural appraisal. Foreign NGOs and nonprofits were contracted to run site-based projects near newly formed nature reserves; these projects, called integrated conservation and development projects (ICDPs), aimed to combine economic development and ecological conservation.[3]

My anthropological research in Madagascar has focused on unskilled, male laborers of the island's ICDPs. Conservation agent is the official job title of these ICDP employees. Through the creation of this job category, a new kind of worker-peasant emerged. The conservation agent was not solely someone who would perform the manual tasks involved with establishing a national park, such as protecting its boundaries and building footpaths and village accommodations for ecotourists. He would also model environmentally sustainable practices and disseminate conservationist ideology to members of his own ilk—that is, to other subsistence farmers and fishermen. Over the course of my ethnographic fieldwork, carried out over several periods between 1994 and 2002, I examined conservation agents' relationships to their structural superiors, their ideas about the mission of conservation biodiversity, and their strategies in reconciling their lives as both wage workers of an international conservation network and peasants with deep ties to the moral economy of tavy, the "slash-and-burn" technique for cultivating rice practiced by the Betsimisaraka and other ethnic populations of the island's east coast.

Low-wage conservation labor represents an integral means by which capitalism "greens" itself in biodiversity hotspots of the global South. Malagasy workers have approached the greening of capitalism pragmatically, seeking to take advantage of the values of international donors in order to find and retain jobs. At the same time, rural people are not blind to the worsening conditions in which they live, the effects of deforestation and exploitation. Therefore many espouse the principles of ecological conservation if not the structure and means through which it has been imposed.

The Greening of Development
Planners of biodiversity conservation in Madagascar have projected that the start-up of market-based activities in some rainforest areas will reduce economic pressure on remaining rainforests. If peasants have a

source of revenue, they will be less likely to raze and burn the forest to grow rice, and eventually vegetation and species population levels will regenerate. If protected natural areas can draw in a greater flow of tourists over time, local residents will be able to take advantage of a market for locally made woven crafts, as well as for the rustic accommodations of the village, offering an "authentic" cultural experience. In addition, protected areas provide sources of state revenue, including the price of entry tickets and the fees paid by scientists to conduct research and biological prospecting in primary forests. The promotion of ecotourism and the rents of scientific research represent facets of the "ecological turn" in industrial expansion.

Another more controversial facet of this trend is the practice of "offsetting" the ecological costs of mining and logging with remedial activities. This is the current strategy of mining companies in Madagascar, such as Rio Tinto, whose activities exact a heavy toll on the island's biodiversity. Rio Tinto's proposed conservation offsets include the replanting of exhausted land with native seeds and the protection of a habitat near the site of mining activity. Conservation policy planners maintain that non-extractive, environmentally benign forms of generating revenue, as well as offsets, lay the foundation for sustainable development, the goal of the United Nation's Brundtland Commission of 1987.

Many scholars have been critical of optimistic portrayals of sustainable development strategies as being something inherently new, and they argue that the greening of industry and the effort to raise environmental consciousness equate to smoke and mirrors, essentially a change in capital's self-representation, nothing more.[4] Capital's ecological turn reflects another moment in which competitive advantage "is solved not by changing the means of production but by changing how meaning is produced, or how the relationship between persons and things is construed and managed."[5] But since the structure of the capitalism stays intact, the internal contradictions that serve to fuel the creativity and crises of capitalism endure.

For ecological Marxists, environmental crisis is the "second contradiction of capitalism."[6] This is distinct from the first contradiction, that of the demand-side crisis arising out of the tensions between capital and labor. The first contradiction stems from capital's drive to increase the amount of surplus value it can extract from labor. An increasing number of workers are either laid off or paid less relative to the task burden. Consumers therefore buy less, and capital's profits suffer as a result.

The second contradiction manifests itself on the supply side. This can happen when the material conditions of capital's production are poorly maintained and one sees the deterioration of workers' health, soil fertility, or infrastructures such as roads, ports, and machinery. It also appears when people organize to impose demands that raise costs for capital or reduce its flexibility.[7] Attempts to solve problems of the second contradiction have included the restructuring of the land-labor relationship, the transformation of industry's image, and the delivery of better benefits or compensations. "Second contradiction" crises are usually diagnosed as management problems, and these problems in turn can present another source of dynamism for capitalism.[8] As Sian Sullivan notes, environmental crisis inspires novel products and services such as "offsetting, payments for ecosystem services, natural capital, green-indexing, biodiversity derivatives, green bonds, [and] environmental mortgages."[9]

It is perhaps easy to write off capitalism's "greening" as nothing more than an assortment of superficial changes. But to do so minimizes the impact of greening discourse on people's consciousness. It elides the ways in which potential workers approach capitalism's new identity strategically as job seekers and ideologically as subjects and inhabitants of a degrading landscape. In Madagascar, even if rural people resist conservation interventions or greet them with cynicism, they are aware of the opportunities afforded by a mastery of the discourse. They are also aware of real environmental problems, including increased flooding, more ferocious hurricanes, leached soils, and a growing scarcity of wild protein, all of which have made survival more challenging.

Below I examine some of the ways rural Betsimisaraka workers in Madagascar's conservation sector have balanced their skepticism of outsiders' intentions with their desire to understand the island's ecology through a "modern" (neoliberal) lens. I focus specifically on the staffs of two ICDPs, one at the Andasibe-Mantadia protected area and the other at the Mananara-Nord Biosphere Reserve, to reveal how conservation agents have resisted the structure of conservation and development from within while also assimilating aspects of the conservationist discourse. Their experiences speak to the subjective transformation of rural labor under neoliberal conservation efforts in Madagascar, offering insight into trends occurring in tropical biodiversity hotspots around the globe.

The ICDP Paradigm

In the late nineteenth and early twentieth centuries, French colonial officials denigrated Malagasy employees of the fledgling forest service,

judging their acumen and skills inferior to that of scientifically educated Europeans, in spite of the fact that the Malagasy workers inti-
mately knew the forest ecology, having been raised in the vicinities of
the respective forestry stations. The Malagasy workers were also agile,
strong, and acclimated to the tropical conditions, unlike the French,
who suffered from malaria and dengue fever, and had difficulty walking
the forest terrain.

This structural bias concerning forestry and conservation labor has
persisted into current times. An education in forestry, environmental
science, or social science is more highly valued and compensated in the
conservation and development bureaucracy than knowledge acquired
from inhabiting the rainforest, but when it comes to physically protecting endangered plant and animal species, manual workers carry out the
tasks. Under neoliberal policy, moreover, ICDP workers are expected to
be true believers in the global mission. What staff members think about
the environment and the purpose of conservation matters in a way
that it had not under colonial rule. The tensions between workers and
management related to workplace conditions, tasks, and compensation
often serve to undermine rural people's acceptance of conservationism,
and this also goes for conservation agents and other ICDP staffers.

In 1994, I arrived in Madagascar to study the lives of Betsimisaraka
peasants. The Betsimisaraka had unwittingly found themselves the
objects of conservation and development interventions a couple years
earlier when an ICDP installed itself in the region to manage a newly
created national park, Mantadia, as well as the existing special reserve
for the indri lemur, the largest primate species in Madagascar.

The Betsimisaraka (literally, "the many who will not be torn
asunder") are the largest ethnic population of the east coast of
Madagascar, while the Merina are the main ethnic population of the
central highlands. The politics of ethnicity play an intrinsic part in the
division of labor in Madagascar, including the conservation and development bureaucracy. The Merina have controlled most state offices
since Madagascar gained independence in 1960. Before French coloniza-
tion in 1896, the Merina monarchy had effectively colonized most of the
island and subjugated the coastal populations.

In recent years, most high-level positions within ICDPs and the
conservation-and-development bureaucracy in Madagascar have gone
to university-educated nationals—the majority of whom are Merina—
while consultancies go to expatriates. Lacking post–secondary school
education, manual workers have sought to add value to their labor by

acquiring skills and knowledge that could elevate their rank in the bureaucracy. They have learned the importance of education and educated language to upward mobility.

A bit about the transition to neoliberal conservation: In the late 1980s, international NGOs took over the responsibility for managing national parks and nature reserves from the state forest service, the Département des Eaux et Forêts, which international donors considered ineffectual and corrupt. Jobs with the ICDPs continue to be desirable to Malagasy citizens because wage jobs are hard to find in Madagascar. ICDPs also appear to offer safer work conditions than, for instance, poorly regulated mining operations or the textile and wood factories in the free trade zones, and ICDPs provide relatively good benefits and salaries. Yet when the manual workers who had been employed by Eaux et Forêts were retained to work for an ICDP, as was the case at the Andasibe-Mantadia protected area in the early 1990s, these men lost their tenured civil service positions to become contractual workers for the particular NGO.

The ideological model of the ICDP entailed a more "bottom-up" approach to conservation and development that contrasted with the heavily top-down strategies of conserving forests during the colonial era. The bottom-up approach meant that ICDP staffs would solicit the input of local residents and take their priorities and complaints into account so that the ICDP activities would proceed collaboratively with local communities. The ICDP paradigm emerged after critical assessments of "fortress conservation," in which the state prohibits subsistence activities within the boundaries of a protected area.[10] ICDP designers intentionally took stock of the interconnection of rural poverty and biodiversity loss and realized the importance of ameliorating poverty to get peasants to adopt conservation practices. Planners envisioned ICDP workers encouraging local villagers to adopt conservation practices by imposing penalties for rule breaking while also allowing villagers to have a voice in ICDP activities. In exchange for the implementation of local development activities by the ICDP, for example, veterinary services, nutrition classes, training in beekeeping, improved fishing techniques, and the creation of tourist-grade crafts, as well as the collaborative construction of bridges, dams, and schools, the ICDP insisted that the villagers respect the rules forbidding them to clear forest or harvest timber or protein from legally protected areas. In addition—and this was key in terms of villagers going along with the plan—village communities were promised a portion of the ticket fees for entry to the protected areas.

Much emphasis was placed on the perks of increased tourism. If ecotourism could become profitable, not only with direct revenue from ticket fees but also through foreign visitors' staying in local hotels and buying villagers' crafts and produce, peasants would see the direct benefits of conservation rather than having to wait for the distant, elusive promise of a better life that would result from leaving the forest alone. However, around 1994, a few years into the new conservation program, the parastatal agency set up by donors to coordinate ICDPs and protected areas, ANGAP (Association Nationale pour la Gestion des Aires Protégées, National Association for the Management of Protected Areas), rescinded its promise to give up a hefty portion of the ticket revenue. Apparently ANGAP needed all the funds for its own operating costs.

Two decades into the ICDP approach, rural Malagasy people continue to resent conservation interventions largely because they involve placing fertile forested land into the state's hands.[11] Nonstate actors have also worked through the vehicle of the state to increase their control over Malagasy territories.[12] Another major problem, which had not by the late 1990s been brought up in scholarly or institutional evaluations of conservation in Madagascar, was the spirit of discontent and resistance among ICDP workers.

Through a series of events, chance acquaintanceships, observations, and interviews with low-wage workers about problems concerning the bureaucratic structure of conservation and development programs, I began to look more closely at the conflict between manual labor (mostly comprised of men from coastal—or what Merina people consider to be "black"—ethnic populations) and the expatriate and Merina bosses of ICDPs. Conservation agents (and their counterparts, development agents, whose role was eventually phased out) were hired from the resident populations of protected areas. They had value as "insiders," since they knew the terrain and local species, knew what kinds of clandestine activities go on in protected areas, and had social ties to communities of the area so residents would be more likely to respect their authority. Since one of their main job duties involved cracking down on people caught trespassing the boundaries of protected areas, they found their loyalties divided between appeasing their ICDP bosses, who paid their salaries, and maintaining good relations with their kin and neighbors.

The Work Strike of 1996
The event that really opened my eyes to the implication of ICDP labor tensions was a strike organized by lower-tier workers of the ICDP of

the Andasibe-Mantadia protected area in December 1996, the details of which were recounted to me when I returned to Madagascar in the summer of 1997 and visited my former field site.[13] The men who struck had the official job titles of conservation agent and unskilled laborer (*ouvrier*). My research assistant and I had gotten to know several of them from my earlier fieldwork there (1994–1995), so they were forthcoming about what prompted the strike and how it unfolded.

According to the conservation agents at Andasibe-Mantadia, the strike was triggered by actions taken against one of their coworkers in December 1996. Charles, the guard of the orchid park inside the special indri lemur reserve, was fired for abandoning his post at night. Normally, he manned the orchid park with a partner, but his partner had stayed home ill one night and Charles had to stand watch alone. He had fled his post because, like most residents of the region, he was afraid of the forest at night, believing it to be haunted by capricious spirits and ghosts (Malagasy distinguish several supernatural beings).

Charles's coworkers in the ICDP understood why he had left, but they still thought it wrong to have left the orchids exposed to theft. Orchids, like other endangered species in Madagascar, are lucrative goods on the black market. After Charles was fired, his former coworkers fumed at the moves of the ICDP director, a Merina man whom the workers called a "shark" (*antsantsa*) or "crocodile" (*voay*). They felt he ought to have first given Charles a warning, as stipulated in their work contract. Resentments against the director had accumulated to the point that the lower-tier workers were fed up. They decided to go on strike.

The thirty-nine strikers included the ouvriers and conservation agents. They felt they were paid inadequate salaries and the bosses did not respect the terms of the contract regarding sick leave, medical benefits, training, and the provision of supplies for long outings in the rainforest, such as rain gear and plastic gel sandals, the only good shoes for the forest terrain. The strike of December 1996 coincided with a point in the life of the ICDP when ANGAP was about to take over the reins of the project from an American nonprofit organization and its Malagasy NGO partner.[14] At that point, the national director would begin to lead the project without the Americans. The strikers worried about how ANGAP's takeover would shake up the existing personnel.

The work strike exasperated the American chief of the project, his Haitian-American deputy, and the Merina director. They were especially irritated when they learned that several of the striking workers had traveled to the capital, Antananarivo, to consult with experts at the National Trade Union Syndicate, a holdover from the socialist era. Representatives there had assisted the ICDP workers in formalizing their own union, the first of its kind in Madagascar, comprised of contractual ICDP employees of a foreign-managed project.

The ICDP workers felt that their work on the project was worth more than that of the (mostly Merina) office workers since they were "the ones who protected the forest" and interacted directly with villagers in the area. The conservation agents and ouvriers took pride in their species knowledge of the reserve as they recounted the events to my research assistant and me. When ANGAP assumed control of the ICDP around January 1997, before any of the strikers' demands had been addressed, ANGAP authorities laid off the main organizers of the strike.

Other participants in the strike received pay cuts. What I found especially interesting in the conservation agents' accounts of the strike was their unselfconscious embrace of the tenets of conservation, expressing a desire to protect the forest, to get out in the "field" (the deep forest) rather than staying around the office building doing repairs and other odd jobs, and to witness species they had never seen before. Their desires seemed newly acquired, compared to what they had wanted and thought about during the recent past under socialism, when they were civil servants of the forest service and before biodiversity conservation had become a national concern. During that time, the political discourse emitted from the national television and radio stations had proclaimed the value of workers: the worker was a rights-bearing individual; the peasant, pride of the nation, was through the production of food the agent of national self-determination.

While president, Didier Ratsiraka broke with the colonial past by adopting the socialist rhetoric of contemporary African leaders, advocating isolationism and self-sufficiency, promoting peasant commodity production, and cultivating ties to the Soviet bloc countries, China, and North Korea.[15] When bankruptcy forced Ratsiraka to turn to the Bretton Woods institutions in 1987, international donors introduced a different valuation of labor and nature. The terms "peasantry" and "proletariat" had become muted, thus affecting the social aspirations and sense of entitlement they stirred in people. In their place emerged the terms "natural heritage," "biodiversity," and "community." Even the word "environment," not directly translatable into Malagasy, inspired a neologism: *tontolo'iainana*, "the lived-in world," to convey the general meaning of our natural surroundings. Rather than appropriating the term as its coiners might have intended, Malagasy people have used the term specifically to refer to protected areas, spaces surveilled by a conservation authority.[16] I noticed that when conservation agents used the term "tontolo'iainana," they did so in front of a specific audience— Merina consultants and officials, other Malagasy bosses—to demonstrate environmental knowledge and solidarity with conservation actors.

Conservation agents and other aspiring employees of the conservation and development sector grasped hold of the environmentalist vocabulary and sustainable development vision. Manual workers were reinvented, and reinvented themselves, through the emergent environmentalist discourse. By 1996, after the impeachment of Albert Zafy and an early presidential election that returned Ratsiraka to power, Ratsiraka presented a new slogan for the island nation: "A Humanist and Ecological Republic."[17] Labor's value in conservation and development institutions now hinged on workers' knowledge of the attributes and locations of species, as well as on their commitment to conservation and development.

The work strike at Andasibe-Mantadia illuminated some of the internal tensions within the conservation and development bureaucracy and some of the strategies workers have used to remain employable, but the strike did not reflect the everyday ways in which rural workers have negotiated their desire to gain benefits from the conservation sector with their aversion to damaging their social relationships in the village.

I carried out a later period of ethnographic fieldwork (2000–2002) in the Mananara-Nord Biosphere Reserve on the northeast coast, where I examined the lives of conservation agents who had never staged a strike or unionized. These men, in contrast, made do by straddling the moral economies of tavy and conservation, making compromises when and where it was necessary to satisfy the demands of the ICDP bosses or the expectations of their kin.

Life in a Biosphere Reserve

The work strike at Andasibe-Mantadia and similar ones around the island in the mid-1990s showed how Malagasy workers rejected the terms and structure of neoliberal programs, but by the early 2000s it had become clear that the strikes, not surprisingly, had done nothing to change business as usual. Yet by ignoring the external manifestations of the structural inequalities, sustainable development planners have been undermining their goals of protecting species from extinction and primary habitats from ruin. In the UNESCO Biosphere Reserve of

Mananara-Nord, where the island's pilot ICDP was launched in 1989, lower-tier ICDP workers had ample opportunity to steal time from their conservation jobs because the majority of them were directly or indirectly invested in tavy, as well as in cash cropping and petty trade.

Nearly the entire district of Mananara-Nord, excluding the town of the same name, had been incorporated into the 140,000 hectares of a UNESCO Biosphere Reserve. A population of more than a hundred thousand resided in approximately two hundred hamlets. The core of the reserve constituted the 24,000 hectares of protected rainforest. Betsimisaraka residents used the word *biosphère* to refer to both the national park and the ICDP that managed the entire reserve. The biosphère was to residents both a thing and an assemblage of social relationships that linked the area to a global environmental network. Staffed by local employees, funded by European donors, supervised by a Dutchman, monitored by Malagasy officials and grant managers, the biosphère became an unwelcome authority to villagers.

The implementation of the ICDP in 1989 met with fierce opposition by villagers. People did not want to give up the forest land to a national park, nor did they want to stop doing tavy in the forest. Hiring local residents onto the ICDP was in part an effort by project managers to diffuse tensions. Residents also insisted that the director of the project not be Merina but a local, implying someone Betsimisaraka or Tsimihety, another ethnic group of the northeastern coast.

During the fourteen months I stayed in the region, a range of ten to eighteen men served in the "conservation component" of the ICDP. The variation was due to resignations and new hires over that period. Most of the conservation agents had joined the project in the late 1980s or early 1990s, when the establishment of the reserve required intensive labor and diligence was at a high pitch. After the boundaries of the park had been mapped, tree nurseries built, habitant species inventoried, and trails cut, the ICDP's momentum slackened. The conservation agents complained to me about the fact their tasks were poorly coordinated in the project. The Malagasy director did not seem to have a clue as to what the workers should be doing on a daily basis, and the Dutch head of the project, acting as a codirector, was usually busy writing reports. Both he and the Malagasy director spent an inordinate amount of time at meetings in the port city of Tamatave or in the capital, Antananarivo.

As a result, most members of the conservation crew who lived in the mountainous villages spent most of their time tending to their tavy fields and rice paddies, as did their family members and neighbors. For the majority (about two-thirds of the crew) who did not own land in the region and lived in villages on the vehicular road or in the town of Mananara-Nord, some participated in sharecropping, others bought rice from peasants with land, others carried out petty trade or odd jobs, one fished regularly with nets acquired by the ICDP, and all attended the mandatory project meetings at the ICDP headquarters in Mananara-Nord.[18]

Constantly surveilling villagers so they did not enter and clear land in the national park, take timber, or hunt birds and lemurs was impractical. To do so would foster ill will toward the ICDP. Plus, conservation agents were quick to point out; the ICDP bosses were not running things fairly. They complained that the bosses were very slow to reimburse agents for any out-of-pocket medical expenses. Of the two project vehicles, one was in constant disrepair and the other was often absent, used by the Malagasy project director on his long overland trips south into Tamatave. This meant that conservation agents stationed in villages far from town had to find their own transportation into town if they wanted to collect their monthly salary.

Rather than pay for a bush taxi, an expense the ICPD was supposed to reimburse but no longer did, manual workers opted instead to go on foot, a trek that took between five and eight hours for agents living in villages on the western side of the reserve. Agents over the age of thirty-five complained that they were too old for this type of work, the long walks through the forest and between villages. Their age, however, did not slow them from working industriously in their rice fields and groves. Especially aggravating to the lower-tier ICDP workers was the lack of raises over the previous four years. The project was also negligent in providing workshops for conservation agents to enhance their skills, particularly foreign-language training, which would enable more of them to guide tourists into the national park and earn tips. In the Mananara-Nord Biosphere Reserve, the labor structure and process compelled conservation agents to negotiate conflicts of interest that occasionally flared up in ways that betrayed their ICDP job duties (and contributed to deforestation) or betrayed the ideal of solidarity espoused by rural Betsimisaraka people.

The Forest Sweep

At specific times, the ICDP bosses demanded very difficult work of the conservation agents. Two tasks in particular were dreaded by conservation agents for their negative repercussions. One was to man a barrier at a village called Anove, located on the main road leading into Mananara-Nord. At the barrier, conservation agents had to check trucks for contraband timber taken out of the reserve. This in itself was not difficult, but manning the Anove barrier took conservation agents away from their homes for several weeks at a time, usually at critical periods of the agricultural cycle when men's work was essential, such as clearing and burning scrub. It is important to note that conservation agents who practiced tavy did not always make incursions into the primary forest; they sometimes reused their plots from the prior season. However, they did clear forest areas that, they claimed, were not part of the reserve proper.

A dreaded task, carried out infrequently, was the forest sweep, or *déguerpissement,* when cultivators who cleared land in the national park were tracked down and forcibly removed by conservation agents teamed with gun-toting national police (*gendarmes*). Delinquents were brought to the local authorities to receive fines, community service, or, in the worst case, jail time. The déguerpissements were passionately decried by local residents and conservation agents' reputations in their respective villages were damaged for months afterward.

The sweeps were supposed to take place every year, but popular opposition to the biosphere project in Mananara-Nord had pressured the ICDP bosses into canceling the sweeps for three successive years. In fact, the ICDP only had conducted two large-scale déguerpissements since the establishment of the biosphere reserve in 1989. The ones carried out in 1998 and 1999 created political fallout as politicians in Mananara-Nord condemned the biosphere reserve for taking away peasants' land and forcibly removing them from their ancestral territory. The ICDP opted to not conduct a sweep in 2000. But in the fall of 2001, as the ICDP staff faced the anxiety of UNESCO handing over the reins of the project to the national park service, ANGAP, the ICDP bosses organized a flurry of activity in the national parks. Teams of conservation agents and gendarmes convened to receive their supplies of food, tents, and rain ponchos for spending the next several weeks in the heart of the rainforest.

The déguerpissement was dangerous work. Peasants were headstrong, the conservation agents asserted. Many refused to abandon their newly cleared plots. They sometimes inflicted curses (*manaña aody*) on the approaching conservation crews by leaving hexed charms on footpaths walked by the conservation agents and gendarmes. The conservation agents fretted about this afterward, ready to attribute ill luck to a curse. Sometimes peasants would brandish their machetes as the ICDP teams approached their homesteads. One conservation agent took to carrying a cheaply made pistol in case of assault.

The long recess since the last déguerpissement in 1999 had emboldened rice farmers to clear land in the reserve's core. In September 2001, the conservation agents took issue with the bosses' decision to conduct the sweep at that time of year, when peasants had either already cleared land or were in the midst of burning. Damage to the forest had already occurred, and arresting farmers after the fact only provoked the population. Another problem for conservation agents was the laxity of the local officials. Conservation agents resented the dishonesty of officials who were supposed to impose penalties on forest clearers but were easy to bribe. When the 1999 déguerpissement took place, for example, local officials had not enforced conservation laws or sentences against rule breakers.

In 2001, Etienne, a conservation agent, told me that to him the most enjoyable aspect of his ICDP job was "protecting the forest" (*fiarovana atiala*) because "there are little children who will live to see it." He disliked policing the forest and resented the fact that the agents' labors seemed wasted by the lack of follow-up by town authorities. "I don't like the corruption of the state," he said. "Reports are falsified, especially at court. People are let off. Nothing changes. The forest clearers don't get enough punishment. That's what makes me bitter."

The social repercussions of carrying out the déguerpissement were significant. Serge, a conservation agent based in the town of Mananara-Nord, explained that villagers treated him like a complete outsider after the sweep: "There are those who are lazy to leave the forest interior. Half of them are not that resentful but half of them are really angry at the biosphere workers. If a lot of people manage to cut down the forest, then a lot of these forest clearers get penalties.... The half who are really angry—they'd refuse me a drink of water." Jafa, another conservation agent, admitted that during his participation in the sweep, people from his village shunned the small shop he ran with his wife.

Despite being ostracized in their villages and criticized as traitors, and despite empathizing with the peasants since they also believed that the forest was their rightful ancestral inheritance, the conservation agents behaved in an unexpected manner during the déguerpissement. I was surprised to see conservation agents assume an air of self-righteousness and even condescension toward "delinquent" peasants, and even their familiars, during the forest sweep of September 2001.

They displayed a supercilious attitude toward rule breakers that seemed genuine (that is, not for my benefit as an expatriate). Was it an attitude of defensiveness that gave them courage to carry out the sweep? Did it reflect a form of cognitive switching triggered by the necessity of having to carry out a task that betrayed the ethos of solidarity (*fihavanana*) intrinsic to village life? Were the self-righteousness and the ostensible satisfaction in protecting the forest for future generations' expressions of subjective transformation?

Such questions call for more ethnographic investigation over time. Since 2009, when a coup d'état ousted the pro-conservation president, Marc Ravalomanana, the situation in Mananara-Nord and regions north of there has been complicated by the plunder of the national parks of rosewood timber by Chinese and Malagasy merchants who hire cheap labor, including labor brought in from China, to fell the trees for export to China, Europe, and the United States. As tourism has slacked off due to the political instability, conservation and development projects have confronted more daunting obstacles to protecting biodiversity. Efforts to promote green capitalism in villages are offset by the urgency of policing nature reserves more vigilantly as people eke out their livelihoods.

Conservation's Contradiction

As my ethnographic work revealed to me, manual ICDP workers tried to make ends meet with wages that did not cover household expenses. They always worried about sudden loss of employment if their ICDP contracts did not get renewed. So most of the conservation agents stay tied to the subsistence economy of tavy, either buying rice cultivated by kin members or cultivating it themselves. This was a troubling contradiction of transnational conservation efforts in Madagascar, the fact that ICDP workers themselves engaged in tavy, the land use most blamed for biodiversity loss and soil erosion. In their eyes, the dual life as worker-peasant was justified by the precariousness of their contractual employment and the constraints put on their upward mobility into salary tiers that might provide a good enough income for them to abandon tavy altogether. Truthfully, however, the tavy economy represents more than a mode of production in eastern Madagascar. It is intrinsic to people's ritual obligations to ancestors and spiritual beliefs. Therefore, conservation agents were all the more reluctant to detach themselves from the moral economy of tavy. After the forest sweeps or other penalties they had to impose, at which time they assumed the cloak of the oppressor, conservation agents suffered the consequences humbly, waiting for the resentment to subside.

The neoliberal era of sustainable development planning in Madagascar set into motion the ascendency of biodiversity protection as a foreign aid priority. This motion had collateral effects on labor, however, insofar as the conservation and development discourse introduced new forms of value and new pathways of self-valorization while suppressing the key words of socialist discourse. Neoliberal conservation planners claim a more humanist approach, but the humanism hinges upon society's acknowledgement of the ecological priority. The institutional conservation discourse creates a fixed contingency. People have a right to a better material life—and this is to derive from an improvement of ecological conditions rather than the actualization of class equality. The institutional discourse dismisses the possibility of the latter as a path to ecological sustainability.

Manual laborers seeking jobs in the conservation and development sector have strategically sought to represent themselves as protectors of the nation's national heritage while also finding themselves in less secure, contractual jobs that expect a high degree of self-initiative. Yet for all the lack of defined, coordinated tasks in the day-to-day, manual workers are the only ones who implement the tasks of cataloging species, policing boundaries, penalizing rule breakers, and planting native tree species. If salaries and benefits for manual laborers in the conservation and development sector do not in themselves mirror donors' sense of urgency in protecting biodiversity, one is led to assume that what the job lacks in monetary compensation is offset by the ecological benefits that accrue to low-wage workers. One might assume that a committed conservation worker would undertake this kind of work for *his own good*, for the good of the nation, for the good of the globe.

Implicit in the representations of green capitalism is the idea of making sacrifices today for a brighter future. If corporate industries are urged to model such sacrificial behavior through the implementation of conservation offsets, so too can low-wage workers carry out the tasks of modeling conservationism, policing nature, and promulgating the tenets of sustainable development to their kin and kindred because they are inhabitants of these endangered landscapes themselves and stand to gain in the long term. As far as short-term gains go, the poor bear the far heavier burden of sacrifice.

CHAPTER 7

Sintracarbón: On the Path to Revolutionary Labor Unionism and Politics in Colombia

Aviva Chomsky

For the past fifteen years, international solidarity organizations have been working with Afro-Colombian and indigenous communities displaced and affected by the giant Cerrejón coal mine in northern Colombia. Initiated by Exxon in the 1980s, the mine was sold to a consortium made up of three of the largest multinational mining companies in the world: BHP Billiton (Australian), Anglo American (British-South African), and Glencore (now Xstrata, Swiss). Almost all the coal is exported, primarily to the United States, Canada, and Europe.[1]

The mine is located in Colombia's poorest department (province), La Guajira. The people who live there are Wayuu indigenous people—Colombia's largest indigenous group, who have maintained their language and culture over the five hundred years of Spanish conquest—and Afro-Colombian and mestizo peasants, many of them descendants of communities of escaped slaves who settled there in the eighteenth century. La Guajira enjoyed little infrastructure or state presence. Most of the inhabitants farmed small plots, hunted, fished, and worked as day laborers on larger farms or ranches until the arrival of the mine began to inexorably devour their land and contaminate their air and water.

The open-pit coal mine employs mostly skilled workers from outside the immediate area. Not until 2006 did the union at the mine, Sintracarbón (the National Union of Workers in the Coal Industry), take note of the operation's effect on the surrounding communities. In August of that year, the union's president met with a Witness for Peace delegation that was investigating the impact of the mine on the local communities. He was shocked by the stories he heard from the international delegates and the community members, and invited representatives of the solidarity organizations to return in November to help build relations between the union and the communities and to support the contract negotiations scheduled to begin that month.

It was a courageous step for Cerrejón's workers to reach out to the poor and marginalized communities that are in many ways victims of their employer's very existence. It was even more courageous—in some ways unprecedented—when workers voted to include a demand in their bargaining proposal that the company recognize the collective rights of the affected communities to negotiation, relocation, and compensation—three things the company has been adamantly denying.

International supporters organized ourselves to support what we saw as a pathbreaking and important commitment by the union to use the collective bargaining process to press the company on issues of human and community rights. We formed an International Commission in Support of Sintracarbón and the Communities Affected by Cerrejón (ICSSCAC). We requested—and received—a meeting with the mine's president during our November delegation, at which we delivered a fat folder of letters from unions, NGOs, and elected officials from around the world demanding that the company negotiate in good faith with the union and acknowledge the rights of the communities. The union sent us daily updates on the negotiating process, which we distributed widely. We organized actions at the headquarters of the three companies that own the mine, and pressed some of the energy companies that purchase the coal in the United States and Canada to express their desire for a peaceful, fair, and negotiated solution.

What follows is a selection of correspondence between the union and the international support group leading up to, and during, the entire process.[2] It reveals the union's growing commitment to the communities and the importance of the international support and publicity we were able to provide during the negotiations. All of us felt we were creating something new, exciting, and full of potential at a time when labor movements worldwide are struggling against extraordinarily unfavorable local and global environments.[3]

José Arias is one of the new leaders of Sintracarbón. He is currently interunion secretary. In his union work he has focused on the social issues facing the Guajiran people, and he has struggled tirelessly for a more just and equitable treatment for the villages in the vicinity of the mine.

Jaime Delúquez Díaz is president of Sintracarbón and a member of the executive committee of the International Federation of Chemical,

Energy, Mine, and General Workers' Unions (ICEM). He has been a tireless leader in the struggle to create a new Colombia based on principles of social justice.

Freddy Lozano Villarreal is from Barranquilla, Colombia. He has been a union leader in Sintracarbón for twelve years, and is currently secretary general of the Puerto Bolívar section. He is forty-eight years old and has worked for Cerrejón for twenty-one years.

Jairo Quiroz Delgado is a community social psychologist and is currently secretary of media and publicity for Sintracarbón. He has been involved in human rights struggles for many years.

September 15, 2006

Dear Avi,

The National Union of the Coal Industry, "SINTRACARBÓN," is preparing to present a negotiating proposal to the corporation Carbones del Cerrejón. Our proposal contains some basic points for discussion including the health, education, and welfare of the communities in the mining region, the workers' lack of economic resources, and other issues.

Avi, we know about your commitment, and that is why we are asking you to join with other supporters to accompany us in this conflict, so that we can carry out a field project together with the workers and the communities in the area of the mine that are affected by the coal operation.

Fraternally,
Jaime Delúquez
President, Sintracarbón

Friday October 27, 2006

Dear Avi:

Sintracarbón has created a commission to accompany your delegation during its entire stay in Colombia. Our organization considers the presence of this international delegation to be of transcendental importance. We are convinced that it will be beneficial for the communities and for the workers at the mine. We would like to consult with you and with members of the communities how to best develop our plan of action.

Fraternally,
Jaime Delúquez

NATIONAL AND INTERNATIONAL DECLARATION ON THE IMPACT OF THE CERREJÓN MINE EXPANSION ON THE COMMUNITIES IN THE MINING AREA

During the week of October 30 to November 3, 2006, a delegation of the National Union of Coal Workers (Sintracarbón) worked together with several international NGOs and the Wayuu indigenous rights organization Yanama to investigate the living conditions and health conditions in the communities in the area of the Cerrejón mine.

The delegation met with the communities of Patilla, Roche, Chancleta, Tamaquito, Albania, and Los Remedios, as well as the indigenous Provincial reservation and the displaced population of Tabaco. It carried out health clinics, conducted a public health survey, and listened to testimonies and life stories in all of these communities.

These communities are being systematically besieged by the Cerrejón company. The company begins by buying up the productive lands in the region surrounding the communities, encircling each community and destroying inhabitants' sources of work.... The United Nations has established categories of "poverty" and "extreme poverty," but these communities have been reduced to the conditions that we could call the "living dead." They do not have even the most minimal conditions necessary for survival. They are suffering from constant attacks and violations of their human rights by the Cerrejón company—a systematic process of annihilation to create despair so that they will negotiate from a position of weakness, desperation, and hopelessness, and agree individually to the company's terms.

Each of these communities has been reduced to a zone of misery. They have no schools, hospitals, or basic public services. Their water supply is unfit for human consumption. We also saw evidence of many cases of respiratory diseases, skin infections, mental health problems, and arthritis.

Upon finishing this stage of the investigation we conclude that the reality is far worse than we had imagined. The multinational companies that exploit and loot our natural resources in the Cerrejón mine are violating the human rights of these communities.

Sintracarbón has committed itself to the struggle of the communities affected by the mine's expansion. We invite all other unions and social organizations in Colombia and especially in La Guajira to join in the struggle of these communities for better conditions and quality of life and to take on the communities' problems as our own problems.

As a union committed to the struggle of these communities, we have established the short-term goal of working to help unify the affected communities, to participate in their meetings, to take a stand with the local and national authorities regarding the absence of public services in the communities, to begin a dialogue with the company about the reality we are now aware of, and to take a public stand locally, nationally, and internationally about the situation of the communities affected by the Cerrejón mine and its expansion.

SINTRACARBÓN STANDS WITH THE STRUGGLE FOR JUSTICE FOR THE COMMUNITIES AFFECTED AND DISPLACED BY THE CERREJÓN MINE! ¡¡¡¡SINTRACARBÓN PRESENTE!!!!

Barranquilla, November 8, 2006

Compañera Avi Chomsky
   Warm greetings:
   All of us here in La Guajira would like to thank you and the members of your international delegation who we had the privilege of accompanying in the important task of bringing a voice of hope to the members of the communities surrounding the Cerrejón mining complex.
   Beginning now we as a union are proposing that just as the company has a social responsibility for the way it runs its business, our union has a moral and political responsibility regarding the destruction that the Guajiran communities are suffering at the hands of Cerrejón. The company generates huge profits through the misery, poverty, and uprooting of these populations. The communities have to pay a very high price for the company's profits.
   Once more we sincerely thank you for your solidarity and your cooperation. We are convinced that only the unity among the different peoples of the world can allow us to confront these economically powerful and inhuman multinationals in the name of the communities that have the misfortune to be located in the path of the mine's expansion.
   Finally, I'd like to share some words by Che Guevara, which I think respond to a question that Tom asked, with respect to the meaning of the word "compañero": "We are not friends, we are not relatives, we don't even know each other. But if you, as I, are outraged by any act of injustice committed in the world, then we are compañeros." However,

we also now consider you all to be our friends and our relatives. Forever united.

Jairo

- -

Excerpt from Sintracarbón bargaining proposal, presented to the company on November 20, 2006:

CHAPTER XI

NEW ARTICLE 16. SUPPORT FOR SINTRACARBÓN'S PROGRAM IN SUPPORT OF THE COMMUNITY:

Upon the signing of this Contract, the Employer will support Sintracarbón's program in relation to the communities, aimed at bettering the quality of life in La Guajira Department.

FIRST PARAGRAPH:

Upon the signing of this Contract, the Employer will carry out improvements on the road from Cuestcitas to Riohacha according to the norms established by the Ministry of Transportation.

SECOND PARAGRAPH:

Upon the signing of this Contract, the CERREJÓN company, in accordance with international law and the Colombian constitution with respect to indigenous and Afro-Colombian communities, will implement and carry out a policy of RELOCATION and INDEMNIZATION for all of the communities affected by the coal complex.

CHAPTER XII

NEW ARTICLE 18. FORUM ON COAL POLICY:

Upon the signing of this Contract, the Employer will finance the organization and implementation of a forum about coal policy that will allow for the dissemination of information about the environmental, socioeconomic, and health impacts of mining on the communities in the region.

- -

Message from Freddy to Avi, December 18

On Sunday December 17 we held another meeting with the communities. Patilla, Tabaco, Chancleta, and Roche attended, as well as Jairo Quiroz, José Arias, Francisco Blanco, and Freddy Lozano from Sintracarbón.

Sintracarbón presented a report explaining step by step what we have been doing up until now, and noting that this week of December 18 the issue of the communities will be coming up at the negotiating table, and that the person in charge of monitoring dust emissions in the mine expansion process left because of accusations made by the union.

Tamaquito explained in their report that they had made requests of the Barrancas authorities but had had no response. Their community kitchen has been taken away. José Arias of Sintracarbón will be following up on this situation.

COMMITMENTS: We will meet again on December 24 in Roche, and on December 30 in Patilla.

At the beginning of January we will hold a larger meeting with the leaders of the communities and Sintracarbón to organize a public demonstration in support of Sintracarbón's bargaining proposal.

Communiqué 28

STATEMENT TO THE PUBLIC
Sintracarbón denounces the intransigent position that the Cerrejón company has been taking before our just bargaining proposal that we presented on November 20, 2006. During 31 days of negotiations the company has not presented serious responses, nor have they showed the will to negotiate.

We summarize below the most important points of our bargaining proposal:

* HEALTH: Among the company's workers there are approximately 700 who are currently suffering health problems. Their health coverage is being permanently altered with the complicity of Colombia's health plans (EPS Coomeva and ISS ARP), with the blessing of the Colombian state.

* EDUCATION: The high cost of education, the privatization of the education system, and the disappearance of the public universities make it impossible for workers' sons and daughters to gain access to higher education without putting an enormous burden on their economic situation.

* WAGES: The most recent labor law reforms, Laws 50 and 789, along with the loss of purchasing power because of inflation, have reduced Colombian workers' salaries, and Cerrejón workers have not been immune to these problems. This situation has plunged many of our workers into insolvency.

* TEMPORARY WORKERS: We are asking that all workers in the Cerrejón coal complex be contracted on a permanent basis. Temporary workers are exploited; their fundamental rights are continually violated. Cerrejón has ignored this situation.

* COMMUNITIES: As a consequence of the expansion of the mining operation, neighboring communities like Patilla, Roche, Chancleta, Tamaquito 2, Provincial, and Los Remedios have been turned into ghost towns. They have lost the capacity to survive through herding, farming, and fishing. They have not had the opportunity to collectively negotiate reparations for the loss of their cultural patrimony, the loss of their ancestors, and everything else. The towns of Tabaco, Manantial, Caracolí, and others, have been abused and their human rights violated. These communities were displaced from their natural environment. These are Afro-Colombian and indigenous communities that were forcibly removed by the army and police. Their property was destroyed. Our union Sintracarbón denounces these acts and reiterates its intention to make sure that no further abuses occur against these communities and that the slums and cordons of poverty in La Guajira do not continue to grow.

In the face of all the above, Sintracarbón emphatically protests the intransigence of the multinationals that are looting our non-renewable energy resources, and their lack of will to negotiate and to make proposals that will satisfy the needs of the Cerrejón workers.

LONG LIVE OUR JUST BARGAINING PROPOSAL!
DOWN WITH THE INTRANSIGENCE OF THE MULTINATIONAL BOSSES!
LONG LIVE THE STRUGGLE, ORGANIZATION AND UNITY!

Communiqué 33

Today, Thursday, January 11, our compañeros who live in Riohacha participated enthusiastically in a large protest against the Cerrejón company's lack of will to negotiate a resolution to our just bargaining proposal.

The CUT [National Union Confederation] La Guajira section and other civic, popular, union, and student organizations participated, as well as people from the communities affected by the mine including Patilla, Roche, Tamaquito 2, Provincial, Los Remedios, and the displaced community of Tabaco. Sintracarbón thanks all of the above for their solidarity and participation and exhorts the people of La Guajira to offer us their support and collaboration in the coming days in the case that we find ourselves involved in a strike which would have a huge magnitude and impact.

During the week of Jan. 15–20 we will be organizing a strike vote. We urge all workers to exercise their right to vote.

Communiqué 35

January 16, 2006; calling for a strike vote

In addition to labor demands, our petition includes social demands, such as those regarding subcontracted/temporary workers, and those regarding communities. The communities near the mine, and the communities displaced by the mine's expansion, also have the right to collective negotiations. All of the communities should be relocated, preferably in conditions better than their current conditions. They should be paid compensation for the loss of their cultural patrimony, the loss of their ancestors. The current approach of individual negotiations should be halted. The current approach has only led these communities to fill the slums of La Guajira. This is the supposed "land and communities" policy followed by Cerrejón and applied by BHP Billiton, Anglo American, and Xstrata/Glencore in other parts of the world where these multinationals exploit non-renewable resources and sow destruction, poverty, and misery in their wake. The Cerrejón company and its enormous profits should not be based on leaving behind sick workers and impoverished communities.

January 20, the union reported the results of the strike vote:

Strike vote results:
Out of 3,100 members, 2,421, or 78 percent, voted. 2,382, or 98 percent of those voting, voted in favor of a strike.

January 21, letter from Jairo to Avi

Our collective work with the communities is beginning to show results. On Monday, January 22, we will be discussing the communities issue at our negotiating session. Eder Arregocés of Chancleta, who spoke for the communities at the Congressional hearings on Friday, will be there to represent the communities.

The work that you have done internationally, our speeches on Thursday at an international event in Bogotá attended by representatives of the International Labor Organization and Anglo-American, and the Congressional hearings on Friday, have pushed the company to moderate its position in the negotiations.

We need your support more than ever this week. The fact that the company has agreed to discuss the issue of the communities is an important advance. We need any kind of pressure you can exert, through political figures and all of the organizations that have been supporting our union in the negotiations.

It is very important that we keep up this arduous struggle, and your support is also very important. Together we will succeed, in spite of the harassment and the threats that we are being subjected to.

Fraternally,

Jairo Quiroz Delgado

Communiqué 44

STRIKE IMMINENT AT EL CERREJÓN

In spite of the Cerrejón mine's enormous profits in recent years, with the selling price of coal over US$60 a ton, and with 28 million tons of coal in sales last year, the company has refused to come to a negotiated agreement with our union. During 45 days of negotiations the Sintracarbón negotiating committee has reiterated its desire to come to an agreement that would satisfy the workers' needs as expressed in our bargaining proposal. During the entire negotiating period Cerrejón has said nothing but NO to the needs that our union has expressed.

IF WE ARE FORCED TO STRIKE, WE WILL STRIKE!

FOR OUR JUST BARGANING PROPOSAL!

UNITY, ORGANIZATION, AND STRUGGLE!

January 23, 2007

Message from Freddy to Avi

Avi, I just want to say a thousand thanks for the torrent of solidarity we have received, letters which in addition have gone to the company. Today we feel that we are no longer alone. I would like to ask you for one more thing, a message from the International Commission that I can read to the delegates in the meeting that we are holding in Riohacha on Thursday the 26th. It would be very important for the people at the meeting to hear a message of support from the international community.

Again, thank you and we are not alone!

January 24

Message from the International Commission

Many of us met Sintracarbón in August 2006, when the union's president, Jaime Delúquez, accepted our invitation to participate in an International Conference that we organized in Riohacha on the impact of mining in La Guajira. The conference included international delegates, academics, members of NGOs, unionists, and representatives of communities affected by Cerrejón.

We are an international coalition of people and organizations that feel involved, one way or another, in coal mining. Some of us are from the United States and Canada, where we import large amounts of Colombian coal for our power stations. Others are from Australia, Switzerland, and England, the countries where the multinationals that own Cerrejón have their headquarters. Some of us are from regions affected by the same multinationals that have investments all over the world. Some are members of unions that are struggling for the same thing Sintracarbón is struggling for: the right to decent work, with decent pay and benefits.

But we are also aware that our struggles depend on others' struggles. We want decent work—but we also want to create a world in which everybody has the right to decent work and a decent life. We want to have electricity—but we don't want it to be produced at the cost of displaced communities and murdered unionists.

In our November delegation to accompany Sintracarbón, in which we visited the communities affected by the mine, we saw clearly that the Cerrejón workers shared our goals. Just as they committed themselves to finding a way to support the rights of the communities, we committed ourselves to supporting our collective struggle for a mining industry that respects the rights of everyone involved.

This is why we created our International Commission to support Sintracarbón in its negotiations, and this is why we today reiterate our strong commitment to maintain and strengthen our support for the union and for the communities affected by Cerrejón. Another world is possible, and we hope that together we can continue to create it.

¡POR EL JUSTO PLIEGO DE PETICIONES DE SINTRACARBÓN!

¡UNIDAD ORGANIZACIÓN Y LUCHA!

¡LA COMISION INTERNACIONAL, PRESENTE!

The International Commission in Support of Sintracarbón and the
Communities Affected by El Cerrejón (ICSSCAC)
Solifonds (Switzerland)
The Berne Declaration (Switzerland)
Grupo de Trabajo Suiza Colombia (Switzerland)
Colombia Solidarity Campaign (Britain)
Atlantic Regional Solidarity Network (Canada)
Langara College Student Union (Vancouver, BC)
Helen Berry, Public Service Alliance of Canada
Aviva Chomsky, Salem State College*
Jeff Crosby, North Shore Labor Council*
Sydney Frey, New Haven-León Sister City Project*
Tracy Glynn, Fredricton Social Network
Daniel Kovalik, United Steelworkers of America
Garry Leech, Cape Breton University*
Lynn Nadeau, HealthLink
Steve Striffler, University of Arkansas*
Cecilia Zarate-Laun, Colombia Support Network
*Affiliation for identification purposes only

January 27

Message from Freddy to Avi:

The workers' commitment to the communities' issues is strengthening daily. In Riohacha on Thursday, before the Assembly, we held a
large demonstration in front of the La Guajira provincial government
headquarters. Representatives of Patilla, Chancleta, Roche, Tamaquito,
and Tabaco participated. Eder and Jaime spoke on behalf of the communities and the union, respectively.

Last week in Bogotá, in a meeting organized by the ILO, in which
Sintracarbón participated along with Billiton and Xstrata officials, we
discussed the issue of the communities. Also, let me reiterate: we will
not accept a contract that does not include a solution for the communities affected by Cerrejón.

Communiqué 50

Today, Wednesday, January 31, the negotiating committees of Cerrejón
Llc and Sintracarbón finished the revision and redaction of the new

Collective Bargaining Agreement. At 3 pm the two parties signed the Agreement, which will be in effect for the period 2007–2008.

The signing of the contract signals the end of the conflict that began on November 20, 2006, when Sintracarbón presented its bargaining proposal before the Ministry of Social Protection.

Sintracarbón reiterates its sincere gratitude to all of the union members, delegates, union leaders, social, student, popular, and union organizations, the national union confederation CUT, and its La Guajira and Atlántico regional sections, the Democratic Pole party, the displaced and affected communities, the international community, the ICEM, and other international organizations, for their unlimited support, without which it would not have been possible to arrive at a negotiated settlement through dialogue.

We believe that the results show a positive outcome, according to our fundamental objectives in the negotiation, from the perspective of wages, educational benefits, social welfare and social security, subcontracted and temporary workers, and communities. In addition, Sintracarbón recovered its capacity for mobilization and its credibility in the local, national, and international spheres, as well as its capacity for struggle and mobilization of its members.

February 1, 2007

Message from Jairo to Avi:

Jaime asked me to tell you that the communities issue was a very difficult one at the negotiating table. The union would not give in up until the last minute; in fact it was the very last point to be agreed upon.

Initially Cerrejón's position was that it would not discuss the communities issue at all at the negotiating table. Finally, because of the work and collaboration of the international community, it agreed to discuss it, and for this we thank you and the rest of our international supporters.

The results may not be everything we hoped for, but knowing these multinationals, we feel it is a political advance. From now on the union will participate in everything related to the company's social programs, and it will have a presence at the negotiations with the communities.

Before signing the final document, Jaime discussed it with Eder (Arregocés, from Chancleta, who is representing the communities in José Julio's absence), and he agreed with it.

We also understand that this is a long-term struggle, and you can rest assured that Sintracarbón will continue to work on this issue together with you.

Note: The company refused, in the end, to include the issue of the communities in the collective bargaining agreement. Instead, it offered a side letter inviting the union to participate in the company's social programs. On its face, the letter offered little, and it evaded the demands that the union, the communities, and the international supporters had so vigorously pressed for. But as Jairo expressed in his letter above, it opened an important door to union participation in the communities' ongoing struggle with the company.

A subsequent message from Jairo illustrates the ongoing conflict, as well as the long-term commitment the union has made to support the communities.

April 5, 2007

On Tuesday, April 3, the Sintracarbón Executive Board met in Chancleta with members of the different communities affected by Cerrejón. The meeting went well. We listened to what the community members had to say, their dissatisfactions and disagreements about the union negotiations with the company and its results for the community.

Sintracarbón accepted some of the criticism, but we also emphasized, as we have before, that the main protagonists in this struggle are the communities. The international community and Sintracarbón are aware of their struggle, and we stand in solidarity with you with the sole goal of improving the conditions and quality of life in the communities. We believe that collective negotiations, with our participation and help, may be able to achieve what the communities' desire: relocation in better conditions and reparations. The meeting was productive and cordial, and at the end the communities understood the importance of our accompaniment, and that our contract negotiations with the company were part of the struggle, a valid tool, but that we all understood that the communities' problems could not be resolved solely by that means.

One of our board members invited several municipal officials from the DEMOCRATIC POLE party, a political party of the left that has committed itself to this struggle.

We agreed on a plan of action, which we will explain to you in detail soon. One thing we agreed on is to carry out a summit of social organizations in one of the communities affected by the mine.

A representative from Tamaquito reported that the people there are being harassed by the army. We will be requesting a meeting with the military commander in the area, with the participation of several national and international human rights organizations and NGOs in order to discuss this problem.

Five years later, the different international solidarity groups have maintained close relations with both the union and the communities, and have tried to contribute to amplifying their voices both inside Colombia and in the international community. The union has continued to accompany the communities and to steadfastly support their right to collective recognition and relocation.

The union was a founding member of RECLAME, the Colombian Network on Large-Scale Transnational Mines (Red Colombiana Frente a la Gran Minería Transnacional). The organization's name is often translated into English as "Colombian Network Against Large-Scale Transnational Mining" but the union points out that the wording is important. "How can a mining union oppose mining?" I asked Jairo in a meeting with another Witness for Peace delegation in 2011. "We're not against mining," he insisted. "The name of the organization is 'Frente a la Gran Minería Transnacional.' We are not against mining—we are confronting mining. And we are against transnational mining. We are against the multinationals that are looting our territory. We think the mines should be nationalized, and should be operated in the interests of the people."

In 2010 the Cerrejón mine began to circulate a plan to greatly expand production, affecting many more local communities. Central to the plan was a project to divert twenty-six kilometers of the Ranchería River, the region's major waterway. In August 2011, a group of Afro-Colombian, indigenous, and community organizations, joined by Sintracarbón, formed the Comité Cívico de La Guajira Frente a la Gran Minería Transnacional, "in defense of the communities in the area of the mining complex and affected by the mine." The committee emphasized "the connection between the mining process and the land, the environment, the royalties, and the future of the department, which now more than ever are suffering from the threat of obliteration at the hands of the Juan Manuel Santos government's mining and energy steamroller." It mobilized particularly in opposition to the diversion of the river.

In June 2012 I asked Igor Karel, the new president of Sintracarbón, the same question I had asked Jairo the summer before. Like Jairo, he insisted that the union does not oppose mining. "Of course we care about our jobs. But diverting the river—that is impossible. The river is water. Water is life. Without life, there are no jobs," he said quietly.

Toward the end of 2012 the mine announced that it was abandoning its expansion plan, at least for now. It cited the low price of coal, rather than the enormous mobilization against the planned expansion, as the reason for the change. The mine continues to move forward with an expropriation process against one of the villages that has refused to abandon its territory in the existing mining area. Community and international activism continue to grow, and the union continues to play a central role in both.

CHAPTER 8

The Formation of a New Independent Democratic Union in Argentina: The Subte Transport Workers Union

Darío Bursztyn

Historical Background

The formation and historic path of working-class organizations and trade unions in Argentina is unique among South American countries. From the mid-nineteenth century, working-class radicalism in Argentina was inflected by the arrival of radical, anarchist, and communist exiles from Germany, France, Spain, Italy, and Eastern Europe. In 1850 a typographers' union was formed in Argentina and, by 1870, an International Workers Association was established and consolidated by exiles from France following the 1871 Paris Commune.[1] Argentina's rapid economic expansion, spurred by British capital, significantly increased the demand for European immigrant labor. As in other settler countries, European working-class émigrés had been radicalized by conditions in their home countries and arrived in Argentina with expectations of improving their standard of living through social mobilization. These crystallizing class antagonisms were instrumental in expanding the size and influence of the flourishing and politically diverse Argentine workers' movement, which included anarchists, syndicalists, and communists who struggled for improved conditions against the dominant capitalist class.

The economic structure of Argentina in the nineteenth century was defined by the dominance of local landlords and British imperial interests, which tried to establish a semi-colony in Argentina analogous to Australia. England and Europe needed food and the vast temperate climate of the Pampas region was ideal for mass agricultural cultivation and cattle production. Situated near the southern Atlantic at the center of the Pampas region, Buenos Aires was perfectly located as a port and as the terminus of the railway for the development and expansion of the fertile region through the transshipment of food, agricultural products, and cotton products to the burgeoning European market. From the late 1850s to the early twentieth century, construction of Argentina's extensive rail network north and south of Buenos Aires was instrumental in the growth of exports to Europe.

European immigration from Italy and Spain in the late nineteenth century was essential for propelling the mass growth of Argentina's population, displacing indigenous people and working in the country's agricultural and transportation industries. The flourishing city of Buenos Aires was the destination for impoverished and persecuted migrants from the two countries, who also frequently harbored revolutionary philosophies of socialism and democratic organization. The first unions to form during this period were organized on the basis of solidarity among their members and the ability to provide benefits to widows and orphans of workers and help to newcomers. The unions, organized through syndicalist and communist groups, formed rank-and-file committees and organizations to fight for labor rights, including the eight-hour workday and living wages. The capitalist class responded to the rapid and widespread radical organization of the working class with state repression that reached a crescendo in the early twentieth century, culminating in the Semana Trágica (Tragic Week) in Buenos Aires, when worker protests were countered by police, leading to the killing of seven hundred and injury of two thousand workers. Subsequently police cracked down on worker radicalism, arresting about fifty thousand workers.

Diverse radical influences from the rise of the Soviet Union and the Spanish revolution contributed to the growth of Argentinean militarism in civil society and were the basis for the rise of the military populist Juan Perón after World War II. From 1946 to 1955, Perón mollified workers with social benefits while abolishing radical anarchist, communist, and socialist unions seeking to expand democratic working-class organizations, replacing them with Peronist unions. The benefits that the state established under Perón molded a strong working class, strong unions, and a high level of organization, even if the bureaucracy barred workers from leading or participating actively in the movement.

When Perón was overthrown in 1955 and the unions and parties forbidden, workers continued to remember this "golden age" of greater worker democracy. The Peronist Resistance shifted to a left nationalism, with admiration of the Cuban revolution and other anti-imperialist movements of the 1950s and 1960s. However, as in other eras of Argentine history, the presence of a strong state apparatus restricted the growth of labor militancy through police repression and social benefits to the working class.

Argentina's Radical Neoliberalism

The election of Carlos Menem as president of Argentina in 1989 augured a new era that stripped workers of their social benefits through instituting neoliberal reforms under the guise of market democracy. As president, Menem (1989–1999), reformed the constitution to facilitate his running for a second term and pardoned key officers imprisoned for crimes committed under the military junta (1976–1983). Seeking support from the working class, Menem concealed his plans to apply neoliberal economic policies to reduce inflation and ultimately to peg the Argentine currency to the U.S. dollar. As president, he implemented policies with support of the state bureaucracy that neglected worker interests—leading to lower wages and flexible working conditions that benefited business interests. These policies included the introduction of short-term and part-time contracts without social benefits, freezing the annual discussion of salaries between unions and employers, and massive privatization of state companies, including railways, water services, electricity, gas, oil, ports, airports, rivers, telephone companies, radios, dockyards, and beyond. Consequently, thousands of employees were laid off.

The fall of the Soviet Union prompted radical workers to concede that no alternative to capitalist domination was possible and that they should await the benefits of neoliberalism to flow from the rich to all of society. Local business formed joint ventures with direct foreign investors that relied on the withdrawal of the state, fewer workers, and monopolistic contracts. Under neoliberalism, the state lowered taxes and controls on foreign capital, permitting investors to reinvest profits in tax havens abroad. The state was reduced to a minimum and education and health services were severely eroded and, in many cases, services were subcontracted to low-wage employers.

In response to these policies, opposition expanded among old and young workers who demanded the renovation of unions rooted in class struggle and democracy. New alliances were established among leftists and Peronists to demand working-class rights. Workers recognized the indestructible nature of bureaucratic unions and the necessity to form "asambleas de base" (popular assemblies) as a direct democratic alternative within factories, offices, and new unions. Delegates, or *delegados*, were chosen in a growing number of production units, reigniting a social construction of the early 1970s. As the movement expanded, the activists expressed aversion to what they viewed as a state that failed to defend worker rights, union bureaucracies that actively supported privatization and employer domination over workers, and growing disinterest in the fate of the Argentine working class.

Argentina was the first country in the Southern Hemisphere to confer workers' benefits unthinkable thirty years later in other countries. Consequently it was logical that new forms of working-class organizations emerged to defend past achievements and fight for new needs. In the context of the 1990s termination of economic benefits and worker rights, workers demanded and formed new democratic labor organizations—notably within the subway (Delegados del Subte) struggle.

Class Struggles in Argentina

Inherent to capitalism and its inequitable structure is the struggle between the owners of the means of production and the workers, who have only their labor power. Thus, capitalists buy and sell specific commodities that accrue labor-added value through the production process and are exchanged through the circulation process. This creates a permanent state of conflict: working classes challenge the power of capitalists with demands to improve their working and living conditions, and experience some gains followed by periods of retreat. On the capitalist side the same ebb and flow occurs but with the priority being to maintain the greatest degree of exploitation of the lower classes.

However, the stages of capitalism and the ways workers organize themselves are not fixed. During the Industrial Revolution and the subsequent implementation of Taylorism and Fordism, the ruling socioeconomic class appeared unified, and the proletariat had to fight protracted, dramatic battles in order to establish the first unions, labor parties, and mutual benefit societies, later winning historic gains such as the eight-hour workday and the prohibition (almost) of child labor. We shall not attempt here to detail the history of each stage, but it must be said that even as the working class has made superb efforts toward achieving workers' rights and political gains, and even confronting those in power to displace the capitalists in order to build a more equitable society, capital is obliged constantly to increase productivity in order to sustain or enlarge the surplus. It's exactly at this point that capital enters a self-destructive cycle: increasing productivity necessitates a greater investment in technology (fixed capital or "dead" capital, in Marxist terminology), which at the outset gives one capitalist entity an advantage over other capitalists at the same level or in the same industry; that advantage eventually extends to the country, and even globally, whatever scale allows for an absolute profit rate.

However, that profit is merely provisional, since the improvement in technology incurred by one capitalist compels the others to follow suit. Journalist Daniel Schäfer described a recent example of this phenomenon at Volkswagen in the *Financial Times*:

> The carmaker is one of a range of German companies that face the daunting task of maintaining their technological edge while being confronted with the need to reform their cost and labour structures. For Germany's automotive and engineering sectors, the industrial heart and soul of Europe's biggest economy, the threat is that they will fall behind in competitiveness after emerging from the global economic crisis with overcapacity and unchanged staff levels."[2]

Capitalism, by nature, prevents profits from falling, resulting in the necessity to constantly cut labor costs through wage cuts and new technology. However, capital is obliged to offer better pay not only for more specialized work that can be performed only by certain individuals, but also for work that the entire capitalist class values, performed at a higher speed with minimal financial risk.

Following the international oil crisis of the 1970s, the hegemonic industrial countries of Europe and North America and even in some more peripheral countries such as Argentina were forced to reduce wages and implement labor-saving technology to maintain profitability through outsourcing manufacturing to the global South where labor could be exploited at a higher rate. Meanwhile, domestic production shifted to largely automated industries, including information technology. Some consequences for labor were as follows:

- The proliferation of software and IT production centers with relatively high salaries
- The growing technological advances of manufacturing with a subsequent increase in productivity and reduction of total payroll.
- The breaking of labor unions and alternative political parties, circumscribing mass struggle through the prism of parliament, government legislation, and wherever possible eliminating traditional forms of collective bargaining.

Concomitantly, capital claimed the following achievements through militarism and financialization:

- A deepening of the industrial-financial-military alliance that diverted large amounts of funds toward the monetization of investments, removing those funds from the production circuit
- The creation of debt instruments for peripheral capitalist countries like Argentina, which, through interest and amortization, resulted in a huge foreign debt owed by the global South to the North
- An accelerated urbanization centered on megadevelopments such as shopping malls, banking centers, and other service providers

In this frame Argentina's railway infrastructure was neglected, and, in its stead, roadways were expanded and subsidized, with increased support for the industries related to private transportation. There was a dramatic transfer of the key position and relevance formerly held by cargo trains to automobiles and long-distance buses.

In Argentina, the economic development and investment in regional urban areas was ignored, as Buenos Aires, the center of the national economy, expanded into a megalopolis dominated by the service sector and encircled by three industrial belts. By the late 1980s Buenos Aires region became Argentina's major financial, service, and industrial center, concentrating trade-industrial and financial consortiums that demanded efficient service structures with qualified workers. Christian Topalov observes that the capital city is a productive, socialized force that centrally concentrates workers through transportation networks and must provide the financial capital for the extended reproduction of the workforce. He argues that the strength of the city is the result of the spatial connection provided by transportation to and from the industrial and financial enterprises.[3]

Mass Transit and Capital Development

Transportation is vital; there is no question it is the master key for the development of the socioeconomic structure of capitalism. In Buenos Aires, particularly in the heart of the city, where financial and communication services are based, the subway—*Subte* in Argentinian slang—is the predominant form of transportation. Struggles between competing capitalists—for instance, a producer of railway materials versus an automotive producer—have been the only factor thwarting the expansion of the subway system, which expanded with support of the National Treasury and through dubious international loans. To promote urban development and to facilitate public transit of workers, the state sought the expansion of Line E, which originally terminated at Bolivar Station, in downtown Buenos Aires, to complete the North-South connection to expand the power of financial and development interests, who maintain hegemonic power over the city.[4] The capitalist transformation of Buenos Aires, the importance of transportation, and the need for speed—form the basis for understanding the political and economic relevance of the labor struggles in the transportation industry from the 1980s to the 2010s.

What Stops When the Subte Stops?

The extended reproduction of capital at the heart of the city grinds to a halt: that hurts the capitalists and sets the stage for a major battle.

> With the strike of telephone workers and the series of conflicts at the Subte, service workers of demonstrated their strength by obstructing a segment of the communications and strategic transportation sectors in a large city such as Buenos Aires.... This is a phenomenon that has many parallels around the world. Its relevance for the working class is that the workers not only can stop the production itself, as they have done before, but can also interrupt the capitalist business as a whole when they stop the services (i.e., subway and telephone service). And moreover: the confluence of both strikes means a general strike de facto, since you cannot go to work without transportation.[5]

> We are a strategic means of transportation because we stop the production of the City of Buenos Aires.... In the book by Virginia Bouvet, one of our colleagues; there is a strong statement that expresses exactly what I mean. It says, "We stop the forty most important blocks of Argentina." And it's exactly like that. It is chaotic.[6] —Ariel Mastandrea, Delegado from Line C

The Subte workers' power resonates because their struggles extend beyond traditional unions, which seek economic demands, to those of worker participation and self-activity. As such, the Subte workers are engaged in a two-pronged fight against hegemony. The subway employees have created their own union, the Delegados del Subte (Asociación Gremial de Trabajadores del Subte y Premetro, AGTSyP), through gaining autonomy from the main transportation union, Unión Tranviarios Automotor (UTA), which primarily represents bus drivers. Delegados del Subte has asserted the UTA ignored its interests and demands. The second primary effort engaged by the Subte workers is the assertion of the importance of their position in the production process of the city of Buenos Aires, and thereby making demands that question the hegemony of the capitalist class. The Delegados del Subte organized through an independent, counterhegemonic process of self-awareness that leads to strategies to overcome the economic-corporative dynamic of exploitation. Antonio Gramsci used "hegemony" to describe the capacity of the dominant social group to attain and maintain power over a given society, not only by preserving the ownership of production means, often using repression to do so, but also, in particular, by controlling the institutions of communication—namely, the media. Such control is most effective when it becomes normalized as "common sense," with this social consensus representing the triumph of the dominant class.[7]

Delegados del Subte are motivated by building class solidarity with workers' struggles in other bureaucratic unions through expressing independent, direct-democratic organizational forms, in which every last decision is made by workers' assemblies. The dominant bureaucratic unions, however, have opposed the resistance of the Delegados del Subte as it reveals the servile nature of traditional unions and foments dissention among rank-and-file members who have challenged their bureaucratic leaders. Subte workers' foremost adversary since the 1980s has been the UTA, the largest transportation union in Buenos Aires, which they view as defending capital and large corporate efforts to promote neoliberal policies rather than upholding the class interests of members. In the 1990s, subway service in Buenos Aires was turned over to Metrovías, a private company, as part of President Menem's neoliberal privatizations, as wages declined and working conditions had become increasingly arduous. The privatization sparked the Delegados (delegates, or *delegados de las bases* in Spanish) to launch a counterhegemonic struggle.

Before the Delegados were expelled from UTA, they served as active shop stewards, and Subte workers thought that they had dynamic representation. Given that UTA had ignored the Subte workers, the Delegados efficiently filed grievances and pressed rank-and-file interests directly with management. According to Pablo Peralta, Delegado from Line A, "because the Delegados were removed, a 'conflict of representation' emerged between workers and the UTA."

The issue faced by an insurgent union is how to develop an independent organizational system outside the dominant system, mirroring a council communist form of representation within the Subte union. The

Argentine media represented the Delegados as agitators, demonstrating the media's support for the dominant class interest, which requires subservience, discipline, and public promotion of the bourgeois discourse. Strength and consensus maintain hegemony, Gramsci argued, and it is to that purpose that the organs of public opinion operate. The media are the link that allows the capitalist infrastructure and superstructure to work together congruently. In this way the complicit media provides the most immediate guarantee of the survival of the capitalist system.[8]

How Did the Media Depict the Subte Strikes?

A subway strike is not the same as a strike in a company that constructs buildings or in a factory. The Subte occupies a conspicuous position. And that's why the media show what they want. But in spite of their wishes, since our strikes are always breaking news, they can't deny the importance of our demands. —Pablo Peralta, Delegado from Line A

Visibility is essential for a strike that involves about 3,000 workers and brings the life of the city to a halt, affecting more than a million and a half people per day. In addition to this window of visibility, good fortune can also play a role in the success of a strike.

If you stop a factory, life goes on. But if you stop the heart of the capital of the country, you have chaos that nobody can hide. This can only happen with our strike, and something of the sort happens with buses, trains, or teachers. You know, the Subte is used by 1.7 million people daily; it is unique and non-substitutable. You can see that other fights and other strikes could be broken after a certain time because people get tired of extreme struggles, but when we stop, we have in, let's say, ten minutes time, all the TV and radio journalists around. Not even Ford or Kraft workers can get this attention. The media can ignore industrial disputes, but cannot contain the Subte strike. —Ariel Mastandrea, Delegado of Line C

When we go on strike, the people going to work must take accordion buses, you have thousands of cars in the streets.... So definitely when the Subte stops, the city trembles.—Claudio Delle Carbonara, Delegado of Line B

This new union defending Subte workers was not created in a month; its development took years, so it's interesting to flash back through its history and, at the same time, have knowledge in hindsight as to how neoliberal policies played out. This is why it is relevant to consider the way the media depicted the measures taken by protesting workers—general strikes, part-time strikes, free access to the trains, and more—since those depictions affected the construction of the "common sense," in Gramscian terms. This is referring to the mechanism by which the subordinated classes' viewpoints mirror those of the leading class, rather than their own, and only by arriving at class consciousness can they liberate themselves from that domination.

Movement of Delegados del Subte

There are two milestone struggles in the movement to create the Delegados del Subte, (1) November 2004–February 2005, and (2) July–December 2008. To understand how those historic moments transpired, it is necessary to understand subway conditions in Buenos during the 1970s and 1980s.

Subway workers introduced their claim to have their own union amid the massive mobilization of the Argentine workers' movement in June–July 1975. The masses were against the economic policies that Isabel Perón tried to launch.[9] Some weeks earlier, during the general strike of April 5, 1975, transport workers created the Coordinadora Interlíneas (a guild of all workers of the subway lines), which was later dismantled by the dictatorship that followed the military coup in 1976. The Delegados de Subte guild comprised representatives from the five subway lines as well as representatives from garages, and one part of the antibureaucratic bus drivers represented by the UTA.

When the Argentine military government ruled from 1976 to 1983, all the Coordinadoras (workers' guilds—the most renowned were the Coordinadoras Interfábricas) suffered prosecution, with militant members imprisoned and disappeared. In the meantime the UTA embraced leaders who conformed to their interests that were not in opposition to business, capital, and the government.

During 1982 the Subte workers again took up the struggle for their rights and confronted the UTA, demanding—once more—an organization of their own. At that time they created the Representatives Board, for which they elected delegates per line and area, mainly militants from the Communist Party, Movimiento al Socialismo, Partido Intransigente, and Peronists. Even before the end of the dictatorship they asked for better salaries and the recognition of "unhealthy job conditions." Their most powerful demand, however, was to reinstate the historic six-hour workday, granted by Juan Perón in 1944 when he was minister of labor. That decision was made in response to unhealthy working conditions, although subsequent administrations—whether democratic or auto-cratic—weakened it, as did the private company, Metrovías, which has run the subway since 1994.

During the administration of General Juan Carlos Onganía (1966–1969) the workday went from six to seven hours, and the unhealthy working conditions benefit was canceled. In 1973, Peronists in the House reestablished the worker protections, but in 1976, under the dic-tatorship of Jorge Rafael Videla the seven-hour day was restored in the subways. The extension of the workday was in place until 1984, when president Raúl Alfonsin reinstated the six-hour workday, though the "unhealthy conditions" issue was tabled, with the promise of new studies of the working conditions that weren't conducted, in the end. In 1994, Menem's administration went even further than the military govern-ments: lengthening the workday to eight hours, and only in 2003 was the former benefit regained.

> As of 1995, in secrecy some comrades began to gather to meet outside of the subway, under clandestine conditions, because when management learned of any organization, people were dismissed.... Many of us remembered the history of the subway workers from the stories of the few who remained from earlier decades, and from them we knew that they worked six hours and all about the unhealthy conditions.... The newly formed organization was a mix of those who had some militancy in leftist parties, young people who entered the subway workforce after 1994. —Claudio Delle Carbonara, Delegado from Line B

The development of neoliberal policies in Argentina beginning in the late 1980s, demonstrated clearly how the conditions imposed by international financial institutions weakened workers' organizations, "increasing the metamorphosis of the classic bureaucratic unions tied to the corporations, and enhancing their ability to adapt to the state's new reality. Unions became more concerned about the income they received through the social and health services they could provide through collective bargaining agreements than defending workers' rights."[10]

In response, activist workers began holding clandestine meetings, which were the genesis of the Cuerpo de Delegados de Subterráneos de Buenos Aires, the initial name of the new union.

You know that the struggles of the subway workers have gone on for many years. At the beginning the leaders were from the Unión Tranviarios Automotor, but progressively the comrades won more and more elections and the Delegates Guild, with the twenty-one comrades, was born. —Ariel Mastandrea, Delegado from Line C

It's (Not) All about Money

The antibureaucratic workers in the Subte workers initiated an insurgency in 1997 when one of the delegates from the ticket counter division called a strike to protest frequent dismissals. Today, antibureaucracy continues to embody the essence of the Cuerpo de Delegados. Eventually, they achieved the six-hour workday as well as salary increases that put them among the best-paid workers in the country, and yet they embrace the adage, "It's not all about money," meaning not everything can be bought and sold.[11]

Our union aims to achieve better economic conditions and better salaries, and that is the main difference from the UTA, which sides with the corporation and looks down at the needs and hardships of the majority of the workers. They negotiate with Metrovías which slice of the cake is for them, and only when the workers really agitate do they take up the claim; otherwise they do not exist. We may or may not be right, but we listen to the demands of our comrades. —Pablo Peralta, Delegado from Line A

You can't intervene on a daily basis or even affect the workers' consciousness if you are not aware that the struggle does not end with unionism, in the protest itself. —Claudio Delle Carbonara, Delegado from Line B

In condemning the conditions that UTA failed to resist, Delegado Carlos Pérez states:

After 1997 the Subte workers had their ideological debates. Bureaucrats and some "leftist friends" said there were no conditions to fight for the six-hour working day, and since we were in an eight-hour regime, they said we had to claim for the seven-hour day that was in the Labour Agreement. In fact, the union played a traitorous role: they jeopardized a general assembly called to discuss the six-hour workday and higher salaries. That was the beginning of deeper ruptures between workers and bureaucrats.

In the struggle for the six-hour workday, in 2002 the Delegados organized strikes, mobs, street blockades, and press conferences. The decision was in the hands of the Buenos Aires City Hall, which in September finally voted in favor of the "Unhealthy Working Conditions Law," although it was vetoed by Mayor Anibal Ibarra.

> We in the subway are all affected. Our environment is unnatural, under the surface. It is true there's no carbon dioxide because the trains are electric, but we do have lead, the atmosphere has many things that you don't have "above." But what does Metrovías argue? The subway has less contamination than the streets that have carbon dioxide. That's a medical debate. However, our retirees have an average survival of five years when they retire. At the Subte there are different illnesses, such as phobias, with all the related consequences—panic attacks, hormonal problems… there's no natural light! And that is key for the mood as well. —Ariel Mastandrea, Delegado from Line C

In October 2002, a month after the mayor's veto, workers tried to enter City Hall while the Unhealthy Working Conditions Law was being discussed but were beaten by the police. On October 25, newspaper reports appeared as follows: "Yesterday there were sudden strikes at the five lines of the Subte. Today normal service will resume—incidents at City Hall when the House discussed the working regime for the Subte" (*Clarín*); and "Two wounded in front of City Hall—Violence and arguments downtown" (*La Nación*).

The year 2003 was also marked by the battle for the six-hour workday. The Unhealthy Working Conditions Law continued to be vetoed; workers demanded the six-hour day with no salary reduction, plus a wage increase, and a clear "no" to the automated ticket dispensers Metrovías wanted to impose in order to reduce the payroll. The UTA signed an agreement with Metrovías allowing for the creation of flexible working conditions and a salary scale far less than the expectations of the subway workers, who replied by staging new strikes.

With this context, it is easier to understand the struggles of the Delegados del Subte in the milestone years of 2004 and 2008. At that time, it is important to note, the subway workers' claims were not covered in the media. According to Mauricio Torme, "The populist rhetoric of the government and two years of growth in the economy after a large period of recession veiled the conflict."[12]

Previous conflicts were interpreted by the media as being a simple discussion between workers and capitalists, and any coverage stressed the "dreadful situation for the passengers" of the subway. On February 24, 2001, *La Nación* reported, "Chaos, subways stopped one hour. It was due to a union conflict and affected almost seven hundred thousand people." The other major newspaper reported, "Protest of Metrovías workers after the company eliminated the guards on the trains of Line B. An unexpected strike caused problems for the passengers."

The Delegados are aware of the power of the media:

> They will try to play against you so you must devise how to oppose them with your argument, and use the media in your favor. We won the battles with public opinion, which is dramatic. We have a very tight argument and we talk to the public very firmly, not responding to what [the media] asked but the message we wanted to spread. You know, it takes years, but in the end you learn how to do it. —Roberto Pianelli, Delegado from Line E

As of November 2004, el Cuerpo de Delegados de los Trabajadores del Subterráneo gained the effective representation of the subway workers while cutting ties to the UTA leadership, before they were expelled in 2008. The Cuerpo de Delegados called for assemblies in each work area to discuss the demand of a salary raise. The majority voted for the following:

1. Raising wages by 50 percent, to be shared collectively between the lowest and highest salary categories;
2. Demand the government reinstate the Unhealthy Working Conditions Law;
3. 1.5 percent bonus for each year worked;
4. Increase in the payroll to cover service demands;
5. Higher pay for workers employed at night.

These demands broke the pattern of concessionary contracts signed by the government, Metrovías, and the leaders of the national unions grouped in the CGT (Confederación General del Trabajo) and bought into visibility the conflicts that had previously been silenced by the government and the media.

From that moment on, the Delegados engaged in a three-front battle: the company (Metrovías), the government, and the union, all the while seeking to influence the press, which retained a hostile position toward subway workers, "Drawing a dichotomy between workers and passengers, with damage being done to the latter. They constantly used references to 'sudden strikes' to emphasize that, even though the strikes had been previously announced by the Cuerpo de Delegados."[13]

The conflict frequently made headlines. *La Nación* reported on December 8, 2004: "Eight hours without Subte and complete chaos, even though the Labor Ministry made an obligatory conciliation." And on February 5, 2005, *Clarín* described the scene, quoting a passenger: "'But these people earn good money. Why do they stop? I have to do social work to get basic compensation and they make a strike. It's a shame,' said Estela, while watching on the subway TV that a driver earned $2,107, a guard $1,512, and a ticket seller $1,442 a month."

> We already know that in many of our battles the media are important. I think that we can win the fight in the union but we have to win the battle in the media too. Because when a journalist says, "But why a strike that affects 1.7 million users that take the subway if your problem is a domestic fight in the union?"... Public opinion is very important because with the public opinion they can take us out in a minute. We are really very careful when we make a strike. And we design our message to communicate with the [subway] users and with the public opinion that doesn't use the subway.... We know that having them against us is a huge problem. —Ariel Mastandrea, Delegado from Line C

> The media want to create a confrontation between the other workers and us. They have giant economic powers behind them, completely against the workers, so they stir it up.... Though it's true that many users get angry. We try to have some politics for the passengers and tie our claims to theirs, because in fact they are the same! We don't ask for anything but better working conditions that mean better service. —Claudio Delle Carbonara, Delegado from Line B

> It is clear that the subway user is a salaried worker too. And there are some moments that are not right for a strike. You can't do that when the long-distance bus drivers decide to strike. That's not a good situation because then everybody is against you. —Roberto Pianelli, Delegado from Line E

2008: Year of Rage

The relation of forces between the workers and the three fronts they faced had changed by 2008. On one front, the rise to power of President Cristina Kirchner put the government in a stronger position and coercion was used when they wanted, including the sending of police brigades to the subway during strikes.

But the unity among the Delegados forced the government to agree to their demands for pay raises, equalization of salary, and promotions. By December, to intimidate the workers during elections for new union leadership, a new element had been added, the insertion of "gangs all over the Subte lines with the support of Metrovías," Delegado Claudio Delle Carbonara wrote in the *La verdad obrera* weekly report. The workers described the UTA and government's efforts to threaten them as "fake and illegitimate."

What was the rationale for the Subte workers for separating from UTA? Every day the UTA more aggressively opposed comrades, up to the moment that the UTA said "It's over." It was not the Cuerpo de Delegados who broke with the dominant union. The UTA expelled the twenty-one Delegados and at that moment the workers made the decision to form an independent union: "We said, 'It smells like shit, we can't go on this way. Let's make a new union.' But the UTA led us to this by mid-2008 by informing the ethics committee that the expulsion of the Delegados was necessary because they didn't respect the union's direction. You know, this led to such aggravation among our people against them! Because in fact they were expelled for fighting for the six-hour day, for better salaries, etc. So it was like saying to the workers, 'We are expelling them because they did it.'"

That was the perfect chance for the media to create negative opinion against the Cuerpo de Delegados. They were willing to publish whatever secretary of transportation Ricardo Jaime—one of Argentina's most corrupted characters, later imprisoned—declared. *La Nación*, December 12, 2008: "We said to Metrovías that they have all our support to continue with the service," and then the paper continued, "Even the general secretary of the CGT, Hugo Moyano, intervened yesterday against the Delegados that pushed for the strike, calling it 'deplorable' and anti-democratic."

> After we expanded our organization, deepened it, and stopped the Subte, the journalists had to speak with us—we were the players. This has to with different stages of our battle, ways of organization, and relation of forces we could impose sometimes. During 2003 and 2005 it was the peak, the best range of victories, also because of the general political noise in the society. We molded an organization that took advantage of that and was strong. After 2006 we had to

lower our profile because the state was stronger, the government was able to show another relation of forces, less favorable to us. — Claudio Delle Carbonara, Delegado from Line B

The Formation of the Cuerpo de Delegados del Subte

The Asociación Gremial de Trabajadores del Subte y Premetro (AGTSyP), was born in September 2008 as an alternative to the UTA. This new union was a legitimate creation of workers seeking for an organization to defend their rights, and they fulfilled every step the state demands to be recognized as an independent union.

> We were forced to make the decision to create our own union, because the union expelled the workers from the union—UTA. Very few of them were affiliated to the union before we took this step. — Claudio Delle Carbonara, Delegado from Line B

The union publishes a newsletter, *Prensa Subte*, and maintains a website, "Metrodelegados" and a radio program. For members of the Cuerpo de Delegados de los Trabajadores del Subterráneo the independent union is the only way to maintain a self-directed organization and a means to enlarge the struggle to other sectors, breaking the hegemony of the union bureaucrats and the vertical organization of the industry and the unions that mirror the structure of the capitalist class. The Delegados insist on an independent union that is organized by the workers themselves and represents the interests of all the members.

> I believe that we should deepen our democratic organization even more, and also our debate on the program or mission for our union, which is not yet legally established. It is not yet defined and I think it must be not only democratic but also class-based. —Claudio Delle Carbonara, Delegado from Line B

Democracy is embraced as one of the key values of the new union, reinforcing that they made the right choice when they decided everything must be discussed by the assemblies.

> Assembly is the way we decide all the coming steps. That was something that distinguished us from the bureaucrats. That's what we demanded in the UTA when we were or weren't Delegados. Because that is a way to pull the masks off those chumps that pretend to represent the workers' interests and they don't. We follow this methodology

because quitting that would be giving up our own identity; we would never be the same. —Claudio Delle Carbonara, Delegado from Line B

Take the Constitution maintenance garage—Line C. They have an assembly every Saturday morning, because that's the only day they are all at work since Sunday is a free day. In other Lines, the assembly is once a month, others have a different schedule... because what must be said is that all the Delegados go to work. —Ariel Mastrandrea, Delegado from Line A

This is another important issue they handle: bureaucrats don't work, and since they don't go to work they know nothing about the daily needs of a worker at the Subte.

We work and we understand it must be like that. The fact that you work puts you in the day-by-day experience of the worker. I mean, you can work at the Subte but if you stay five years with a license, and work in a union office, it's obvious you will have a reduced idea of what issues a worker has. Also, we believe it's wrong to have privileges for being a representative: you were not elected to have privileges but to have responsibilities. —Ariel Mastandrea, Delegado from Line A

Attempting to create a common definition for the union produces different ideas, specific to the background and political experience of each interviewee. Some talk about "base unionism" and others "class unionism." Altogether, the main common themes are antagonism toward the bureaucrats, pride in being part of a class, and equality among members.

You may be a militant in one of the leftist organizations, or you may not. You can have different political views, but what you cannot defend is a position that is not democratic and class-based. Because we faced many battles and we know that every demand has to do first with the company, then the bureaucrats, but at the end you have the state. —Claudio Delle Carbonara, Delegado from Line B

The Metrodelegados website helps to knit worker relationships in the subway with worker struggles in other unions. They are not isolated.

We try to keep a relationship with other unions and national unions, staying as far away as we can from prejudices. That doesn't mean we don't have an opinion on the way they work. —Roberto Pianelli, Delegado from Line E

They communicate with other workers and convince them to join the union through direct relationships among rank-and-file workers. The union newsletter reveals the solidarity developed among Subte workers:

> A new union, with 1,774 workers who enable it to exist with the satisfaction of knowing that there's something better and today is the right day to begin to build it. According to the workers' union, we began almost by chance to create our own organization, a long time ago. Every time we trusted the collective will of workers, on the commons, we became stronger and were able to take control of our destiny. Now we have the opportunity to grow, to give full life to our organization, to make it reflect our history. We will need the willingness and the time of many—of all those able to give their commitment to build working teams in each of the provisional secretaries of the new union. We invite you to join, to be part of the new era.

The union collects dues directly from the workers and through mutual recognition of the importance of maintaining independence; rank-and-file members understand the need to support the union through direct payment to the union, rather than a dues check-off system. "With 1 percent of your basic salary you support the new union, and we'll create a common fund with the administration of all the comrades who had dealt with finances until today, and all those who want to join them.[14] It is evident that this has been quite a journey for the workers at the Subte. Although their current situation reflects positive expectations and a new sense of dignity, there are many obstacles to overcome to maintain the functioning of the independent union.

> We do not have the legal dues check off, even though we have fulfilled all the requirements. The government has decided to gum the works. And another step would be to have the guild's support. We're facing the chance of being only a union, legally inscribed, but not having more than that. It's a tough issue. —Pablo Peralta, Delegado from Line A

While Delegados disagree on the most efficient means to collect dues to maintain the Subte union, their strength reveals member perception that they must contribute to maintain the functions of the subway workers organization and their desire to contribute to its strength rooted in rank-and-file participation.

According to Delegado Claudio Delle Carbonara, from Line B, "I believe we have to define the organization as not only democratic but at the same time class-based, and link to other comrades who are fighting to change the structure of this society."

III.
ORGANIZING AUTONOMY AND RADICAL UNIONISM IN THE GLOBAL NORTH

CHAPTER 9

Syndicalism in Sweden:
A Hundred Years of the SAC

Gabriel Kuhn

Origins and Overview

In 1898, Landsorganisationen (LO), Sweden's biggest trade union confederation, was founded by members of the Social Democratic Party. The relations between LO and the Swedish Social Democrats remain very strong to this day.

In 1909, LO entered its first major confrontation with Svenska Arbetsgivareföreningen (Swedish Employers' Association, SAF). The reasons were lockouts and salary cuts, which the employers attempted to justify as necessary means during a time of economic recession. From August 4 to November 13, 1909, the so-called Storstrejken (Great Strike) effectively put a halt to industrial production and service industries in the country.[1]

When the Great Strike ended, none of LO's demands were met and thousands of workers had lost their jobs. Many among LO's rank and file accused the leadership of organizing the strike half-heartedly and not putting enough pressure on the employers. LO lost almost half of its membership. It was in this historical context that Sveriges Arbetares Centralorganisation (the Central Organization of Sweden's Workers, SAC) was founded in 1910 as a radical union alternative.

The SAC's founding congress took place in Stockholm in June 1910. A photograph from the event shows thirty-six men and one woman assembled. Apart from delegates sent by various unions, the participants included members of the socialist press and representatives of Ungsocialisterna (the Young Socialists), a radical wing with anarchist tendencies that had left the Social Democratic Party in 1908. The Young Socialists and the SAC were closely connected and laid the foundation for organized anarchism and syndicalism in Sweden.

The SAC was founded as a syndicalist organization. Guiding examples were the French Confédération Générale du Travail (CGT) and the Industrial Workers of the World (IWW), founded in the United States in 1905. The main organizational unit of the SAC is the Lokal Samorganisation (LS), roughly a "local federation." A single LS unites all workers in a municipality and is comparable to the traditional *bourse du travail*: an independently organized group of workers determining their own workplace struggles and means. Many LSs—some of which had already formed before the official foundation of the SAC—had a radical outlook and favored direct action over negotiation. At the end of 1910, the SAC counted twenty-one of them.

The SAC's name is somewhat misleading. Far from being a centralized organization, the SAC mainly functions as an administrative umbrella for the LSs, which maintain a very high level of autonomy. Federalism has always been a key principle of the organization.[2] While the SAC's founding documents include explicit commitments to "socialist principles" and the "fight against capitalism," and while many individual SAC members throughout history identified as "libertarian socialists" or "anarchists," the organization itself never adhered to any particular political worldview and has always been open to all workers, regardless of political conviction or affiliation.

History

Most of the SAC's early members came from the stonemasonry, forestry, mining, and construction industries. In 1911 a LS formed in Kiruna, a small mining town far north of the Arctic Circle, representing the single biggest LS in the country.

The SAC grew rapidly and had more than thirty thousand members in the 1920s. Membership peaked in 1924, when thirty-seven thousand workers were registered as LS members. Throughout the 1920s, Sweden reputedly had the most labor conflicts of all European countries.

In 1922, the journal *Arbetaren* (The Worker) was founded, which serves as the organization's main publication to this day. Until 1958 it was published as a daily, since then as a weekly journal. In 1922, the SAC also joined the newly founded anarcho-syndicalist International Workers' Association (IWA).

In the mid-1930s, the SAC still had around thirty-five thousand members. Considering that there also existed a rival syndicalist organization at the time, Syndikalistiska Arbetarfederationen (Syndicalist Workers' Federation, SAF), an SAC offshoot that also boasted several thousand members; this was the pinnacle of syndicalist organizing in Sweden. The SAF was founded in 1928 by P.J. Welinder, a Swedish-born IWW veteran who had returned to the country of his birth. Welinder saw the SAC as too compromising. He advocated confrontational tactics and opposed all collective bargaining agreements, professional administrators, and even strike funds: strikes needed to be militant and deal strong blows to the employers, rather than ending in drawn-out conflicts demoralizing the workers. When Welinder died in 1934, the SAF lost its driving force. In 1938, the remaining members rejoined the SAC.

SAC membership numbers dwindled during World War II, when Sweden was governed by a broad coalition—excluding only the Communist Party—and operating under emergency wartime laws. Workplace organizing became difficult and many SAC members were persecuted for protesting the politics of appeasement that characterized Sweden's relationship to Nazi Germany until 1942–43. Some syndicalists, including the chief editor of *Arbetaren*, Birger Svahn, received prison sentences or were sent to labor camps. The labor camps had been established for drafted radicals whom the government wanted to keep separated from the regular troops.

Despite the difficult circumstances and the significant decrease in membership, the SAC played an important role during the war, as it was one of the few oppositional forces in the country. *Arbetaren* was the most confiscated Swedish journal during World War II. Although never completely banned, many of its issues were seized by the authorities on the day of publication.

After the end of the war, the SAC was weakened but still functioning. Since almost all of Europe's syndicalist organizations had been crushed or forced into exile, the SAC took on a leading role in international syndicalist organizing. As of 1938, the IWA's secretariat had moved to Stockholm, where it remained until 1953.

The relationship between the SAC and the IWA became increasingly strained, however, during the 1950s. When moderates, such as the German-born Helmut Rüdiger, who had come to Sweden after the defeat of the republicans in the Spanish Civil War, gained more and more influence in the organization, the SAC was accused of "reformism." For the circle around Rüdiger, the survival of the SAC depended on providing a viable alternative to the social-democratic LO rather than on stubbornly clinging to anarcho-syndicalist principles that needed revision in the light of a modernizing workforce and the postwar economic boom. While the merits that the SAC had won in its opposition to Nazi

Germany had given the organization moral credit, it was not necessarily regarded as a still relevant labor organization.

The most controversial aspect of the SAC's so-called *nyorientering* (new orientation) was the establishment of a government-supported unemployment fund. For many of the IWA's member organizations this contradicted the values that the IWA had been founded upon, and the ideological rift between the SAC and the IWA become more and more apparent. In addition, members of the Spanish CNT, historically the strongest organization within the IWA, were unhappy with the SAC's role in the conflict between the underground CNT activists in Spain and the CNT factions in French exile—a sensitive issue for all syndicalists in the 1950s. All of these tensions came to a boil at the 1958 IWA congress in Toulouse, France, after which the SAC and the IWA parted ways. The relationship between the SAC and the IWA remains complicated to this day, although much of the old bitterness has disappeared and individual IWA member organizations have reestablished contact with the SAC.

During the 1960s, the SAC was finally able to reverse the trend of continuously losing members. For the first time in decades, membership numbers increased. Nonetheless, there was still a sense of stagnancy and a lack of ideological orientation. After the turbulent developments of the 1940s and 1950s, the organization struggled to define a new identity. This changed with the political developments of the late 1960s, when young radicals saw the SAC as a useful tool for broad leftist organizing. A trend started that continued until the early 2000s: LS activities moved more and more from workplace organizing to general political issues, including nuclear energy, environmentalism, feminism, and the queer movement. In 2001, many LSs were strongly involved in the protests against the European Union summit in Gothenburg, which brought some of the heaviest street fighting and police violence that Sweden had seen in decades.

Antifascism also became a focus of the 1990s. Sweden was haunted by the violence of armed extreme right-wing groups. After the Stockholm LS member Björn Söderberg successfully protested the inclusion of a right-wing extremist in the shop council of his workplace, he was shot dead outside his home on October 12, 1999. Söderberg's death was the zenith of extreme right-wing militancy and spurred mass demonstrations across the country. It also triggered a broad effort to clamp down on right-wing extremism, supported by all political parties and the media. Although the campaign was fairly successful, right-wing extremism remains a serious concern. In 2008, two SAC members and their two-year-old daughter barely escaped an arson attack on their third-story apartment in Stockholm. They managed to escape over the balcony with the help of their neighbors.

Söderberg is honored at a yearly event at the La Mano monument in Stockholm, erected in 1977 in commemoration of the Swedish volunteers in the Spanish Civil War. The SAC also awards a yearly Civilkuragepriset (Civil Courage Prize) in Söderberg's memory.

Around 2000, an increasing number of SAC members vocally bemoaned the shift from workplace struggles to broader leftist agendas. They began campaigning for a return to the organization's roots, to workplace organizing and class struggle. At the 2002 congress, according resolutions were passed concerning both the organization's activities and its organizational structure. In terms of the former, no one challenged the interrelatedness of forms of oppression and the necessity to incorporate analyses of, for example, male dominance into workplace struggles, yet there was a strong demand to focus on campaigns that were directly workplace-related. In terms of the organizational structure, the administrative body was to be made more dynamic: the number of employed ombudsmen was to be cut and a rotation system enforced for the remaining administrators, which include the general secretary, the treasurer, and the chief editor of *Arbetaren*.

Some of the changes were met by resistance within the organization. Numerous debates and conflicts followed. However, rather than weakening the SAC, they helped identify and lay out a new direction for the SAC. Today, most of the strongest tensions have been overcome. SAC membership, which had dropped to about 5,500, is slightly on the rise again, a feat that very few current syndicalist organizations can claim. The makeup of the membership is also changing, with an increasing number of women and young people involved. About fifty LSs are currently active, spread out over the entire country. The biggest is the Stockholm LS with about one thousand members.

Organizational Structure
There are two central aspects to the organizational structure of the SAC, geography and branch.

Geographically, the LSs of the same region are united in districts, which often share a common infrastructure, provide mutual support, organize regional campaigns, and send delegates to nationwide meetings.

On the branch level, the smallest unit is the shop branch, which unites all SAC members at a specific workplace, regardless of trade. For example, the SAC branch at Stockholm University includes lecturers as well as cleaners. A union branch unites several shop branches that work in the same industry. For example, the Gothenburg Social and Health Services Union Branch unites shop branches from hospitals, homes for the elderly, welfare centers, and so on. Finally, a nationwide federation unites all union branches of the same industry.

The central body of the SAC serves predominantly administrative purposes. Most duties are handled by a seven-member Arbetsutskott (Executive Committee, AU) which meets biweekly. The AU members are elected at the SAC congress, to which each LS sends one delegate plus additional delegates for every one hundred members.[3]

Although some significant changes have occurred in the last century, the foundations of the SAC's organizational structure—LS, AU, CK, and congress—have essentially been the same since its founding.

The Challenges Ahead

Jan Abrahamsson drives maintenance trains for the Stockholm metro system and belongs to the new generation of SAC organizers. He joined the SAC in 2001, was a board member of the Stockholm LS from 2007 to 2011, and has been an AU member since the 2009 congress.

Abrahamsson welcomes the changes within the organization. When I meet him on a snowy Stockholm winter day, he insists that the SAC is in a better condition than it has been in many years. At the same time, he does not deny that in order to make the SAC a serious alternative to LO, much remains to be done. The SAC has many obvious advantages over LO: it is more democratic, it allows for much more worker independence and a wider variety of means, and it does not need to consider party interests. Yet, in order to grow in a service-oriented society, the SAC must prove that it also can achieve more for its members. Abrahamsson matter-of-factly concedes, "If workers can get the same out of active organizing or of simply paying a membership fee, many will choose to simply pay the fee."

Abrahamsson believes that the way forward must encompass three main aspects. First, self-determination must be strengthened as a value among the workforce. The SAC can contribute to this in terms of education and agitation. Second, the SAC's ability to intervene in workplace struggles needs to be improved. This implies ongoing restructuring within the organization. LS members need to know how to act fast and on their own initiative. Abrahamsson sees this as an ongoing process, in which the first important steps have been taken. Third, the public image of the SAC needs to be altered. Sometimes, SAC members enter public debate with a fierce rhetoric that is not necessarily supported by the level of organizing within the union. Abrahamsson calls this being "hard on the outside and soft on the inside." He wishes for the exact opposite: "Soft on the outside and really committed on the inside!"

A particular problem facing the SAC in recent years is a growing urban-rural divide. While the restructuring of the SAC has led to a new wave of activism in Sweden's three major cities, Stockholm, Gothenburg, and Malmö, this is not necessarily the case in small towns and rural areas. In many ways, the trend merely reflects the general urbanization of Swedish society and the concentration of young activists in the urban centers. With respect to the LSs this means that changes in process implemented in Stockholm, Gothenburg, or Malmö cannot necessarily be replicated in the smaller LSs. However, there are also structural challenges. The smaller and more isolated LSs have bigger difficulties adapting to recent shifts, for example, the disappearance of the district ombudsmen. These problems need to be addressed in order to prevent the SAC from turning into a primarily urban organization—a development that would contradict its very roots in the forestry and mining industries.

Abrahamsson stresses another aspect vital to the organization's future: internationalism. A key value of classical syndicalism and the workers' movement in general, internationalism takes on new urgency in a world of increasing labor migration, international trade treaties, and neoliberal corporate rule.

The SAC has taken some steps in that direction. Still excluded from the IWA, SAC delegates have in recent years participated in meetings of the Red and Black Coordination, an informal alliance of non-IWA-affiliated syndicalist organizations, including the Spanish Confederación General del Trabajo (CGT), the French Confédération Nationale du Travail affiliated with the Fédération Anarchiste (CNT-F), the UK branch of the Industrial Workers of the World (IWW), the Greek Union of Libertarian Syndicalists (ESE), the Polish Workers' Initiative (IP), and the non-IWA-affiliated current of the Italian Unione Sindiciale Italiana (USI). In September 2011, a Red and Black Coordination conference with the title "Undocumented Workers and the Criminalization of Trade Unions" was organized in Malmö.

The SAC's internationalist efforts are not only evident in networking attempts with syndicalist organizations, however. They are also expressed in a variety of campaigns, reflecting Abrahamsson's demand that internationalism needs to serve as a "practical weapon." Two of the most prominent SAC campaigns of recent years have been directly related to this: the organization of undocumented workers and the campaign Rättvis vinhandel, "Fair Wine Trade."

SAC Campaigns and Activities
The Organization of Undocumented Workers
The organization of undocumented workers began with the founding of the Papperslösasgruppen (Group of the Undocumented) by members of Stockholm's LS in 2004. The internationalist aspect of the effort is evident: undocumented workers in Sweden are migrant laborers without work permits. Fittingly, the Stockholm LS invited Decio Machado Flores, a Spanish CGT comrade with a long experience of organizing undocumented workers, to the founding meeting.

Although undocumented workers in Sweden come from a broad range of countries, the vast majority of those organizing in the SAC originate from Latin America. There are two main reasons for this. First, radical Latin American organizing in Sweden dates back to the 1970s, when many political refugees escaping the military dictatorships in Chile, Uruguay, and Argentina arrived in the country. To this day, some SAC publications have a Spanish-language section. Second, most of the current Latin American immigrants to Sweden are not political refugees but people looking for more economic prosperity. Few of them are threatened with imprisonment, torture, and murder, or with famine and starvation in the case of being deported. This means that they are more willing to take risks in workplace struggles than refugees from Africa, Asia, or the Middle East, who often try to avoid deportation at all costs.

Lotta Holmberg is a veteran in working with migrants and refugees and a founding member of the Group of the Undocumented. When I visit her in one of the working-class suburbs of southern Stockholm, she still gets excited about the founding meeting, which was held in the building of Arbetarnas Bildningsförbund (Workers' Education Association, ABF). One hundred people came, at least half of whom were undocumented workers, despite the threat of police and migration officers infiltrating the event. Many of the Latin Americans present were experienced organizers and took initiative right away, which delighted the meeting planners. According to Holmberg, the idea had never been to organize *for* undocumented workers, but to provide an infrastructure that would allow them to organize themselves. Soon, one LS in the greater Stockholm region consisted almost exclusively of undocumented workers.

The effort to organize undocumented workers dates back to syndicalism's earliest days, with the movement's opposition to the exclusive focus on the skilled workforce in union organizing. It was considered important to protect—and, when necessary, even to establish—the rights of temporary and migrant workers and to "organize the unorganizable." Today, this translates into efforts at organizing the precarious workforce, a task in which syndicalist principles have a clear edge over mainstream union policies. Undocumented migrant workers are currently the most precarious of Europe's workforce.

The magnitude of this challenge for mainstream unions became apparent in the reactions that met the Group of the Undocumented. LO, as well as representatives of political organizations, including Vänsterpartiet (Left Party), accused the Stockholm LS members of validating a black labor market and undercutting wages. The criticism seems problematic on multiple levels: First, it is based on a notion of protectionism that should have no place in progressive politics. Second, what are the alternatives? As Holmberg succinctly states, "If you are afraid of undocumented workers undercutting wages, there are only two options: either you organize them or you deport them." Third, the accusations simply aren't true. Organizing undocumented workers helps stabilize wages, at least if this is a clear objective.

In the case of the SAC, a method was revived that had been used several times in its history, first in 1913: the *registermetod* (register method). Historically, the register method was used as an alternative to collective bargaining agreements. The SAC would decide on a minimum wage in a certain trade or industry. Employers who did not accept the wage were picketed and made the target of public campaigns. The same principle is used today to ensure a fair wage for undocumented workers—not least because in their case collective bargaining agreements are not an option.[4]

Despite these points of contention, most SAC members agree that the register method has proven an effective tool in strengthening the rights of undocumented workers. Apart from the labor conflicts it has helped to win, it has also made the plight of undocumented workers public. Three struggles in Stockholm were particularly important in this process. They all concerned the service industry, where many migrant workers suffer meager wages, long working hours, and a hostile work environment. At the same time, the service industry is highly vulnerable to public campaigns as these directly affect customers and, therefore, business.

In 2007, the popular Indian-Pakistani restaurant Lilla Karachi in central Stockholm owed thousands of Swedish crowns in wages to one of their undocumented workers, an SAC member. When negotiations with the owner brought no results, the restaurant was picketed. SAC members and sympathizers, at times more than one hundred, tirelessly held banners and handed out flyers. After seven weeks, the money was paid.

The Lilla Karachi case was a breakthrough for the SAC. After this success, it often sufficed for SAC members to threaten similar campaigns in order to settle conflicts. Very often, business owners would simply comply with their demands. Not in all cases, however. At the luxury restaurant Josefina in Stockholm's posh Djurgården district, nine SAC members complained about poor working conditions and outstanding wages in 2008. The owner refused to negotiate, and Josefina was picketed. When the restaurant closed for the winter, the conflict had not yet been resolved. After Josefina reopened in the spring of 2009, thousands of participants in the SAC's May 1 rally vowed to resume the campaign. With that, the owner agreed to pay the demanded compensation of roughly US$30,000.

The longest of the three struggles concerned the restaurant, hotel, and entertainment complex Berns in central Stockholm. This struggle also received most media attention. The conflict began in 2007, when the SAC demanded the payment of outstanding wages to seven cleaners at the Berns complex. Initially, one day of picketing sufficed for Berns to comply. After that, however, the conflict escalated over the relationship between Berns and the employment agency it had used to hire the cleaners. Berns was accused of illegal agreements with the agency and eventually of trying to blacklist all syndicalists.

A popular nightlife spot, Berns was picketed on Fridays and Saturdays from evening until the early morning hours, weekend after weekend. More than once, the police tried to disperse the picketers. Many were arrested. Eventually, a "security zone" was installed around Berns, which only a limited number of SAC activists were allowed to enter at a time. Meanwhile, Berns owner Yvonne Sörensen Björud hired bodyguards and closed the premises on May 1, fearing violent syndicalist attacks. The SAC activists resorted to more creative means. Garbage bags filled with crumpled Berns advertisements, ripped from walls around town were dumped outside the main entrance. Artists canceled shows at Berns and a number of events changed venues out of solidarity with the SAC campaign, among them a one-week conference about Swedish archives after employees of the Arbetarrörelsens arkiv (Swedish Workers' Archive) threatened to boycott the event.

The bourgeois press wrote about "mafia methods" and "extortion." A prominent consultant, Lars-Olof Pettersson, and a well-known journalist, Willy Silberstein, even published a book entitled *Syndikalisternas nya ansikte* (The Syndicalists' New Face) comparing the SAC's methods to those of "biker gangs." Meanwhile, conservative politicians made a point of frequenting Berns on the weekend. They had already scheduled their lunch meetings at Lilla Karachi and Josefina when those establishments were picketed, earning them the unflattering moniker "support eaters." Berns claims that it has lost up to US$700,000 in revenue due to the SAC's protests.

The conflict is ongoing after more than five years. It has caused debate even among sympathetic union activists. Some wondered whether Berns was being unfairly targeted. The main villains, so the argument went, were the employment agencies, after all. They were the main profiteers off the undocumented workers' vulnerability. However, apart from the fact that employers are often perfectly aware of the employment agencies' practices, there is a simple reason why employment agencies are hard to target: many of them lack a physical presence. As Ruben Tastas Duque, a driving force behind reviving the register method, stated in a December 2010 interview with the labor law journal *Lag & Avtal*: "Many small employment agencies have no office. It is not meaningful to picket a house in some suburb. No one would take notice."

The struggles by undocumented workers in Stockholm have left a significant mark on the SAC as a whole. In 2008, a Papperslösakommitté (Committee for Undocumented Workers) was established by Gothenburg's LS. In 2009, the first undocumented worker was elected as an AU member. Moreover, the struggles and the public attention they received have attracted new SAC members and reenergized many longtime syndicalists who had not been particularly active in years.

However, significantly, the resurgence of direct action is not limited to Stockholm. In 2005–2006, several picket lines were organized in Malmö, where picketers were often attacked by the police with batons and pepper spray. On December 1, 2006, a picket line at the sushi restaurant Izakaya Koi, whose owner had been accused of abusing and firing a member of Malmö's LS, led to legal charges against twenty-six protesters for criminal conversion and for disobeying police orders.

The accused had allegedly blocked all entrances to the restaurant. On November 2008, twenty-five of the "Malmö 26" were declared guilty and sentenced to thousands of crowns in fines.

The organizing of undocumented workers has not only won cases for migrant laborers and given a boost to the SAC as an organization, but it has also had an impact on union organizing of undocumented workers in general. Most significantly, the early hostile reactions from LO changed as soon as the Stockholm LSs Group of the Undocumented earned public sympathy as well as attention. In 2008, LO, together with a number of smaller trade union federations, established the Fackligt center för pappersslösa (Union Center for Undocumented Workers). Lotta Holmberg is convinced that the Group of the Undocumented influenced the decision to open the center. She sees this as an example of how syndicalist organizations can still have an impact on general union and labor politics even when they appear to be marginalized.

Fair Wine Trade
The organizing of undocumented workers has not been the only encouraging development within the SAC in recent years. Another inspiring initiative, not least with respect to internationalism, is the campaign Rättvis vinhandel (Fair Wine Trade).

In Sweden, the government retains a monopoly on the sale of beverages with an alcohol content of more than 3.5 percent. All wine imports are handled by the state-run company Systembolaget. Systembolaget's selection includes a broad range of Chilean, Argentinean, and South African wines. Labor conditions for vineyard workers in these countries remain poor. Therefore, the SAC Shop Branch of Systembolaget Employees (Driftsektion för Systembolaganställda, DFSA) initiated the Fair Wine Trade campaign at the end of 2010. Aims of the campaign are to establish cooperation between the DFSA and various trade unions organizing vineyard workers in Chile, Argentina, and South Africa; to change vineyard labor conditions; and to put pressure on Systembolaget and other wine monopoly holders in the Nordic countries to actively support these efforts. (Finland, Norway, the Faroe Islands, and Iceland have regulations similar to Sweden.)

In June 2011, a vineyard workers' conference was held in Santiago de Chile with delegates from the DFSA, the South African grassroots farmworkers union Sikhula Sonke, the Argentinean Unión Socialista de los Trabajadores, several unions organized in the Chilean Asociación Nacional de Mujeres Rurales e Indígenas (ANAMURI), and representatives of Systembolaget and other Nordic wine monopoly holders. According to Emil Boss, a DFSA member who had just returned from a trip to South Africa when I spoke to him, much had been achieved during the campaign's first year: labor conditions were improving at fifty vineyards; regular cooperation between the unions involved in the campaign had been established; Systembolaget began to sell Fair Trade wines at all their shops; and, finally, the company released an ethical code for wine production on January 1, 2012. However, vineyard workers were not included in formulating the ethical code and there were no provisions for including them in supervising its implementation. Emil Boss argues that ethical codes remaining under exclusive company control tend to change only the most visible parts of the labor process, namely the labor environment. They do not necessarily affect wages and insurance packages; they do not necessarily strengthen the role of unions, workplace democracy, and workers' rights; and they do not necessarily provide sufficient protection from discrimination at the workplace. As a result, the Fair Wine Trade campaign continues to demand a much stronger integration of unions in transforming the conditions for vineyard workers.

The Fair Wine Trade campaign holds much future potential, not least because DFSA, as one of the SAC's most successful shop branches, has several years of experience in challenging Systembolaget's employment policies and labor conditions.

DSTS: Organizing Underground

Another SAC shop branch that has proven the ongoing effectiveness of syndicalist organizing is Driftsektionen Stockholms Tunnelbana och Spårvägar (the Shop Branch for Stockholm's Metro and Rail Services, DSTS). Founded in 2003, DSTS has grown steadily and is today a significant factor in workers' rights struggles in the Stockholm metro and railway system. It is perhaps no coincidence that DSTS is one of the most active SAC shop branches. There is a long history of radical organizing among railway workers in Sweden—they were the first to employ the register method in 1913. Today, of the ten thousand people working in the Stockholm subway and along the local railway lines, many are migrants and students working part-time. Thus, there is a relatively high potential for radical sentiments, further fueled by the inherently democratic aspect of providing transport for hundreds of thousands of citizens, which translates easily into demanding democratic workers' rights. In addition, local transport services have become a focal point of resistance to privatization since their operation began to be contracted to corporations in the 1990s. Today, Stockholm's metro is operated by the Hong Kong–based MTR Corporation, while many services of the local railway lines have been contracted to ISS Trafficare.

DSTS first drew attention by calling for wildcat strikes in October 2005 after the general secretary of the LO transport and communications branch, Per Johansson, was dismissed by Connex (Veolia), the metro operator at the time. Since 2005, several strikes have been organized by DSTS, the latest in January 2011. Demands have ranged from a healthier working environment (a number of subway workers have to work in mold-infested locations) to more reasonable work schedules. In addition, DSTS has supported numerous workers in labor conflicts related to work accidents and punitive transfers.

As DSTS approaches its ten-year anniversary, it is for many an encouraging example of workers' self-organization remaining possible and effective, not simply as a one-off campaign, but as a continuous means of improving labor conditions and defending workers' rights.

Around the Country

Although many of the SAC's most acknowledged recent campaigns have been centered in Stockholm—where most of what's acknowledged in Sweden is centered—activities have gone far beyond the city's confines. The following are recent examples of SAC campaigns outside the capital:

In 2010, the SAC shop branch at the University Hospital in Lund, affiliated with Malmö's LS, organized strikes of hospital personnel demanding better labor conditions for the hospitals' cleaners, who are employed through the multinational facility service company ISS.

In March 2011, Malmö's LS launched a picketing campaign against Assistansia AB, Sweden's biggest employment agency for personal care assistants. Assistansia AB was accused of providing poor training, neglecting workplace safety, and obstructing union organizing. There were solidarity actions all over the country, which gathered broad popular support. Assistansia AB complained about a "defamation campaign." Rather than making any concessions, the company changed its name to Humana at the end of 2011.

In the spring of 2011, teachers belonging to the Gothenburg LS went on strike at the women's youth detention center, Björnbacken, in Gothenburg, after the state department in charge of youth detention centers introduced new teaching schedules limiting both teachers' free time and course preparation. The teachers argued that the latter would inevitably impact the quality of their classes. The strike was the first at a state-run institution in Sweden in decades. Circumstances were stacked against the teachers: they could not cause a loss of profits and there was limited parental and social support for the students. Klas Rönnbäck, chairman of the Union Branch for Teachers and Pedagogues affiliated with Gothenburg's LS, stated in an interview with *Arbetaren* on September 1, 2011, that the strike proved that detention at Björnbacken was more important than schooling. Nonetheless, the strike was not without consequences. After several weeks, a compromise was reached that included revisions to the teachers' new schedules.

Publishing

Arbetaren still appears once a week with a print run of about 3,500 copies. The SAC members' journal, *Syndikalisten*, appears once monthly, and some local LSs maintain their own newsletters and journals, such as *Organisera*, published by Stockholm's LS. The SAC has also been running the publishing house Federativ since 1922. It remains the most important Swedish-language source for texts on syndicalism and anarchism.

Education

The SAC administration and various LSs regularly organize courses and workshops, including introductory meetings for new members, conferences on how to found an LS, study circles on general workplace organizing, and classes in everything from labor negotiating to how to effectively use social media.

A number of LSs also organize regular lectures and panel discussions. In December 2011, South African scholar Lucien van der Walt presented his book *Black Flame: The Revolutionary Class Politics of Anarchism and Syndicalism*, coauthored with Michael Schmidt, in Stockholm and at the Joe Hill House in Gävle. In February 2011, the Stockholm LS organized a one-day event exploring the relationship between syndicalism and anarchism on the occasion of the Kronstadt uprising's ninety-year anniversary.

Infrastructure

Both the SAC headquarters at Sveavägen in central Stockholm and local LS offices remain important meeting places for a wide variety of people. The SAC's generous sharing of its infrastructure and resources with underfunded groups of the extraparliamentary left confirms the organization's ongoing importance in broader social movements.

In Gävle, the LS office is located at the Joe Hill House, the childhood home of the famed IWW singer and poet who was born Joel Hägglund in Gävle on October 7, 1879. The Joe Hill House, located in the picturesque old town of Gävle, about 150 miles north of Stockholm, serves as a museum, café, and events center.

Syndikalistiska Ungdomsförbundet

Syndikalistiska ungdomsförbundet (Sweden's Syndicalist Youth Federation, SUF) was founded in 1993. It is entirely independent from the SAC, but the organizations work closely together and membership overlaps. The SUF has about twenty-five chapters across the country and publishes the journal *Direkt Aktion* four times a year. Recently, it has been very active in precarious labor issues. It is also involved in broader leftist struggles such as squatting, antifascism, and sexual politics.

From 1930 to 1955, the SAC had its own youth organization, Sveriges syndikalistiska ungdomsförbund, also abbreviated SUF. It disbanded during the 1950s restructuring of the SAC.

Into the Future

The SAC is often hailed as the only organization founded on anarchosyndicalist principles that can claim uninterrupted activity for more than a hundred years. This is no small feat. Although membership numbers have significantly dropped since the 1930s, they remain high enough for the SAC to remain a factor in Swedish labor politics. It remains a well-established and well-known organization without comparison in Central and Northern Europe.

As mentioned above, membership numbers have experienced a slight rise in recent years. The SAC's May 1 rallies across the country gather several thousand sympathizers annually, up to five thousand in Stockholm alone. The high-publicity campaigns in recent years have further contributed to syndicalism's being far from a mere footnote to Swedish history.

In September 2012, the SAC's thirtieth congress will be held in Gävle. The theme is "For the SAC's Second Century." The main challenges are the continuation of the internal reorganizing process, the urban-rural divide, and the extension of international collaboration. The congress will be an important step in determining the future of the organization. Hopefully, the SAC will continue to stand strong against the neoliberal threat.

CHAPTER 10

Doing without the Boss: Workers' Control Experiments in Australia in the 1970s

Verity Burgmann, Ray Jureidini, and Meredith Burgmann

"It has often been said in the working-class movement that the workers can do without the boss, but the boss can't do without the workers."[1]

This observation was made by Pete Thomas, editor of the Australian Miners' Federation weekly newspaper, *Common Cause*, in his history of the work-ins and takeover at the Nymboida Mine in northern New South Wales between 1975 and 1979.[2] Joe Owens, a union organizer involved in the 1972 Sydney Opera House work-in, described workers' control as "a political strategy in which workers gain experience and also gain the knowledge that they have within themselves the ability to conduct their own affairs, the ability to run their own jobs."[3]

Experiments with workers' control occurred in many countries during the late postwar boom period, commencing with the occupation of factories in France during the turbulent events of 1968 and reaching their high point in the early to mid-1970s.[4] These actions encouraged renewed interest at that time in earlier waves of alternative work organization, most notably the factory occupations and workers' councils in Italy after World War I.[5] Australian union activists in the 1970s would likely have been aware at least of British experiments in workers' control, especially those of the Upper Clyde and Lucas Aerospace at the beginning of the decade.[6]

The Australian contributions to the wave of workers' control episodes around the world at this time were no copycat affairs. Rather, there were shared circumstances that, in each country, encouraged similar spontaneous displays of working-class audacity that were expressed in workers' control experimentation: the corresponding and mutually reinforcing combination of heightened industrial militancy and a crisis in employer and state authority. In the case of Britain, this phenomenon was described as an "industrial relations crisis."[7] These conditions were peculiar to the late 1960s and 1970s and differed from those of economic crisis, which is currently producing significant upsurges of workers' control experiments. With Argentina and Venezuela leading the way in recent such episodes, the Spanish term *autogestión* has become increasingly common in workers' control scholarship in the early twenty-first century.[8]

Experiments in workers' control can be seen as practical declarations of the autonomy of labor from capital. Theoretically, the notion of working-class autonomy has been elaborated most cogently by the "autonomist" stream within Western Marxism, and is associated especially with Italian philosopher Antonio Negri. Harry Cleaver coined the term "autonomist Marxism" to describe the threads of the Marxist tradition that have emphasized the "self-activity of the working class" and the autonomous power of workers: the constant tendency of the working class to oppose the command of capital, to go beyond the mere reaction to exploitation and to take the offensive in ways that shape the class struggle and define the future.[9]

Instances of autogestion, including the antipodean examples, were emblematic of the extraordinary working-class militancy of the late postwar boom period, the crucible in which autonomist-Marxist theory was itself forged. As a product of 1960s–1970s Italy, an exceptional moment in proletarian self-activity, autonomist Marxism possibly overstates the autonomous power of workers. This chapter inquires whether the experiences of workers engaged in other instances of autogestion—apart from the notable Italian phenomena—confirm or counteract the autonomist-Marxist emphasis on the significance of such actions and the sensational effects on those involved. To do so, it investigates Australian workers' control experiments during the 1970s, focusing on three case studies: the Sydney Opera House work-in of April–May 1972; the Whyalla Glove Factory sit-in of November 1972 and subsequent formation of a workers' cooperative that lasted until September 1973; and the Nymboida mine work-in and takeover under workers' and union control from February 1975 to August 1979.

The Sydney Opera House Work-in, 1972

Construction of the Opera House took about thirteen years (starting in 1959) and the work-in occurred during the final phase of construction. During the construction of the Sydney Opera House, a conventional industrial dispute—protesting the dismissal of a worker and demanding a wage increase—escalated and culminated in the workers expelling management from the site and continuing work under workers' control from April 8 to May 15, 1972. A week before the work-in commenced, the *Australian* reported under the headline of "Workers 'Forced' Short Week" that construction workers employed at the Opera House had threatened to dismantle the revolving stage if they were not granted a thirty-five-hour week on forty-eight hours' pay.[10] Joe Owens, one of the organizers, confirms this was no idle threat. He recalls that when management at the Opera House was confronted with the workers' campaign for the wage increase, "They threw their hands in the air in alarm and despondency and said it couldn't happen. However, the workers forced it upon them. I recall that at one point the managers were reneging on the deal that the riggers and fitters on the job went onto the revolving stage and started dismantling it, began to pull it down. That quickly changed some tunes and subsequently the work in itself for the 35 hour week paid for 48 was a success."[11]

Owens and John Wallace, another organizer involved, wrote an informative account of the work-in experience, appropriately titled *Workers Call the Tune at Opera House.*[12] They recall that the suggestion for a "work-in... a complete takeover of the job" was met with astonishment and even laughter in the meeting held to discuss how to win the dispute. "However the eventual outcome of the debate was, in fact, a work-in—the dismissed man taken back onto the job in defiance of the management." Employer threats to remove the dismissed man proved hollow "and it was realized that the authorities on the job did not know where to go next."[13] A subsequent meeting was held at which the call to take over the job completely was proposed and passed by a large majority.[14]

Force was needed to commence the takeover: "independent destructive action," in Negri's words.[15] Workers broke open a toolbox in the Opera Theatre with a crowbar and obtained the equipment necessary to do the work.[16] Or undo the work. To have men standing around would have a disastrous effect on morale, so the workers resolved that if work on construction ran out due to the absence of engineers, work already performed would be *"de-constructed* or dismantled."[17]

Employees entered the work site by walking past a supervising engineer and a foreman, who informed each man there was no work available: "The management pickets (a reversal of the usual roles!) must have realised that authority was slipping from their grasp."[18] It was. The workers elected a foreman and safety officer, and the job was reorganized because certain tasks could not be continued in the absence of engineers. Owens told the press the situation was absurd: "We've got men ready and willing to work. All we need is a supervising engineer, but the Department of Public Works says we can't have one."[19] Work that could continue did so, and very well, according to Wallace and Owens: "No-one ran to the foreman for trifling decisions which foremen generally demand to make. The leading hands and individual workers found new confidence in themselves. They became self-acting and just went ahead with the task in hand."[20] They recall that by the second day, company foremen were "completely ignored" and "although they tried to intervene on one or two occasions, they were told firmly by the men concerned that they were not needed and could go and sit in the office, go home or throw themselves in the harbour, but just keep out of the way." One foreman took it upon himself to dismiss three of his former underlings, "but of course this was disregarded and the workers continued their tasks unconcerned at this."[21] In the first few days of the work-in, management put up little fight and agreed to pay for the Saturday work-in with a lump-sum payment and for both Monday and Tuesday at normal rates. The workers, according to Wallace and Owens, "were jubilant at this victory for nerve and solidarity."[22]

Greater productivity and better work practices evolved during the work-in. In demanding forty-eight hours' pay for thirty-five hours' work, the workers had pronounced that, under workers' control, this level of productivity would occur under worker control. The supervising engineer had ventured the opinion it was virtually impossible to achieve such a goal. However, the rate of production exceeded management's expectations. At the end of the first week, figures proved that a forty-eight-hour production rate had in fact been achieved. How? According to Wallace and Owens, through a reduction in absenteeism, abolition of demarcation among work roles, and, in general, more efficient organization of production by the workers themselves.[23]

Wallace and Owens describe work life under workers' control:

> The enthusiasm was unbelievable and work processed at a rate unknown on the job. The absence of imposed discipline, together with the camaraderie created a harmony… that surpassed anyone's expectations.… It was like being released from prison after years of hard labour. Boredom and the hatred of oppression were gone, leaving an exhilarated feeling of release. Even the most menial tasks were performed with enthusiasm.[24]

Even when management expected the work-ins to end, the workers wrote, "To go back to a daily drudge under the old management, from the stimulating conditions of the last few days was a very depressing thought, to say the least."[25] Wallace and Owens conjecture that workers' control must bring workers to a point when they not only question a company's right to make a profit, but also question their own role in a capitalist society: "To many of the workers at the Opera House, this is exactly what happened. Conditioned all their lives to seek more money and more possessions, success for some of them was to live like those at the top. So they questioned the need to work, to meet a programme, to discipline themselves. Many heated debates took place around this important question of discipline."[26]

The nature of work also changed under workers' control, according to Wallace and Owens:

> Once the workers had taken over the powers of management the pressures normally existing on other jobs disappeared. No-one had disciplinary powers, the... foremen and non-supervising engineers were fully integrated into the workforce, not only fulfilling their functions as engineers etc., but in complete harmony with the workers. Lines of demarcation had completely disappeared, with tradesmen doing traditional labourers' work, and vice versa. Barriers which have been skilfully used over the years to divide workers completely disappeared, staff-men for the first time in their lives realised that after all they too were workers, and accepted their role in the workers' community.[27]

The form in which the thirty-five-hour week operated "substantially increased the real control the workers had over production on the job. In the final analysis, almost all of the power of management on the job rested with the workers."[28]

On April 18, the subcontractor in charge of building the revolving stage departed, declaring that worker self-management was "no longer an economic proposition" but a demand for employer control.[29] When all workers were handed dismissal letters the same day, "that was not going to be taken lying down and the meetings next day confirmed this attitude with a vengeance."[30] On April 20, the building superintendent and security guards attempted for the first time to stop the men from walking onto the job, but the workers went inside, brushing past guards as they did so.[31] That day, thirty-two builders' laborers and fitters, members of the Builders Labourers Federation and the Amalgamated

Engineering Union, occupied the revolving stage in protest at being dismissed. Owens told the press they would continue to occupy the site at the normal starting time each day while negotiations with management were in progress to reinstate them.[32] After receiving a delegation of the workers six days later on April 26, minister of public works Davis Hughes told the deputy leader of the opposition Labor Party that the men were "very troublesome."[33]

On May 1, these troublesome workers assembled outside the work site at 7:30 a.m., charged the gates, entered in spite of security guards attempting to close the gates, and occupied the revolving stage. This "sit-in strike," as the *Sydney Morning Herald* called it, continued each workday until May 5, when a new contractor arrived.[34] However, the men remained troublesome after new management took control. The first day under new management saw a series of protracted negotiations on redundancy payments, with the sums upped each round, until agreement was reached on payments so generous they extracted the majority of employer profits from the revolving stage.[35] The new contractor agreed to guarantee payment for all wages for time lost since the departure of the previous contractor; an increase was also given to all workers on site of ten dollars a week; and, as work did not recommence until May 16 because of an electricians' strike, all workers were paid for this time lost as well.[36] Enormous pressures were brought to bear by the workers on the Opera House and its contractors to stop the thirty-five-hour week, but it prevailed. Wallace and Owens explain: "All that had to be done was to convince management that if the workers could completely organise their jobs themselves, the amount of work expected from a working week of 6 days could be achieved under these conditions in 35 hours." So, the new contractor was told that payment for forty-eight hours was expected.[37]

The result of this militancy was that builders' laborers and fitters on the Opera House site won forty-eight hours' pay for a regular thirty-five-hour week, the right to elect their foremen and regulate production, big redundancy payments, four weeks' annual leave with a 25 percent bonus, and other concessions. These wages were won "by workers' control tactics and the unity of the workers on the job."[38] Owens told the press the terms of the settlement were "most satisfactory."[39]

The Whyalla Glove Factory Cooperative, 1972–1973
At the James North Glove Factory in Whyalla, a South Australian town three hundred miles northwest of Adelaide, twenty women machinists

were faced with redundancy by the closure of the factory late in 1972. They challenged the company's prerogative to withdraw its operations at will and ten of them occupied the factory. When these women machinists streamed into the manager's office at the commencement of their sit-in, the manager, J.E. Larven, was clearly shocked. Those involved attest that Larven realized he had lost control of the situation.[40]

Peter Duncan, a Labor MP, attended this occupation on November 20, 1972, in his role as counsel for the Miscellaneous Workers Union (MWU), which represented the women. He told the South Australian Parliament that Larven "completely lost control of himself and started punching people in all directions.... [He] was a boxing instructor and he evidently decided to use his prowess on the employees."[41] The workers, however, stood their ground—or, rather, sat on it. Barry Cavanagh, MWU South Australian state secretary at the time, whose wife's nose was broken by Larven, recalls:

> While the manager, Larven, was going berserk, outside the factory the workers streamed inside.... Larven eventually went and locked himself in his office and made frantic phone calls.... Then the Ship Painters and Dockers arrived with their secretary who had a particularly strong record of militancy and mobilized members to demonstrate solidarity with workers during their sit-in (He was a little bloke, but built like a drop of water upside down).... Larven had no more authority. In a show of solidarity and material, all of a sudden a procession of Ship Painters and Dockers streamed into the factory through the window later followed by mattresses, guitars, food, T.V. sets, and other amenities to show solidarity and give material support to the workers.[42]

The next morning, there were hundreds of unionists and onlookers gathered in front of the building. When Larven arrived, he found the pathway to the factory blocked. Police informed him that they would escort him through, but if anything went wrong, they could not guarantee his safety. Larven decided to get back into his car and go home.[43] At this point, about a hundred members of the Federated Ship Painters and Dockers Union went out on strike in sympathy, while an ad hoc committee of unionists at the sit-in at the factory announced to the press that, in support of the women machinists, they would attempt to close down all industry in Whyalla.[44]

This occupation of the Whyalla Glove Factory aligned with the general aims of the MWU, which was committed to militant strategies, including converting sit-ins into workers' cooperatives.[45] The MWU had been moving leftward since the early 1960s, emblematic of the radicalization of unions occurring during this period. A former Seaman's Union official observed: "They were becoming far more militant and serious about challenging the bosses and winning, and therefore becoming more disliked... by employers."[46]

Employer disdain for unions was echoed in the mainstream press, encouraging the common perceptions of this time that unions were too powerful and heavy-handed. Certainly, the reporting of this occupation in the Adelaide *Advertiser* focused on the strong record of militancy among workers in the Ship Painters union, implying the violence was all theirs, with captions such as "Whyalla Unionists Invade Factory."[47] In contrast, an editorial in the normally conservative Whyalla newspaper was surprisingly responsive to the extent of local support for the women:

> Even the most implacable opponents of direct action on the industrial front can hardly quarrel with the motive behind the latest show of protest by unionists in Whyalla. The sit-in at the James North glove-making factory in Norrie Avenue, started by the firm's sacked women employees and supported by outside male unionists, was promoted to keep jobs open, and only that.... The violence that occurred was quite unnecessary, as also was the locking of the showroom and—it would seem—the closing down of the factory.[48]

The sit-in concluded after five days, when the South Australian government responded to this militant action by ordering gloves and thus guaranteeing a month's work, which gave the MWU time to assist the workers in organizing themselves as a cooperative. From the beginning of 1973, the women machinists formed the Whyalla Cooperative to run the factory under workers' control. It remained in successful operation for nine months and was increasingly profitable with each month's operations. In September 1973, it was taken over by private interests with the agreement of the workers, who were all guaranteed employment under the new owner.[49]

It is possible that the women's decision not to continue with this successful cooperative was prompted by factors beyond their working environment, suggesting a particular set of difficulties for women engaged in workers' control experimentation. Some of the women's husbands complained about their extra involvement in their workplace disrupting the family routine.[50] The husbands' response suggested it was acceptable for wives to earn supplementary income, but that to actually own their means of production was too confrontational. The Whyalla women did not endure discrimination in the reactions of male unionists, in contrast to the experiences of women in similar circumstances in England.[51] However, some of them did suffer, though to a lesser degree, from disgruntled husbands.

Gender issues were also at play in other ways. In establishing their cooperative, the women's aspirations to complete autonomy were not quite fully realized, as they decided to appoint as manager a recently retired foreman, Jim Gettings, for his experience and ability to service the machinery and repair minor breakdowns. The women paid Gettings six times what they themselves earned on average.[52] So a form of patriarchal domination, however limited, persisted in the workplace. Gettings did not have the normal managerial prerogatives, in that all decisions affecting the cooperative had to be ratified by the workers. He was "manager" in name only. His occasional attempts to persuade the workers he should have the power to hire and fire without collective approval were consistently denied. Likewise, when he sought more power to discipline workers, it was insisted that all decisions be discussed collectively. The women elected a committee of three to represent them collectively, which had meetings with Gettings to discuss operations on a day-to-day basis. All decisions concerning the cooperative were made with worker consultation, and usually unanimous agreements were reached.[53]

Clearly, authority relations between shop-floor workers and "management" in the Whyalla Cooperative were not as repressive as those in the capitalist enterprise of James North Glove Factory's former owner James North. The "surplus control" beyond that necessitated by the cooperative production of use-values, which the capitalist typically assumes, was absent. In the cooperative, such surplus control was eliminated along with the capitalist/owner, and the workers no longer needed to suffer the repressive authority relations as under James North. In principle they could set their own speed of production, rates of pay, conditions, and so on, without the watchful eye of "the boss."[54] Particularly revealing was the fact that, according to the women, in the cooperative the "manager" often helped with the cutting, after which a worker completed the sewing.[55] In contrast, when Gettings was named manager of the new private company, his attitude and manner changed dramatically. He became authoritarian and demanded to be called "Mr. Gettings." However, none of the women took any notice, and they continued to call him Jim.[56]

In the Whyalla Cooperative, as at the Sydney Opera House, productivity was improved by cooperative work practices. On the shop floor, there existed collective authority and a commitment to collective production. If an individual worker was not pulling her weight, instead of being reprimanded by an authoritarian manager, the whole group would talk to her and, according to one interviewee, "give encouragement rather than abuse or threats."[57] Interestingly, Gettings conceded there was greater "conscientiousness" in the cooperative; when private ownership resumed, he observed, "They didn't care. They played up— always going to the toilet, arguing, complaining."[58]

Interviews with the women confirm Gettings's opinion that they worked better and more cheerfully before the reprivatization. Although the existence of a male manager meant that gender inequity diminished somewhat the pleasurable experience of workers' control, the women all described the atmosphere during the period of the Whyalla Cooperative as cordial and casual. Morale was high. For instance, whenever a production run was completed and the truck arrived to pick up goods for transporting to Adelaide, they would have a small party to celebrate.[59]

The reason for this contentment was that work practices were refreshingly altered and creative responses encouraged. Diversifying from glove production to other items such as surgical gowns, the ingenuity of the workers was given free rein, and they successfully standardized production as they learned how to make each new item required. The allocation of tasks in the cooperative was very different from that in the private firm. For example, when new attachments arrived for special hemming work, it was assumed that whoever wanted to learn and perform the new operation could do so. If more than one expressed interest, workers would rotate the work, which provided learning opportunities and also breaks from the monotony of repetition.[60]

Moreover, because the workers on the shop floor were in control, conflicts rarely occurred. Nancy Baines was elected "supervisor" among them, but, as she explained, "You can't 'supervise' people who are their own bosses," because "you can't give them orders." She recalled the role of supervisor became more akin to "organizer and quality control"; she would deliver the materials to each machinist, inspect the work for flaws, and help out when an operator was having problems with the work.[61]

Interviews with the cooperative members confirm the gratifying nature of the experience: One stated, "In James North I took pride in the gloves which I made but nobody else's…. In the cooperative I took pride in the whole organisation."[62] For another woman, her involvement in the cooperative spoiled her thereafter for wage labor. She declined to work after private ownership was resumed by Spencer Gulf Clothing, because it was not a cooperative. She said, "I don't want a bridge between my wages and the product. The company is the middle-man and you can't see any profit unless it is a cooperative—and therefore, for me, there is no incentive to work for the SGC or any other company."[63]

The Nymboida Mine Takeover, 1975–1979

Pete Thomas maintains that the work-ins and takeover of the Nymboida mine were "a resounding example of workers' capacity for self-reliant effectiveness"; they showed how well they could do without a boss.[64] On February 7, 1975, Nymboida Collieries Pty Ltd announced the closure of its small mine in northern coastal New South Wales because it was insufficiently profitable, and issued dismissal notices to the thirty workers, whose years of service ranged from ten to twenty-six years. All twenty-five miners were Miners' Federation members.[65] The company also intimated it would not pay the workers some $70,000 they were owed in severance pay, annual leave, and other entitlements. At a meeting on February 16, the workers decided to go to work as usual the following Monday and operate the mine themselves, in defiance of the closedown decree.[66] Miners' Federation Northern District president Bill Chapman said the miners had launched their work-in "to show that the mine can be worked and should not be closed."[67]

"REFUSE TO TAKE SACK; NYMBOIDA MEN WORK-IN" was the headline in the journal of the Miners' Federation, *Common Cause*, on February 17, 1975. An Australian Broadcasting Corporation documentary on Nymboida described the militant mood of that first day of the work-in:

> As work began on that first morning, the atmosphere was bright. The men had taken their decision; they had nothing to lose except their jobs! On that first morning, the company in Brisbane lost control of its mine. By threatening dismissal, it had made the men bitter; now they were defying the orders from Queensland. Legally the men were trespassing. These were not their skips, this was not their railway but, with money owing and livelihood threatened, there was no way the police or the owners were going to get in.[68]

With the company responding by withdrawing the dismissal notices, Miners' Federation general president Evan Phillips described the work-in as "an inspiration to all of us."[69] The Miners' Federation Central Council passed a unanimous resolution that voiced its "warmest congratulations" to the members of the Miners' Federation and other unions at Nymboida colliery "on their historic work-in action," which had brought credit to all concerned: "It is new and compelling evidence of the right of the workers to have a decisive say in the industry's affairs."[70] The Miners' Federation position was as follows: "We are determined not to allow the mine to be closed."[71] Plaudits from labor movement organizations poured in, congratulating the workers at Nymboida on their successful resistance to dismissal notices.[72] The militant tenor of Miners' Federation statements continued as the work-in proceeded successfully. "The Nymboida actions have been a demonstration that the working class has rights and intends to enforce them," stated Miners' Federation general secretary Bill Smale, adding, "This is a cardinal principle and we have to battle it through."[73]

After a few weeks of the work-ins, on March 11 the company agreed to hand over ownership of the mine to the Miners' Federation; in return, the workers did not demand that the company pay the workers for lost wages—which the workers had regarded as lost, anyway. Nymboida was operated by the workers and the Miners' Federation for more than four years, until the end of August 1979, when the local council power station it supplied was closed. It was known this would eventually happen, for reasons both economic and thermodynamic, but the extra years enabled the workforce to plan for it and, when the time came, there were sufficient funds to pay the workers what was due them. Under workers' control, the workers received at least the standard rate of pay in the mining industry, the "mechanical-unit rate," an objective not attained in the industry generally.[74] Merv McIntosh, the first miner to retire under workers' control, claimed his departure with full benefits proved the men could work the mine "better than the company could have done."[75]

Others at the face of the coal mine agreed. On his retirement as a union permit manager at the mine in 1978, Jack Tapp told *Common Cause* that the Miners' Federation had provided "the opportunity to prove that the workers can take over an enterprise that a company has given away as not being worthwhile."[76] Even the inspector of collieries in the State Mineral Resources and Development Department, Elwyn Jones, described as "tremendous: use any superlative you like" the job that the Nymboida workers did in taking over a pit considered "completely non-viable" and making it a viable proposition for four and a half years.[77] Miners' Federation Northern District president Jim Hayes said, at the farewell party for Nymboida mineworkers and their families on August 24, 1979, "You have proved that workers, banded together, can succeed where others, such as the old company, had failed in maintaining the mine."[78]

Productivity had improved immediately under workers' control.[79] By October 1975, Nymboida's production was six hundred to seven hundred tons of saleable coal a week, compared with about five hundred in the latter part of the Nymboida company ownership, despite machinery being "almost of vintage age."[80] Permit manager Jack Tapp told *Common Cause* that the men "proved to be as good pillar-coal men as any I have met in the industry," and they achieved "maximum production."[81] *Common Cause* offered the obvious explanation that "production has been enhanced by the fact that the workers are imbued with a new spirit of working for themselves, with a free rein to their capacities and initiatives."[82] Miners' lodge secretary Cliff Bultitude said they knew it would be difficult because of the old equipment, but "Everyone is keen to get the results and to show what can be done."[83] Not just pride, but necessity also increased output. Mineworker Pat Huxley, interviewed on ABC-TV, made the revealing comment that, at Nymboida, everyone had to work to make it pay; and, to laughter, added that it wasn't like a private mine, "where you can carry a lot of dead labor."[84] Predictably, there was reduced absenteeism. When a reckoning was made in June 1979 on the amount due for days of sick leave entitlements not taken, it was over $12,000.[85]

Observers confirmed these reasons for improved output. The Australian reporter for a London magazine visited Nymboida under workers' control and explained the enhanced productivity: "When men work freely, profit comes as a natural by-product to benefit everyone, while property, regarded as their own, will be responsibly cared for to keep it in first-class condition and maintenance. This applies to every piece of mining equipment and accessories."[86]

Likewise, collieries inspector Elwyn Jones connected the improved production figures to the "total difference—cheese and chalk" in the attitudes of the men before and after the Miners' Federation took control. After the takeover, the workers had a sense of personal involvement, of doing things for their own benefit instead of for the benefit of some remote and aloof company.[87]

Those on the ground also argued that cooperation intrinsically aided productivity. In February 1978, the first permit manager after the workers' takeover, Jack Tapp, described the differences between working for the boss and the Nymboida experience: "While there is a permit manager, he is a Federation man and decisions have to be made in full consultation with the workers, benefitting from their experience of the mine and their ideas. Normally at mines, managers' talk at the men; at Nymboida, on the other hand, it is a matter of talking with them. Working with them helped me to learn more."[88]

Another permit manager, Dennis Clarke, stated in August 1979: "There has been complete teamwork, and it's this which has made Nymboida a successful operation. Everybody knew what was going on, in organisation and production, and this helped them to contribute in the best way and with a feeling of self-satisfaction. It's been an example of how a mine can be run. Nymboida has shown that this sort of thing can work, and work well."[89]

Pete Thomas was convinced that absence of authoritarian workplace relations aided productivity: "Those at Nymboida proved what workers can do, by their own skills and resources, by their own initiative and resolve, working for themselves and depending on themselves, free from the frustrations that come from exploitation by employers."[90]

The miners reveled in the absence of exploitation. "I woke up this morning," one Nymboida miner told a reporter, "thinking how I own a share in this myself. I enjoyed thinking that."[91] In the first week of workers' control, Bill Chapman told *Common Cause* that, on Thursday, March 6, the miners "came out of the mine beaming again."[92] Jack Tapp reported on March 17 that the feeling among the men was "good, really good," that they were saying, "It's fine to be working for themselves instead of a boss."[93] In mid-April, Miners' Federation official Rex McGrath commented on the enthusiasm among the men at Nymboida.[94] Under the headline, "NYMBOIDA: they're working for themselves and enjoying it," *Common Cause* quoted Jack Tapp: "The mine has settled down to normal working conditions—except that there is no owner, other than the Federation—production is steadily rising, and safety is paramount in the minds of all workers.... Nymboida is workers' control at its best, where the men are working for themselves and enjoying the experienced."[95] Les Ohlsen, who worked as a deputy in these early stages of the Miners' Federation takeover, described the men's spirits as "way up."[96]

Six months after the takeover, *Common Cause* journalists visited Nymboida and found the workers' morale still high. Pat Huxley said, "Take a few pictures of us working here with a happy look on our faces; then send the pictures to the old Nymboida company, and ask them if they've got any other mines which the Miners' Federation can take over." Cliff Bultitude stated, "The blokes are pretty happy with the set-up." Pike Johnstone, about to retire, reckoned the months of the work-ins "were great." Vane Ross remarked on the "fun and humour among the boys."[97] In June 1976, *Common Cause* conducted follow-up interviews. Lodge president Vic West stressed the "big difference" felt by the workers: "There isn't a boss breathing down your neck. There is more contentment." Frank Smidt, who had worked there since 1951, agreed the work was now more rewarding, because "You know now what's going on, and you have your say in it." Louis Szabo referred to the "bad old days" and insisted, "It's good now; better than it was under the company."[98]

Interviews in the final months before the closure in 1979 confirm the positive nature of the experience. Earle Fernance related the rewarding aspect of greater responsibility: "There has been a good feeling here. When there is any trouble with the equipment, we know what has to be done and we do it. We've all learnt to do a whole lot of things—just about anything."[99] For John Austen, increased camaraderie came with the absence of oppressive relations of production:

> It's been better all round as a Miners' Federation mine than it was under Nymboida Collieries. Before, we were just cogs in someone else's mine; now we've been all together, making up the whole thing between us.... If you work for a boss, then you're always wrong. It's been different here in the last few years. And in the lodge itself there has been a stronger feeling of being together, of mateship.[100]

Autonomy, Self-Valorization, and Political Crisis?

Whether prompted by economic crisis as at present, or by industrial relations crisis as in the 1960s and 1970s, autonomist-Marxist theory seeks to demonstrate that workers are willing to brave severe obstacles successfully without the boss. Workers' control episodes, according to the autonomist-Marxist perspective, remind us that the working class can do away with capitalism and create a different sort of society, but capital will always require a working class. Labor existed prior to capital and could therefore do so again, whereas capital is inescapably dependent on labor for the creation of surplus value, or profit. Capital cannot exist without labor, but labor is a subject potentially independent of capital.[101]

The working class, according to Negri, is a "dynamic subject, antagonistic force tending toward its own independent identity."[102] In contrast to the dominant, classical Marxist tradition that emphasizes the power of capital, autonomists such as Negri insist that Marx's analysis affirms rather the power of the creative human energy Marx called "labor"—"the living, form-giving flame" constitutive of society.[103] In Negri's words, "Labour is the essence of capital. It always has been so. It is also the essence of man, inasmuch as man is productive capacity."[104] Autonomist philosophy thus emphasizes the self-sufficiency of the proletarian masses: their ability to conceptualize, produce, and organize their own forms of struggle—their fundamental autonomy from the command of capital.[105]

During the Opera House work-in, labor functioned better without foremen, work was organized more efficiently, productivity was greater, and work practices were better. At the Whyalla Cooperative, the workers benefited and output improved with the elimination of oppressive authority relations; there was a greater commitment to collective production and greater conscientiousness in the cooperative than under privatized control before or after. At the Nymboida mine under union control, productivity improved under cooperative rather than oppressive relations of production.

The workers' control episodes examined here are expressions of working-class autonomy. They illustrate the point stressed in autonomist-Marxist theory that, no matter how difficult or doomed the experiment, the desire to do without the boss is latent and capable of periodic realization. The autonomist perspective is undoubtedly overly optimistic, tending to ignore the immense practical and political barriers to workers' control. Nonetheless it offers the valuable insight that autonomy is always a logical possibility, and cogently explains why this is so. It explains, too, why labor aspires to autonomy, despite hardly ever attaining it.

The autonomist concept of "self-valorization" is also a useful attempt to describe and understand the exhilaration of the workers and the qualitative changes they enjoy under workers' control. Negri developed the concept of self-valorization to describe the process by which labor power expresses its autonomy and presents itself forcibly as a social subject rather than as a mere object of exploitation. It refers to the needs, demands, and values generated autonomously within working-class experience to supplant the alien and coercive needs and values imposed upon workers by capitalism. It generally leads to demands for changes in the nature of work as well as for the reduction of working hours and higher wages.[106] Negri defines self-valorization as "to put the soul to work, to understand the positive, creative, radically alternative side (of the refusal of work)."[107]

These three experiments in workers' control differed in their immediate causes and outcomes, but all shared an infectious, self-empowering enthusiasm indicative of the experience of "self-valorization." Accounts of these episodes of working-class autonomy all emphasize the elation of the workers as they engaged in positive, creative, radically alternative forms of productive labor. At the Opera House work-in, the workers reveled in the stimulating new conditions, feeling like they had been released from prison. The women at Whyalla found the period of the cooperative refreshing; they took pride at last in their creative labor. Work at Nymboida after the union takeover became much more enjoyable and rewarding; contentment and morale were high.

Finally, the autonomist-Marxist analysis of the crisis of capital in the late postwar boom period speaks to the crisis evident in Australia in this period. These episodes of worker control in labor unions (autogestion) were the most dramatic indicators that Australia was experiencing its own version of the "industrial relations crisis" identified overseas at this time. In addition to workers' control experiments examined here, others in Australia in the 1970s, briefly summarized here, exhibited remarkable resilience.

At the Harco Steel factory on the western outskirts of Sydney, a dispute in November 1971 that challenged the boss's prerogative to hire and fire at will evolved into a four-week "stay-put" under workers' control—in the knowledge that management wanted a strike to give them grounds to dismiss the workers involved—to demonstrate that the boss was "surplus to their requirements."[108] From May 8 to 10, 1972, about sixty miners took over the Clutha Development mine at South Clifton in defiance of its official closure on May 5, ensuring the mine was reopened for a further period; all workers were returned to the payroll and promised work at other mines after the impending closure.[109]

In May 1974, sixty-seven construction workers on a shopping center a hundred miles north of Sydney at Wyong responded to the dismissal of a laborer by occupying the site. They announced from the jib of the crane that they would remain there until the job was reopened for all workers. Having expelled the developer, they organized work along self-management lines; they even asked local residents whether they would prefer a hospital to a shopping center. The workers' control episode at Wyong Plaza lasted six weeks and only ended after the company agreed to generous allowances and conditions, including the right of workers to be consulted on "hire and fire" decisions.[110]

The Nymboida experiment directly inspired follow-up militant miners' actions, including, as *Common Cause* termed it, an "invasion" of Canberra, the national capital, to demand unemployment benefits for locked-out miners, and other work-in tactics. One work-in was at Pelton colliery near Cessnock in September 1975.[111] Another was at Coal Cliff on the New South Wales south coast in August 1975, which lasted three days, until the employer agreed to negotiations. It was described in *Common Cause* as "a defiant challenge that goes into the proud records of the mining unions and the trade union movement generally."[112]

The ten-day occupation of the Sanyo television factory in Wodonga in June–July 1978 reduced the number of retrenchments and increased the payments made to those who departed.[113] Union Carbide workers at a plant in Altona, a Melbourne suburb, staged a fifty-one-day sit-in from August 27 to October 16, 1979, after Union Carbide announced it would replace union workers with use scab labor as replacement workers to operate the plant in response to overtime bans in support of a thirty-five-hour-week campaign. Upon occupation, at least 31 workers were sacked and 150 were suspended. With workers at other companies financially supporting the Union Carbide workers, the sit-in ended with the offer of reinstatement of all sacked workers and the lifting of all moves by the company to deregister the union.[114]

In the late 1970s, white-collar workers organized in the Administrative and Clerical Officers' Association who were employed in the federal Department of Social Security staged a series of work-ins. In 1980, they decided against a "traditional work-in" and instead backed up their demand for improved staffing levels by refusing—for more than two years—to recover overpayments made to social security recipients, which cost the federal government many millions of dollars.[115]

And there were more. Industrial relations scholar John Dalton stated in a conference paper in 1980 that "occupations are becoming an accepted part of the Australian industrial relations scene."[116] He notes in his discussion of the 1979 Union Carbide occupation in Melbourne that it occurred without prior planning, a result of built-up anger at the use of staff scabbing during a dispute.[117] The left-wing newspaper *Direct Action* commented, "It is doubtful whether many workers... have ever had the power that comes from occupying an $80m. plant."[118] The extent of the problem for capitalists is indicated starkly in an undated telegram sent during this period to an employer from the Plumbers and Gasfitters Employees Union of Australia:

RECEIVED TELEX BUT UNFORTUNATELY REPLY IMPOSSIBLE AS WE THE WORKERS OF ENERGY SERVICES HAVE SEIZED THE COMPANY OFFICES AND TAKEN COMPLETE CONTROL. OFFICE STAFF HAVE BEEN

LOCKED OUT. MANAGEMENT LOCKED OUT... DARE TO STRUGGLE, DARE TO WIN, IF YOU DON'T FIGHT YOU LOSE.[119]

This text clearly expresses exhilaration over an autonomist escapade, indicative of the repressed working-class desire to do without the boss, however short-lived such a reprieve might be.

Negri argues such adventurous displays of working-class power were characteristic of the "political crisis" in relations between capital and labor during the late postwar boom. The Keynesian "planner state," which commenced with the New Deal period in the United States before spreading globally and remaining dominant until the 1970s, was no longer able to contain the working-class desire for autonomy.[120] Negri describes Keynes as "perhaps the most penetrating theorist of capitalist reconstruction, of the new form of the capitalist state that emerged in reaction to the revolutionary working-class impact of 1917."[121] Though triggered by the 1929 Wall Street crash, Keynesian policies primarily attempted to avoid revolution by making the working class function within an overall mechanism that would "sublimate" its continuous struggle for power into a dynamic element within the system.[122] Keynes's theory "recognises and makes use of the power of the working class, in all its autonomy. The class can be neither put down nor removed: the only option is to understand the way it moves, and regulate its revolution."[123] We can therefore sum up the spirit of the theory of effective demand: "that it assumes class struggle, and sets out to resolve it, on a day-to-day basis, in ways that are favourable to capitalist development."[124]

Yet, in the long run, working-class resistance of exploitation was uncontainable.[125] The degree of working-class struggle ultimately brought about a transformation from planner state to "crisis state,"[126] because of the "tendency of the power balance to consolidate in favour of the working class."[127] The 1960s witnessed "the *quantitative* emergence of disproportionate wage struggles, and, as a result, an upsetting of the 'virtuous circles' of proportions on which Keynesian development depended."[128] In the 1970s, "The wage variable developed its own independence, its own autonomy"[129] such that "a kind of economic-political dual power came into existence."[130] This was expressed dramatically in occupations and workers' control experiments, in the extraordinary confidence displayed and direct-action methods adopted.

The three main episodes of autogestion discussed above indicate how the working class had become so assertive under Keynesian policies that the mediating functions of the planner state could no longer contain its militancy. The vulnerability of the planner state, threatening the functioning of the state's institutions, highlighted the position into which capital had been driven by working-class struggle: "The process that initially saw the working class wholly within capital today sees capital wholly within the working class. The precarious existence of capital's institutions and the exhaustion of their mediating functions derive precisely from this situation."[131]

In 1972, the federal government minister for labour and national service, Phillip Lynch, expressed the frustrations and anxieties of Australian employers in the face of such high degrees of working-class confidence. Sometimes he cajoled: "What must be understood by the trade-unions is the effect which industrial unrest can have directly on the employment market, the profitability of companies and the economy as a whole."[132] Other times he ranted, as when the *Sydney Morning Herald* headlined his speech, "MINISTER WARNS OF UNION BLUDGEONING."[133] Davis Hughes, minister for public works in New South Wales, was of a similar mind. He informed the Productivity Council of Australia on April 27, 1972, that industrial unrest was to blame for Australia's productivity not being as good as it should be.[134]

Like employers elsewhere, Australian bosses were particularly alarmed by the audacity expressed in occupations and workers' control episodes. In response to the Opera House work-in, for example, the New South Wales Employers' Federation declared its opposition to "the whole concept of workers' control" and stated that industry should be entitled to proceed about its lawful business "without intimidation, coercion or extortion." Their editorial in the April 1972 issue of *Employers' Review* continued, warning that workers' control, encouraged by "misguided" union leaders and communists, would result in "a Mafia-type monopolistic Power," which would deny management the job only it had been trained to do.[135]

The mainstream media nervously noted the degree of working-class defiance. The *Newcastle Morning Herald* in 1975 described as "a challenging view" the following passage it quoted from Pete Thomas's *The Nymboida Story*: "No longer can an employer assert an unquestionable right to decree whether workers should work or be sacked, whether a plant or mine should be opened or closed, with these decisions being based solely on what might best suit the employer's own interests." The *Herald* feared the Miners' Federation was determined to give this challenging view "a prominent place in the lore of industrial action and principle."[136]

They were forceful and forcible reminders of the fact that workers can do without the boss—however precariously in an otherwise capitalist society—and provided glimpses of an alternative universe in relations of production. Joe Owens sagely observed that workers' control "isn't a strategy to overcome this society and change it into a socialist society but it does give workers confidence and in it is the seed of the new society that can be practised in the old."[137]

CHAPTER 11

Revolt in Fast Food Nation: The Wobblies Take on Jimmy John's

Erik Forman

DAMMIT.

Third gear was slipping. The car was going to need a new transmission soon, I could tell. Where would I get the money for a new transmission? It would cost more than the $700 I had paid for the car the year before. That's most of what I made in a month juggling two food-service jobs. I eased the stick into fourth and kept the gas pedal to the floor, coaxing the car up to seventy as we rattled and careened down I-494.

"How're you feeling, dude?" I asked my coworker Bart, sitting next to me in the passenger seat, his knees forced to his chest by the Lilliputian dimensions of the subcompact passenger compartment. My other coworker Nick was jammed into the back.

"Pretty fucking good, man. I just can't wait to see the look on Monica's face when we bust in there. She is going to flip!" Bart said.

It was 11:30 a.m. on September 2, 2010. Bart, Nick, and I were on our way to the Jimmy John's restaurant we worked at in St. Louis Park, a first-ring suburb of Minneapolis. We were on a mission to confront our boss. Across the city at exactly that moment, groups of workers in eight other shops were stepping away from the sandwich lines and cash registers, leaving delivery orders sitting out on the counter, and confronting their bosses, too.

This was the first public action of the largest unionization effort in the history of the sprawling U.S. fast food industry.

Bart began rehearsing for the confrontation. "We, the undersigned employees of Jimmy John's-MikLin Enterprises Inc., demand that you recognize the Jimmy John's Workers Union-Industrial Workers of the World as our sole collective bargaining agent in order to negotiate for improvements in our wages, hours, and working conditions. A petition signed by the overwhelming majority of your employees is attached."

The page-long letter went on to detail demands for a litany of basic improvements in our lives. Like most fast food employers, Jimmy John's paid workers minimum wage, and sometimes not even, deducting pay for uniforms and never paying workers for overtime or mandatory meetings. Store managers wielded absolute power inside their little fiefdoms, firing workers on a whim or cutting their hours, and sending workers home early when business slowed down. Workers scrambled to get enough hours to pay rent. With shifts as short as two hours and wages at the legal minimum of $7.25/hr., almost everyone was on food stamps to survive. Workers were frequently fired for staying home when they were sick, or were forced to work with ailments ranging from a cold or the flu to pinkeye and a collapsed lung. We never got our legally mandated breaks. There was no holiday pay, health insurance, vacation time, or benefits of any kind. Male managers commonly made sexual remarks, and some even fired female workers who refused to sleep with them. The company systematically excluded African American workers from working as delivery drivers, a position that meant more take-home pay than working in-shop. The job itself was unsafe, with delivery drivers on bicycles getting hit by cars almost on a monthly basis, and then sometimes being denied workers' compensation benefits. The federal legal minimum as established by wage and hour, discrimination, and occupational safety laws would have been an improvement over the status quo at Jimmy John's.

Some stores were slightly better than others. Ours was worse. Within the four walls of our sandwich shop in a half-empty new upscale "lifestyle center" in the suburbs of Minneapolis, our manager, Monica Sesley, ruled with an iron fist. She demanded total obedience from her twenty-five employees, even when she showed up drunk and bossed workers around. She wasn't only strict, she was also abusive. "I'm going to bring a shotgun and shoot you," "Your mama should have had an abortion," "I'm going to stab you"—these were the threats she peppered her dictates with. If you questioned her, you would end up with fewer work hours the next week or simply disappear from the schedule completely.

At 11:45 a.m., we finally pulled into the parking lot, got out of the car, and strode purposefully into the store. Monica was running one of the two cash registers. Two or three workers were staffing each sandwich line; delivery drivers were running in and out with orders. Monica didn't look at me as we walked behind the counter and into the kitchen area. She knew something was up.

On Monica's left, Jen and Candace, two union supporters, stared at the cold table in front of them, trying to hide their enormous grins in their aprons. They had been waiting for this moment.

Dwayne, a large African American man who was prepping meats at the slicer, crowed, "I know the movement when I see it!" as we zeroed in on our boss. I wondered to myself what it would take for Dwayne to join the movement, not just watch. He had said he supported the union but had stalled on signing the petition or coming to a meeting. He had recently gotten out of prison and was worried about losing his job. Management knew this, too, and took advantage of the vulnerability of workers with criminal records or in halfway houses by denying them raises and giving them no say in their schedules. I had told Dwayne I understood his position, and that we would have his back if the company tried anything.

I looked to Tiffany, prepping sandwiches at the cold table on Monica's right. She avoided eye contact. She had signed the petition a few weeks before but flaked out on the mass meeting last week. Her commitment to the union was shaky. She took a two-hour bus ride to work each day from the poorest neighborhood in St. Paul, spending almost a quarter of her daily income from a four-hour lunch rush shift on bus fare. Sometimes she got marooned at work after the last bus at night and had to walk for hours to get home, or else blow her entire day's wages on a taxi. She was angry, but her solution was booze, boys, and betting that she'd land in franchise owners Mike and Rob Mulligan's good graces.

Antoine, another African American in-shopper who had signed the petition, also avoided eye contact. He had a son to take care of and was selling drugs to make up the difference between minimum wage at Jimmy John's and what he needed to pay rent and put food on the table at home. A couple weeks before, he had opened up to me as I drove him home. He needed a change and supported the union, but he wasn't ready to confront the boss.

"Monica!" I said loudly and assertively, over the odious racket of piped-in classic rock that every Jimmy John's blares on loop.

She didn't turn around.

"Monica!" I repeated.

She half-turned and mumbled, "I'm with a customer," as she beckoned the next person in line to the register.

"We need to talk. *Now*," I intoned. "We're here and we need to talk with you in the back for a minute." We wanted to surround her and were concerned that one or two of the many family relatives she'd hired on recently might interfere while we were delivering the demands. Nepotism was her way of organizing the shop against a mutiny.

"Okay," she said quietly, but didn't move.

"Monica, do you want us to do this right here or are we going to talk in the back room?" I looked to Jen and Candace. "Should we talk with Monica in back?"

"Yeah, let's do it," said Jen.

"Okay, we'll be waiting for you in back, Monica," I said and the five of us walked to the back room.

After a minute, Monica trundled back to talk with us. She was trembling slightly; she wasn't her usual, abusive self.

I wanted to set the tone. "Monica, we're here to inform you that workers at Jimmy John's have formed a union. Our right to organize is protected by the National Labor Relations Act—any retaliation from you or other managers is illegal. The union will be monitoring your conduct in the weeks ahead. If you choose to break the law, we will hold you accountable for your actions." I stopped; it was Bart's turn. We wanted to make sure everyone spoke.

Monica looked like she had been hit by a truck. She was speechless. Bart hesitated, and then began. He was nervous, too. He read the opening passage of the letter and then continued into our demands: "fair wages and fair wage increases. This means a fair and congruent starting wage, proper compensation for overtime and a protocol for scheduling raises that is timely, consistent and equitable." It took Bart a good five minutes to read the entire page of eight-point text, detailing demands for better pay, an end to arbitrary firings, tip jars for in-shop workers, adequate gas mileage and maintenance reimbursement for drivers, minimum shift lengths and fair scheduling, an end to sexual harassment, an end to racial discrimination in hiring drivers, the ability to take time off, paid time off, holiday pay, free uniforms, breaks, a free sandwich on our shifts, affordable health care, and respect and dignity. It was a laundry list of grievances that had been festering for years.

Monica seemed to be going into shock, swaying back and forth like a drunk while looking at the ground with a thousand-yard stare.

The purpose of a march on the boss is to give workers a taste of their own power, to turn the table on an oppressor by confronting them directly through worker solidarity. By this measure, our going-public action was an unqualified success. For the next week, our typically boisterously abusive boss didn't say a word.

Going Downtown

Bart, Nick, and I sealed ourselves back inside my tiny Geo. As we pulled onto the highway en route to the next action, I looked in my rearview mirror, reading the landscape behind. Two corporate office towers in the Minneapolis exurb of Minnetonka interrupted the horizon, punctuating a confused mess of strip malls and shoddy 1970s housing stock. I had delivered sandwiches to all those buildings; I knew that world. High in their office suites, the soft-handed corporate class subsisted on takeout and delivery food while tapping away at computers, monitoring streams of data linked to the various flows of the capitalist economy. They were the technicians of market research, product development, sales, advertising, accounting, insurance, finance, investment, law, real estate... the liberal arts of late capitalism.

Down below, service sector scrubs like us did the dirty work—preparing and serving food, stocking shelves, cleaning hotels and other buildings, driving taxis, ringing up customers, caring for higher-paid workers' children, and all the other jobs that must be done to get the world ready for another day at work.

Despite a world of difference, jobs at both the top and bottom of the office park towers are typically lumped together as "services," a catch-all category that absorbs more than 70 percent of the workforce in the United States and other highly industrialized countries. However, the use of the blanket term "service sector" papers over a much more profound trend—the bifurcation of employment in the United States into a small number of full-time, high-wage service jobs in various areas of corporate administration, and the cancerous growth of a vast low-wage service sector staffed by an army of wage slaves who are bound to these dead-end, meaningless jobs by mountains of debt.

The rise of the low-wage service sector is tied directly to the decline of higher-wage, largely unionized industrial employment in the 1970s, when the dislocation of workers through deindustrialization and the entry of large numbers of women into the workforce provided a labor force ready to work for low wages—and because of their low wages and long hours, ready to buy cheap food. Seeing a new opportunity to profit while returns on traditional investments lagged, capitalists began pouring money into a ballooning low-wage service sector. The number of fast food restaurants exploded from the late 1960s to the 1970s. McDonald's grew from 710 outlets in 1965 to more than 3,000 by 1977.[1] In a clear sign of the times, by 1982 McDonald's employed more than twice as many workers than US Steel.[2]

It was in this brave new world that Jimmy John Liautaud (yes, there really is a Jimmy John) opened a sandwich shop with his daddy's money in 1983 in Champaign, Illinois. According to the mythology of the Jimmy John's PR department, Liautaud came from humble beginnings, finishing second-to-last in his high school class at Elgin Academy, a private school that costs $19,000 a year. And starting a business from nothing, with a $25,000 loan ($60,000 in today's dollars) from his rich restaurateur dad. He was in the right place at the right time to get aboard the fast food gravy train just as it began to leave the station. By 2012, there were more than 1,400 franchised Jimmy John's stores across the United States, bringing in over $1 billion in revenue annually, a new store opening every day.

The multimillionaire Jimmy John Liautaud says, "I'm not a greedy American pig, I'm a hard-working, bread-baking, meat-slicing delivery guy who happens to be immensely successful."[3] The facts tell a different story. The orange-tanned oligarch is a caricature of a fast food captain of industry. He goes on safaris in Africa to hunt endangered species.[4] He has donated over $223,500 to right-wing candidates since 2001, pouring $10,000 into the campaign coffers of racist Arizona sheriff Joe Arpaio.[5] He is infamous among Jimmy John's workers for showing up at stores drunk and demanding to be waited on hand and foot.[6] An assistant store manager who attended "Jimmy Camp"—the corporate training that all Jimmy John's managers go through—reports that Liautaud said, "I don't want anyone named Jamal or Tyrone running one of my stores," and instructed managers to always put a "pretty girl" at the cash register. When the state of Illinois increased corporate tax rates to close the budget deficit in 2011, he threatened to move the company's headquarters out of the state, whining, "I could absorb this and adapt, but *it doesn't feel good in my soul* to make it happen."[7] In October 2012, Jimmy John told FOX news he planned to cut his employees' schedules to below twenty-eight hours a week in order to skirt Obamacare's employer-provided healthcare mandate.[8]

Jimmy John owns 67 percent of the company he named after himself and stamps the corporation with his own reactionary persona. The store interiors are festooned with pseudovintage metal signs trumpeting the supposedly classic American values of working hard for the boss and mindless consumption. One plaque screams, "WE deliver sandwiches, YOU eat sandwiches, GOD bless America," turning the act of ordering a sandwich into a celebration of the totalizing ideology of the American system of suburban consumerism, apparently ordained by God himself. Feeling excluded from the sacred orgy of consumption by the poverty wages of service industry work? Another sign squawks,

"Life is not fair—get used to it!" And, in case you think that a life based on consumption might be too effeminate, or that caring about food might be a little too *French*, another sign invokes the tired right-wing trope: "Sure my sandwiches are gourmet, but the only thing *French* about me is the way I kiss." If you don't like reading the signs, too bad, because Jimmy John's does not allow workers to read books, newspapers, or magazines in the store. If you would prefer to hold a conversation, that's too bad, too, because the music is so loud all you can do is eat a sandwich and read the signs. God bless America.

Can Fast Food Workers Organize into Unions?

With abhorrent conditions and an expanding workforce of nearly three million workers by 2012, one would think that the fast food industry would have long been a magnet for unions seeking to stem the tide of membership decline, and that fast food workers themselves would be beating down the doors of the labor movement to fight for decent pay, benefits, and fair treatment at work. Yet the U.S. fast food industry is almost entirely nonunion.

For seventy years, most union campaigns in the United States have relied on the provisions of the 1935 National Labor Relations Act (NLRA), passed in response to a series of insurrectionary strikes in 1934. The NLRA sought to avoid these "obstructions to the free flow of commerce" by removing class struggle from the shop floors and streets and confining it to offices and courtrooms. Under the government-run procedure, the bare-knuckled confrontations that had previously forced bosses to negotiate would be replaced by workplace-based elections for union recognition supervised by the National Labor Relations Board (NLRB). Union organizing was to become a "gentleman's game."[9]

As long as the threat of mass direct action loomed behind labor struggle, the ruling elites were willing to deal with unions inside the NLRA framework of class compromise. In the postwar era, leaders of the industrial monopolies that controlled U.S. economic life sought to form an unholy alliance with the trade unionists that C. Wright Mills dubbed the "New Men of Power." In exchange for dues check-off[10] and a bureaucratic grievance procedure, the ascendant labor bureaucracy agreed to allow corporate managers to assert their prerogative to organize the shop floor and signed no-strike clauses guaranteeing labor peace for the duration of the contract.[11]

By replacing robust direct action with the dead letters of bureaucratic procedure, the labor movement traded its birthright for a mess of pottage. As closed-door negotiations and courtroom hearings replaced mass meetings and work stoppages, the fighting capacity of the unions atrophied. The defanged labor organizations were ill-prepared for the withering corporate assault that began in the 1980s. As a result of union-busting, outsourcing, and the growth of the low-wage nonunion service sector, private sector union density plummeted from 24.2 percent in 1973 to 6.9 percent in 2012.

Since the passage of the NLRA in 1935, employers have figured out a way to game the system to stymie unions with the aid of a new breed of antiunion consultants. Euphemized by its profiteers as "union avoidance" or "positive employee relations," union-busting has become big business in the United States. A 2009 study found that 75 percent of employers hire a third-party consultant when faced with a union campaign.[12] Union-busters stall NLRB elections by launching challenges to the size of the bargaining unit, and then barrage workers with "captive audience" meetings and one-on-ones that serve up a psychological warfare cocktail of threats, disinformation about the union, promises that things will change, sob stories seeking to humanize the boss, and targeted firings.

Employer resistance has turned the NLRB process into an exercise in collective suicide for unions. There are other options; the labor movement has a rich history of organizing outside the NLRB, but most union leaders have all but forgotten the origins of their organizations in the battles of sit-downs and general strikes in the 1930s. The art of rank-and-file organizing, passed down from the radicals of the nineteenth century to IWW militants in the 1910s, and then from the Wobblies to the radical organizers of the 1930s, was lost.

Solidarity Unionism

By the end of the 1990s, years of continued decline had prompted an increasing number of labor activists to begin looking outside the mainstream for a source of union renewal. An amalgamation of rebel rank-and-filers, dissident staffers and officers, radical left activists, punk rockers, and angry workers began coalescing to rebuild the legendary Industrial Workers of the World. They sought revolution from below— organizing the rank and file of the existing unions, and building new worker-driven unions among the 87 percent of U.S. public and private sector workers who were not in a union as of year 2000.[13] After plenty of mistakes and modest growth through organizing campaigns in the early 2000s, the IWW achieved breakthrough notoriety with a union effort at Starbucks in New York City. Starting out with a bid for recognition at one store with an NLRB election, the campaign was stalled by the usual tricks of bargaining-unit gerrymandering. But instead of throwing in the towel, the workers at Starbucks opted to continue the campaign using an innovative organizing philosophy known as "solidarity unionism."[14]

The central tenets of solidarity unionism are simple—the power of the union comes from solidarity among workers and their ability to take action to fight for their demands. You don't need union recognition or even a majority to win gains from the boss. In practice, IWW solidarity unionism campaigns have three major hallmarks. First, IWW organizers almost always work in the shop they are organizing. We don't rely on professional organizing staff. This means that the experience and know-how gained through organizing remains embedded in the working class. Second, while most unions simply ask workers to sign cards or vote in an NLRB election, we focus heavily on developing our coworkers as leaders with a high level of involvement in the campaign, with the goal of unleashing workers' most powerful weapon: shop-floor direct action. The union is active on the shop floor every single day, shoring up confidence, addressing fears, and building solidarity among their coworkers in order to organize a guerrilla war of small-scale actions against the boss over shop-level issues. Third, in IWW campaigns, the organizing committee of workers calls all the shots, rather than union officers, staff, lawyers, or PR consultants. These differences may seem minor at first, but they have profound implications for the kind of movement we are building. By building a union run by workers, IWW organizing prefigures a world where power is in the hands of workers.

History set the stage with the rise of a massive—and massively exploitative—fast food industry, a bureaucratic labor movement in retreat, and the stirrings of a renewed Industrial Workers of the World. Now, the drama only waited for someone to act.

Building the Union

In 2007, Mike Wilkowicz was twenty-two, fresh out of college, and looking for a way to change the world. He had been involved in campus politics, getting pepper-sprayed and arrested for protesting the closure of the University of Minnesota's General College, which had provided an opportunity for working-class students, predominantly people of color, to access higher education. He had protested the Iraq War and, like so many activists of our generation, watched in despair as the war began despite the largest protests in human history on February 15, 2003. In 2006, he joined the IWW.

In February 2007, Mike joined his friend and fellow IWW member Wil Ericson in getting a job at Jimmy John's with the intent to organize. The Minneapolis-area MikLin Enterprises Jimmy John's franchise had seven stores at the time. Owned by Mike and Linda Mulligan and managed by their son Rob, this "family business" was no Mom-and-Pop. Mike Mulligan had retired in 1999 at the ripe old age of fifty-four, after making a fortune in fourteen years as a vice president of Supervalu, now the second-largest owner of grocery stores in the United States. His wife operates a real estate business specializing in relocating moneyed corporate executives to the Minneapolis area. They reside together in a $1.3 million villa on the shores of the exclusive Lake Minnetonka in the exurb of Minnetrista, far from the squalor of urban poverty caused by the poverty wages companies like Jimmy John's pay. The 96.3 percent white population of the town had a median household income of $126,302 in 2009, more than twice the state average.[15]

Mike Mulligan turned up at promotional events in the stores maybe a couple times a year, usually driving a different luxury car each time. He turned the day-to-day operations of the franchise over to his son, Rob, a rich kid who had squandered his private-school upbringing on a party-boy lifestyle. Rob was saved from his own haplessness when his dad bought him a Jimmy John's franchise in 2001. With the help of government small-business loans and federal stimulus money, they expanded their poverty-wage sandwich plantation to ten stores as of 2010, giving the feckless Rob Mulligan control over the livelihoods of more than two hundred workers.

Starting the union was a learning process of trial and error for Mike and his friend Wil. Initially, instead of following the IWW model of meeting one on one with coworkers to have deep conversations about their issues, Mike invited coworkers to parties, and brought up the idea of a union when everyone was drunk enough to feel confident talking about anything. It was an effective way to get workers to open up about workplace issues. It was less effective at securing commitments that everyone would remember the next day. Nevertheless, using this method, a small core of workers started coming together for the first meetings of what would one day become the IWW Jimmy John's Workers Union.

The first union meeting was a mess. Mike sums it up this way:

What we did do at the meeting:
- Drink beer
- Start late

- Slightly outnumber the non-JJ workers in attendance
- Decide to write a letter without tasking anyone to write it or collect signatures

What we did not do at the meeting:
- Choose a facilitator/chair
- Take notes
- Follow an agenda
- Accomplish a whole hell of a lot[16]

With the first meeting under his belt, Mike started bringing more workers into the committee. He began maintaining lists of contact information for coworkers, mapped out relationships in the shops, and started approaching people about organizing. The hope was that workers would meet, discuss their problems, plan an action to win a demand around a small issue, and bring in more workers who were inspired by that victory—all the way until they had a strong union capable of winning major gains through larger direct actions.

It didn't quite develop that way. After a few months of rambling, beer-infused get-togethers, the committee began to fall apart. But just as meeting attendance was dwindling, the union got a massive push from the usual source: management.

On June 10, 2007, management fired Kate, a committee member, because she had strep throat and couldn't come to work. Her boss at the Riverside Jimmy John's said the district manager (DM) had told him to fire her because she was "missing too much work lately" due to having strep, and that it was "easier to get a new dog than to teach an old dog new tricks."[17]

As soon as word about the firing got around, six Jimmy John's workers and five supporters from the IWW met up on Kate's front porch to plan an action. At 11:30 the next morning, IWW members and friends of the workers flooded the Riverside store's phone lines with calls complaining about Kate's firing. The workers wanted to keep the union campaign under wraps, so no one mentioned the IWW. The calls jammed the phone lines, shutting down the store's delivery operation during the busiest period of the day.

Next, the five committee members arrived at the shop and demanded to speak with the manager. The boss came out of the back room sputtering excuses and recriminations. In front of their coworkers, the workers calmly presented their demand for Kate's reinstatement.

The boss huffed and puffed but said it was out of his hands and that he'd have to call in the district manager. After a brief wait, the DM showed up along with Rob Mulligan. They rapidly tried to take control of the conversation with empty rationalizations to derail the workers' from presenting their demand, but one of the committee members blew up, filibustering the bosses with a two-minute rant about the unfairness of it all. From there, the other workers were able to state the demand. They didn't get the bosses to give in, but they did put them on the defensive.

After the action, Kate decided she didn't want her job back, so the union called off further actions. In a sense, it was a defeat—Kate was not reinstated. But in a broader sense, the action was an enormous success. The committee had shown a shop full of Jimmy John's workers that you can stand up to your boss, and keep your job, as long as you do it together.

Over the next year, the committee took action time and again. At one store, workers won consistent hours simply by writing their own schedule and presenting it to the boss. In another shop, the workers banded together and got a boss fired for sexually harassing their coworkers. In another case, they confronted a boss when he tried to fire a committee member.

There were also low points. High turnover rates made building the committee a Sisyphean task. Looking for ways to consolidate their gains, eventually the workers decided to adopt one element of traditional union-ization campaigns—the authorization card. By late 2008, they had gotten around forty cards signed, but the organizing committee had dwindled.

Once again, provocation by the boss brought the campaign back to life. On March 23, 2009, the boss at the Calhoun Square Jimmy John's punched one of the workers for refusing to cut a sandwich diagonally rather than straight across. Brandon, the assaulted worker, happened to be a member of the IWW. Outraged, all the workers in the shop stopped work, called Rob Mulligan, and announced that they wouldn't resume working until the boss was fired. Meanwhile, another IWW member mobilized friends and comrades via text messages to occupy the store's lobby. Within an hour, twenty-five people had packed the tiny Calhoun Square Jimmy John's.

Faced with a work stoppage and quasi-occupation, Rob Mulligan fired the boss, but also fired the worker who had been assaulted. That evening, the union had its largest meeting yet, with sixteen workers showing up to figure out next steps. They decided to circulate a peti-tion and file a charge with the NLRB. Incredibly, the NLRB ruled that the work stoppage was not legally protected because the workers hadn't clocked out. The ludicrous ruling was a taste of things to come from the legal system. Brandon didn't get his job back, but the spontaneous work stoppage had reignited the fire in the campaign.

Seeds

Over the summer, several more workers joined the committee, two directly from the shop floor, and others who decided to start working at Jimmy John's to help build the union. Some unions call this "salting." In the IWW, we have begun calling this practice "seeding," because our goal is to put down roots so that solidarity can grow among the workforce, eventually blooming into class consciousness through collective action, creating more "seeds" for future campaigns.

The first new "seed" was a brainy recent college grad looking to transition from campus activism to long-term workplace organizing. Next, an organizer joined after the mainstream union campaign he was involved in at a hotel had folded. Another, Max, got hired while fighting charges of "Conspiracy to Riot in Furtherance of Terrorism" along with seven other organizers of the 2008 Republican National Convention protests. Two others were caring, social-justice minded graduates of a local alternative high school. In November 2009, I got hired at the new West End store, creating a bridge to the experience I'd accumulated in the IWW campaign at Starbucks (my other job).

As of June 2010, we had 49 cards signed out of around 180 total workers in the franchise. As we planned our final push to build an indestructible pro-union majority, we decided to switch from using cards to a petition that would list our demands. The advantage of a petition is that workers can see that others have signed it, creating a sense of momentum and solidarity, and our petition kept the focus of the campaign squarely on the workers' demands rather than on the NLRB's legalistic procedure. With active organizers in eight of the nine stores in the franchise at that time, we steadily accumulated signatures through the dog days of summer. We felt confident enough to set a date to go public—Labor Day weekend.

But even as union support solidified, debate raged in the committee as to how exactly we would bring the Mulligans to the table. Mike Wilkowicz was adamant that we should file for an NLRB election. Many other committee members wanted to stay outside the NLRB system, favoring a combination of escalating direct action and community support. Unable to agree, we postponed the decision. We planned to call a mass meeting at the end of August of all the workers who had signed the petition in order to finalize our demands. Then, on the Thursday before Labor Day

weekend, we would pull off work stoppages in all the stores simultaneously, present our demands, and seek to negotiate with the Mulligans.

On August 29, forty Jimmy John's workers packed the living room of
the house Max lived in. By then, we had eighty workers on the petition—
not quite a majority, but we knew we could get there. The atmosphere
was electric. We struck several subcommittees, all run by Jimmy John's
workers, to distribute the work of waging a public campaign against
the company: the War Committee, tasked with coming up with actions
to propose at general meetings; the Solidarity Committee, a group of
community supporters who would build support outside the shops; a
Media Team to handle press work, and a Social Team to plan parties and
other social events for workers and supporters. After more than three
years of underground organizing, we had built an organization that
could wage a guerrilla class war reaching every store in the franchise.
We were ready for battle.

Zero Hour

And so, on Thursday, September 2, I found myself careening down the
highway toward my suburban Jimmy John's with two coworkers while
union members in eight other shops stopped work and confronted their
managers with our list of demands. Elsewhere, a union member flipped
the switch and launched jimmyjohnsworkers.org, while another blasted
out our press release to journalists across the country. The IWW Jimmy
John's Workers Union was born.

At 3:00 p.m., workers from all nine stores mustered up at a coffee
shop a block from the franchise's flagship store and main office at Block
E. We reported on the confrontations in each of our shops. At one store,
the manager had actually run away from a group of five workers, forcing
them to chase him into a corner in order to deliver the demand letter. In
another, the boss had spent the next hour in a panic, pacing around the
store, screaming, "Fuck! Fuck! Fuck!"

Everything was going according to plan. We had taken the company
by surprise.

At 4:00, about fifteen of us trooped into the Block E store and headed
to the back office to demand negotiations with the Mulligans. We had
telephoned ahead to tell them we were coming and expected to meet,
but the bosses were nowhere to be found. They had fled.

So, we took the next step of our escalation plan—a mass picket at
the Block E store with more than a hundred IWW members and supporters timed to shut down the expected dinner rush from that evening's

Minnesota Twins game. The mood was ebullient as choruses of the IWW anthem, "Solidarity Forever," ricocheted through the canyons of downtown skyscrapers.

There was no response from Mike and Rob Mulligan, save a short statement to the press. They said: "We are very proud of our employment record in Minneapolis and take issue with the claims by the IWW. We value our relationship with our employees and offer competitive wages and good local jobs. We are dedicated to providing a fair, equal, and diverse workplace environment."

They also posted a "help wanted" ad on Craigslist.

Although they talked tough in public, in the shops the company had been forced deep on the defensive. Almost immediately managers began giving workers raises, ranging from twenty-five cents to two dollars an hour, unheard of in a company that literally never granted pay increases. Taken by surprise, Jimmy John's did not fire a single worker in the first few weeks of the campaign.

We had the bosses on the back foot. It was time for the next step. Our immediate priority was to reach out to the roughly 40 percent of the franchise's workers we hadn't been able to talk to about the union previously, either because we had thought they would be hostile or rat us out, or we simply hadn't been able to contact them.

We also kept up the pressure on our target. The next step in our escalation strategy was a revival of a labor movement classic. On Saturday, September 4, we formed a roving picket of bicyclists, rolling from store to store, bringing balloons and candy to our coworkers behind the counter to keep up spirits. The critical mass-style action culminated in an unpermitted block party, shutting down business at the Calhoun Square Jimmy John's in the heart of the Saturday night Uptown club scene.

The struggle received widespread media attention, becoming symbolic of the labor movement's zero hour—a potential turning point that could interrupt years of decline with a breakthrough into new, unorganized, highly exploited sectors. The only thing holding us back was the unresolved debate in the core of our organizing committee about the overall campaign strategy. We were also starting to run out of runway, burning through the first week of actions that we had planned before going public.

To Be or to NLRB?

Against the advice of virtually the entire IWW, Mike still had his heart set on filing for an NLRB election. His reasoning was that the company would never come to the table unless they were forced to by law, and that we needed the stamp of legitimacy an NLRB victory would provide. Mike was also confident we would win, even though our final push since going public had garnered only a narrow majority of workers signed on in support.

On the other side of the debate, we argued that (a) there was no guarantee we would win an NLRB election and a good likelihood we would lose, based on abundant historical precedent; (b) even if we won the election, we would be no closer to realizing material gains; (c) the election timeline would give the company additional weeks and months to weaken us in the shops; (d) negotiations brought about through an election could lead to binding arbitration, which would take decision-making power completely out of our hands and would likely saddle us with a no-strike clause that would prevent future direct actions; and (e) focusing on the NLRB to gain legitimacy shifted the focus from the collective power of workers to the power of the government, contradicting the central message we were trying to convey: workers can change the world when they take action together.

We proposed alternative ways to achieve legitimacy through a highly public demonstration of union membership, like an ad in the paper and a poster with our demands and every supporter's photo, or an election through a "Community Labor Relations Board" assembled of respected local public figures that would oversee an election on our timeline. We also figured that no matter what happened, we would still need to be able to shut the company down if we were going to win major gains. Looking at the examples of the 1934 Minneapolis truckers' strike and the 1936 sit-downs, we put every possible tactic on the table—a franchise-wide strike, organizing down the supply chain to cut off the flow of raw materials, work-to-rule, targeted consumer boycotts to hurt business, a demonstration or encampment at Mike Mulligan's mansion, pickets at the stores, lockdowns, a sit-down strike, blockades of deliveries—nothing was off-limits in discussion.

These were the options: a clear pathway laid out by the NLRB that would give the campaign legitimacy and would force the bosses to talk to us, or a vague plan to escalate the struggle into a strike, occupation, or other protest tactic. We were at the end of the road paved by traditional organizing of the last seventy years and without a map for how to go forward.

At our weekly Sunday organizing committee meeting on September 5, 2010, we debated the issue for the last time. Through hours of discussion, those who wanted to go for an election put forward a semi-compromise position: file for an NLRB election in the next week *and* continue fighting for our demands and union recognition with direct action. We took a vote and the motion carried, with eight in favor, five against, and two abstaining. We were committed to filing for an election with the NLRB while continuing the escalating actions.

With the certainty of a union election on the horizon, we continued ratcheting up the pressure on the Mulligans. Starting on Labor Day, the campaign crashed onto the national stage with a week of actions at Jimmy John's locations across the United States. In Minneapolis, we organized a concert on the University of Minnesota campus, and then marched to a nearby Jimmy John's location and disrupted business with another picket. After the picket wound down, we closed out the night with a massive party at a local underground venue. The crowd was dotted with JJWU T-shirts emblazoned with our slogan, "Wages So Low, You'll Freak," an irreverent riff on the company's PR line, "Subs So Fast You'll Freak." For the first time since the 1934, union organizing was *cool* in Minneapolis.

Two days later, on Wednesday, September 8, we kicked up the pressure another notch by attempting to call unionized building trades workers off the job to stall construction at a new Jimmy John's store. Some of the workers were sympathetic but felt that if they walked off the job, others from their union would scab on them. After an hour of blocking a truck carrying building supplies and arguing with the police and the contractor, we decided to call it a day.

Up to this point we had been a few steps ahead of the bosses, but they were catching up. As our first week of actions drew to a close, the company posted the first of many antiunion letters in the back room of the store. It said, in part: "It's illegal for an employer to deal with a union that doesn't in fact represent a majority of the company's employees. This is why we have not met with them. It seems clear to us that the IWW is asking us to meet because they apparently don't have enough support to call for a democratic secret ballot election."

We recognized something new in management's propaganda. Sure enough, on September 10, we got word that a union-busting consultant named Rebecca Smith had arrived.

The Union-Busters

On September 13, we went to the NLRB office with our petition and filed for an election. A week later, the company's antiunion consultant began the first cycle of captive audience meetings. At first, the antiunion propaganda was way off the mark. Before a roomful of young, low-wage fast food workers, Rebecca Smith screened an ancient video from the 1990s featuring mulleted workers in industrial settings, complaining that their union didn't listen to them and that it had bargained away perks like paid holidays. Most of us didn't have mullets, and none of us had paid holidays. In the question and answer session following, our irreverent, punk rock– and hip hop–influenced workforce mocked Smith, calling her "Teacher" and carrying on side conversations. The first captive audience was a flop, but the antiunion campaign rapidly got much more vicious and effective.

Ghostwritten letters "from" Mike and Rob Mulligan, defaming the union, began accompanying our paychecks. Managers claimed that they had to institute a "wage freeze" because of the union, then told certain workers that the freeze was preventing them from getting raises they would otherwise have received. The company tightened policy, writing up workers for being a few minutes late. They sent workers home for slight dress code infractions. In a spiteful response to our demand for the right to not come to work if we were ill, the company began punishing workers by forcing them to stay home for seventy-two hours when they called out sick.

The next week, they began a second round of captive audience meetings, bringing in a second union-buster, named Joe Brock. This time they divided the group based on their assessment of who was pro-union, neutral or undecided, and anti, with a different message for each group.

Brock showed us a PowerPoint presentation that jumbled together quotes and photos found online to red-bait the IWW as an "Anarchist Socialist" organization bent on destroying capitalism—and Jimmy John's with it. They admonished us, "The IWW is for self-management. That means your sweet manager Monica here would be out of a job!" Smith at one point yelled at Max, the committee member who had stood trial for his involvement in the anarchist RNC Welcoming Committee in 2008, "Why don't you go throw a Molotov cocktail?" when he disrupted her antiunion speech. They combined an aggressive stance toward the IWW (Brock at one point called me a "faggot" and screamed "You're a fucking liar!" during a captive audience meeting at my store) with a buddy-buddy approach to the other workers.

In addition to the captive audience meetings, the union-busters attempted to paint the IWW as a violent organization and pinned an allegation of sabotage on us. When a cooler broke at the Calhoun Square store on September 12, the company's district manager, Jason Effertz, showed up and ordered workers to slice the spoiled meat and serve it. The "PIC" ("person in charge"—what Jimmy John's calls shift supervisors) on duty refused and was sent home with the threat that she might face discipline. In response, the union organized a campaign to blast management with phone calls, and put out a press release as workers and supporters marched to the store with flowers to thank her for standing up for public safety. Within hours, she got a call from Rob Mulligan informing her that her job was no longer in jeopardy.

Unwilling to stomach a union win, the company began circulating rumors that the IWW had sabotaged the cooler. From then on, any time any little thing went wrong in a store, the company said IWW sabotage was to blame. In one store, the hoses to the soda machine got hooked up wrong so that Coke came out of the Sprite spigot, and so on. Jimmy John's claimed this was an act of IWW sabotage. Most workers found this as hilariously absurd as we did, and "sabotage" became a running joke in the franchise whenever anything went wrong.

Most of the red-baiting was dead on arrival with our coworkers. After one meeting where Smith had decried the IWW preamble's words, "It is the historic mission of the working class to do away with capitalism," as anarchist demagoguery, a worker approached an organizer and said, "That makes me so angry. I've been reading about this stuff in school. That's not anarchist, it's Marxist. There's a difference!" Another worker said, "I'm so confused. They say the IWW is all about anarchy and destruction. I'm *all about* anarchy and destruction... but I just don't know about this union idea." Disruptions of the captive audience meetings were frequent—whether organized by the union or spontaneous. At the beginning of one meeting, a worker asked Joe Brock, "Have you ever heard of the band Garbage?" Brock replied, "Um, yes?" The worker then shouted, "Because that's what this is—garbage!" That ended the meeting.

Seeking a proxy to advance the antiunion message, the union-busters aimed to split the workforce along racial lines by designating two African American workers as antiunion spokespeople. The company stoked tensions by distributing antiunion buttons. At least one manager cornered individual workers and asked them if they would wear the pins. Some workers were so scared and conflicted that they wore both pro- and antiunion pins.

Actively antiunion workers were never more than a very small minority of the workforce. What was most devastating to the organizing was the increase in tension in the shops caused by the constant back-and-forth of letters, accusations, and arguments, and the impact of selective policy-tightening, threats, and a couple of targeted firings. Jimmy John's had turned into a war zone. This is the goal of union-busting campaigns—to make life at work so unpleasant that workers just want the union question to go away.

Keeping It Together

To maintain the solidarity and organization we had built, we decided to produce a series of posters to show workers their own numbers and power. On September 30, we put up the first "WE ARE THE UNION" poster in the back of all our stores, featuring photos of union supporters and quotes about why they were for the union. We set a goal of getting every single union supporter onto the poster, producing a new one each week leading up to the election, each with more photos on it. It was compelling visual evidence of the rising tide of solidarity that we hoped would bring us across the finish line victorious. Collecting the photos and quotes was also a justification for meeting with coworkers one on one, having deep conversations with them about their concerns and fears, re-agitating them over the problems that had motivated us to organize in the first place, and shoring up their commitment to the fight. Three days before the election, we finished the final poster, with the names and photos of seventy workers—approaching a majority in its own right. We also asked our coworkers to fill out a survey identifying the workplace issues that were most important to them, seeking to inspire workers to imagine the changes that were possible.

We did our best to stay on the offensive and keep the spirit of the union alive by continually involving our coworkers in actions highlighting our core demands. One of the most successful mobilizations was a collective violation of the company's ban on tip jars, a sore point for in-shoppers and the source of pay inequality with tipped delivery drivers. It was even worse on "dollar sub" promo days, when radio advertising brought hordes of customers to the stores, severely increasing the workload of in-shop workers despite the same minimum-wage pay. On the dollar sub day in September, union volunteers distributed Styrofoam cup "tip jars" and flyers to lines of customers, explaining the importance of giving the minimum-wage workers gratuities. The action was a hit. Customers left cups with tips in them on the counter faster than management could clear them away. At the end of the day, management was foaming at the mouth in anger, and the workers had around eighty dollars each in tips—quadruple their daily income. Direct actions like this demonstrated the union's ability to win gains for workers, shifting the debate away from the bureaucratic yes-no vote in the NLRB election and toward collective action against the company's unfair policies.

Our actions provided the media with fodder for a continuous narrative of a scrappy union of low-wage workers fighting to turn the tides of a forty-year war against the working poor. Unions, community groups, and hundreds of individuals signed a pledge to boycott Jimmy John's if called upon to do so. Our "air war" of building community support and destroying the Mulligans' credibility and legitimacy was so successful that by the time the election rolled around, customers were wishing us luck with the union fight as they waited in line for their sandwiches.

Once the election date was set for October 22, the union-busting intensified with a constant cycle of captive audience meetings, tightening of policies, retaliation, threats, and all the other weapons in the antiunion arsenal. We decided to hedge our bets on an election win, possibly slow down the union-busting onslaught, and cost the company money by filing a battery of Unfair Labor Practice charges over the illegal threats and interrogations that were becoming commonplace in the shops. Also, we wanted to build a paper trail and narrative in the public sphere that the company was breaking the law, so if we lost the election the public would understand the defeat as a result of illegal union-busting, and we could eventually get the results thrown out. We filed our first ULP charge, covering fourteen violations of the NRLA, on October 1. It was to be the first of many.

On Saturday, October 16, the final cycle of captive audience meetings began. We knew these would be "twenty-fifth hour" speeches in which the owner, and likely also his wife, would give an emotional appeal to workers to keep the big, bad, lying IWW out of the family business Mike and his son had poured their lives into. Like clockwork, Mike and Linda Mulligan appeared at all the stores, imploring the workers to give them another chance and to keep the IWW out. Mike told us his story of growing up on a farm, going into corporate America, retiring by age fifty-four, and starting MikLin Enterprises for his dissolute son.

It was then time for our own twenty-fifth hour. Instead of a teary speech from a sixty-five-year-old patrician, we had a concert. We called it "Jimmy Jams Vol. 1." The night before the vote, we lined up one band from each Jimmy John's store to perform at Jimmy Jams in a converted warehouse building in Northeast Minneapolis. Around a hundred people showed up, including workers from almost every store. We hoped the show on the eve of the elections would solidify commitments and give us one last bit of momentum before the expected photo finish.

That night, we assessed our support at 103 "yes" votes, 45 expected "no" votes, and 45 undecided/maybe votes. By this count, as long as we got out the vote, we would not lose. I was still nervous. It was going to be close.

Election Day

On election day, our side worked to ensure that all union supporters had access to transportation and followed through on their pledge to vote. The other side had similar plans. In each store, managers ordered all the workers on shift to take a company-provided shuttle to the polling places. They were making a bet that they held an absolute majority among the entire workforce, so they were going to force the entire workforce to vote.

I spent the day as the union's observer at the polling place in St. Louis Park. Mike monitored the polling place in Block E. On my right sat a gray-suited NLRB bureaucrat and a younger NLRB intern. On my left sat Tiffany, the company's election observer—Tiffany, who had signed the petition two months prior. She had gotten a promotion and a transfer to a store closer to her home, and likely other incentives to side with the company.

Workers began trickling in. As we checked off their names on the list of eligible voters, I thought about the massive work of organization that had gone into it all. Years of meetings, a few complete collapses of the campaign, thousands of conversations, hundreds of committee meetings, uncountable hours of life, dozens of job actions, scores of news articles, and an antiunion campaign that had cost Jimmy John's more than $84,000 all lay behind us. We had come so far. A union with no staff, no money, and little experience stood toe to toe with one of the largest fast food empires in the United States. Because of us, millions of poverty-wage workers had seen that it is possible to fight back. I knew there was a good chance we would lose the vote. But in my mind, we had already won; we had already changed the definition of what is possible for low-wage workers.

The primary impact of a win at the polls would be a boost in morale. The committee had not agreed on a plan in the event of a defeat. When the polls closed, I was ready for whatever the fates had in store, but I knew it didn't look good. One of my pro-union coworkers arrived at the polls literally moments after they had closed. Another hadn't made it because she had to drill for the National Guard that day. Not good signs, as we had very little margin for error. We packed up and drove downtown to the vacant Hooters that had served as the other polling location. More than a hundred workers and supporters gathered in the cavern-like interior of the shuttered restaurant to watch the count. The two union-busters were there, looking nervous. Mike, Rob, and Linda Mulligan were there as well, also looking nervous. We were nervous, too.

The NLRB agents began pulling ballots out of the sealed ballot bags, reading each vote aloud. Time seemed to slow down. NO-NO-NO-YES-NO-YES-YES-NO-YES. The Board agent's emotionless voice echoed through the airless room.

We lost, eighty-seven to eighty-five. Two pro-union ballots were uncounted because the company claimed one worker had been hired after the cutoff date for eligibility to participate, and the other had been fired and we were in the process of filing NLRB charges to try to win reinstatement. But even a tie goes to the employer under the NLRA. We had lost.

The union regrouped that night at a party that bore more of a resemblance to an Irish wake. But once the tears had a few days to dry, the core of the committee was ready to move forward again.

Organizing Beyond the NLRB

With the election behind us, we were back to where we had been two months earlier, but with a wealth of new experience. The committee resolved to move forward with the fight for our demands, returning to the path of direct-action-only organizing we had left when we had voted to file for an NLRB election on September 10. We also decided to file objections to the election, citing more than thirty NLRA violations. But the legal fight was peripheral to the main questions confronting the campaign: How would we get the company to the table? What kind of actions would we take? How could we win? How would the campaign be structured? We had few models to draw on, save what we had read about the pre-1935 unions that depended exclusively on direct action,[18] recent IWW successes, and our own experiences.

We settled on a process of defining a set of demands that we would fight for, one by one, with creative direct actions. We would organize through the structure we had developed over the last three years: weekly general meetings with committees for specific projects, all run by Jimmy John's workers. We codified the top ten issues that workers had rated as "very important" on our pre-election collective bargaining survey as the "Ten Point Program for Justice at Jimmy John's." In addition to fighting for the demands, we began circulating the Ten Point Program as a new petition. Our goal was to rebuild majority support for the union in order to solidify our legitimacy as a collective voice of workers. After a slow build to a majority through actions around the ten issues, we planned to implement, once again, an escalating campaign to force the company to negotiate.

While we were developing the Ten Point Program, discontent was once again rising in the shops. Many of the eighty-seven workers who had voted against the union had been taken in by promises that things would change if they kept the union out. As weeks and months of "back to normal" went by, these workers began to get wise to the fact they had been sold a bill of goods. There were no raises, no changes to the scheduling practices, no promotions, no nothing.

To pick our first fight, we identified one issue from the Ten Point Program as both uniquely winnable and weighty in the lives of our coworkers: direct deposit. At Jimmy John's, workers were forced to show up in person to collect their paychecks on payday. The $3.50–$6.00 in round-trip bus fare, plus the likelihood that the checks would arrive late, added up to a major inconvenience in the lives of Jimmy John's workers. We began circulating a new petition for direct deposit. This time the company was on high alert for issues that could escalate into pickets, strikes, and public pressure. Word got back to management that the petition was going around. On November 19, before we had even submitted the demand, the company gave in. The bosses were scared shitless of a resurgent union campaign. We claimed victory and began looking for other issues to organize around.

The Sick Day Campaign

The holidays came and went and we found ourselves in the deep Minnesota midwinter. This had traditionally been a difficult time to maintain momentum. Temperatures drop to 0° F (–18° C) or lower, snow and ice make travel difficult, and short days send many people into seasonal depression. As temperatures fall, instances of flu and colds rise. It's the off-season of organizing. But this year, we were invigorated in early January by the nullification of the tainted election results. Vindicated by the government ruling that the company's law-breaking had poisoned the election, we looked through our Ten Point Program and decided on the next issue to focus on: sick days.

At Jimmy John's, workers were required to find their own replacement if they needed to call out or go home sick. Since the stores were already staffed by a skeleton crew, usually no one was available. Also, living paycheck to paycheck, most workers couldn't afford to lose a shift. So people came to work and made sandwiches while sick. We had conducted a survey of Jimmy John's workers and found that, on average, each worker works 4.1 days per year while sick. That meant that on any given day, an average of two workers in the franchise were working while sick—a disgusting fact that would likely make customers think twice before biting into a sandwich full of cold and flu germs.

The campaign began with a simple phone call to Rob Mulligan from a worker representing the union in mid-January 2011. The union made two demands: the right to call in sick without fear of being fired, and paid sick days so workers wouldn't have to choose between having money for rent and being able to stay home to get well. When Rob dodged the issue, we escalated a step to confronting him with the demand whenever we saw him. He gave excuses, asked us for examples of restaurants that provided paid sick days, and kept repeating that he couldn't meet with the union. It was time for another escalation.

In February, workers started sporting "Sick of Working Sick" buttons while making and delivering sandwiches. We put up a poster in a prominent place in the back room of each store, encouraging workers to call a union hotline if their manager asked them to work while sick, putting management on notice that we were watching.

Still, Rob Mulligan refused to make changes. In fact, not only did he refuse, but two workers were fired for calling in sick even as we were escalating the campaign. It was a provocation; we decided it was time to show the company we meant business.

One of the members of the committee created a poster with two identical photos of a Jimmy John's sandwich. The captions read, "This is your sandwich made by a HEALTHY Jimmy John's worker. This is your sandwich made by a SICK Jimmy John's worker. Can you tell the difference? That's too bad, because Jimmy John's workers don't get paid sick days. Shoot, we can't even call in sick," and listed owner Rob Mulligan's phone number, asking the public to call him to "Let him know you want healthy workers making your sandwich."

On March 10, four members of the committee knocked on the franchise management office's door in the back of the Block E Jimmy John's and confronted Rob Mulligan. We laid out what Rob already knew—workers worked sick every day at Jimmy John's because they couldn't afford to take a day off, and there was usually no one who could cover their shift. Rob didn't respond much, but it was clear from a few nods that he recognized the reality of the problems we were describing. He told us that the company was revising its sick day policy but wouldn't give us any details or guarantees. This was the first indication that we had begun to move the company. We told him the company had ten days—until March 20—to fix the sick day policy or we would "plaster the city" with posters exposing the health risk of eating at Jimmy John's.

We left the office feeling that the past six months of constant class warfare in the shops might have finally pushed the company to deal with us more reasonably. We were completely wrong.

The next day when we all started work at our respective stores, we were confronted by a posting that accused us of "attempting to force [the company] to unlawfully recognize and bargain with the IWW by driving customers away from Jimmy John's.... We will not cave to the IWW!"

With no acceptable response from management by March 20, union members posted three thousand of the sick day posters in neighborhoods around stores in the franchise. The next day, the Mulligans fired six of the core organizers, including myself, for involvement in the sick day poster action, decimating the organizing committee. It was clear this was a calculated move to "decapitate" the union by taking out the people they perceived as leaders. The Mulligans knew they might lose in front of a judge, but they preferred an expensive, lengthy battle in court to an expensive, lengthy battle on the shop floor.

We tried to give them both. In the days after we were fired, we confronted Rob Mulligan directly in the Block E store, organized phone zaps that shut down the delivery intake system, mobilized pickets across the country at Jimmy John's, and held a "quarantine Jimmy John's" demonstration at a local store to continue the fight for paid sick days. We considered a more dramatic escalation, but the reality set in that there was almost no amount of pressure we could bring to bear on the bosses that would force them to reinstate us, and anything more aggressive might alienate the fragile support base we had been rebuilding.

For the second time in the campaign, we fell back on the legal system, filing an Unfair Labor Practice charge contesting our firings in March 2011. It took over seven months for us to get a response from the NLRB. Finally, in November of that year, the NLRB "found merit" in our charges. Jimmy John's refused to settle, so we were headed to trial.

On February 14, 2012, almost an entire year after we had been fired—a year of battling the company in unemployment hearings, scrambling to find work, scraping by to make rent, and straining to hold together the organizing committee—the trial began before an administrative law judge in a windowless office building courtroom in downtown Minneapolis.

We won... sort of. The judge ordered Jimmy John's to reinstate the six fired workers with back pay and expunge from the record the warnings given to other participants in the sick day action. The bitter irony is that this was the fullest remedy the NLRB could offer. No fines. No jail time. Just the wages we would have made, minus interim earnings, and reinstatement to our shitty jobs. Within weeks, the company announced it would appeal the rulings rather than comply, meaning we would not be back on the job for even longer as the appeal made its way first to the NLRB, and then likely to higher, even more conservative courts.

Once again, the legal route proved a dead end.

As weeks stretched into months, and months became years, the campaign slowly returned to a now familiar cycle of meetings, organizing around shop-level grievances, and small-scale job actions. The workers have defended each other from discipline, blocked firings, and won small demands at the store level. The company continues playing defense, slowly giving ground on the various demands of the Ten Point Program.

Like a seed beneath the Minnesota snow, a culture of solidarity and resistance lives on among the fast food proletariat of Minneapolis. However, the question remains as to how this seed can blossom into a mass movement to put an end to the exploitation of low-wage service workers, bypassing the dead end of relying on politicians and courts. Although we don't have an easy answer, the experience of the IWW at Jimmy John's can provide us with a few clues.

Toward an Insurgent Organizing Model

The JJWU election and subsequent non-NLRB campaign represents a bridge in the labor movement between what everyone once said could not be done and what everyone now agrees *must* be done—organizing the low-wage mass industries of fast food and retail. Our campaign developed in a specific interregnum, after the end of the effectiveness of the old way of organizing through the NLRB, but before the beginning of a new workers' movement based on strategies adapted to a brave new world with no de facto right to organize. What can the experience of the JJWU tell those who seek to invent labor's future?

The most significant advances of the JJWU were due to its most radical departures from the conventional organizing model: the empowerment of the rank and file in a largely autonomous organizing

committee, and a constant focus on fighting for demands and addressing grievances through direct action. Because workers were highly
engaged in every aspect of the campaign, the JJWU was able to organize effectively and continually win substantial gains with direct action
despite extremely high workplace turnover rates, far-flung worksites,
some close relationships between workers and bosses, weeks of intense
union-busting, and an unsuccessful union election. Even the firing of
most of the core organizers was not enough to destroy the union. This
level of militancy can only be built by organizers who are thoroughly
embedded in the segment of the working class they are organizing, in
line with the largely forgotten tradition of the Knights of Labor, IWW,
and early CIO.

The combination of empowered organizing committees armed
with an arsenal of direct-action tactics constitutes the basis of a new,
insurgent organizing model. As economic conditions worsen, larger
numbers of workers will become politicized, opening up a dramatic
possibility of using this model to build a workers' movement in areas
beyond the reach of staff-driven campaigns relying on a collapsing legal
framework, card-check deals, or other leverage. It is our task to arm this
new generation of working-class militants with training and support,
putting the implements of class war directly in the hands of a new insurgency in every workplace and neighborhood.

The Jimmy John's Workers Union has demonstrated that with a
little training, a little encouragement, and a big dream, a small group
of committed workers can change the world. It will be messy. Workers
won't win every battle, but that's not the point. The most important
outcome of organizing is its impact on the participants. The road to
victory will be long, but if workers are able to make their own decisions,
they will be able to draw their own conclusions from the consequences.
Long after the headlines have faded, after the court cases have been
closed, and after fired workers go on to other jobs and projects, what
remains is the ineffable—the forging of a new generation of working-
class militants in the crucible of struggle. If we achieve this goal, then all
others will eventually follow, and in the end—we will win.

CHAPTER 12

The IWW Cleaners Branch Union in the United Kingdom

Jack Kirkpatrick

"Pay us fairly or we'll fucking strike!"

She's serious.

Normally bubbly and funny, right now she is *pissed off*. The big man at the other end of the table smiles and holds his hands up in front of him imploringly. But he does look shaken. The area manager across from him looks even more shaken, watching his boss to see what happens next. The other five cleaners smile quietly. *That* was funny.

The young chap pretending to be a union official (he's wearing a suit and everything) chokes off his laughter, ignores his thumping heart, and speaks sincerely to the fat man, cutting off his reply. "They're pretty angry, y'know? I mean, from their perspective this has been dragging on for a while. Our union is totally democratic. I can't stop them. You *might* need to move faster than that."

It's another month before the union official finds out that, even if they win, the woman doesn't get a penny extra—she's already earning £8.00 an hour. In her own words: "This is for my colleagues."

At the end of the meeting, the workers and their twenty-eight-year-old "union official," Tom, head down the stairs in silence and out of the shop through the "partners' entrance." Over in the square they meet up with Dan, another young union activist. Dan is also a filmmaker and Tom has asked him to try and get some sound bites or even footage of the workers midcampaign. The tension of the meeting has broken now they're out, and is replaced by relieved laughter. Tamy is back to her jokes and a bit shy, but, along with Abraham, Kwesi, Abidemi, and even the soft-spoken Maria, she speaks into the microphone:

"We need this, you know? It's not fair!"

Before they go their separate ways, Tom reinforces what he's said before. These workers need to be sure their colleagues are definitely on board and will stick together. If it comes to a strike, it needs to be solid. Anger and determination flash in Tamy's eyes: "Don't worry; they'll strike if I say so. I'll bloody *make* them strike!"

Cleaning Workers and Exploitation in London's Neoliberal Economy

This is November 2012 and the workers are six cleaning supervisors who work in a retail shop. But they work *for* a cleaning company, owned by a major multinational corporation, contracted by a broker, who in turn is contracted by the shop—prestige British retailer and "workers' partnership" John Lewis—to arrange the cleaning of their stores. The cleaning supervisors—and they do clean, but they also get a little extra pay to "supervise" the other cleaners—are all immigrants, and they're all angry.

They're angry because of something that went down four months earlier, on London's Oxford Street. Walk down Oxford Street any day of the year, and you'll be bumped along with the crowds of consumers like flotsam on white water. It's always noisy with the rhythms of stamping feet, beeping horns, and gunning engines. But on Friday, July 13, 2012, above the traffic came the rhythms of whistles, drums, and chanting. West of Oxford Circus and east of Bond Street, scarlet flags and homemade banners marked the spot right outside the flagship store of John Lewis. This was the first lawful strike carried out by the Industrial Workers of the World in the United Kingdom.

The strike at John Lewis was the latest and highest-profile action by the "new kid on the block" union, whose Cleaners Branch had grabbed first the attention of the left media, then local followed by national media, with their visible and militant campaigns. Not that the Industrial Workers of the World (IWW)—known colloquially as "the Wobblies"—is a new union. The first time an employer twitched nervously after hearing that the Wobblies had shown up in their business was more than a century ago, back in 1905.

In the United Kingdom today, just over a quarter of all workers—roughly six million people—are in a union. This includes men and women, young and old, migrants, workers of color, unskilled and service sector workers; in theory, anyone and everyone. But the devil's in the details. Four million of those union workers are in the public sector. The vast majority are in professional, administrative, or skilled roles. They work in government, education, defense, health care, energy supply, and transportation. They left university with degrees and they are in the middle-income bracket. They are likely to have permanent contracts with pay progression, pensions, sick pay, and above-minimum holiday and redundancy terms. It is true that they are more likely to be women than men, and (just about) more likely to be Black or Asian than white. But they are very unlikely to be young, of other ethnicities, or recent immigrants. The Trades Union Congress estimates that one in five UK workers is low-paid with no collective representation.

Let's be clear, I am not claiming it's a life o' Riley for *any* workers. Right now, we are all taking a very serious kicking. But, as a UNISON[1] branch secretary who—like most of his union member comrades—is soon to retire, said to me recently, "I have a smile on my face and my tongue in my cheek.... We have to accept that we are living in a world where some of us will cope with these changes, and others who won't. And the ones that won't are not union members. We can only look after our own."

He's right. Down here we won't cope. Down here among the millions of private service-sector workers in the United Kingdom, only a tiny minority are unionized. Here, minimum wage—or less—is the norm. Largely unskilled and easily replaceable, often with short-term or "zero-hours" contracts, for us, insecurity is king. Subcontracted and on shifts throughout each of the 168 hours in every week, millions work more than one job just to get by. We rent a room from a private landlord in a house that used to be council-owned and affordable. We share with other families and get kicked out with only a month's notice. We claim benefits to supplement our income—if we're here legally—while our bosses make billions. The "management style" consists of threats, aggression, and intimidation while verbal abuse and sexual assault by customers and managers are commonplace. Half the time we don't even get paid, and we get sacked with no recourse. Consequently, a minority have unions, better conditions, and at least the potential for resistance (whether they appreciate that or not). The rest of us ain't got shit. In other words, we find ourselves in a situation with similarities to that which saw Chicago give birth to the IWW on June 24, 1905.

At that time just 5 percent of workers in the United States were unionized. If you were white, male, and skilled, you might have been a member of your trade—or "craft"—union. Representing only the men doing a specific job in a given industry, each of these unions "looked out for their own," leaving everybody else to fend for themselves. They were brought together in the elitist, conservative, and pro-capitalist American Federation of Labor (AFL). Women, migrants, and millions of laborers and unskilled, itinerant workers weren't welcome. The very few Black workers who were in unions were separated from the white workers by law.

New Relevance of the IWW to Workers

That was until 1905, when the radical Western Federation of Miners gathered three hundred socialists, anarchists, and other radical trade unionists in Chicago in what would forever after be known as the First Convention of the Industrial Workers of the World. The IWW was an aggressive challenge to the bosses—and the AFL. Hearts firmly on sleeves, WFM leader William "Big Bill" Haywood spelled out their purpose:

> Fellow Workers, this is the Continental Congress of the working-class. We are here to confederate the workers of this country into a working-class movement that shall have for its purpose the emancipation of the working-class from the slave bondage of capitalism. The aims and objects of this organization shall be to put the working-class in possession of the economic power, the means of life, in control of the machinery of production and distribution, without regard to capitalist masters.[2]

Toward this goal the union set about organizing all workers in each industry, regardless of race, gender, craft, religion, immigration status, or politics, into the same industrial union. These were to be part of the overall IWW, uniting all workers in "one big union" capable of overthrowing capitalism through a general strike, and managing the economy democratically afterward.

Seeking to empower the workers themselves, the IWW preferred to win disputes through militant, worker-led direct action instead of empowering "representatives" to bargain for them. Likewise, they ignored political representation, preferring strikes, sabotage, and boycotts. Their commitment to equality and solidarity was solid. While the right-wing media were shocked that the IWW "pushed their women to the front," IWW women retorted, "The IWW just didn't keep us at the back."[3] Famous IWW branches such as the Local 8 Philadelphia longshoremen's branch were led and almost exclusively made up of African Americans and migrant workers, and many migrants, as well as women, gained prominent leadership and organizing positions. Speaking to a timber workers union conference, Big Bill urged them to break the law and invite the African American workers to join them: "You work in the same mills together. Sometimes a black man and a white man chop down the same tree together. You are meeting in a convention now to discuss the conditions under which you labor. Why not be sensible about this and call the Negroes into the Convention? If it is against the law, this is one time when the law should be broken."[4] The timber workers agreed and later voted to join the IWW.

Following militant and successful strikes, such as the famous 1912 Lawrence, Massachusetts, textile workers strike, the union grew quickly. In 1913 it launched the Agricultural Workers Organization, gaining well over one hundred thousand members in two years, as full-time organizers brought in a hundred members a week each. The Lumber Workers Industrial Union came next, winning the eight-hour day with their 1917 strike, and from 1913 through the mid-1930s, the Marine Transport Workers Industrial Union organized thousands of longshoremen on ports around the United States and the rest of the world.

Unsurprisingly, the union faced an unparalleled level of suppression, led by employers and carried out by the U.S. government, media, police, military troops, and vigilantes—including the Ku Klux Klan. Members were kidnapped, assaulted, jailed for crimes they didn't commit, and murdered. With the IWW having publicly opposed the U.S. entry into World War I ("Capitalists of America, we'll fight against you, not for you!"), the government moved in for the kill in 1917. As IWW wage strikes took hold in the timber, farming, and distribution sectors—all vital to the war effort—the union was accused of treachery. Forty-eight union halls were raided, 165 people were arrested, and 108 faced trial for various crimes under the new Espionage Act, including nonmembers. All were found guilty and sentenced to twenty years in jail. Bill Haywood escaped to the Soviet Union, where he died a lonely, broken man. Violence and repression continued into the 1920s and a major split in 1924 marked the end of the IWW's heyday. As the new Congress of Industrial Organizations (CIO) picked up the mantle of industrial unionism—albeit a less radical version—it looked like the end of the IWW.

Yet almost a century later, in 1996, 1,300 people from thirty diverse communities were gathered together in York Hall, Bethnal Green, to "commit to working together for the common good," launching The East London Citizens Organisation (TELCO). Later expanding into London Citizens and then Citizens UK (the organization now has chapters across London as well as in Birmingham and Milton Keynes), TELCO pioneered the use of something akin to Alinskyist/ACORN-style community organizing in the UK. Building coalitions of faith and community groups, as well as trade union branches, by recruiting and training "leaders" who go on to organize and train other leaders, Citizens describes itself as "building the power of civil society."

Bankruptcy of Traditional U.S.-Style Unionism

Around the same time, British trade union leaders were waking up to the fact that corporate rebranding, prepaid credit cards, and other gimmicks were not enough to reverse the twenty-year decline in membership that had started in the 1980s. They decided to look stateside, where proponents of "the organizing model" and "new unionism" had, to some extent, triumphed over the "new realists," who preferred a more conservative and partnership-minded "service model." Put simply, where the "new realists" proposed to retain membership through good relations with the employer and the provision of services to the members, the "new unionists" proposed to reinject a "social movement feeling" into the unions by engaging workers themselves in running issue-based campaigns. This was to be achieved by heavy resourcing of full-time organizers who would engage workers one on one, identifying the issues they cared about and moving them to become increasingly active based on their own motivations and experience. Mobilization would build momentum, and gradually more and more workers would become active.

This model was largely conceived by the Service Employees International Union (SEIU), who in the mid-1980s launched the Justice for Janitors campaign, immortalized in Ken Loach's film *Bread & Roses* (the title a reference to the IWW's 1912 Lawrence textile strike). Justice for Janitors sought to mobilize "the active 1 percent" into vibrant and creative action that would draw others along, building the campaign. The campaign learned its creative direct-action tactics—as well as its slogan, "¡Si se puede!" ("Yes we can!" from the United Farm Workers of America [UFW]). From the late 1960s onward, the UFW had organized huge numbers of migrant farm workers through what has become known as "community unionism," using creative tactics pioneered by the IWW decades earlier. Through vibrant campaigns such as Justice for Janitors, the SEIU became the fastest-growing union in the United States, with 225,000 cleaners joining, not to mention home-care workers, health workers, and others. Unsurprisingly, UK union leaders started paying attention.

In 1998, the British Trades Union Congress launched its "Organising Academy," based on U.S. AFL-CIO Organizing Institute, purportedly to prepare and train gifted college graduates to recruit workers into unions.[5] Over the next ten years it would train 240 full-time organizers with a view to changing the culture within the unions and reinjecting that "social movement feeling." Partially successful, this development crossed paths with the community organizing initiated by TELCO and, with a little more inspiration from across the water, led to the launch of London's own "Justice for Cleaners" campaign. In 2000, TELCO leaders got together to discuss the U.S. "living wage" campaigns run by unions including the SEIU and community organizations such as ACORN, and agreed to work toward a similar campaign in the United Kingdom. In January 2001, the public service union UNISON asked the Family Budget Unit to calculate what would be a real "London living wage." In September that year TELCO published *Mapping Low Pay in East London* and in November hosted a thousand-strong assembly at York Hall, which heard the TUC general secretary restate the case for the living wage. The following month, activists occupied an HSBC bank branch to protest the low pay of cleaners at Canary Wharf. The London Living Wage campaigns had started.

A century before, the IWW had responded to the consolidation of economic power into fewer hands and bigger companies by stating the need for international organization on an industry-wide basis along the supply chain. Research by Jane Wills at Queen Mary University—the UK's first "living wage university"—tells us that if anything, this is truer today than ever. In an age of globalization and subcontracting, workers' actual employer might be several times and even thousands of miles removed from where the real power over their terms and conditions lies. In this reality, where "the market" (by which I mean a handful of billionaires) holds the real clout, traditional collective bargaining can be almost meaningless. Global industrial unions such as IndustriALL are one response to the situation and the London Living Wage campaigns are another.

London Living Wage Campaigns and Immigrant Self-Organizing

The London Living Wage Campaigns are led by London Citizens, a broad-based organization of more than eighty faith groups, trade union branches, schools and community organizations (including my own Department of Geography at Queen Mary, University of London). The campaign has pioneered new forms of community unionism within the UK. At its best, the campaign has worked by adopting a twin-track approach to labor organization. While trade unions (UNISON, in the case of the hospitals, and the Transport and General Workers Union Justice for Cleaners campaign in the case of Canary Wharf and the City) organized from below, recruiting workers to the campaign, the wider alliance simultaneously targeted the "real employers" in the NHS trusts, finance houses, and universities.[6]

From the word go in 2001, TELCO activists targeted the financial institutions of Canary Wharf, as many of TELCO's members worked as cleaners and security guards amid the glistening glass that has long since replaced the site of the 1912 dockworkers' strike. The T&G stationed two full-time organizers at Canary Wharf and began unionizing the cleaners. With the bureaucratic leaders of TELCO uncomfortable with the pressure from financial firms, the cleaners were forced to organize on their own without outside help against the subcontracted cleaning companies in the district. But London citizens weren't the only community that the T&G's Justice for Cleaners campaign mobilized.

A majority of the cleaners organized by the T&G were migrants, mostly of African and Latin American descent. The Latin American Workers Association (LAWAS) first existed in the 1980s but was relaunched in 2003, with its mission stating, "We are workers, we are Latin American, and we are immigrants. These are the pillars of our identity and why we fight." LAWAS was organized by and for Latin Americans living and working in the United Kingdom with a strong focus on education about workplace rights, union organization, and immigration issues. Starting out in parks and pubs, in 2004 LAWAS accepted the offer of an office and basic facilities in the T&G's building. Deeply connected to their community, particularly around the Elephant and Castle area of London, LAWAS became a major recruiter for the union. Despite not being an "official" part of the union's democracy, LAWAS spearheaded successful projects such as language classes and immigration rights assistance, significantly building T&G's reputation in the community.

Over the next few years, Justice for Cleaners and the broader London Living Wage campaigns achieved a series of high-profile victories. Jane Wills reported in 2007:

> The most significant victories cover more than 5,000 workers in London. These include 1,000 domestic and catering staff in east London hospitals, who are now paid the living wage... around 3,000 contract cleaners at Canary Wharf and in the City of London; at least 250 contract cleaning staff at Queen Mary and the London School of Economics... about 1,000 support staff working for Barclays Bank;

several hundred workers contracted to the GLA family, including Transport for London; and a smaller number contracted by third sector organisations such as the Child Poverty Action Group and the IPPR.[7]

With success after success, it looked pretty rosy, but these roses had thorns. Since the mid-1990s, U.S. union "reform movements" (union members' campaigns for greater internal democracy and member control) such as Teamsters for a Democratic Voice, and their supporters in the activist publication *Labor Notes*, had been critical supporters of "the organizing model" as it was actually being practiced. Willing to head into uncomfortable territory, their point was subtle but damned important. Yes, the model was a big improvement on the "powerful provider of services" model preached by the new realists. But, while it was succeeding in "organizing the un-organized" (or at least recruiting them), something at its core was a little off.

Organizers might rely on "member involvement" to build their campaigns, but in reality the campaigns remain theirs, with actual control in the hands of the full-time union organizers—and *their* bosses. With union leaders ultimately still tied to "partnership" with employers (in reality, no such thing), the militant posturing needs to be kept within limits. What might be occasionally sensible strategic reasoning is often not communicated to members and all they know is that tactics suddenly change on short notice with militancy turned off and on like a tap. There are only so many times you can be marched up the hill.

Paternalistic attitudes are common on the Left and the problem isn't just that it's patronizing. It's a thin line between organizing and educating in a spirit of solidarity (a real exchange among equals) and believing your own hype that these workers are vulnerable, *they* don't know their rights, *they* need *your* help. Sometimes, *they* just don't know what's good for 'em and *you've* got to keep control. Except that the workers who built LAWAS didn't just land from outer space. They were union activists in Chile and Colombia, lifelong fighters. The only naivety shown by these workers, if any, might have been that they believed the rhetoric of the unions—and the unions got more than they bargained for.

Justice for Cleaners Campaign

Problems in the Justice for Cleaners campaign arose when workers joined who didn't fit the strict strategic rules on which buildings and employers the campaign would focus on. Big buildings within certain areas fit the criteria, small ones elsewhere didn't, and when cleaners—including one LAWAS leader—tried to organize at the National Physics Laboratory, they got short shrift. The campaign was proving a little *too* successful, with the good news spreading by word of mouth in the community. What's more, workers no longer stick around for ten years in the same building. The cleaners work three jobs and move around regularly, with frustratingly little support from trade unions, understanding their legal and bureaucratic limitations as working-class organizations. When cleaners organized themselves at the BBC, the recognized union there (BECTU) refused to support them, accusing Unite (by this point formed by a merger of the T&G and Amicus unions) of stirring things up to poach members.

The problems got more serious when the victories began to ring hollow. The cleaners employed by Mitie at Willis Insurance Group won the London Living Wage in January 2008. But, in what's become a familiar move, the employer decided to cover the costs by changing shifts and reducing the staff, making fewer workers do more. As one senior cleaning industry figure told me, "We're not going to reduce our margins. It's that simple." Workers were moved about through negotiation (scattering the organized workforce in the process) and, after a temporary move, six were laid off. At this point the workers surprised the union—and the union didn't like it. Redundancy in the United Kingdom is usually met with resignation, but not this time. The cleaners leafleted the desks of the office workers and called protests, expecting the union's support. Instead, Unite "banned" their protests and told them to back off.

Meanwhile, Alberto Durango, a Colombian migrant and LAWAS volunteer, was a Unite shop steward at Schroders Bank, employed by Lancaster Office Cleaning. By arranging their own demonstrations—and despite being given the runaround by Unite—he and his colleagues resisted company plans to reduce the workforce, argued in court that his sacking was in retaliation for union organizing, and he was reinstated. At the same time, Alberto met the cleaners from Willis and others who felt the union wasn't up to scratch.

LAWAS began to get on Unite's nerves by unconditionally supporting all these cleaners' struggles, and pissed them off further by refusing to toe the line on immigration. The vast majority of cleaners organized by Unite (and other unions) were in the country legally. But the reality was that huge numbers of cleaners in London were (and are) undocumented—they don't join the union because they know the score. With the cleaners' campaign in full swing, employers decided to use the UK

Border Agency to instill a bit of fear, teaching these foreigners to pipe down. Immigration raids became common and LAWAS stated clearly what Unite refused to admit: border controls don't stop people from coming into the country, but they might just keep them docile while they're here. The raids were an open attack on the union.

In 2007, Citizens UK had launched Strangers into Citizens, a broad-based campaign to demand legal status for undocumented migrants who fulfilled certain criteria. Unite supported the campaign, but much to the union's annoyance, LAWAS took a view more suited to the needs of migrant workers, rejecting the criteria and making their point during the big Strangers into Citizens demonstrations by raising banners proclaiming, "No One Is Illegal." In 2008, as if to drum the LAWAS point home, Lancaster—angered by Alberto Durango's activism—called in the cops. Alberto was arrested and held for two days before being released without charge. While he was detained, police asked him about the campaign at Willis—where he didn't even work—and it became obvious to activists that a blacklist was at work. Alberto should have been able to return to work after being released, but Lancaster sacked him without justification.

The wrong workers were joining. They weren't grateful for their "living wage" when it meant they paid for it in reduced hours, and had to work with fewer employers, while working more intensely. They took action without permission and didn't do what they were told. They opposed border controls full stop. In short, they were a pain in the arse. And it was obviously LAWAS's fault. So, in 2009, Unite kicked LAWAS out of their office. The national officials told their subordinates they were not to support the Willis cleaners or Alberto Durango. When Chris Ford, a Unite branch organizer, who went on to mobilize support for the organizing drive, invited Alberto and the Willis cleaners to a meeting of the "United Left" caucus in Unite, they were told upon arrival that they had no platform to speak ("no-platformed"). The union went so far as to circulate a leaflet at the National Shop Stewards Network conference—in the name of Justice for Cleaners, despite not having been put to a vote of the branch—telling the rest of the movement not to support these extremist troublemakers. To these cleaners at least, their time in Unite had come to an end.

Revival of the IWW

Meanwhile, for the union that should have died in the 1920s, it had been touch and go. At various stages looking up, and then falling back on life support, the IWW had been kept alive thanks to romantic labor historians, true believers, and anticapitalist radicals. Maintaining a few union contracts in the United States and seeing small upswings in the 1960s and 1970s, the union was relaunched in the UK in the late 1990s. By 2005, there were a couple hundred Wobblies in the United Kingdom, general branches in a few major cities, and even one or two workplace branches (Leicester Adult Education College, for one). Branches typically discussed revolutionary politics and joined demonstrations by other unions and causes, but a 2007 organizing drive at a Sheffield cinema prompted the union to raise funds and apply for the Certificate of Independence needed to lawfully seek union recognition by an employer. This didn't happen in time and the cinema decided to recognize the GMB union in order to undermine the Wobblies. But, it *did* happen and, along with other organizational reforms led by syndicalists and trade union radicals, including the creation of a labor law/representation training program and centralized administration, the union was technically capable of the bare bones of workplace organization.

Throughout 2009–2010, the battles over Unite's Justice for Cleaners campaign were still raging. The Willis cleaners were holding weekly demonstrations and Alberto Durango was sacked by Lancaster for a second time, this time at United Bank of Switzerland. With Unite refusing support, the Left filled the void as radical trade unionists, Socialists, anarchists, Greens, and others—including London Wobblies—built the Cleaners Defense Committee (CDC), which organized demonstrations and other support for the Unite pariahs. When Alberto and the other LAWAS cleaners began to discuss leaving Unite, Wobblies in the CDC made a tentative suggestion.

The IWW promised a legal union structure ready and waiting, an anarchist culture that meant the cleaners would be free to organize as they liked, a militant outlook that would back up direct action, and a few hardworking volunteers to help with administration and training. Alberto was sold, but not everyone agreed. Some argued against "red unions," urging the cleaners to stay in Unite and fight; others proposed LAWAS itself register as a union, becoming a "Latin American Workers Union." Recognizing that the problems facing the cleaners were the same for cleaners of all nationalities, Alberto argued against this but was determined to leave Unite behind. IWW leaders, some with TUC (Trades Union Congress) union backgrounds, gave an honest appraisal of the union: "We told them, 'IWW is really small, we've got no money, no lawyers, etc. But we can do the admin and the training, we've got the legal structure you need and there are no paid bureaucrats; you can do what you want.'"

Some of this honesty came back to bite the Wobblies, and maybe other aspects were not fully appreciated by the cleaners' leaders, but in 2011, LAWAS members voted to leave Britain's biggest trade union for Britain's smallest and joined the Industrial Workers of the World. The IWW Cleaners Branch, as it became known (technically speaking it was the London IU640 Cleaning and Allied Industries Branch), was initially formed by around forty cleaners and a few other LAWAS members, while Unite was winding down its Justice for Cleaners campaign. For a while, not much happened, but when it did it carried echoes of IWW history and in a fitting setting, too.

London's opulent Guildhall was built between 1411 and 1440 as a powerful symbol of England's elite upper classes. In 2011 the cleaners working in the Guildhall were employed by subcontractor Oceans and paid minimum wage—when they were paid. London Citizens had previously uncovered that Oceans cleaners at one London university had worked without being paid for months—these workers eventually reclaimed some fifty thousand pounds in owed wages—and the same was true at the Guildhall. Added to the constant management bullying and petty discipline that would never happen in other industries, the workers had had enough.

The famous IWW Lawrence textile strike of 1912 wasn't organized by the IWW, at least not at first. Just as cleaners at the start of the twenty-first century find their living wage victories undermined by staff layoffs, longer hours, and more work, the early-twentieth-century mill workers of Lawrence, Massachusetts, feared they would end up paying for a new law shortening the working week. True enough, when this apparently positive law was enacted, at least one mill owner reduced his workers' wages. The Polish women in his mill walked out and were joined by twenty thousand migrant mill workers around the town within the week. Local IWW organizers were on the scene quickly and assumed leadership, organizing a strike committee of leaders from each of the ethnic groups—but it was the workers who started the strike.

At 5:30 a.m. on June 14, 2011, the Guildhall cleaners turned up for work—and stopped right there. Taking organized wildcat strike action, they refused to work until their wages were paid. Thanks to the LAWAS grapevine, and showing the value of locally rooted community unionism, when the workers repeated their strike the next morning Alberto Durango and a fellow IWW organizer were there to meet them. The workers joined the IWW on the spot and when the union's use of the normal grievance procedure failed to produce results, the IWW called for a day of action. On July 15, the cleaners again refused to work for free, while, in what would become Cleaners Branch standard practice, a noisy demonstration of other cleaners, IWW members, and trade unionists from elsewhere rattled the management from outside. Alberto, Chris Ford, and three Guildhall cleaners entered negotiations with the extremely annoyed managers and came out victorious.

Over the following year, the migrant workers of the IWW Cleaners Branch took on neoliberal capitalism and won. Going from strength to strength, the scrappy little DIY union organized hundreds of workers into campaigns, saved jobs, and won wage rises while protecting terms and conditions. In an age of austerity, across the secretive and frankly very strange world of the City of London, David was quite successfully kicking the crap out of Goliath.

Or at least that's how it was painted from the outside. To some extent that was true; but inside the new movement tensions were brewing as "egos and megaphones"—to paraphrase techno DJ and ex-IWW activist Teknocracy—battled it out.

While the campaign at the Guildhall continued for almost a year with demands for a London Living Wage, removal of racist, bullying management, and recognition of the IWW union for collective bargaining purposes, other campaigns seemed to start almost weekly. During 2011 Alberto Durango got a new job with cleaning contractor LCC at Heron Tower and set to work organizing a campaign for the London Living Wage. A quick victory followed, as the company agreed at first and then tried to cut hours, backing down in the face of IWW demonstrations. Meanwhile, activists from the IWW's London General Membership Branch, LAWAS, the Justice for Cleaners campaign, and the anarcho-syndicalist Solidarity Federation were running workers' advice clinics, language exchanges, and arts events, all of which brought new members into the Cleaners Branch. Other contacts came directly via Alberto, as word of mouth often led angry workers to his door.

IWW and Occupy London

In late 2011, the IWW was joined by Occupy London activists to demonstrate outside the Old Bailey, where one pregnant worker had been abused, her husband, a cleaning worker, sacked, and another woman bullied so badly she went to hospital. The demonstration and union negotiations succeeded in removing the managers in question. Back at the Guildhall, the minimum-wage cleaners joined an international day of action against the new contractor, Sodexo, demanding the London Living Wage. In what would become another trademark move, the union secured a supportive Early Day Motion in the Houses of Parliament from left-wing Labour MP John McDonnell, drawing attention to the cause. However, as the new contractor bullied union activists out of their jobs, discussed recognition with the more amenable GMB union, and a winter sit-in by a handful of workers looked increasingly desperate, the IWW Cleaners Branch hit its first brick wall. Not that many people noticed except the workers, presumably, as new campaigns came thick and fast and the inexperienced majority of IWW activists struggled to keep up.

In early 2012, Alberto was once again sacked from his job as a new contractor took over at Heron Tower, refusing to honor the previous agreement despite the UK's TUPE (Transfer of Undertakings/Protection of Employment) legislation. At the same time, the IWW was launching London Living Wage campaigns at Exchange Tower and Thomson Reuters in Canary Wharf, as well as at NTT Communications in the City. When the entire cleaning workforce at NTT was viciously sacked in response to their campaign, they joined a noisy and militant demonstration outside Heron Tower demanding Alberto's reinstatement, along with the then RMT[8] regional organizer Steve Hedley and other left-wing trade union leaders. These union leaders, as well as John McDonnell, MP, lent vocal support to most IWW campaigns throughout 2012, regularly billed as speakers on demonstrations, but their presence was not always comfortable for some anarchist members of the IWW.

Within weeks, the contractor at NTT had bottled it, reinstated the sacked cleaners, and met their demand for a London Living Wage. Meanwhile, Alberto's ex-bosses reached a settlement agreement with him. Over at Canary Wharf, the cleaners at Thomson Reuters and Exchange Tower were suffering severe bullying and intimidation, with managers at the former screaming at their workers, "Are you stupid?" and telling them, "If you want to earn more, go get another job." However, with Early Day Motions in Parliament and militant demonstrations on the streets, on top of recent victories at Guildhall, NTT, and Heron Tower, Exchange Tower soon gave in, removing managers and paying the London Living Wage. Managers at Thomson Reuters were also removed, although the Living Wage campaign doesn't seem to have been successful there (information on unsuccessful Cleaners Branch campaigns is hard to come by), despite the cleaners' winning the support of the National Union of Journalists, which represents Thomson Reuter's journalists.

Internally though, tensions were building. Alberto initiated the removal of non-cleaners and professional activists from the Cleaners Branch. Some of those removed—female LAWAS activists—have suggested that the close presence of white, male professional activists was never challenged but rather appreciated. However, those white males (strictly speaking) never had a vote as members of the branch (though their informal influence is obvious). In any case, it was only a few months later that Alberto left LAWAS and the Cleaners Branch after more disagreements.

In the wider union, strict anarchist members were uncomfortable with organizational and administrative reforms initiated by others. Despite the fact that these reforms—such as an improved administration, the adoption of direct-debit for dues payments, and the attempt to create "departments" to take on specific functions—were accepted by the union's delegate democracy, many felt that IWW officers were overstepping the mark and centralizing power. In fact many of the reforms were designed to improve democracy and participation (or at least facilitate worker organization at a shop-floor level), but ideological perceptions led to conflicts nonetheless.

Arguments often revolved around disagreements over the political relevance of practical actions. Does doing this or that contradict principles? Does it endanger or enhance the democracy of the union? These turned into battles—often waged on e-mail threads—between more dogmatic members and others (both anarchist and non-anarchist) and frequently became bitterly personal. In late 2011, the Cleaners Branch attended a meeting at the Houses of Parliament organized by John McDonnell. Plenty of anarchists declared that attending breached IWW principles and endangered the revolutionary potential of the union; others were sure this positively raised the profile of the Cleaners Branch and pointed to the historical IWW's regular attendance at governmental meetings to argue their corner. The appearance of conflict—Wobblies against Wobblies—which appeared openly on the internet ratcheted tensions further.

Long and Arduous Path to Victory

Meanwhile, the sudden necessity to "do the business" created an almost constant state of panic among leading IWW activists. Legal casework for Cleaners Branch members, engaged exclusively by Chris Ford, Alberto, and one or two others, became a point of contention. While there were attempts to train reps among the workforce and develop shop stewards in the workplace, in reality these never really came to fruition, with branch leaders having to dedicate the vast majority of their time to campaigning. Volunteers from LAWAS and the General Membership Branch tried to help, but they lacked experience or organizational ability, meaning casework wasn't done properly, organizing opportunities were not spotted, and activists burned out. Worst of all, occasionally volunteers failed to show up to run the regular workers' advice clinics, leaving disgruntled workers waiting for hours—and sometimes even failed to show up to members' hearings. The union was running before it could walk, but Chris, Alberto, and the Cleaners Branch had little time for baby steps.

In 2009, a group of bus drivers had left Unite to join the militant Rail, Maritime and Transport Union. The RMT, however, had a century-old demarcation agreement with Unite and honored this, refusing to support its new members. While some of the drivers created their own union, others joined the IWW, forming a Bus Workers Branch. In 2010–11 the IWW sanctioned the creation of the London Regional Committee, bringing together delegates of the Cleaners Branch and the Bus Workers Branch (the newly created national Print and Creative Workers Branch pulled back for reasons that other leading Wobblies came to appreciate later). With tensions high and the General Membership Branch under "assessment" (an ad hoc procedure whereby the national union would investigate the administrative and financial procedures of a branch), those involved in the London Regional Committee decided not to accept their membership.

IWW officers were accused of enforcing the rules when it suited them (i.e., forcing an "assessment" procedure on the General Membership Branch) but ignoring them at other times. Maybe this was true to some extent, but IWW officers have responded that someone had to be first, and that the assessment procedure would eventually be used to ensure all branches met their responsibilities. It seems the truth is that IWW officers were just as concerned about the local officers running the Regional Committee and the Cleaners Branch as they were about the General Membership Branch.

The difference was that the former two were central to the serious workers' campaigns kicking off across the city, and to the consequent perceived development of the IWW. Crucially, as any experienced organizer understands, they also had the personal contact with the workers.

Despite other Wobblies attending Cleaners Branch protests and parties, in reality Chris and Alberto were the organizers and few others knew the people one to one. The gulf in activity between the Cleaners Branch and the rest of the union became a serious concern for the union's officers, who privately discussed the possibility that Chris and Alberto might eventually lead a split, but decided that without serious one-to-one contact and organizational relationships with the workers there was little they could do about it in the short term.

Cleaning Workers' Organizing Unions

Regardless of these internal difficulties, IWW campaigns continued to kick off. In March, protests were held outside Bloomberg, where an IWW activist had been placed under surveillance by the contractor Oceans and was threatened with being sacked for "encouraging her workmates to join a union." The company backed down following protests, and the IWW represented other workers in grievances around bullying and racism.

March 2012 also saw the first serious attempt to bridge the gap between the needs of the very real union campaigns being waged in London and the lack of experience and appreciation of the situation within the rest of the IWW. Proposed by the Cleaners Branch (though originally suggested by other IWW leaders), the 2012 IWW Strategy Conference brought together around 10 percent of the union's membership to debate the future of the IWW. Despite initial membership suspicions of a setup and betrayal, the conference proved a positive and useful event, helping to heal rifts; the membership reached agreements to prioritize organizing in nonunionized workplaces, prioritize training and the building of industrial branches ahead of general membership branches, and consider paying union organizers in the future. However, a motion to become a "sovereign union, the Industrial Workers of Great Britain," failed.

May brought a high-profile campaign at St. George's Hospital, University of London, as workers—suffering the usual low pay and bullying management—and their supporters held noisy and militant demonstrations, organized a three-hundred-strong online petition, and secured the familiar Early Day Motion in Parliament. They eventually won the London Living Wage with no threat to hours or workloads. Not for the first time though, the campaign brought the IWW into conflict with another union, as UNISON claimed they had campaigned for and won the wage rise as the recognized union. This prompted at least some cleaners to deny this in a public statement defending their IWW union, while Chris was put under pressure at his day job educating trade union reps at the Workers' Educational Association.

In early June, the rhythms of the Cleaners Branch samba band, which appeared at demonstrations, were echoing off the walls of the London School of Economics as cleaners harangued the facilities manager in a protest against reduction of hours and bullying. Later that month cleaners were outside the Royal Bank of Canada, where cleaners had been promised the living wage but were not being paid it, and instead were facing cuts to hours, extreme increases in workload, and what they described as "racist bullying"; the whole workforce was allegedly sacked after they joined the IWW. And, on the last weekend of the month, the rhythms of the drums, horns, and chants of the IWW Cleaners Branch were drowning out the noise of traffic and consumerism on Oxford Street, outside the flagship store of the famous UK retailer John Lewis.

John Lewis, hailed by deputy prime minister Nick Clegg as a "model for the British economy," makes ethical capital out of the fact that it is a cooperative, with "partners" all sharing in the profits—and the running—of the business. But the cleaners are subcontracted and don't share these rights; John Lewis contracted the broker MML, which in turn contracted the cleaning company ICM, which in turn is owned by the multinational Compass Group. Like their fellow workers across the city, the John Lewis cleaners were earning minimum wage and facing 50 percent job cuts and 50 percent workload increases. The campaign began familiarly enough, with loud and proud protests outside the store, scarlet flags, and vuvuzelas, along with an Early Day Motion in Parliament. Then, for the first time in the United Kingdom, the union announced it was going to ballot for strike action—just as the Olympic Games were set to bring thousands of extra consumers into the capital.

With an 80 percent turnout and 90 percent "yes" vote, the ballot result was solid and the date for the first strike was set. On July 13, 2012, twenty-eight cleaners refused to work. They were joined as usual by between fifty and one hundred supporters, including other cleaners, other Wobblies, students, anarchists, Socialists, and other trade unionists. Ignoring the United Kingdom's antiunion laws, the organizers sent flying pickets of supporters to other stores while demonstrators, including RMT regional organizer Steve Hedley, led an invasion of the store. A second day of strike action and protests took place the following Friday, with police protecting the store and flying pickets sent to the head office.

Although the Cleaners Branch had been steadily gaining media coverage throughout the last year, the strike at John Lewis was breaking news. This famously "ethical" employer, a favorite of the British middle classes, was treating its migrant cleaners as second-class citizens—and they were fighting back. Coverage wasn't just confined to the left-of-center *Guardian* and *Independent*. Favorable reporting appeared in the right-wing, Murdoch-owned *Sun*—Britain's most-purchased newspaper—and videos were broadcast on the BBC. John Lewis partners even appeared in online videos criticizing their employer for its treatment of the cleaners. Passersby were shocked by the banner stating, "CEO = £300 PER HOUR, CLEANER = £6.19 PER HOUR, JUSTICE?" but it was the leaflet distributed, featuring two union logos, that raised Wobblies' own eyebrows. The first logo was the famous universal label of the IWW. The second was a new logo, one for the "Industrial Workers of Great Britain."

The split was announced by Chris Ford in the press release declaring the workers' victory. Though a living wage had proved a step too far, the cleaners had resisted the job cuts and won a 10 percent pay raise, backdated three months. Wobblies should have been celebrating. Yet in the same moment, Chris announced that the victory was being used as "a springboard to relaunch the Industrial Workers of Great Britain." The IWGB was first launched in 1909 by supporters of the Workers' International Industrial Union; originally as a split from the IWW led by the U.S. socialist Daniel Deleon in 1908, after demanding that the union adopt "political means" in addition to direct action. After growing rapidly around Glasgow, and playing a role in the start of the Red Clydeside period, the IWGB had disappeared by the mid-1920s. Chris claimed the Cleaners Branch had decided to relaunch in this way, having "outgrown the activist network that is the IWW."

Over the next few weeks, Chris and Alberto claimed that the Cleaners Branch, along with the London Regional Committee as a whole, had democratically agreed to this move. It looked as if the cleaners who had left a big union for a small one were now leaving for an even smaller one. But gradually it became evident that the reality was far hazier. Bus drivers and printers came forward to say they had never agreed to the move and, for what it was worth, were still Wobblies. Other cleaners came forward with complaints about a lack of democracy in the running of the Cleaners Branch. While even leading Wobblies seem unsure of where the truth lies, it seems likely to be somewhere in between, with one cleaner telling me, "Meetings were held but never very formal. The workers who came were whichever ones had a campaign at that time."

More confusion seems to have been created by arguments about what would happen to Cleaners Branch finances, as when Chris announced the split the IWW moved fast to secure its members' assets. It appears that this subject is still touchy. Regardless, it also seems that who was or wasn't a member was never quite clear (another echo of the IWW's ramshackle history) and, for this reason, while there were definitely some who followed Chris and Alberto into their new organization, a large number of others remained members of the IWW, possibly without even knowing the split had even occurred. As internet wars—and discomfort between activists in London—continued in the background, the IWW Cleaners Branch was alive but severely injured.

Two months later, the IWW got an e-mail. A cleaning supervisor working at Peter Jones in Sloan Square, London—another flagship store owned by John Lewis—wanted to meet someone from the union. A young African named Kwesi met IWW activist Tom in the Square and led him into the store through the partners' entrance, up in a service elevator, through corridors, and eventually into a tiny office, where Kwesi's five cleaning supervisor colleagues were waiting. They worked at four John Lewis sites across South London, including a major distribution depot and the company's head office in Victoria, as well as the famous Peter Jones store. Cleaners from Peter Jones had effectively scabbed the Oxford Street IWW strike in July, but they said they didn't really understand what they were doing—cleaners are moved around regularly.

The cleaners at these four sites were unaffected by the Oxford Street victory—with the exception that they were now angry. They, too, were on minimum wage (the supervisors were paid between £6.70 and £8.00 per hour, randomly) and suffering from cut hours and increased workloads. Adding insult to injury, their manager had laughed off their complaints, telling them "Latin Americans might strike, but you Africans won't" (they weren't all African, for starters). Tom told them every single one would need to join the IWW and be ready to strike; he recommended they think it over and meet him again the following day. Kwesi greeted him the next afternoon with signed forms for 95 percent of cleaners at the four sites, saying the sites were united, they would refuse to negotiate separately, and they needed to use the Christmas shopping period for maximum leverage. The campaign was on.

IWW Solidarity Unionism for the Twenty-First Century

In typical IWW fashion, the Wobblies flew by the seat of their pants. Having never done this before, Tom spent hours on the phone to a mainstream union organizer friend of his (who had been instrumental in forming the IWW Cleaners Branch in the first place), stitching together the legal complexities and procedures in his head and snatching copies of templates used by the other unions to hop the legal hurdles placed in the way of protected industrial action in the United Kingdom. The time frame was tight. It was already October and to be able to threaten industrial action in the run-up to Christmas and the January sales, the union should have submitted their pay claim already—but it was just about doable.

The pay claim was sent, demanding the same backdated 10 percent pay raise that had been won at Oxford Street and a time frame for discussions toward a living wage and full sick pay. The multinational Compass Group sent its HR guy to buy Tom breakfast while insisting that each site be discussed separately. The cleaners refused and the company bottled it, pledging to meet with four representatives. In late October, all six of the cleaning supervisors (they insisted) sat around the table with Tom, ICM management, and the Compass Group HR man.

The debate went in circles, until one of the cleaners finally lost her temper: "Pay us fairly or we'll fucking strike!" This is the real promise of the Wobblies in the twenty-first century: ordinary people, denied power for so long, feeling fully emboldened by the direct experience of their own collective strength and—metaphorically or otherwise—giving the big boys a bloody nose.

Two weeks later the IWW Cleaners Branch declared a dispute and served notice of their intention to ballot. Just as the election ballot was about to be sent to the membership, the company called them back in. The managing director made an offer, the cleaners rejected it, and, ten minutes later, they had won: a 10 percent pay raise for the cleaners, backdated five months, and a wage of at least £8.00 per hour for all supervisors.

Minutes later, outside in the courtyard, Tamy was on the phone, cheering and shouting. "We won!"

Kwesi, smiling broadly, leaned over to amaze Tom. "She hasn't even won anything. She was already on £8.00 per hour." And that is the reality of a true twenty-first-century Wobbly, someone who might never have heard the slogan, but who sure as hell knows the meaning of "An injury to one is an injury to all."

So, what now for the One Big Union? Well, for starters, the members of the Cleaners Branch weren't the only Wobblies to be organizing and fighting back over the last two years. In late 2011, an IWW group was formed at a university just west of London. Initially a small group of "dual-carder" (i.e., members of both the IWW and their relevant TUC union) academics and library staff, the university IWW group kicked off when the cleaners—subcontracted, demanding proper contracts, and sick of bullying, nepotism, and payroll problems—joined up. Less gung-ho than some of the Cleaners Branch leaders, but a great organizer and equally committed to collective direct action, the academic worker-organizer at the university gave the cleaners the options via their one English-speaking colleague, ranging from a legalistic grievance procedure to wildcat direct action, stating the benefits of direct action but also making clear the dangers. The Polish cleaners laughed. "We were in Solidarity! The police beat us very hard, over and over again, but we kept fighting. We are not afraid."

The wildcat strike took the university by storm. The mainstream unions attacked the Wobblies, the HR team didn't know which way to turn, and the workers won their contracts. Over the following year, the university IWW has begun a student- and worker-led campaign for a living wage, dealt with several instances of bullying, and has recently managed to secure the removal of at least one of the culprits. What's more, Somalian cleaners have recently joined their Polish fellow workers in the union, and one of them has recruited other cleaners around the local area to the IWW. This, in turn, has led to the union's recruiting Somali cleaners in a prestigious West London Catholic high school as well as workers in the retail sector. These developments are encouraging, as they show the union slowly trying to build its reach within the local community and beyond the university that was its starting point.

Back in London, activists primarily from the London General Membership Branch have organized a high-profile campaign at BMA House, the headquarters and conferencing facilities owned by the British Medical Association. The campaign for a living wage and union recognition has yet to achieve its main goals, but it has seen workers holding demonstrations, gained nearly six hundred signatures on a petition, spurred members of the public to write to newspapers on its behalf, and gained the support of many BMA branches and members. Despite intimidation from management, the majority of the cleaners are now IWW members and have recently collectively petitioned their employer to protest what they maintain is the unfair dismissal of one of their colleagues.

Meanwhile, as I write this chapter, the London IWW is launching a campaign to secure the reinstatement of a bus driver and IWW rep who has been sacked, officially because of a disagreement with a motorist but more likely because he has been instrumental in drumming up resistance among drivers to new, inferior contracts and the "race-to-the-bottom" creation of a two-tier workforce, itself a consequence of privatization. In other areas, Pizza Hut workers in Sheffield organized an international day of protest, winning a nationwide increase in their mileage compensation as well as new health and safety equipment (in a return to the past of Wobbly sabotage, anonymous workers contributed to the latter victory by smashing up their old, damaged equipment, forcing management to replace it). In a Bristol community center, workers are organizing around health and safety issues and demanding union recognition, while in Reading and London, shop workers have won their jobs back after being unfairly dismissed, won back their unpaid wages, and secured the removal of bullying managers.

But I think this is just the tip of the iceberg of the IWW's potential today. Any historical comparisons I have drawn throughout this piece are not coincidence. Analogies between the economic and social realities at the beginnings of the twentieth and twenty-first centuries, as well as the needs of a model of union organization that suits those realities, have real merit. Sure, everything *looks* different; we lead different lives, with new technologies, fancy clothes, and stuff like that. But substantively we're in a very similar position. Globalized and consolidated corporate power, expansion of massive inequality, global migration, a rapidly shifting and changing economy, low pay, job insecurity, low skills, low union density (not to mention organization), especially in the unskilled sectors—all these elements are parallels.

The IWW has a lot to offer: an international, supply-chain based vision; a unionism that is 100 percent based on empowering ordinary workers via the life-changing experience of taking collective direct action; a rough-and-ready message that speaks to the experience, levels of education, and languages of our people; and a cultural "union way of life" that provides real social and emotional value to people. Maybe those are the lasting lessons of the original "new unionism," introduced by the Wobblies and other industrial syndicalist movements of a century ago.

If one looks a bit deeper and there's another side to these historical movements that is often overlooked. In hindsight, they might appear quite rough-and-ready, ramshackle, and based on a raw militancy and direct-action spirit. But for its time the IWW was intensely modern, futuristic even. The original Wobblies studied the power structure of the industries they wanted to organize, understood the weak links, and mirrored the organization of their employers. They stuck stickers on boxcars, sang popular songs, and used theatre; today they would be all over Twitter and YouTube, making agitprop for the twenty-first century. If a strike historically could be started by a rumor, and social media has coordinated street protests and revolutions across the world, then could union members spark and coordinate self-organized wildcat action via the amplification of their outrage on Twitter?

Most importantly, what might have appeared chaotic and out of control was actually a reflection of a sophisticated understanding, something that teachers, managers, systems theorists, social media marketers, union organizers, and even governments are talking about today. The role of social media in recent "horizontal" movements from Cairo to Wall Street, London to Madrid, has led commentators from Paul Mason to Carne Ross to study the dynamics of "the network." To build a powerful collective takes a deep engagement with the individual; the people's actions are based on a balance of their motivations and their fears. The job of the organizer is to shift that balance, ensuring that the people's experiences strengthen their motivations and diminish their fear. The IWW's focus on mass leadership development through education on the job and empowerment through collective direct action (as opposed to "one-step-removed" representation)—and "self-ownership" of that action—demonstrates the IWW is best suited for shifting the balance away from fear in favor of motivation. Only when the workers can't be controlled will they be able to control their world. An IWW organizer wrote recently,

> Right now, the majority of the left (radical and less so) are conservative, scared, stuck in ideas and traditions that are taken for granted. The working class movement is in crisis, the unions are stuck, and it's time for a radical, futuristic view. The basic social relationship of capitalism remains the same, but the organisation of society and the economy, not to mention our own "employers," is very different even to what it was even 20 years ago. Fuck catching up, we should be setting the new agenda.... The IWW's growth and success, and its role as a space to experiment, is exciting. We're getting slaughtered; we've got to do something, we've got to shake things up. Whatever the future holds; right now, the Wobblies are back.[9]

CHAPTER 13

Against Bureaucratic Unions: U.S. Working-Class Insurgency and Capital's Counteroffensive

Immanuel Ness

The American political economy is characterized by a procedural form of democracy that emerged in the late eighteenth century to serve the interests of business and capital. While a range of socialist ideologies gained the allegiance of workers, students, and intellectuals from the late nineteenth century to the present, state opposition has always imperiled the development of democratic organizations of working people. This chapter argues that, by embracing collective bargaining through the National Labor Relations Act (NLRA) of 1935 and the Democratic Party, organized labor deprived workers of their capacity to contest capitalist and state power. The class compromise with capital closed out any possibility for building a mass-based labor movement. Rather than advancing the interests of workers, the NLRA accords circumscribed workers' aspirations for democratic syndicalist and autonomist unions.

Redefining Class Compromise

In examining the long-term failure of organized labor from the 1930s to the present we must note the capitalist state's fierce opposition to an organic autonomous workers' movement that formed among unions affiliated with the Industrial Workers of the World in the early twentieth century. In the absence of an authentic labor party, union leaders set a tragic course that marginalized a militant workers' movement after the rise of the Soviet Union in the 1920s. In effect, since the 1930s, no faction or tendency in organized labor outside of the cadre of union leaders in the Communist Party and then the Democratic Party has had a significant role in the political system. Instead, self-organized workers expressed dissent through wildcat strikes and, from the 1980s to the present day, through direct action and tactical procedures in the workplace, often meeting severe force and sanctions by capital, the state, and their own traditional unions.[1] From the mid-1930s through World War II worker-activists and union organizers who were instrumental in building insurgent unions were forced out or left newly formed industrial unions, disillusioned by the centralization of power and the erosion of syndicalist rank-and-file power on the shop floor. As local control waned, national unions became more and more beholden to management and government cooperation. The growth of a bureaucracy within organized labor in the years following the labor insurgency of the 1930s constrained worker self-activity. This set the stage for organized labor to remove leftist organizations and also jettison almost all support for genuine rank-and-file workers' movements in the imperial world.

Alternatives

From its inception in 1905 the IWW represented the primary alternative to contract unionism over the first two decades of the twentieth century. Over the next fifteen years IWW members and activists engaged in a genuine form of democracy that provided the basis for the mass-industrial model adopted by the American Federation of Labor (AFL) and Congress of Industrial Organizations (CIO). Adhering to militant tactics that recognized the pressure points within business and the dominant state, the Wobblies unleashed a model of labor unionism that conferred power upon workers rather than union bosses. Wobblies privileged the working class over the party, and its unions were impelled to respond to workers rather than impose strictures on obedient members. Their model eschewed differences in all phases of working-class life, from craft unionism in mass production to racial, ethnic, and gender differences among workers. Fiercely opposed by capital, by reformists such as Daniel DeLeon of the Socialist Labor Party, and by the AFL, the IWW model of wall-to-wall working-class organization was soon recognized by traditional unions as the most effective means of challenging capital and state hegemony.[2]

The IWW practiced class struggle through the equivalent of workers' councils: in the community and at the point of production, disavowing the legitimacy of the state and at the same time recognizing that any agreement with business was temporary. Branch unions of the IWW vigorously negotiated with employers but were never deluded that agreements would permanently lead to labor peace with the capitalist class. They knew that capital and business would always seek to erode the strength of workers. As such, they embraced a policy of sabotage, direct action, and the general strike as a means to counter corporate hegemony. The IWW also advocated the organization of the entire working class beyond the factory gates—including precarious workers employed in hotels and restaurants, and even those employed casually. Although Melvyn Dubofsky has disparaged IWW tactics as whimsical, flawed, and lacking the capacity to sustain and consolidate a mass workers' movement, the early twentieth-century syndicalist model of mass-production workers' organization was ultimately adopted by the AFL unions.[3] Rejecting union hierarchy and centralization of leadership, the IWW achieved major gains for U.S. workers into the 1930s, as organizing marginalized workers in transportation, mining, agriculture, and other key industries represented an alternative to the traditional unionism consecrated by the New Deal. Traditional unions expanded dramatically and achieved continuous wage gains for their members through disciplining activist workers. As Nelson Lichtenstein shows, after CIO unions relinquished the right to strike during World War II, national and local leaders had to contend with the militancy of disgruntled members who opposed incentive schemes and the prohibition of strikes.[4] The AFL and CIO policies of compromise were rejected by members almost immediately after they were formed, evidenced by the sit-down strikes of 1937–1938, unauthorized wildcat strikes during World War II, and rank-and-file activity.

No doubt organized labor went on to improve their wages and conditions and militant leaders gained greater voice in mass production industries, but they also ceded their power as labor bureaucrats collaborated with FDR, the Democratic Party, and big business. The NLRA ushered in a descent into labor-management collaboration severely restricting worker rights that accelerated from the 1970s to the present. While under the NLRA traditional unions may plan the terms of a contract to provide ultimate leverage, they are bound by restrictions on their right to strike during the course of the contract. Worse still, over the ensuing eight years, most unions surrendered their right to strike even if the employer violated the terms of the contract. In the postwar era even as the strike remained among the most potent means of building workers' power, most unions have signed away the right or are unwilling to use it. From the 1970s to the 2010s, the suppression of rank-and-file unions by capital, the state, and organized labor sapped working-class enthusiasm for joining existing trade unions that denied them an independent voice to improve wages and conditions in their workplaces.

Traditional Union Conservatism and the No-Strike Pledge

The no-strike pledge represents the conservatism of organized labor as embodied in the NLRA, especially in the CIO. Comparing labor militancy and labor organization during World Wars I and II and the postwar era reveals the shifting terrain that workers faced during both conflicts and the possibilities for mass working-class militancy.

The apogee of strike activity among U.S. workers occurred after World War I and World War II, periods when the federal government, national union federations, and management thwarted any work stoppages in the burgeoning organized sectors of the economy that would interfere with war production. Upon U.S. entry into World War II, a no-strike pledge was exchanged by trade unions in exchange for a no-lockout pledge by management. The agreement was sanctioned by the Roosevelt administration as well as AFL and CIO unions, given that the United States was fighting with the Allies against Nazi Germany and that any drop in U.S. production might adversely interfere with the war effort.[5]

The American working class has had a proclivity for direct action through strikes and work stoppages to improve conditions, which continued after the passage of the NLRA in 1935 and even after the end of World War II (Table 13.1). Even as democratic rights were restricted by the state, management, and unions, militant workers retained a strong militancy even in the height of war. While World War II work stoppages were not sanctioned by AFL and CIO unions, as of 1944 thousands of workers in various industries nonetheless went on strike without union authorization, in demand of wage increases, which had been frozen by FDR for the duration of the conflict. In the postwar era union contracts often included provisions outlawing the right to strike even when employers violated collective bargaining agreements. By the early 1980s, after President Ronald Reagan authorized the use of replacement workers for striking air traffic controllers, even if union leaders were willing to authorize strikes, they had lost their capacity to improve conditions and wages for their members due to a growth of sanctions against workers, and their unions engaged in direct action and strikes.

From the beginning of the twentieth century until the 1980s, U.S. unions and workers had more work stoppages that tended to last longer than industrial countries in Europe. In the five years preceding World War II, many workers and unions engaged in mass strikes throughout the economy, including sit-downs, for union recognition and new contracts to increase wages and improve working conditions.

TABLE 13.1 Work stoppages involving 1,000 or more workers, 1947–2011

Year	Number of work stoppages	Number of workers involved* (thousands)	Number of days idle** (thousands)
1947	270	1,629	25,720
1950	424	1,698	30,390
1955	363	2,055	21,180
1960	222	896	13,260
1965	268	999	15,140
1970	381	2,468	52,761
1975	235	965	17,563
1980	187	795	20,844
1985	54	324	7,079
1990	44	185	5,926
1995	31	192	5,771
2000	39	394	20,419
2005	22	100	1,736
2010	11	45	302

* Number of workers involved includes only those workers who participated in work stoppages that began in the calendar year. Workers are counted more than once if they are involved in more than one stoppage during the reference period. Numbers are rounded to the nearest thousand.
** Days idle include all stoppages in effect during the reference period. For work stoppages that are still ongoing at the end of the calendar year, only those days of idleness in the calendar year are counted.

Source: Derived from U.S. Bureau of Labor Statistics (2012). Work stoppages involving 1,000 or more workers, 1947–2011. http://www.bls.gov/news.release/archives/wkstp_02082012.htm

World War I: Federal Government Responses to Labor Militancy

The United States did not enter World War I (1914–1918) until April 1917. During the World War I era, labor unions in the United States engaged in an upsurge of strikes as demand for munitions expanded and workers demanded increased wages and advanced the effort to establish the eight-hour workday. In addition, labor shortages in key industries essential for advancing the U.S. war effort increased the power of worker demands. Workers who were members of the International Association of Machinists (IAM) were prominent in the major wave of strikes and collective bargaining at a time when craft labor was integral to military industries, and Democratic president Woodrow Wilson was more sympathetic than his predecessors to the legitimacy of labor unions. President Wilson signed the Clayton Antitrust Act of 1914, restricting employer court injunctions and antitrust lawsuits against strikes and other forms of labor union–concerted activities. The passage of bills supporting organized labor contributed to expanded labor militancy. However, on April 2, 1917—at the beginning of Wilson's second term—the United States entered World War I, leading to fresh efforts by government, business, and labor unions to restrict strikes and work stoppages. Despite the declaration by AFL president Samuel Gompers that strikes would be used "only as a last resort," strikes continued to surge in 1917.

In September 1917, President Wilson established the Mediation Commission to diminish wartime strike activity. The failure to limit wartime strikes in the year following U.S. entry into World War I initiated a new government effort to restrict strikes with Wilson's creation of the National War Labor Board (NWLB) in April 1918, with representatives from business, labor, and government. The main objective of the NWLB was to contain strikes in shipbuilding and railroads, nationalized by the U.S. government in 1918. In the year following the end of World War I, mass strikes broke out in the industries. The NWLB was able to control strikes, initially through reaching agreements with workers, emboldening workers in other key craft industries to walk off the job. Capital soon gained the upper hand by dividing skilled from unskilled workers and repressing most worker-concerted activities.[6]

Nativism, the Offensive against U.S. Syndicalism and the Left

The growth of white nativism during World War I contributed to racist and anti-immigrant sentiments and aided employer efforts to destroy unionization campaigns and rank-and-file efforts to improve wages and working conditions. Whereas the wartime demand for manufacturing spurred employers to negotiate with workers from Southern and Eastern Europe after strikes and labor actions, militant workers and immigrants from Mexico were typically not afforded the same provisions. A significant feature of the attack against unions from 1915 to 1919 was a systematic assault against the IWW platform to organize mass production workers across racial, ethnic, and gender lines. IWW rank-and-file members organized direct action in industries that were not essential to the wartime effort, namely agriculture, mining, and timber. Through their inclusive policy that embraced racial and ethnic minorities, the IWW mobilized Black workers and immigrant workers from Mexico and Southeast Asia. The federal government was intolerant of the IWW due to its anarcho-syndicalist guiding principles of direct action and its opposition to contracts, collective bargaining agreements, and the capitalist state. With the passage of the Espionage Act in 1917 and Sedition Act in 1918, the federal government stoked opposition to the IWW and its members. Perhaps the most notorious example of government despotism was the support of local military efforts to defeat and forcibly deport IWW miners in Bisbee, Arizona, in July 1917.

The primary expression of communist sentiment in the United States from the late nineteenth century to the present has been through nebulous, non-electoral political organizations. Even the Communist Party (CPUSA), which participated in U.S. electoral politics, garnered negligible popular electoral support. Ironically, in the 1930s, when working-class militancy was at its apogee, the party failed to mobilize this support—and instead favored a "united front from above" strategy that embraced the Democratic Party, opposition to fascism, and the New Deal. The most widely accepted explanation for the failure of a labor party to form in the United States was initially advanced by Werner Sombart and his acolytes, who promoted "American Exceptionalism."[7] Conversely, in the 1930s era of mass industrial insurgency, a socialist alternative was dashed by the CIO's support of the New Deal and the Democratic Party. Leaders of insurgent workers unions were influential in sublimating worker militancy through supporting the provisions of the NLRA and modest and incomplete New Deal reforms that immediately weakened the capacity of workers to confront capital directly. In the early 1930s, the CPUSA and other left parties opposed the New Deal as inimical to the welfare of the working class, but by 1931 the Communist Party had begun to waver, and in 1935 it tacitly approved the NLRA and the New Deal.[8]

Thus, opposition to collective bargaining that limited workers' direct action and strikes—a central plank of working-class radicalism upheld by the IWW—was dissolved in 1936 by the Comintern without justification for this policy shift being conveyed to workers or members. Stanley Aronowitz interprets Comintern policies as nothing short of devious, particularly for rank-and-file members of the party who were offered no explanation for policies that compromised their capacity for democratic participation in the workplace and unions, or for its slavish support of the Democratic Party. The mold of labor-management relations was cast, preventing workplace representation from the late 1930s to the present.[9] Plainly, while communist union leaders in the CIO were in part driven by supporting the war against the Nazis from 1935 to 1945, union leaders in the federation were more absorbed with maintaining their power vis-à-vis management through suppressing workers' dissent in local unions and communities. The baldly contradictory policies advancing a mass party while supporting the Democrats eroded the power and legitimacy of the CPUSA and set the stage for the bipartisan anticommunist witch hunts a decade later.

Refashioning Historical Interpretations of Labor Power in the U.S.

The political and economic power of organized labor in the United States has declined to a nadir not witnessed since the first two decades of the twentieth century, when the craft-based unions recognized the necessity to focus on industrial representation or risk absolute defeat. At that time, private sector union membership in the United States hovered around 7 percent. With the growth of industrial unionism, by 1954 union density had risen to 35 percent. But as of 2010, membership in the private sector had officially dropped to 7.5 percent, though substantial evidence demonstrates that trade union density was hovering around only 4 to 5 percent in the private sector. What forces can account for this dramatic decline?

Clearly, the institutional constraints of the U.S. electoral system prevented a third party from emerging, but the Left also consented to the Democratic Party as stand-in for a workers' party. In exchange, labor leaders were bought off by some of the capitalists and proffered as official representatives of the U.S. working class. Institutional constraints do not preclude short-term tactical means to advance working-class interests. In the 1930s, at a crucial historical moment of revolutionary worker upsurge, direct-action tactics by workers were viewed by labor leaders as an impediment to cooperative political relations with the Democratic Party and union collaboration with management. Left leaders in the CIO may have been committed to defending the Soviet Union from Nazism, but the greater concern was defending and controlling their own turf from militant workers in mass production industries who were more committed to solidarity in opposition to government edicts and employer collaboration. Lacking viable organizational alternatives to the CIO, workers could only express their militancy directly on the local plant level.

Parliamentary or legislative tactics like organized labor's support for the NLRA are not fully about ideological purity and people must, at times, recognize that compromise is sometimes in the best interest of a class. But in retrospect there was no turning back from working-class struggle once labor law was concretized by capital, the state, and trade unions in the 1930s. The NLRA reforms constrained militancy and created a sense of hopelessness among workers who achieved a voice through direct action on the shop floor. As a consequence, the tactics of the leaders of the labor movement were strictly a matter of compromise, whereas the bourgeois parties in the United States were divided in crafting the program—even one favorable to the bosses, preferring to deny the labor movement any rights. Once the New Deal legislation was sanctioned by the judiciary, business was already engaged in an all-out struggle for political and economic hegemony as labor unions tied the hands of the workers.

Generally, if the socialist Left accepts these terms, then labor tactics are transformed into a sideshow that does not take into account the objective militancy of the working class. In replacing tactics with strategy, organized labor could only defend the established law from the onslaught of capitalist forces while members were immediately under assault by the state and capital. Thus the New Deal set into motion a labor regime deeply rooted in compromise and collaboration while the capitalist class engaged in unremitting warfare. Through sanctioning of this maneuver, organized labor made it clear that it had no interest in building a class-based movement of the working class.

Labor Studies Defining and Worker Power

Political scientists are preoccupied with measuring the power of labor unions, as they are concerned with any interest group that lobbies and contributes to parties and elected officials to advance institutional interests. Within this framework, how do serious scholars explain the rapid decline in labor union density in the United States? Some mainstream and liberal scholars contend that industrial unionism is declining because workers in the United States are uninterested in joining. This skeptical public sentiment among workers is reinforced by political legislation that saps and erodes the capability of labor unions to form.[10] Others contend that labor unions have fared quite well in the United States, particularly in view of their strong capacity to influence government legislation as an interest group. Contrary to widely held belief, they argue, the Democratic Party has been a staunch and effective ally of organized labor.[11] Moreover, some analysts asserted that as union membership has continued to decline without end, organized labor could not expect to receive anything near the level of support they have seen in the past from the Democratic Party, which has become less willing to defend labor union interests. As a consequence, labor unions would have to become social-movement unions and expand by mobilizing their membership. Paul Johnston's first-rate ethnographies of the ascendancy of activist unions in California during the 1980s demonstrated that labor union growth was possible if only it turned to a progressive mobilizing strategy.[12]

This social-movement union concept was taken up by labor organizers in the 1990s. After witnessing a generation of union decline, organized labor, for the first time since the 1930s, sought a new strategy to increase membership through new organizing. In 1995, John Sweeney, president of the Service Employees International Union (SEIU), led a palace coup that ousted AFL-CIO president Lane Kirkland, promising to revitalize the labor movement through new organizing campaigns. Sweeney pledged to rebuild unions through strategic campaigns targeting growing industries and vulnerable employers.

Rather than engaging in grassroots mobilizing of new members on the ground, most unions opted for opportunistic efforts to leverage employers through corporate campaigns and by training as labor organizers astute, altruistic college students, who allegedly knew more than the workers and often neglected workers themselves in corporate campaigns.[13] Many other unions grew by mergers and raiding, as is well documented in the work of Steve Early, which exposed opportunistic union leaders who regarded workers as dues-paying members and engaged in rapacious trusteeships of insurgent locals, while neglecting member interests. Instead of building a militant rank-and-file labor movement, union leaders sought to consolidate power in a spurious effort to increase labor union power or working-class support.[14]

However, by the turn of the twenty-first century, misguided optimists argued that organized labor had turned the corner by adopting the correct strategy to rebuild its strength through mobilizing members on a grassroots level, and that this would significantly advance its influence over the Democratic Party. Peter Francia, for instance, believed the state was so amenable to pressure from interest groups that unions had only to increase organizing efforts at the grassroots level in order to inexplicably expand their power and influence.[15]

Others took a darker view. In 2004, Leo Troy correctly predicted that industrial-style labor representation was in a process of unrelenting free-fall due to global economic restructuring. The view was disparaged in academia by liberal-left supporters of industrial unions who did not anticipate the rapid outsourcing of global industrial production from the United States to the Global South, where wages were lower and most labor unions prohibited. While industrial unions would continue to represent a shrinking share of the labor force in the United States, Troy argued, service and public sector unions would supersede them in membership. Given these unions' dependence on state largesse, he observed that the Democratic Party was becoming the equivalent of labor parties in European social democracies. Troy's position was in the minority among scholars, yet his prediction that the center of labor union strength was shifting to public or private sector workers who depended on government largesse to grow and maintain wage strength proved correct.

Troy's belief that the Democratic Party was crucial to the expansion of service unions was also accurate, as both labor unions and the party gained mutual benefits of wage growth and votes.[16] But Troy was gravely mistaken about the "labor" nature of the Democratic Party, which was anything but the handmaiden of the U.S. working class. In the final instance, the Democratic Party always defended the interests of capital. While less rapacious than Republicans in undermining the doctrinal elements of the labor law, Democrats were just as adamant in advancing free trade agreements and neoliberal policies, as has been evident throughout the global financial crisis from 2008 to the present. In 2009, after President Obama's victory and with Democratic control of the House of Representatives and Senate, union membership in the private sector declined to its lowest point in over a century. As union power eroded in the private sector, public sector government workers, portrayed by Republicans as overpaid union members, were targeted by business and elected officials. While the Republican Party is most responsible for the new assault on public sector workers, Democratic officials certainly engaged in explicit if less overt efforts to undermine government workers.

Labor and the Crisis of Capital

In 2010, when state budgets across the United States were in deficit, Democratic governors were almost as assertive as their Republican counterparts in slashing budgets for crucial social services that undercut public sector unions. The difference between Democrats and Republicans seemed primarily one of technique. In 2011, Scott Walker, governor of Wisconsin, used a full-throated political challenge to eliminate collective bargaining rights for state workers. Other governors even went further. In Indiana, Governor Mitch Daniels signed into law right-to-work legislation with great fanfare and exulted in the rebukes from liberal media, even though they often hold workers in the same negative regard, and after the 2013 national elections, Michigan governor, Rick Snyder followed with right-to-work legislation. If Republican governors used a sledgehammer to attack public unions, Democratic governors attacked unions with drone strikes, evading the radar of the compliant media. With significant corporate support, New York's Democratic governor, Andrew Cuomo, who had also received the endorsement of the union-supported Working Families Party, threatened to fire public sector workers unless they agreed to concessionary contracts. While Republican governors and legislators may have been more vocal in breaking the backs of labor unions, Democrats were shrewder; recognizing that workers who depended on the state would not sign concessionary contracts, Cuomo crushed public sector unions through legislation and threats of dismissal. To punish unions representing low-wage public sector workers, funded by federal, state, and city dollars, Cuomo, with the support of Michael Bloomberg, New York City's oligarch mayor from 2002 to 2013, simply capped spending and, in so doing, eliminated pensions and healthcare for home care workers employed by nonprofit agencies.[17]

The New Deal: Class Compromise or Truce?

The dominant historical and social science perspective is that the New Deal represents the U.S. class compromise that ended the hot war between workers' aspirations to form labor unions and capital's desire to exercise despotic control over the workplace. Recent historical analysis documents the immediacy of the business assault on unions after passage of the NLRA, with mobilization initially on the state level, leading to the passage of the Taft-Hartley Act in 1947. As Marc Dixon writes:

> Following the labor upheavals of the 1930s, employers and their associations took their case to state legislatures across the country, making labor, and Right-to-Work in particular, a heated political issue. The political battles that ensued resulted in a wave of legislative restrictions on unions and helped contain the labor movement to a decidedly narrow geographic and industrial space. Restrictive labor laws were not adopted solely where union organization was weak, but rather where unions were actively organizing to solidify their movement as a national force and, indeed, where there were notable openings for union activism.[18]

The dominant liberal narrative is that in an environment of widespread labor unrest, workers' militancy frightened the U.S. capitalist class into negotiating a compromise with putative representatives of workers, who had the power to mollify the insurgency that had spread throughout the nation. The demand for recognition caused prominent corporate leaders to yield to workers selected rights that did not interfere with employer absolutism in the workplace. As the workers' movement gained momentum, astute capitalists gradually allowed workers in the mass production industries to form labor unions with which they would negotiate bargaining agreements. In due course the national government enacted the NLRA. But even as the capitalist class created a structural mechanism to mediate class struggle, workers' militancy escalated and it was not until 1938 that labor unions could finally contain mass action in plants and enterprises.

Some employers continued to resist unionization and, between 1936 and 1938, workers continued to engage in ever more militant sit-downs and general strikes in Toledo, the Bay Area, Minneapolis–St. Paul, Flint, San Francisco, and St. Louis. Although liberal scholars such as David Plotke outlandishly contend, without evidence, that workers' control was never sought out or even popular among industrial workers in the 1930s and 1940s,[19] the historical record entirely controverts this position. While the Flint sit-down strike ushered in a twenty-five-year period of tranquility in most auto plants, Sidney Fine's well-documented account of the Flint sit-down strike finds that the experience activated worker militancy that persisted in many plants: "UAW members... were reluctant to accept the customary discipline exercised by management," and they "ran wild in many plants for months." Union committeemen aggressively pressed the grievances of union members upon oftentimes unyielding foremen, and as a UAW member later conceded, "Every time a dispute came up the fellows would have a tendency to sit down and just stop working."[20]

These mass labor actions revealed that many workers considered unionization as synonymous with control over the enterprise. In fact, many newly unionized workers who engaged in sit-down strikes were surprised to learn that their unions, as sanctioned by the NLRA, set up a framework that restricted their autonomy and established a formal system of labor relations limiting working-class power on the shop floor. Although workers remained militant through the late 1940s they were forced to play by the rules of capital.[21] The NLRA was not a class compromise but a constellation of tactics implemented by management and union leaders, serving as representatives of labor, to quell worker militancy. For all practical purposes, the terms of the act were relevant from about 1940 to 1990. Immediately after the act's passage in 1935, employers in Texas and the U.S. Southwest who opposed the accords sought to undermine the system through a range of tactics aimed at weakening the law and working-class gains as a whole.

Trade Unions and Organizational Subservience to the Democratic Party
Outside the United States the ideology of communism strongly influenced early twentieth-century workers. In the United States, anarchist, socialist, communist, and Marxist ideologies were severely repressed by the state, and workers engaged in struggles deprived of the symbolism that made the Left so strong in Europe through most of the twentieth century. Although second-generation immigrants formed a large share of the U.S. working class in the 1940s, most were unacquainted with the leftist ideologies that had been so prevalent in Europe but had been beaten back. As such, the failure of communist ideology to take hold was not because of an uninterested working class but the primacy of a politics of working-class organization and class struggle over the politics of ideology.

Working behind the scenes, communist and left labor activists and leaders were unable to assert an organizational force for workers and the labor movement in the Democratic Party, and were ultimately outflanked and crushed after World War II. Indeed, from 1935 to 1945, the CIO leadership was absorbed in restraining the worker power that built the organization through supporting a labor law and collective bargaining that set the limits for rank and file mobilization. The Left could not achieve the equivalent socio-economic rights for workers, as, unlike in European social democracies, in the United States landmark legislation such as the NLRA had limited organizational support from the Democratic Party. In the absence of a labor party, the union movement cannot achieve a social compact that institutionalizes its interests. Why, then, are organized labor and the Left surprised and offended when the Democratic Party is unsympathetic to their institutional and programmatic interests?

This sets the framework for understanding the weakness of the left movements in the United States that prioritized cordial relations with business and the state over the organization of the U.S. working class—especially African Americans. Michael Goldfield provides a thorough analysis of these failures of organized labor and its initial ties to the

Communist Party, whose catastrophic alliance with the Democratic Party was a leading factor in the failure to organize people of color and low-wage workers.[22] The CPUSA, supporting a New Deal order inferior to principles of class struggle, was marginalized through curbing worker militancy and then dismembered itself by McCarthyism after World War II.

Formalizing Contracts and Traditional Unionism

For the same reason that it is irrelevant to contemplate any equivalent to a left or social democratic party in the United States after the 1930s, it is crucial to recognize that the NLRA rendered most forms of alternative rank-and-file unionism inconsequential. While European leftist workers in the early twentieth century engaged in multiple alternative forms of representation—including council communism, anarcho-syndicalism, and autonomism—in the United States, almost without exception, workers seeking unionization had one rite of passage: employer recognition for the eligibility to negotiate contracts for members employed by the corporation. Any possibility of organizing the power of worker solidarity differently was foreclosed upon in the aftermath of the 1935–1938 sit-down strikes, which resulted in the formation of traditional industrial unions obliged to crush rank-and-file dissent and play by the rules of the game as established by the capitalist class. In the absence of a political counterforce to the two capitalist parties, contract unionism heralded the ideological capitulation of the AFL and CIO. The competition between the two rival federations for industrial union members signaled their unequivocal adherence to a system framed by mass production.

Recognition of the mass-industrial model subordinated the craft unions that had been dominant from the early nineteenth to the early twentieth century. The AFL honed its organizing strategy to eliminate the principles that had sustained craft unionism: hierarchy, aristocracy, and exclusion of nonmembers, and instead adopted the mass-industrial union model that was dominant in factories. Institutionalization of contract unionism in the 1930s was reinforced by the state and capitalists, who firmly believed that maintaining labor peace was imperative for regrouping and developing new tactics for repressing labor in and out of the workplace. For national labor unions, the industrial union collective bargaining model also precluded any alternative to the dominance of business unionism over social unionism for more than a generation, aside from independent syndicalist unions in the service sector. These have been typically formed by migrant workers, often originally organized as workers' centers; examples include the Taxi Workers Alliance, the Domestic Workers United, and the Guestworkers United, as well as IWW formations such as the Jimmy John's Workers Union in Minnesota and Brandworkers International (food processing) in New York City. But the labor management regime of the 1930s continued to straitjacket workers into contract unionism in an industrial setting where ideology was not a factor. Left unions and conservative unions alike strove to gain and maintain the identical goal: management recognition and the negotiation of a collective bargaining agreement.

No viable new forms of organization could emerge as a major force as long as the NLRA system was the law—a system that has unraveled by the 2010s and is now in tatters. In this respect, the New Deal was a basis for the establishment of industrial unions and for material advances to white industrial workers. Collective bargaining was the mechanism for distributing private benefits to workers, while the New Deal programs provided social benefits to some of the unemployed, elderly, and poor. But while conditions improved for a segment of the working class, African Americans and ethnic minorities were left out of this agreement.

As much as the New Deal system expanded union recognition and workers' rights, it also restricted the prefigurative workers organizations promoted by the IWW, syndicalists, and those local communist unions committed to anticapitalism and racial equality. In a penetrating analysis, Goldfield reveals that some IWW locals, such as the Sailors International Union and the Woodworkers of America, embraced syndicalism, often adhering to a local, provincial, and anticommunist platform, and yet they engaged in struggles that rejected the inclusion of African Americans in the U.S. Northwest and South. The CPUSA's advocacy for unionism on the basis of multiracial and non-exclusionary membership led many African Americans to affiliate with the party in the early 1930s. Following a 1936 strike the Mine Mill Workers, a communist local in Alabama with a Black leadership and majority, gained white support and campaigned for the eventual reinstatement of 160 fired workers in 1938 despite the company's effort to divide the workers on the basis of race.[23] Similarly, Peter Cole demonstrates that in the early 1930s, key IWW locals embraced multiracial unionism, notably Philadelphia's Maritime Workers Local 8, in which Black workers maintained a majority at a time when the influence of the Communist Party and the Soviet Union was growing, particularly due to the party's commitment to racial justice.[24] From the party's founding in 1919, many IWW activists were initially attracted to the Communist Party and its commitment to class-struggle unionism and racial justice, the pursuit of socialism and democratic working-class politics and opposition to collective bargaining. Those labor unions in the IWW daring to challenge the NLRA system were rendered irrelevant and dismissed as quixotic and utopian.

Following consolidation of the NLRA system in the 1940s, by the end of the decade, the empowered CIO leadership pursued membership growth at any expense, despite the emergence and expansion of unions advocating class compromise and racial segregation. Although in the early twentieth century the IWW could not control provincialism and racism in some locals, after 1950, the more powerful and anticommunist CIO, like the AFL, for the most part ignored the marginalization of African Americans on the local level.[25]

A Workers' Movement for the "Inexistent" and Class Compromise

In *The Rebirth of History*, Alain Badiou, who uses the word "riot" to describe the social movements of the excluded classes, considers the foundation of organization as critical to the majority who are unrecognized until they engage in collective action. With this line of thinking I view the U.S. workers' movement of the 1930s as decisive to the expansion of the rights of Badiou's "inexistent": "If the event, the historical riot, is a break in time—a break in which the inexistent appears—organization is an outside-time in time, which creates the collective subjectivity wherein the existence taken on by the inexistent in the light of the Idea is going to challenge the conservative power of the state, guardian of all temporal forms of oppression."[26]

Likewise, the workers' movement of the 1930s fashioned the basis for an as yet unknown future. Capital and the state both recognized the power that workers wielded through militant demonstrations in industrial zones, sit-down strikes, and general strikes that had been unimaginable in the 1920s. Workers, especially those in low-wage jobs, were subsequently recognized as "existent" but they were stripped of almost all their actual power through the legislative and organizational compromises ushered in by the New Deal. Although it would still take more than a generation to confer rights to African Americans, the protests and "riots" and strikes in the 1930s set the stage for expanding workers' rights. In the New Deal, the state brokered a compact between capital and organized labor, who shared a mutual interest in systematizing the NLRA. Thus, the 1930s workers' movement sought to preserve the potency of worker power through militant rank-and-file labor organizations that would challenge capital's supremacy; this objective was adamantly opposed by the state and capital.

What were the consequences of the truce? In addition to maintaining control over the work process, business almost always refused to recognize unions and challenged elections, negotiated with stubborn resolve, and used the grievance system, which made it impossible for unions to monitor employer abuses, to its advantage. Historian David Brody aptly depicts the antilabor practices of employers as unsurprising: "I do not fault employers or their minions any more than I would the beasts of the field. Business is business."[27] What is so surprising to him is that government leaders have discounted the significance of labor unions and the New Deal social compact.

On the legislative front, capital immediately shifted attention to undermining the NLRA and successfully overturned key provisions of labor union power with the 1947 Taft-Hartley Act. Democratic president Harry Truman opposed the Republican-sponsored legislation as an encroachment on free speech rights but then went on to use its provisions frequently after its passage.[28]

The labor movement was constrained by its own legislation, which qualitatively transformed the expression of working-class power. As evidenced by the wave of unauthorized strikes during World War II, workers were no less class-conscious and militant than before but were drawn constantly into the black hole of collective bargaining.

Rank-and-File Workers Reject No-Strike Pledge

Cooperation between organized labor and the federal government to prevent work stoppages was significantly more extensive during World War II than World War I. Given the wave of labor activism preceding entry into World War II, the federal government sought to ensure the stable production of wartime goods during the period of conflict. Upon U.S. entry into the war, the leaders of the AFL and the ascendant CIO, the two peak labor federations in the United States, accepted a no-strike pledge for the purpose of preventing any unionized industries crucial to the war economy from ceasing production. In addition to preventing work stoppages, the labor federations promised to increase production to advance the war effort. Wartime typically produced labor shortages and thus resulted in increased bargaining power for unions. The no-strike pledge assured the government the union federations would prevent strikes or walkouts during the entire length of the war, considerably eroding the ability of organized labor to negotiate wage increases.

To avert strikes or walkouts, the two union federations agreed to settle and resolve labor-management disputes through the National War Labor Board, created by President Wilson during World War I. Under President Franklin Roosevelt, the War Labor Board was delegated to decide and enforce labor and management agreements, largely keeping wages in check. With the passage of the Economic Stabilization Act of October 2, 1942, at Roosevelt's urging, wages and prices were controlled, preventing workers from exercising their NLRA rights to bargain over wages and working conditions. Apart from rare instances when it was deemed that workers were underpaid relative to others in their industries, labor unions were charged with preventing wage growth.

During World War II, the no-strike pledge eliminated the possibility of any union-sanctioned job action while conferring greater power to labor leadership and leading to an unprecedented growth in union organization, to nearly 70 percent of manufacturing industries in 1946.[29] As the enforcers of the no-strike pledge, unions could punish members who engaged in concerted activities of any kind, and under the union security provision of the War Labor Board, workers paid dues to their unions without being granted effective bargaining and grievance rights in exchange. In effect, unions policed their own members, leading Jeremy Brecher to conclude: "By making the unions dependent on the government instead of their members, it kept them 'responsible.'"[30]

Although strikes were radically reduced, aggrieved workers engaged in unauthorized labor actions that union leaders were unable to control. Under the no-strike pledge, workers who sought wage increases went on strike without union approval. By 1944—one year before the end of World War II—"more strikes took place than in any previous year in American history."[31] The strikes, in most instances unofficial, lasted an average of 5.6 days before employers were forced to offer modest wage increases. In effect, due to losing their legitimacy as representatives, the labor unions were unable to prevent rank-and-file members from striking. By the end of World War II in 1945, mass strikes had erupted throughout the manufacturing industries, leading to wage increases for workers whose wages had been held in check through the complicity of labor with employers and the government. Paradoxically, while the no-strike pledge may initially have prevented workers from striking, it ended up triggering a new strike wave that challenged the authority of the War Labor Board and labor union leaders for many years to come.

As demonstrated through the War Labor Board, any radical possi-bilities for intensifying the struggle through IWW tactics were legislated out of existence. The formalized system of labor relations preserved the authority of the capitalist state even as radical workers were in motion. Thus, organized labor recognized that it could not stray from its task of repressing its own members. Labor could not shift course to advocate social movement unionism, as it was constrained by its obligation to uphold the sanctity of collective bargaining.

In the late 1940s and early 1950s, the McCarthy purges and de-Staliniz-ation rendered the CPUSA powerless as a legitimate force on the left, without any socialist political organization capable of filling the breach; while the Democratic Party gained near monopoly control over organ-ized labor. Unions in the AFL and CIO then went on to support the gov-ernment's foreign policy in opposition to the Soviet Union and any other form of socialism or labor militancy, thereby advancing the interests of U.S. business at home and imperialism and monopoly capitalism abroad. Since the mid-1970s, capitalist globalization has deepened the crisis for traditional unions through the global outsourcing of production to non-union firms and deindustrialization.

Toward a Militant Rank-and-File Future

The U.S. capitalist state identifies democracy and freedom as individu-als' choices made within the market system. These choices are viewed as an extension of civil liberties within a bourgeois state. The capitalist state conflates civil liberties with market choice. At the center of the lib-eral-democratic capitalist and imperialist system, workers have fiercely resisted exploitation through worker-based organizations founded in rank-and-file solidarity.

Since the 1970s, labor unions extracted inconsequential short-term gains when Democrats were in power. In exchange for working-class votes, the party paid lip service to organized labor, which remained loyal to the party. Perhaps the most damning evidence of the Democratic Party's ignominious stance toward organized labor was its shift against the passage of the Employee Free Choice Act (EFCA) just after it gained control of the presidency, the House, and the Senate in 2009. EFCA, "or card check," which would have allowed workers to form unions on the basis of evidence that a majority of workers in a bargaining unit had signed cards indicating their choice to be represented by a union, was opposed not just by Republicans but also by Democrats who had earlier pledged support for the legislation. The failure of EFCA reflects labor unions' propensity to seek solutions through government legislation to the exclusion of members. By the 2010s, as union membership was in free fall, labor could only depend on government to appeal to the conscience of liberals and would-be members.

All those seeking greater labor militancy must recognize that traditional unions are unable to escape the trap set in the 1930s through fidelity to the collective bargaining agreement. While the relevancy of IWW tactics to the conditions of the early twenty-first century are indisputable—direct action, mass industrial action, general strikes, and eventual workers' control over production—radical workers ensnared in traditional unions will fail at this effort as they defy the reality of the legal institutional framework established through the NLRA. With certainty, as advocated by the IWW, new advances for labor will only emerge through defiant actions of autonomous workers in solidarity outside of the traditional trade unions that officially sanctioned and benefited from the old system that is now becoming all but extinct.

Editor and Contributors

Immanuel Ness is professor of political science at Brooklyn College of the City University of New York. His research focuses on labor organization and mobilization, migration, resistance and social movements against oppression from a historical and comparative perspective. Ness is author of *Global Imperialism and Worker Struggles in the Global South* (2014), *Guest Workers and Resistance to U.S. Corporate Despotism* (2011) and *Immigrants, Unions, and the U.S. Labor Market* (2005). He is General Editor of *Encyclopedia of Global Human Migration*, five volumes (2013) and is currently finishing a book on labor migration and global inequality and is conducting research on independent labor organization and the rise of the police state in the global South. Ness is coeditor of *Ours to Master and to Own: Worker Control from the Commune to the Present* (2011). He has written or edited many other books on labor, workers organization, migration, and urban politics with leading publishers. He is editor of the peer-review quarterly journal *Working USA: The Journal of Labor and Society*. He is founder of the Lower East Side Community Labor Organization, and recipient of a special Proclamation from the Council of the City of New York in May 2001. He has worked with the New York State Attorney General's Office on creating the Code of Conduct for the Greengrocery Industry. In 2005, his four-volume work: *Encyclopedia of American Social Movements* was awarded Outstanding Reference Source, Reference and User Services Association, American Library Association. The work was selected as best reference for 2005 from *Library Journal*. He received awards and acclaim for his other reference works, including *Encyclopedia of Third Parties in America*. In 2009, he edited *International Encyclopedia of Protest and Revolution: 1500 to the*

Present, a four-thousand-page, eight-volume collection. E-mail: iness@
brooklyn.cuny.edu or manny.ness@gmail.com.

Au Loong Yu is a labor researcher based in Hong Kong. He is a founding
member of Globalization Monitor, an NGO which promotes public education on the impact of globalization on labor in China. He is the author
of two Chinese language books on China and capitalism, including *From
Bureaucratic Socialism to Bureaucratic Capitalism* and *The World Is Not for
Sale*, and most recently coeditor of *China's Rise: Strength and Fragility*. In
recent years he has contributed essays to journals such as *New Politics*
and *Working USA: The Journal of Labor and Society*. E-mail: auloongyu@
hotmail.com.

Bai Ruixue is a researcher based in Hong Kong with a particular interest in
labor and globalization. She is a member of the editorial board of China
Labour Net and is a regular contributor to *Working USA: The Journal of
Labor and Society* and to the book *China's Rise: Strength and Fragility* edited
by Au Loong-yu and Fred Leplat. E-mail: brx353@yahoo.com.

Piotr Bizyukov works as a leading expert at the Center for Social-Labor
Rights, Moscow. His recent studies are focused on the issues of discrimination in the labor sphere (2007–2008), practices of individual labor
conflicts (2009–2010), monitoring of labor protests in Russia (since
2008), and contingent labor and its consequences for the employees.
He is the author of three books, most recently: *How Labor Rights Are
Defined in Russia: Collective Labor Protests and Their Role in Labor Relations'
Regulation* (2011). His articles are published in leading Russian academic
journals as well as a wide range of newspapers, including *Kommersant*.
E-mail: bizyukov@trudprava.ru.

Meredith Burgmann was an industrial relations academic at Macquarie
University and later Australian Labor Party President (Speaker) of the
NSW Legislative Council. She is an activist and author of books and
articles on misogyny, Aboriginal rights, postwar anticommunism, and
early environmentalism in Australia, including (with Verity Burgmann)
Green Bans, Red Union. Her forthcoming book is on Australia's secret
police (ASIO). E-mail: mburgmann@gmail.com

Verity Burgmann is adjunct professor in Social Sciences at Monash
University, previously professor of Political Science at the University of

Melbourne. Historian, political scientist, and activist, she is the author of numerous books and articles on the labor movement, radical political ideologies, contemporary protest movements, environmental politics, racism, antiglobalization, and anticorporate politics. Her most recent book is *Climate Politics and the Climate Movement in Australia* (2012). E-mail: vnb@unimelb.edu.au.

Darío Bursztyn, born in Buenos Aires, is a journalist and holds a PhD in sociology from the Universidad de Buenos Aires. He has integrated militant and study groups such as Laboratorio Social Argentina, led by Dr. Floreal Ferrara, which published the first book of Toni Negri after his visit in 2003. His research is related to Ecology and Capitalism, Urbanism and Transportation under Neoliberalism, and he has collaborated in research on New IT configurations. He works in Colectivo Editorial Crisis and has translated the books of Dr. Miguel Benassayag and articles by Bifo Berardi, Saskia Sassen, and Alessandro de Giorgi. He also works at Radio Nacional Argentina. E-mail: dariobursztyn@gmail.com.

Aviva Chomsky is professor of history and coordinator of Latin American studies at Salem State University. She is also a member of the North Shore Colombia Solidarity Committee. She is author of numerous books and articles including *Undocumented: How Immigration Became Illegal* (2014); *A History of the Cuban Revolution* (Wiley-Blackwell 2010); *Linked Labor Histories: New England, Colombia, and the Making of a Global Working Class* (2008); coeditor of *The People Behind Colombian Coal/Bajo el manto del carbon*, with Garry Leech and Steve Striffler; *They Take Our Jobs! and 20 Other Myths About Immigration* (2007); and *West Indian Workers and the United Fruit Company in Costa Rica*, 1870–1940 (1996). E-mail: avi.chomsky@salemstate.edu.

Erik Forman has worked to develop solidarity unionism organizing strategies for the burgeoning low-wage service sector as a shop-floor militant in the IWW campaigns at Starbucks and Jimmy John's. He has conducted workshops and trainings on direct action and syndicalist organizing techniques in more than twenty countries.

Shawn Hattingh currently works at the International Labour Research and Information Group (ILRIG) in Cape Town, South Africa as a research and education officer. ILRIG is a labor support organization that works with trade unions and community based movements in southern Africa, which involves providing both popular research and education to these formations. This also includes conducting popular education–based workshops, with activists from trade unions and movements, in which the participants develop critiques of capitalism, the role of the state in society, and neoliberal globalization, and analyzing alternatives that have been, and are being, forged by the working class in struggle, including new forms of organization. Shawn has also been a member of trade unions and community based movements in South Africa and is currently a member of a Cape Town based activist group, Soundz of the South, and a supporter of the Zabalaza Anarchist-Communist Front (ZACF). E-mail: shawn@ilrig.org.za.

Ray Jureidini is associate professor of sociology at the Institute for Migration Studies at the Lebanese American University in Beirut, Lebanon. He has published widely in his areas of research interest: industrial and economic sociology, migration, gender, human rights, racism, and xenophobia. E-mail: ray.jureidini@gmail.com.

Jack Kirkpatrick is a union organizer in County Berkshire, England. After leaving school, he worked for ten years at minimum wage. He is a rank-and-file organizer, anarchist, socialist, and syndicalist. For one year, he was an unemployed squatter and then was a union shop-steward for two years, a paid union organizer for the last two years. Since 2007 he has been a Wobbly. E-mail: readingantig8@hotmail.com.

Ray Jureidini is associate professor of sociology at the Institute for Migration Studies at the Lebanese American University in Beirut, Lebanon. He has published widely in his areas of research interest: industrial and economic sociology, migration, gender, human rights, racism, and xenophobia.

Gabriel Kuhn was born in Austria but soon began moving around with his artist parents. He grew up in various countries, including Turkey, Italy, England, and the United States, but returned to Austria for most of his formal education and a four-year semiprofessional soccer career. In 1996 he received a PhD in philosophy from the University of Innsbruck. Gabriel has been active in radical politics since the late 1980s, and in the early 1990s he worked with the Austrian autonomist journal *TATblatt* and anarchist publisher Monte Verita, before turning his attention to DIY zine publishing. He founded Alpine Anarchist Productions in 2000, a project that distributes pamphlets to this day. Since 2005 Gabriel has been working closely with radical German publisher Unrast. His book *"'Neuer Anarchismus' in den USA. Seattle und die Folgen"* was named "Book of the Year 2008" by Berlin's Library of the Free. Gabriel also contributes regularly to the Swedish anarchist journal *Brand*. He is author of *All Power to the Councils! A Documentary History of the German Revolution of 1918–1919* (2012) and *Soccer vs. the State: Tackling Football and Radical Politics* (2011). E-mail: cheetahkay@yahoo.com.

Steven Manicastri is currently enrolled in the PhD Program of Political Science at the University of Connecticut. His subfields include political theory and comparative politics. He participated in the 2012 Left Forum panel, in which he presented in the panel "Syndicalism and Autonomism: Building a New Labor Movement." He has been a student organizer and labor union activist and is currently pursuing activism in social movements. His academic interests involve Marxism and critical theory, and he is interested in exploring the theories of the Italian autonomous movements as potential frameworks for organizing workers' movements. E-mail: smanicastri@gmail.com.

Irina Olimpieva works as a head of the research department "Social Studies of the Economy" at the Center for Independent Social Research in St. Petersburg. She received a PhD in economic sociology from the St. Petersburg State University of Economics and Finance. Her basic research interests are in the field of labor relations and trade unionism with particular focus on postsocialist transformation. Her recent studies have focused on Russian trade unions as political actors and the phenomenon of social movement unionism. She also works as a lecturer in a number of higher educational organizations of St. Petersburg, among her recently developed curricula is the course "Industrial Relations: Legal Frame, Collective Bargaining, and Deregulation" examining industrial relations models in Russia and European societies (since 2008). Her professional experience includes research fellowships in the Centre for Civil Society Studies (2010), and in the Paul H. Nizshe School of Advanced International Studies (2011–2012) at Johns Hopkins University. Irina Olimpieva is the author of over forty articles published in Russian and international academic journals and a monograph, *Russian Trade Unions in the System of Socio-Labor Relations Regulation: Particularities, Problems, and Research Perspectives* (2010). E-mail: irinaolimp@gmail.com.

Genese Marie Sodikoff is assistant professor of anthropology in the Department of Sociology and Anthropology, Rutgers University, Newark. Professionally and academically, Sodikoff focuses on rain forest conservation and international development in Africa, specifically the Comoros (1989–1991) and Madagascar (1994–2002). Over several periods of fieldwork in Madagascar since 1994, she examined the role of low-wage workers in rain forest conservation projects, and how the relationship between capital and labor has affected the global conservation effort and biodiversity loss. Her teaching and research interests include political ecology, conservation and international development, extinction (both biological and cultural), human-animal relations, historical anthropology, and Africa and the Indian Ocean islands. E-mail: sodikoff@andromeda.rutgers.edu.

Notes

Introduction

1   Frances Fox Piven and Richard Cloward's examination of the formation of the U.S. workers' movement in the 1930s is instructive to today's working class in the global South, where the state is unyielding in support of capital over labor. Only after an uncontainable militant and unruly industrial workers' movement developed did labor leaders and the American state seek restraint through encouraging legislation to subdue labor unrest and create a compliant working class by means of government oversight and promoting submissive bureaucratic unions. See *Poor People's Movements: Why They Succeed, How They Fail* (New York: Vintage Books, 1979), 96–180. On a global scale, industrial workers bear a resemblance to militant U.S. workers of the 1930s more than their U.S. counterparts in the contemporary era.

2   Bill Fletcher Jr. and Fernando Gapasin provide a compelling contemporary analysis of the shortcomings of traditional unionism that has contributed to spiral from a dominant force to one declining in relevance for most U.S. workers. They prescribe a unionization rooted in community and labor alliances which recognize the significance of a broader working class that is inclusive of racial and ethnic diversity, omitted in most works on the decline of labor unions. See Fletcher and Gapasin, *Solidarity Divided: The Crisis of Organized Labor and a New Path toward Social Justice* (Berkeley: University of California, 2009).

3   David Graeber, *Direct Action: An Ethnography* (Oakland: AK Press, 2009), 205. Graeber argues that unions formed in the early twentieth century retained a revolutionary character and sought to exercise dual power through controlling production while retaining the threat of strikes, factory occupations, sabotage, and destruction of machinery. The militancy included resistance to the autocratic power of business and challenged the state's monopoly of violence. However, lamentably, union leaders emerged who were driven to eviscerate workers' rank-and-file activity and, with the support of the state, control and wear down the resilience of workers organizations through co-optation and repression.

4   Daniel Gross and Staughton Lynd, *Labor Law for the Rank and Filer: Building Solidarity While Staying Clear of the Law* (Oakland: PM Press, 2009), 17–23.

5   Kate Bronfrenbrenner et al., *Organizing to Win: New Research on Union Strategies* (Ithaca: Cornell University Press, 1998).

6   Taylor E. Dark, *The Unions and the Democrats: An Enduring Alliance* (Ithaca: Cornell University Press, 1999); Peter L. Francia, *The Future of Organized Labor in American Politics* (New York: Columbia University Press, 2006).

7   Emma Goldman, *Syndicalism: The Modern Menace to Capitalism* (New York: Mother Earth Publishing Association, 2013).

8   Joyce L. Kornbluh, ed., *Rebel Voices: An IWW Anthology* (Oakland: PM Press, 2011).

9   Paul M. Buhle and Nicole Schulman, *Wobblies! A Graphic History of the Industrial Workers of the World* (London: Verso, 2005), 14, 244.

10 Examples include Verity Burgmann, *Revolutionary Industrial Unionism: The Industrial Workers of the World in Australia* (London: Cambridge University Press, 1998); Peter Cole, *Wobblies on the Waterfront: Interracial Unionism in Progressive-Era Philadelphia* (Chicago/ Urban: University of Illinois Press, 2007; and Ralph Darlington, *Syndicalism and the Transition to Capitalism* (Aldershot, Hampshire, England: Ashgate, 2008).

11 For example, see Staughton Lynd and Andrej Grubačić, *Wobblies and Zapatistas: Conversations on Anarchism, Marxism and Radical History* (Oakland: PM Press, 2008).

12 Peter J. Rachleff, *Marxism and Council Communism: The Foundation for Revolutionary Theory for Modern Society* (Brooklyn: Revisionist Press, 1976).

13 Aaron Brenner, Robert Brenner, and Cal Winslow, *Rebel Rank and File: Labor Militancy and Revolt from Below During the Long 1970s* (New York: Verso, 2010).

14 George Katsiaficas, *The Subversion of Politics: European Autonomous Social Movements and the Decolonization of Everyday Life* (Oakland: AK Press, 2006).

15 Ilda Lindell, ed., *Africa's Informal Workers: Collective Agency, Alliances and Transnational Organizing in Urban Africa* (London: Zed Books, 2010); Lynd and Grubačić, *Wobblies and Zapatistas*; and Akira Suzuki, *Cross-National Comparisons of Social Movement Unionism: Diversities of Labour Movement Revitalization in Japan, Korea and the United States* (London: Peter Lang, 2013).

16 David Harvey, *Rebel Cities: From the Right to the City to the Urban Revolution* (New York: Verso, 2012).

Chapter 1

1   For instance, in a 2011 interview with *Democracy Now*, Noam Chomsky said, "I'm not a great enthusiast for Obama, as you know, from way back, but at least he's somewhere in the real world." Given the radical nature of Chomsky's politics compared to mainstream U.S. politics, his opting for a "lesser-evil" vote lays bare the extremity of the need for a viable alternative party in the United States.

2   Sandro Mezzadra, "Italy, Operaism and Post-operaism," *The International Encyclopedia of Revolution and Protest: 1500 to the Present*, ed. Immanuel Ness (Oxford: Wiley-Blackwell Publishing, 2009), 1, http://www.revolutionprotestencyclopedia.com/.

3   Steven Wright, "Mapping Pathways within Italian Autonomist Marxism: A Preliminary Survey," *Historical Materialism* 16 (2008): 111.

4   *Statuto dell'Associazione COBAS—Confederazione dei Comitati di Base* (Rome: Viale Manzoni no. 55, 2009).

5   What remains unanswered is how the established political parties of the Left or the official unions can continue to demand obedience in the face of what can only be described as a betrayal of the ideals behind communism.

6   Paul Ginsborg, *A History of Contemporary Italy: Society and Politics 1943–1988* (New York: Palgrave Macmillan, 2003).

7   Ginsborg, *A History of Contemporary Italy*, 256.

8   Ibid., 257.

9   Ibid., 255.

10 Arthur Schlesinger is well known for his "mass society" theory in social movements. His book *The Vital Center*, published in 1949, is a paranoid representation of the Cold War era,

famous for its contempt of social movements and endorsement of a national security state.

11 Ginsborg, *A History of Contemporary Italy*, 258.

12 Ibid., 266.

13 Donald Sassoon, *The Strategy of the Italian Communist Party* (New York: St Martin's Press, 1981).

14 Ginsborg, *A History of Contemporary Italy*, 292.

15 Ibid., 293.

16 Marcuse's *One-Dimensional Man* argued that all major forms of resistance would be integrated within the capitalist political system, and so the Left would have to look towards the disenfranchised and the marginalized in order to resist capitalist means of production in the developed Western world.

17 Mario Tronti, "Workerism and Politics," *Historical Materialism* 18 (2010): 186.

18 "The philosophers have only *interpreted* the world, in various ways; the point, however, is to *change* it." Karl Marx, "Theses on Feuerbach," *Marx-Engels Reader*, 2nd ed., Robert Tucker ed., (New York: W.W. Norton & Company, 1978), 145.

19 Tronti, "Workerism and Politics," 187.

20 Mezzadra, "Italy, Operaism and Post-operaism," 3.

21 Adelino Zanini, "On the 'Philosophical Foundations' of Italian Workerism: A Conceptual Approach," *Historical Materialism* 18 (2010): 46.

22 Ibid.

23 Lukács's work on reification, or the objectification of living subjects, is a seminal work that is pivotal for understanding capitalist means of production.

24 Zanini, "On the 'Philosophical Foundations,'" 56.

25 Jason Read, "The Potential of Living Labor: Negri and the Practice of Philosophy" in Timothy S. Murphy and Abdul Karim Mustapha eds., *The Philosophy of Antonio Negri: Revolution in Theory* (London: Pluto Press, 2007), 41.

26 Mario Tronti, "Lenin in England," *Classe Operaia* 1 (January 1964), http://libcom.org/library/lenin-england.

27 One of the main reasons why the working class was viewed as "irredeemably integrated" can be attributed to the Frankfurt School of Critical Theory, which, along with Horkheimer's and Adorno's work *Dialectic of Enlightenment*, removed the working class as "the agent of history," arguing that the only form of resistance could come from up-and-coming movements not yet integrated within the capitalist system. Horkheimer would in fact become a political conservative by the end of his life, and was never too convinced of the working class's potential as a revolutionary class, writing in his essay "Traditional and Critical Theory" that intellectuals do a disservice to the proletariat by enthusiastically supporting them without question, which to an extent might be true, but it is also arrogant to think that intellectuals know what the working class wants better than they do. See *Critical Theory: Selected Essays by Max Horkheimer*, ed. Matthew J. O'Connell (New York: Continuum, 1990), 214.

28 Ginsborg, *A History of Contemporary Italy*, 309.

29 Mezzadra, "Italy, Operaism and Post-operaism," 4.

30 Ibid.

31 Steve Wright, *Storming Heaven: Class Composition and Struggle in Italian Autonomist Marxism* (London: Pluto Press, 2002), 110.

32 Ibid., 111.

33 Ibid., 113.

34 Ibid., 114.

35 Ibid.

36 Ibid., 117.

37 Ibid., 118.

38 Ibid., 119.

39 Ginsborg, *A History of Contemporary Italy*, 314.

40 Ibid., 315.

41 Ibid., 316.

42 Wright, *Storming Heaven*, 318.

43 Ibid., 138.

44 Ginsborg, *A History of Contemporary Italy*, 380.

45 Ibid., 376.

46 Ibid., 386.

47 Ibid., 387.

48 Wright, *Storming Heaven*, 212.

49 Dario Azzellini, "Italy, From the New Left to the Great Repression," *The International Encyclopedia of Revolution and Protest: 1500 to the Present*, ed. Immanuel Ness (Oxford: Wiley-Blackwell Publishing, 2009), 5, http://www.revolutionprotestencyclopedia.com/.

50 Steve Wright, "Mapping Pathways within Italian Autonomist Marxism: A Preliminary Survey," *Historical Materialism* 16 (2008): 122.

51 Ibid.

52 Piero Bernocchi, *Dal sindacato ai Cobas* (Rome: Erre Emme, 1993), 106.

53 Gregor Gall, "The Emergence of a Rank and File Movement: The Comitati di Base in the Italian Worker's Movement," *Capital & Class* 19, no. 1 (1995): 14.

54 Ida Regalia and Marino Regini, "Collective Bargaining and Social Pacts in Italy," in Harry Charles Katz, Wonduck Lee, and Joohee Lee, eds., *The New Structure of Labor Relations: Tripartism and Decentralization* (Ithaca, NY: Cornell University Press, 2004), 8.

55 Regalia and Regini, "Collective Bargaining and Social Pacts," 9.

56 Gall, "The Emergence of a Rank and File Movement."

57 Bernocchi describes the phenomenon of state syndicalism in *Dal sindacato ai Cobas*, in which he highlights the key problem with Italy's confederal unions. For Bernocchi the issue is that being a union representative has become a career rather than a form of workers' participation. The union has become another agency that workers have to answer to rather than an apparatus workers can use against their employer (94).

58 Accusing the Cobas of representing highly paid workers is also a moot point. As Marx and Engels say in *The Communist Manifesto*, "The bourgeoisie has stripped of its halo every occupation hitherto honored and looked up to with reverent awe. It has converted the physician, the lawyer, the priest, the poet, the man of science, into its paid wage-laborers." (Karl Marx and Friedrich Engels, *Marx-Engels Reader*, 2nd ed., Robert Tucker ed. [New York: W.W. Norton & Company, 1978], 476.) The Cobas recognize the developments that Marx and Engels predicted as capitalism has progressed.

59 Piero Bernocchi, "Risposte COBAS," accessed April 22, 2012, http://www.pane-rose.it/files/index.php?c8:086.

60 Ibid.

61 Bernocchi, *Dal sindacato ai Cobas*, 108.

62 "CHI SIAMO E COSA VOGLIAMO—Una sintetica presentazione della CUB," *Confederazione Unitaria di Base*. CUB, October 3, 2005, http://www.cub.it/article/?c=chi-siamo&id=3&print=1.

63 Bernocchi, "Risposte COBAS." http://www.idocentiscapigliati.com/2012/10/lettera-ai-sindacati-di-bernocchi-cobas.html, accessed February 20, 2014.

64 COBAS di nuovo in piazza," L'Unione Sarda.it, November 17, 2011 (accessed March 4, 2012)

65 "COBAS, corteo per pochi intimi e scuole ," L'UnioneSarda.it, November 18, 2011, (accessed March 4, 2012).

66 "Universita: La protesta di migliaia di studenti cortei, sit-in, lezioni sul bus emobilitazione," Cobas, November 17, 2011, http://www.cobas.it (accessed March 4, 2012).

67 Mario Neri and Gerardo Adinolfi, "Studenti e Cobas in Piazza Catene alla sede Bankitalia," *La Repubblica Firenze,* November 17, 2011, http://firenze.repubblica.it/ (accessed March 4, 2012).

68 "Cub-Cobas: una pratica unitaria per sostenere una lotta che modifichi radicalmente l'esistente," CUB, February 2012, http://www.cub.it/ (accessed March 4, 2012).

69 Katia Ancona, Laura Mari, and Valeria Pini. "Onda, Cobas e centri sociali contro il G8," La Repubblica Roma March (2009), http://roma.repubblica.it/dettaglio/onda-cobas-e-centri-sociali-contro-il-g8/1610591/1.

70 Piero Bernocchi, "Su alcune interpretazioni della crisi e del capitalismo attuale e sulle prospettive," n.d., http://utopiarossa.blogspot.com/2011/11/su-alcune-interpretazioni-della-crisi-e.html.

71 For more on the concept of state capitalism, see "State Capitalism," an essay by Friedrich Pollock, in which he argues that capital is no longer private; rather, there is an interest on behalf of the state to coordinate the major industries of the country. See *The Essential Frankfurt School Reader*, eds. Andrew Arato and Elke Gelbhardt (New York: Continuum, 1990) 71–94.

72 Bernocchi, "Risposte COBAS."

73 Gramsci, in his *Prison Notebooks*, argued that hegemony can lie either within the state or within the private, but that it is entirely possible that hegemony may lie in both, creating confusion as to which institution to direct action toward.

74 Antonio Gramsci, *Selections from the Prison Notebooks*, Quintin Hoare ed. (New York: International Publishers, 1971), 6.

75 Ibid., 9–10.

76 Antonio Negri makes a persuasive argument that constitutional democracies are, in fact, a way to sever the ability of democracy to fully manifest itself. "Democracy is in fact a theory of absolute government, while constitutionalism is a theory of limited government and therefore a practice that limits democracy." Negri, *Insurgencies: Constituent Power and the Modern State* (Minneapolis: University of Minnesota Press, 1999), 2.

77 Roger Karapin, *Protest Politics in Germany: Movements on the Left and Right since the 1960s* (University Park: Pennsylvania State University Press, 2007).

78 Bernocchi, "Risposte COBAS."

79 Ibid.

80 Statuto dello Slai COBAS—Sindacato dei Lavoratori Autorganizzati Intercategoriale, (Bellaria: Congresso Nazionale dello Slai COBAS 1998).

81 Bernocchi, *Dal sindacato ai Cobas*, 125–26.

82 Bernocchi, "Risposte COBAS."

83 Bernocchi, *Dal sindacato ai Cobas*, 132.

84 Ibid., 130.

85 Ibid., 131.

86 Bernocchi, "Risposte COBAS."

87 Gall, "The Emergence of a Rank and File Movement," 17.

88 Mario Tronti, "Workerism and Politics," *Historical Materialism* 18 (2010): 189.

Chapter 2

1 *Chinese Statistical Yearbook* (Beijing: China Statistics Press, 1998, 2009).

2 Ching Kwan Lee, *Against the Law: Labor Protests in China's Rustbelt and Sunbelt* (University of California Press, 2007).

3 Yu Jianrong, *Zhongguo gongren jieji zhuangkuang:Anyuan shilu (The Plight of China's Working Class: Annals of Anyuan)* (Hong Kong: Mirror Books, 2006), 461.

4 Cheng Guangshen, "Zhongguo gongren jieji de xingqi yu zhongguo geming de qiantu." ("The Rise of the Working Class and the Future of Chinese Revolution") China Labor Research Web Associates, Spring 2011, 21–22, http://www.clb.org.hk/en/. See also

Mingqi Li, "The Rise of the Working Class and the Future of the Chinese Revolution," *Monthly Review* 63, no. 2 (June 2011).

5   *China Labour Bulletin* "Protecting Workers' Rights or Serving the Party: The Way Forward for China's Trade Unions," (March 2009): http://www.clb.org.hk/en/files/share/File/research_reports/acftu_report.pdf.

6   Han Dongfang, "China's Main Union Is Yet to Earn Its Job," *The Guardian* (June 26, 2011): http://www.guardian.co.uk/commentisfree/2011/jun/26/china-trade-union-global-movement?intcmp=239.

7   Yu Jianrong, *The Plight of China's Working Class*, 461.

8   Mingqi Li, "The Rise of the Working Class."

9   For instance, see: *Gaige kaifang shidai de ziben yundong* (Hong Kong: China Cultural Communication Press, 2010).

10 Mingqi Li, "The Rise of the Working Class."

11 Jackie Sheehan, *Chinese Workers: A New History* (London: Routledge, 1998).

12 Elizabeth Perry, *Challenging the Mandate of Heaven: Popular Protest in Modern China*, (Armonk, NY: M.E. Sharpe, 2001).

13 Ibid.

14 Sheehan, *Chinese Workers*, 148–52.

15 Yu Jianrong, *The Plight of China's Working Class*, 461.

16 Ching Kwan Lee, *Against the Law*.

17 Yu Jianrong (2006) seeks the reason for defeat in socialism itself. Mingqi Li (2011) sees the political inexperience of the working class as the reason for the workers' defeat. Cheng Guangshen (2011) believes that workers had too many illusions about the party, which led to their demise. All these authors fail to make a connection between 1989 and the defeat of resistance to privatization in the ensuing period.

18 Cheng Guangshen, *The Rise of the Working Class*, 21–22.

19 Uniden is a Japanese electronics company and one of its plants in Shenzhen experienced five strikes between December 2004 and April 2005. The strikers demanded the founding of a workplace union. See Au Loong Yu, Nan Shan and Zhang Ping, *Women Migrant Workers under the Chinese Social Apartheid* (Bangkok: Committee for Asian Women, 2007).

20 Associated Press, Beijing, "30,000 China Steel Workers in Deadly Clash," *Jakarta Post*, July 25, 2009, http://www.thejakartapost.com/news/2009/07/25/report-30000-china-steelworkers-deadly-clash.html.

21 Jiang Xuan, *Woguo zhongchangqi shiye wenti yanjiu* (Research on China's Medium and Long Term Unemployment) (Beijing: China People's University Press, 2004), 181.

22 Cited in "China Debates the Lessons of Tonghua Tragedy," *China Labour Bulletin*, August 10, 2009, http://www.clb.org.hk/en/content/china-debates-lessons-tonghua-tragedy.

23 "Open Letter to the Public and All the Workers in Honda Auto Parts Manufacturing Co., Ltd.," China Labour Net, June 4, 2010, http://worldlabor.org/eng/node/361.

24 Rena Lau, "Restructuring of the Honda Auto Parts Union in Guongdong, China: A 2-year Assessment of the 2010 Strike," *WorkingUSA* 15, no. 4, (2012).

25 "Nanhai bentian laozi tanpan, jinnian gongzi zaizhang 600 yuan," http://gcontent.oeeee.com/7/1b/71bfbe458113bbc3/Blog/b4f/433268.html.

26 "Open Letter from The Nanhai District General Trade Union and Shishan Town General Trade Union to the Workers of Honda Motors Nanhai Component and Parts Factory," translation posted on China Study Group, June 5, 2010, http://chinastudygroup.net/2010/06/translation-of-an-open-letter-from-the-nanhai-district-general-trade-union-and-shishan-town-general-trade-union-to-the-workers-of-honda-motors-nanhai-component-and-parts-factory/.

27 Feng Chen, "Union Power in China: Source, Operation and Constraints," *Modern China* 35, no. 6, (2009). Chen points to the increase in the number of provincial union heads who have assumed key party and government positions at the same level since then as evidence.

28 Ying Zhu, Malcom Warner, and Tongqing Feng, "Employment Relations 'with Chinese Characteristics': The Role of Trade Unions in China." *International Labor Review* (2011).

29 China Labour Bulletin, "Protecting Workers' Rights."

30 "Guangdongsheng qiye minzhu guanli tiaoli (Oct 1 2011 zhengqiu yijiangao) pinglun ji xiugai jianyi," ("Comment and Suggestions for Amendment on the Draft of Guangdong Province's 'Regulations on the Democratic Management of Enterprises,' October 1, 2011 Draft"): http://www.jttp.cn/a/report/opinion/2011/0219/889.html. See also Zhu, Warner, and Feng, 2011.

31 Chen, "Union Power in China," 666–67

32 S.F. Diamond, "The 'Race to the Bottom' Returns: China's Challenge to the International Labor Movement." *UC Davis Journal of International Law and Policy* 10 (2003): 39–74.

33 Han Dongfang, "China's Main Union."

34 Ibid.

35 Ibid.

36 Unpublished letter.

37 Ron's Blog, "China: ACFTU representing workers on ILO governing body—That cannot be serious." International Union of Food, Agricultural, Hotel, Restaurant, Catering, Tobacco and Allied Workers' Associations website, October 2011, http://cms.iuf.org/?q=node/1076.

38 China Labour Bulletin, "Protecting Workers' Rights."

39 Han Dongfang, "China's Main Union."

40 China Labour Bulletin, "Protecting Workers' Rights."

41 *Shuilai weiquan, weishui weiquan—Lun quanzong weiquan de zhengzhihua ji zhongguo gonghui yundong de chulu* ("On ACFTU's Politicization of Workers' Rights Protection and the Way Forward for Chinese Trade Union Movement) (Hong Kong: China Labour Bulletin, 2008). Chapter four, as translated by the authors.

42 "A Political Economic Analysis of the Strike in Honda and the auto parts industry in China," a report of the Hong Kong Liaison Office (IHLO) of the international trade union movement, http://www.ihlo.org/LRC/W/000710.pdf.

Chapter 3

1 Joseph R. Blasi, Maya Kroumova, and Douglas Kruse, *Kremlin Capitalism: The Privatization of the Russian Economy* (Ithaca, NY: Cornell University Press, 1997).

2 Linda J. Cook, *Labor and Liberalization: Trade Unions in the New Russia* (New York: Twentieth Century Foundation Press, 1997); Sarah Ashwin and Simon Clarke, *Russian Trade Unions and Industrial Relations in Transition* (New York: Palgrave Macmillan, 2003); and V.A. Borisov, *Zabastovki v Ugolnoi Promyshlennosti: Analiz Shahterskogo Dvizhenija za 1989–99 gg* (Moscow: ISITO, 2001).

3 Cook, *Labor and Liberalization*; Borisov, *Zabastovki v Ugolnoi Promyshlennosti*; Debora Javeline, *Protest and the Politics of Blame: The Russian Response to Unpaid Wages* (Ann Arbor: University of Michigan Press, 2003); Simon Clarke, "Trade Unions, Industrial Relations and Politics in Russia," *Journal of Communist Studies* 9, no. 4 (1993): 133–60; Ashwin and Clarke, *Russian Trade Unions*.

4 Sarah Ashwin, *Russian Workers: The Anatomy of Patience* (Manchester: Manchester University Press, 1999); Javeline, *Protest and the Politics of Blame*; Stephen Crowley, *Hot Coal, Cold Steel: Russian and Ukrainian Workers from the End of the Soviet Union to the Postcommunist Transformation* (Ann Arbor: University of Michigan Press, 1997); Stephen Crowley and David Ost, eds., *Workers after Workers' States: Labor and Politics in Post-Communist Eastern Europe* (Lanham, MD: Rowman & Littlefield, 2001); and Paul Kubicek, "Organized Labor in Postcommunist States: Will the Western Sun Set on It, Too?" *Comparative Politics* 32, no. 1 (1999).

5 Javeline, *Protest and the Politics of Blame*, 3.

6   S. Greene and G. Robertson, "Novoe Rabochee Dvizhenie v Rossii," *Pro et Contra* 12, no. 2–3 (2008): 36–58

7   I. Germanov, "Samoorganizatsija rabotnikov I protestnaja aktivnost," in I.M. Kozina ed., *Profsoyuzy na Predpriyatiyach Sovremennoj Rossii* (Moscow: Vozmozhnosti Rebrendinga, 2009).

8   Greene and Roberston, "Novoe Rabochee Dvizhenie v Rossii; K. Kleman, Pod'em Rabochego i Profsojuznogo Dvizhenija, 2007, http://ikd.ru/node/3510; P.V. Bizyukov, *Kak zaschischajut trudovye prava v Rosii: kollektivnye trudovye protesty i ih rol' v regulirovanii trudovyh otnoshenij* (Moscow: ANO Centr social'no-trudovyh prav, 2011); P. Bizyukov, "Labor Protests in Russia, 2008–2011" *Russian Analytical Digest* 104 (2011): 6–9, http://www.css.ethz.ch/publications/DetailansichtPubDB_EN?rec_id=1664; I.M. Kozina, "Postsovetskie Profsojuzy," *Otechestvennye Zapiski* 36, no. 3 (2007): 94–108.

9   David Ost, "Illusory Corporatism: Tripartism in the Service of Neoliberalism," *Politics and Society* 28, no. 4 (2000): 503–30.

10 Arturo Bronstein, "The New Labour Law of the Russian Federation," *International Labour Review* 144, no. 3 (2005): 292.

11 JSITO cited in Sarah Ashwin, "Social Partnership or a 'Complete Sellout'? Russian Trade Unions' Responses to Conflict," *British Journal of Industrial Relations* 42, no. 1 (2004): 26.

12 According to the new Labor Code, the union is deprived of the right to a "veto" when workers are fired at the initiative of the administration; now the union can only state its opinion. Time limits were introduced in conducting collective bargaining at an enterprise, after which the employer can sign only several insignificant points and the agreement will be considered concluded. Agreement on the most important, and therefore most conflictual, points can be postponed indefinitely.

13 "As a rule [a] strike can be called only at the outcome of a fairly formal procedure consisting of several successive stages, none of which can be skipped. The procedure begins with listing in writing, of the workers' demands. The list of demands must then be approved by an assembly of the workers or a conference of their representatives with a quorum of the majority of the workers in the former case or a two-thirds majority in the later case (article 399). Next, the workers' demands are transmitted to the Collective Dispute Settlement Departments (It is worth mentioning that, by early 2004, such Departments had been set up in only nine of 89 'subjects' of the Russian Federation. And following the 'dissolution' of the Ministry of Labor and Social Development, the establishment of additional Departments appears to have been suspended). Only after the conciliation or, as the case may be, mediation procedure has run its course can a strike been called (prior to this the Code does provide that a 1-hour warning strike may be called during the proceedings of the conciliation commission after the later had been in session for five consecutive days and subject to three days prior notice (article 410), subject to a majority vote for by an assembly of the workers or a conference of their representatives (with a quorum of two-thirds at least of the total number of workers concerned). Prior notice of the strike must be given ten consecutive days beforehand, indicating inter alia the date of the start of the strike, its estimated duration, the number of participants, the name of the chief officer of the body representing the workers, etc. (article 410) During the strikes the freedom of work of non-strikers must be guaranteed." Arturo Bronstein, "The New Labour Law of the Russian Federation," *International Labour Review* 144, no. 3, (2005): 314.

14 Linda J. Cook, "More Rights, Less Power: Labor Standards and Labor Markets in East European Post-communist States," *Studies in Comparative International Development* 45 (2010): 170–97.

15 Cook, "More Rights, Less Power," 193.

16 See http://www.fnpr.ru.

17 Unfortunately there are no reliable statistics about free labor unions. According to the Federation of European Employers (http://www.fedee.com/labour-relations/

trade-unions-in-europe/#Russia), the All-Russian Confederation of Labor (VKT) has about 3 million members and the Confederation of Labor of Russia (KTR) 1.2 million members. The Trade Union Association of Russia (SOTSPROF) encompasses a total of 500,000 members. Alternative labor unions are strong among the miners, airline pilots, air traffic controllers, dockers, railway locomotive crews, and automobile industry workers. Although alternative labor unions claim the growth of union membership in recent years they do not provide any statistical proof to this claim.

18 Kozina, "Postsovetskie Profsojuzy."
19 P.V. Bizyukov, "Al'ternativnye profsojuzy: tri jepohi" (Alternative Trade Unions: Three Types), in V. Borisov and S. Klark, eds., *Profsojuznoe prostranstvo sovremennoj Rossii* (The Trade Union Space of Modern Russia) (Moscow: ISITO, 2003). Irina B. Olimpieva,"Rossijskie Profsojuzy v Sisteme Regulirovanija Social'no-trudovyh Otnoshenij: Osobennosti, Problemy i Perspektivy Issledovanija," (Moscow: MONF, 2010); and Irina Olimpieva, "'Free' and 'Official' Labor Unions in Russia: Different Modes of Labor Interest Representation," *Russian Analytical Digest*, 2011, http://e-collection. library.ethz.ch/eserv/eth:5057/eth-5057-01.pdf.
20 I. Kozina, "Korporativnye Profsojuzy: Vzaimodejstvie s Rabotodatelem v Bovyh Uslovijah," in *Profsoyuzy na Predpriyatiyach Sovremennoj*, ed. I. Kozina.
21 Kozina, "Postsovetskie Profsojuzy"; K. Kleman, Pod'em Rabochego i Profsojuznogo Dvizhenija, 2007, http://ikd.ru/node/3510.
22 See TsSTP's site, http://www.trudprava.ru. A special methodology has been developed to monitor protest actions. In the monitoring research approach "labor protest" is defined as an *open form of labor conflict, in which workers at an enterprise (organization, corporation) or a labor group take actions directed at standing up for their social-labor position by influencing their employer or other subjects serving as employers, with the goal of making changes*. The main source of information are reports about protest actions published on news websites, in internet newspapers, and information portals devoted to social-economic themes (about 80 different sources). These reports are extremely timely and usually appear on-line the same day as the protest action occurs. On the basis of the daily monitoring of the announcements about labor and related protests and the cases are being chosen that fit the working definition of a labor protest. Most information comes from specialized internet portals that focus on labor issues and from federal and regional news agencies. Among the most useful sites are: The Institute of Collective Action (http://www.ikd.ru/), Labour Start (http://www.labourstart.org/ru), Rabochaia bor'ba (http://www.rborba.ru) Profsoyuzy segodnya (http://www.unionstoday.ru/ news/), Labor unions' newspaper *Solidarnost* (http://www.solidarnost.org/) and some others. Usually, articles provide information about the place where the protest action (strike) took place (federal district, region, and city); the date that it started and finished; the industry of the enterprise or workers; the reasons for the protest; the forms of the protest; and the results achieved. It is also important to know whether this is the first time that a conflict arose or if it has been repeating over time. Also we record the role played by trade unions and other organizations in labor conflicts. All the data is gathered in a database and then used for analysis.
23 The description of the case "FORD plant" was prepared by a union activist and participant in the strike, Vadim Bolshakov.
24 MPRA was established in 2006. Other members of MPRA include labor union "Edinstvo" (at AvtoVAZ), labor unions of GM, Nokian Tires, and others.
25 The description of this case is based on the research conducted by Irina Kozina ("Postsovetskie Profsojuzy," op. cit.).
26 The description of the case "Pikalevo" is based on the empirical studies conducted by Bizyukov (in *Kak zaschischajut trudovye prava v Rosii: kollektivnye trudovye protesty i ih rol' v regulirovanii trudovyh otnoshenij*, 2011) and B.I. Maximov, "Russia's Phenomenon in Pikalevo," *Sociological Studies Monthly* 4 (2010).

27 This episode can be seen at http://rt.com/news/top-businessmen-not-immune-to-putin-s-wrath (accessed January 2, 2012).

28 The description of the conflict in Mezhdurechensk is based on the empirical data collected by Piotr Bizyucov (in *Kak zaschischajut trudovye prava v Rosii*).

Chapter 4

1   See Arup Kumar Sen, "On a Leash: Then and Now," *Economic and Political Weekly* (December 22, 2012).

2   Mausumi Bhattacharyya has helped me in giving final shape to the text. However, I alone am responsible for the views expressed here.

3   Ambuj D. Sagar and Pankaj Chandra, *Technological Change in the Indian Passenger Car Industry*, BCSIA Discussion Paper 2004–05, Energy Technology Innovation Project, Kennedy School of Government, Harvard University, 2004.

4   See *mint*, September 24, 2012.

5   Mouvement Communiste and Kolektivně Proti Kapitalu, *Workers Autonomy Strikes in India: Maruti Suzuki Strike at Manesar (June, September, October 2011)*, (May 2012): 3–5, http://libcom.org/files/28C59d01.pdf.

6   *Workers Autonomy Strikes in India.*

7   *Gurgaon Workers News* 9, no. 41, http://gurgaonworkersnews.wordpress.com/gurgaonworkersnews-no-941/.

8   *Workers Autonomy Strikes in India.*

9   J.C.B Annavajhula and Surendra Pratap, "Worker Voices in an Auto Production Chain: Notes from the Pits of a Low Road—I" in *Economic and Political Weekly* 47, no. 33 (August 18, 2012): 50.

10 Ibid.

11 *Workers Autonomy Strikes in India*, 17–18.

12 "Towards a Workers' Organization: On the Struggle at Maruti Suzuki," *Gurgaon Workers News*, October 28, 2012. This is the report of a detailed survey conducted by *GWN*. The interviews incorporated in the report were conducted during April to June 2012.

13 Annavajhula and Pratap, "Worker Voices in an Auto Production Chain—I," 51.

14 "Towards a Workers' Organization," *Gurgaon Workers News*, October 28, 2012. See also Amit Sengupta and Sadiq Naqvi, "Maruti Mayhem: Dark Side of the Moon," Hardnews, August 2012, http://www.hardnewsmedia.com/2012/07/5517.

15 Aman Sethi, cited in "Towards a Workers' Organization"; *Workers Autonomy Strikes in India*, 18; Annavajhula and Pratap, "Worker Voices in an Auto Production Chain," (August 18, 2012): 56–57; and Manu N Kulkarni, "Where is *Nemawashi* in Maruti Suzuki?", *Economic and Political Weekly*, September 15, 2012.

16 "Towards a Workers' Organization," *Gurgaon Workers News*, October 28, 2012.

17 Ibid.

18 See Maya John, "Workers' Discontent and Form of Trade Union Politics," *Economic and Political Weekly* (January 7, 2012): 19–20.

19 John, "Workers' Discontent," 20.

20 Ibid.

21 See Jayashankar Menon, "Newly Formed Maruti Suzuki Workers' Union to Demand Wage Revision within a Fortnight," http://smehorizon.sulekha.com/newly-formed-maruti-suzuki-workers-union-to-demand_automotive-viewsitem_7357.

22 *Workers Autonomy Strikes in India*, 6–8.

23 *Workers Autonomy Strikes in India*, 8; "Maruti Manesar plant workers boycott union election," http://www.thehindu.com/business/companies/marutis-manesar-plant-workers-boycott-union-election/article2233110.ece .

24 *Workers Autonomy Strikes in India*, 8–9.; John, "Workers' Discontent," 19.

25 *Workers Autonomy Strikes in India*, 9–11.

26 Ibid., 12–13, 25.

27 "Towards a Workers' Organization," *Gurgaon Workers News*, October 28, 2012., 2; Sengupta and Naqvi, "Maruti Mayhem."
28 See "Militarization of Maruti Workplace" in *Economic and Political Weekly* (September, 15, 2012).
29 See "Third Degree Torture Used on Maruti Workers: Rights Body," *The Hindu*, September 26, 2012, http://www.thehindu.com/todays-paper/tp-national/tp-newdelhi/third-degree-torture-used-on-maruti-workers-rights-body/article3937396.ece.
30 Ibid.
31 Cited in Annavajhula and Pratap, "Worker Voices in an Auto Production Chain—I," 56.
32 Ibid., 53.
33 Ibid.; J.C.B. Annavajhula and Surendra Pratap, "Worker Voices in an Auto Production Chain: Notes from the Pits of a Low Road—II," *Economic and Political Weekly* (August 25, 2012): 52. http://www.epw.in/special-articles/worker-voices-auto-production-chain.html.
34 "Towards a Workers' Organization," *Gurgaon Workers News*, October 28, 2012.
35 Annavajhula and Pratap, "Worker Voices in an Auto Production Chain—II," 49, 52–53.
36 "Towards a Workers' Organization."
37 Ibid.
38 Cited in ibid.
39 Deepal Jayasekera, "India: Maruti Suzuki Union Leaders Given Huge Payouts after Ending Strike," World Socialist Web Site, November 12, 2011, http://www.wsws.org/en/articles/2011/11/maru-n12.html.
40 John, "Workers' Discontent," 20.
41 See Arun Kumar, "India: Maruti Suzuki Launches Witch-Hunt against Workers," World Socialist Web Site, July 23, 2002, http://www.wsws.org/en/articles/2012/07/maru-j23.html.
42 See John, "Workers' Discontent," 20, for the above arguments.
43 See Arup Kumar Sen, "Mode of Labour Control in Colonial India," *Economic and Political Weekly* (September 2002); and "Capital, Labour and the State: Eastern India and Western India, 1918–1939," *Economic and Political Weekly* (July, 2000).
44 *Workers Autonomy Strikes in India*, 12
45 See Sen, "On a Leash: Then and Now," 9.
46 See Arup Kumar Sen, "Workers' Control in India's Communist-Ruled State: Labor Struggles and Trade Unions in West Bengal" in Immanuel Ness and Dario Azzellini eds., *Ours to Master and to Own: Workers' Control from the Commune to the Present* (Chicago: Haymarket Books, 2011), 356–64.

Chapter 5

1 Luli Callincos, *A People's History of South Africa: Gold and Workers, 1886–1924* (Ravan Press: Johannesburg, 1980).
2 B. Nasiorowska, "Improving Safety and Security in Platinum Mining Using the Newest Facial Recognition Technology," ("The 4th International Platinum Conference, Platinum in transition 'Boom or Bust,'" The Southern African Institute of Mining and Metallurgy, 2010). http://www.saimm.co.za/Conferences/Pt2010/129-136_Nasiorowska.pdf.
3 G4S, "Mine Security," http://www.g4s.co.za/en-ZA/What%20we%20do/Services/Mine%20security/.
4 Mikhail A. Bakunin, *The Capitalist System* (Los Angeles: ICC, 1999).
5 The Southern African NGO Network (SANGONeT), "Mining Industry Must Act on Silicosis," November 18, 2009, http://www.ngopulse.org/press-release/mining-industry-must-act-silicosis.
6 Congress of South African Trade Unions, *Cosatu Today: Our Side of the Story*, October 7, 2009, http://www.groups.google.com/group/cosatu-daily-news/msg/16c4c01e2acd8969.

7   Shawn Hattingh, "Mineworkers' Direct Action: Occupations and Sit-Ins in South Africa," *WorkingUSA: The Journal of Labor and Society* 13, no. 3 (2010): 343–50.

8   Ibid.

9   Chanel de Bruyn, "Aquarius' Kroondal Mine Reopened after Protest Action." http://www.miningweekly.com/article/aquarius-kroondal-mine-reopened-after-protest-action-2009-11-23, accessed February 20, 2014.

10 Hattingh, "Mineworkers' Direct Action."

11 James Macharia, "Striking Implats Miners Attack Union Leaders," *Mail & Guardian*, http://www.mg.co.za/article/2009-09-04-striking-implats-miners-attack-union-leaders, September 4, 2009, accessed May 28, 2010.

12 Mametlwe Sebei and Weizmann Hamilton, "Rustenburg Miners' Strike," http://www.socialistsouthafrica.co.za, December 9, 2009, accessed May 28, 2010.

13 De Bruyn, "Aquarius' Kroondal Mine Reopened."

14 Kwanele Sosibo, "Pattern of Violence, Intimidation against Miners." *Mail & Guadian Online*, August 30, 2012, http://za.news.yahoo.com/pattern-violence-intimidation-against-miners-143900383.html, accessed February 20, 2014.

15 De Bruyn, "Aquarius' Kroondal Mine Reopened."

16 Ibid.

17 Chanel de Bruyn, "Illegal Sit-in Halts Production at SA Platinum Mine," *Mining Weekly*, http://www.miningweekly.com/article/illegal-sit-in-halts-production-at-two-rivers-2009-10-19, October 19, 2009, accessed May 28, 2010

18 Kea' Modimoeng, "Protests Go Underground," http://www.timeslive.co.za/business/article164643.ece/Protests-go-underground. November 8, 2009, accessed May 28, 2010.

19 Hattingh, "Mineworkers' Direct Action."

20 Ibid.

21 Martin Creamer, "Two Rivers Two-Day Underground Sit-in Ends after Interdict," *Mining Weekly.com*, January 23, 2010, http://www.miningweekly.com/article/two-rivers-two-day-underground-sit-in-ends-after-interdict-2010-01-22, accessed February 20, 2014.

22 "Cops End Limpopo Mine Sit-in," News 24, January 21, 2010, http://www.news24.com/Content/SouthAfrica/News/1059/45c260d650164982a987b3b16 22e7512/21-01-2010-06-13/Cops_end_Limpopo_mine_sit-in.

23 Martin Creamer, "Two Rivers Platinum-Miners in Underground Pay Drama," January 20, 2010, *Mining Weekly*, http://www.miningweekly.com/article/two-rivers-platinum-miners-being-held-hostage-underground---num-2010-01-20, accessed February 20, 2014.

24 Ibid.

25 Hattingh, "Mineworkers' Direct Action."

26 Ibid.

27 "Coal Strike Starts," *City Press*, July 25, 2011, http://www.citypress.co.za/Business/News/Coal-strike-starts-20110725.

28 Loni Prinsloo, "Illegal strike brings Platmins Pilanesberg mine to a halt," *Mining Weekly*, June, 24, 2011, http://www.miningweekly.com/article/illegal-strike-brings-platmins-pilanesberg-mine-to-a-halt-2011-06-24.

29 "Lonmin Starts Dismissing Striking Miners," *Mining Review*, May 24, 2011. http://www.miningreview.com/node/19469.

30 David Steward, "How Will Future Historians View Marikana?" Politics Web, September 30, 2012, http://www.politicsweb.co.za/politicsweb/view/politicsweb/en/page71619?oi d=329465&sn=Marketingweb+detail.

31 Dineo Matomela, "Lonmin Rehires 6 000 Workers," *Business Report*, May 30, 2011, http://www.iol.co.za/business/lonmin-rehires-6-000-workers-1.1075493 30th May 2011

32 Nelly Shamase, "Striking Gupta Mine Workers Held," M&G Centre for Investigative Journalism, May 4, 1011, http://amabhungane.co.za/article/2011-03-04-striking-gupta-mine-workers-held.

33 Dewald van Rensburg, "NUM Challenged in Implats Member Revolt," Miningmx, February 5, 2012, http://www.miningmx.com/news/platinum_group_metals/Num-challenged-in-Implats-member-revolt.htm.

34 Tito Mzamo, "South Africa: Recent Strike at Impala Platinum Mine in Rustenburg," In Defence of Marxism, March 6, 2012, http://www.marxist.com/south-africa-strike-at-impala-platinum-mine-rustenburg.htm.

35 "Impala Platinum Strike," *Mail & Guardian*, http://mg.co.za/tag/impala-platinum-strike

36 Mzamo, "South Africa: Recent strike at Impala"

37 Greg Marinovich, "Beyond the chaos at Marikana," IOL News, August 17, 2012, http://www.iol.co.za/news/beyond-the-chaos-at-marikana-1.1364787

38 News 24, March 13, 2012, http://www.news24.com/SouthAfrica/News/Mineworkers-barricade-roads-in-Limpopo-20120315.

39 Allan Seccombe, "Three Dead in Aquarius Platinum mine invasion," *Business Day*, August 1, 2012, http://www.bdlive.co.za/articles/2012/08/01/three-dead-in-aquarius-platinum-mine-invasion

40 Sacks, "Marikana prequel."

41 Sipho Hlongwane, "Marikana Commission: NUM in a deep hole over the fight that started ti all," Daily Maverick, November 12, 2012, http://www.dailymaverick.co.za/article/2013-02-01-marikana-commission-num-in-a-deep-hole-over-the-fight-that-started-it-all

42 Sacks, "Marikana prequel."

43 Greg Marinovich, "The Murder Fields of Marikana," *Daily Maverick*, August 30, 2012, http://www.dailymaverick.co.za/article/2012-08-30-the-murder-fields-of-marikana-the-cold-murder-fields-of-marikana; Niren Tolsi, "Miners Killed Like 'Possessed Vermin,' Says Lawyer," *Mail & Guardian*, October 22, 2012, http://mg.co.za/article/2012-10-22-miners-killed-like-possessed-vermin-says-lawyer/.

44 Martin Legassick, "The Marikana Massacre: A Turning Point?" Abahlali baseMjondolo, August 27, 2012, http://abahlali.org/node/9084.

45 Marinovich, "The Murder Fields of Marikana."

46 Tolsi, "Miners Killed Like 'Possessed Vermin.'"

47 Branko Brkic, "Reporter's Marikana Notebook: A Thin Line Between Fear and Hate," *Daily Maverick*, September 16, 2012, http://dailymaverick.co.za/article/2012-09-16-marikana-notebook-a-thin-line-between-fear-and-hate.

48 Marikana Massacre Reports, http://ccs.ukzn.ac.za/files/Marikana%20Massacre%20reports.pdf.

49 SAPA, "77 Arrested in Mine Related Crimes," Sowetan Live, October 15, 2012, http://www.sowetanlive.co.za/news/2012/10/15/77-arrested-in-mine-related-crimes.

50 SAPA, "Miners in Underground Sit-in at Rustenberg Chrome Mine," *Mail & Guardian*, September 28, 2012, http://mg.co.za/article/2012-09-28-miners-in-underground-sit-in-at-rustenburg-chrome-mine.

51 SAPA, "Sit-in at Diamond Mine into Third Day," *Business Report*, October 4, 2012, http://www.iol.co.za/business/companies/sit-in-at-diamond-mine-into-third-day-1.1396724; and SAPA, "300 Strikers Maintain Sit-in at Sishen," *Business Report*, October 7, 2012, http://www.iol.co.za/business/companies/300-strikers-maintain-sit-in-at-sishen-1.1397944.

52 Rahima Essop, "Kumba Iron Miners Face Disciplinary Action," *Eye Witness News*, October 15, 2012, http://ewn.co.za/2012/10/15/Kumba-Iron-miners-face-disciplinary-action.

53 "Exxaro Strike Spreads to a Third Mine," *Business Report*, March 8, 2013, http://www.iol.co.za/business/companies/exxaro-strike-spreads-to-a-third-mine-1.1483325.

54 Kwanelle Sosibo, "NUM Bleeds Both Workers and Lives," *Mail & Guardian*, October 12, 2012, http://mg.co.za/article/2012-10-12-00-num-bleeds-workers-lives.

55 Allan Seccombe, "NUM Spent R1m of Own Money in Bid to End Wildcat Strikes," *Business Day*, October 15, 2012, http://www.bdlive.co.za/national/labour/2012/10/15/num-spent-r1m-of-own-money-in-bid-to-end-wildcat-strikes.

56 Matuma Letsoala, "NUM Plans Disciplinary Action over Baleni Salary Leak," *Mail & Guardian*, May 31, 2012, http://mg.co.za/article/2012-05-31-num-plans-disciplinary-action-over-baleni-salary-leak 31 May 2012

57 Jared Sacks, "Marikana Prequel: NUM and the Murders that Started It All," *Daily Maverick*, October 12, 2012, http://dailymaverick.co.za/opinionista/2012-10-12-marikana-prequel-num-and-the-murders-that-started-it-all.

58 Sosibo, "NUM Bleeds Both Workers and Lives."

59 "Rutenberg Mineworker 'Shot Dead,'" *City Press*, October 5, 2012, http://www.citypress.co.za/SouthAfrica/News/Rustenburg-mineworker-shot-dead-20121005.

60 Rael Solomon, "Harmony Mine Closure a Taste of Things to Come," *Money Web*, January 8, 2012, http://www.moneyweb.co.za/moneyweb-soapbox/harmony-mine-closure-a-taste-of-things-to-come--th?sn=2009+Detail+no+image.

61 Leonard Gentle, "AngloPlat: The Economic Propaganda War and the Battle for Democracy," South African Civil Society Information Service, January 22, 2013, http://sacsis.org.za/site/article/1544.

62 D. Van Wyk, "Overview of Operations," presentation at Community House, Salt River, Cape Town, August 29, 2012.

63 Minopex, http://www.minopex.co.za/overview-of-operations.html.

64 Mikhail A. Bakunin, *Statism and Anarchy* (Cambridge: Cambridge University Press, 1990), 343.

65 Quoted in Daniel Guérin, *Anarchism* (New York: Monthly Review Books, 1970), 68.

66 Bakunin, *Statism and Anarchy*, 178.

67 Michael Schmidt and Lucien van der Walt, *Black Flame: The Revolutionary Class Politics of Anarchism and Syndicalism* (Oakland: AK Press, 2009), 52.

Chapter 6

1 Katharina C. Wollenberg, David R. Vieites, Arie van der Meijden, Frank Glaw, David C. Cannatella, and Miguel Vences, "Patterns of Endemism and Species Richness in Malagasy Cophyline Frogs Support a Key Role of Mountainous Areas for Speciation," *Evolution* 62, no. 8 (2008): 1891; Norman Myers, Russell A. Mittermeier, Cristina G. Mittermeier, Gustavo A. B. da Fonseca, and Jennifer Kent, "Biodiversity Hotspots for Conservation Priorities," *Nature* 403 (2000): 853–58.

2 Peter J. Brosius, "Analyses and Interventions: Anthropological Engagements with Environmentalism," *Current Anthropology* 40, no. 3 (1999): 277–310.

3 Christine J. Walley, *Rough Waters: Nature and Development in an East African Marine Park* (Princeton, NJ: Princeton University Press, 2004); Genese Marie Sodikoff, *Forest and Labor in Madagascar: From Colonial Concession to Global Biosphere* (Bloomington: Indiana University Press, 2012).

4 Martin O'Connor, "On the Misadventures of Capitalist Nature," in Martin O'Connor, ed., *Is Capitalism Sustainable?: Political Economy and the Politics of Ecology* (New York: Guilford Press, 1994); Arturo Escobar, "Construction Nature: Elements for a Post-Structuralist Political Ecology," *Futures* 28, no. 4 (1996): 325–43.

5 Robert J. Foster, "Commodities, Brands, Love and Kula: Comparative Notes on Value Creation in Honor of Nancy Munn," *Anthropological Theory* 8, no. 1 (March 2008): 9–26.

6 Martin O'Connor, ed., *Is Capitalism Sustainable?*; James O'Connor, *Natural Causes: Essays in Ecological Marxism* (New York: Guilford Press, 1998); and Ted Benton, ed., *The Greening of Marxism* (New York: Guildford, 1996).

7 James O'Connor, "Is Sustainable Capitalism Possible?" in *Is Capitalism Sustainable?*, 162.

8 Martin O'Connor, "On the Misadventures of Capitalist Nature," in *Is Capitalism Sustainable?*, 128.

9 Sian Sullivan, "The Environmentality of 'Earth Incorporated,'" paper presented at the conference "An Environmental History of Neoliberalism," Lund University, May 6–8, 2010, http://siansullivan.net/2010/06/16/the-environmentality-of-earth-incorporated/.

10 Dan Brockington, *Fortress Conservation: The Preservation of the Mkomazi Game Reserve, Tanzania* (Bloomington: University of Indiana Press, 2002).

11 Lisa Gezon, "Institutional Structure and the Effectiveness of Integrated Conservation and Development Projects: Case Study from Madagascar," *Human Organization* 56, no. 4 (1997): 462–70; Janice Harper, *Endangered Species: Health, Illness and Death among Madagascar's People of the Forest* (Durham, NC: Carolina Academic Press, 2002); Christian Kull, *Isle of Fire: The Political Ecology of Landscape Burning in Madagascar* (Chicago: University of Chicago Press, 2004); Paul W. Hanson, "Governmentality, Language Ideology, and the Production of Needs in Malagasy Conservation and Development," *Cultural Anthropology* 22, no. 2 (2007): 244–84; Jeffrey C. Kaufmann, ed., *Greening the Great Red Island: Madagascar in Nature and Culture* (Pretoria: Africa Institute of South Africa, 2008); and Eva Keller, "The Banana Plant and the Moon: Conservation and the Malagasy Ethos of Life in Masoala, Madagascar," *American Ethnologist* 35, no. 4 (2009): 650–64.

12 Catherine Corson, "Territorialization, Enclosure and Neoliberalism: Non-state Influence in Struggles over Madagascar's Forests," *Journal of Peasant Studies* 38, no. 4 (2011): 703–26.

13 Genese Marie Sodikoff, "An Exceptional Strike: A Micro-History of 'People versus Park' in Madagascar," *Journal of Political Ecology* 14 (2007): 10–33.

14 ANGAP had been established by donors to replace some of the duties of *Eaux et Forêts*, considered corrupt and ineffectual. ANGAP has since been renamed Madagascar National Parks.

15 Ratsiraka's socialism promised a "proletarian revolution" and the devolution of state power to the people, while the staffs of government agencies swelled. By the 1970s and 1980s, the payroll of Eaux et Forêts had risen to between seven hundred and nine hundred foresters, yet the number was still too meager to monitor the scope of forest burning. For an analysis of the political forces leading to the growth of burning in Madagascar, see Cristian Kull, *Isle of Fire: The Political Ecology of Landscape Burning in Madagascar* (Chicago: University of Chicago Press, 2004). See also Maureen Covell, *Madagascar: Politics, Economics and Society* (London: Frances Pinter, 1987).

16 Sarah Osterhoudt, "Sense and Sensibilities: Negotiating Meanings within Agriculture In Northeastern Madagascar," *Ethnology* 49, no. 4 (2010): 283–301.

17 Longo O. Malaivandy, *Republique Humaniste et Ecologique" Hoe? Na Eritreritra Nateraky ny kabarin'ny Filoha, ny Amiraly Didier Ratsiraka tamin'ny 9 Febroary 1997* (Antanarivo: DLE, 2000).

18 During the ICDP meetings, when the monthly agenda was supposed to be spelled out and tasked, conservation agents never seemed satisfied by the tasks assigned. When it came to "policing the park boundaries" or "teaching agroforestry techniques" or other such extension work, it was too easy to neglect these duties with no one there to supervise them.

Chapter 7

1 This chapter is a revised and updated version of an essay that appeared in *The People behind Colombian Coal: Mining, Multinationals, and Human Rights* (Bogotá: Editosorial Pisando Callos, 2007).

2 Correspondence translated by author.

3 The following descriptions reflect the positions of the participants at the time of the 2006 delegation and contract negotiations.

Chapter 8

1 Eduardo Sartelli "Argentina, socialist and communist workers' movement," in *The International Encyclopedia of Revolution and Protest: 1500 to the Present*, ed.

Immanuel Ness (Oxford: Wiley-Blackwell Publishing, 2009), 1, http://www.revolutionprotestencyclopedia.com/.

2 Daniel Schäfer, "VW: Protective Layers," *Financial Times*, June 17, 2010, http://www.ft.com/cms/s/0/dc36a278-7a44-11df-aa69-00144feabdc0.html#axzz2kvV26AAI.

3 Christian Topalov, "La Urbanización Capitalista: algunos elementos para su análisis," http://www.institutodeestudiosurbanos.info/dmdocuments/cendocieu/Especializacion_Mercados/Documentos_Cursos/Urbanizacion_Capitalista-Topalov_Christian-1979.pdf.

4 Paul Virilio considers speed as essential to the modern city. He argues that speed is essential in winning military or commercial wars. In the commercial sphere Virilio views speed as the most liberating process in capitalism. He asserts that space is losing its essential importance as information can trespass it immediately and facts can be remitted in real time to any part of the globe, and shared in real time as well. See Virilio's *Speed and Politics: An Essay on Dromology* (New York: Semiotext(e),1986).

5 Laura Meyer and Gastón Gutiérrez, "Las luchas obreras y los avances en la subjetividad," (Asociación Argentina de Especialistas en Estudios del Trabajo), http://www.aset.org.ar/congresos/7/08010.pdf, August 2005.

6 This citation and others to follow in this chapter are derived from interviews conducted by author in July 2010.

7 Perry Anderson, "The Antinomies of Antonio Gramsci," *New Left Review* 1, no. 100 (November–December 1976): 5–78. See http://www.cwanderson.org/wp-content/uploads/2011/09/anderson.pdf.

8 Antonio Gramsci, *Prison Notebooks*, vol. 1, Joseph A. Buttigieg ed. (New York: Columbia University Press, 1992).

9 Rodrigazo: Hecho significativo que desencadenó la primera huelga general que el movimiento obrero argentino realizó contra políticas impulsadas por un gobierno peronista; lo que evidencia una profunda crisis en esa alianza social. Se caracterizó como un proceso de luchas dispersas y parciales que logra centralizarse en la forma de huelga general. Su origen tuvo que ver con el Plan Rodrigo, ministro de economía del gobierno de Isabel Perón, quien ejerció su cargo durante cuarenta y nueve días (21-06 al 02-07-1975). Las medidas económicas consistían en reducir el salario de los trabajadores, estableciendo topes en los aumentos que se fijarían en los convenios colectivos a renovarse. Dado que los aumentos superaban dichos topes el gobierno no los homologa dando lugar a los reclamos pertinentes. Diario Clarín, *"El Rodrigazo, un ajuste que dejó sus huellas en los argentinos,"* 2005.

10 See Bianchini, Facundo y Mauricio Torme, "La experiencia organizativa del cuerpo de delegados de subtes: La situación de la clase obrera después de la crisis del 2001: La situación particular de los trabajadores de subterráneos de Buenos Aires, Centro Cultural de la Cooperación Floreal Gorini, n.d.

11 Celeste Rouspil, "Los últimos treinta años" in *Experiencias subterráneas: Trabajo, Organización Gremial e Ideas Políticas de los Trabajadores del Subte*. Colectivo Encuesta Obrera, Christian Castillo, et al. Ed. IPS. 2007. CABA, Argentina.

12 Mauricio Torme and Bianchini Facundo, "El Cuerpo de Delegados de Subterráneos de Buenos Aires y el conflicto salarial de Noviembre de 2004/Febrero de 2005" (Amsterdam: IISG, Labour Again Publications), http://www.iisg.nl/labouragain/documents/torme-bianchini.pdf.

13 Torme and Facundo, "El Cuerpo de Delegados."

14 "El Sindicato Se Hace," Metro Delegado, March 9, 2009, http://www.metrodelegados.com.ar/spip.php?article1741.

Chapter 9

1 The only sectors that were considered exceptions where workers remained at work and did not go on strike were the most essential public sectors, such as healthcare.

2   The "central" in the name refers mainly to the aspect of unity. Along the lines of the CGT and the IWW, the SAC united workers of all trades and industries in one organization rather than in a confederation of several trade unions. Another similarity between the CGT and the IWW was the principle of strict political independence.

3   The congress takes place every three years, unless special circumstances demand an extraordinary congress. An extraordinary congress can be called by the Central Committee (*Centralkommitté*, CK), which consists of the seven AU members plus fifteen delegates representing five electoral districts. Among the duties of the CK is the supervision of the AU. The CK meets four times a year. The employed administrators—general secretary, treasurer, and so on—are also appointed at the congress. Furthermore, the congress delegates vote on all motions that have been brought forward. Major decisions between the congresses are made by referendum. A referendum can be called by the AU, CK, or at least three LSs.

4   The register method is not uncontested within the SAC. Internal criticism focuses on two aspects (1) without enough power to broadly enforce the set minimum wage, the register method can easily backfire and the registered workers will simply be out of work—in the worst case, they will be blacklisted and (2) if the register method is only used for undocumented laborers, it might undermine working-class unity.

Chapter 10

1   This essay was adapted with permission from *Labor History* 103 (November 2012).

2   Pete Thomas, *The Mine the Workers Ran: The 1975–79 Success Story at Nymboida* (Sydney: Australian Coal & Shale Employees Federation, 1979), 36.

3   Joe Owens, Interview with Meredith Burgmann, January 24, 1978.

4   Andrée Hoyles, *Imagination in Power the Occupation of Factories in France in 1968*, Spokesman Books, Nottingham, 1973; Dave Sherry, *Occupy! A Short History of Workers' Occupations* (London: Bookmarks Publications, 2010), esp. 99–112.

5   Paulo Spriano, *The Occupation of the Factories: Italy 1920* (London: Pluto Press, 1975); Gwyn A. Williams, *Proletarian Order: Antonio Gramsci, Factory Councils and the Origins of Italian Communism, 1911–1921*, (London: Pluto Press, 1975); Martin Clark, *Antonio Gramsci and the Revolution that Failed* (New Haven: Yale University Press, New Haven, 1977).

6   Ken Coates, *Work-ins, Sit-ins and Industrial Democracy* (Nottingham: Spokesman Books, 1981); Ken Coates (ed.), *The New Worker Co-operatives* (Nottingham: Spokesman Books, 1976); John Foster and Charles Woolfson, *The Politics of the UCS Work-in: Class Alliances and the Right to Work* (London: Lawrence & Wishart, 1986); Hilary Wainwright and Dave Elliott, *The Lucas Plan: a New Trade Unionism in the Making?* (London: Allison and Busby, 1982); Tony Eccles, *Under New Management: the Story of Britain's Largest Worker Co-operative—Its Successes and Failures* (London: Pan Books, 1981); Ralph Darlington and Dave Lyddon, *Glorious Summer: Class Struggle in Britain 1972* (London: Bookmarks, 2001); Sherry, *Occupy!*, 113–28.

7   Colin Crouch, *Class Conflict and the Industrial Relations Crisis: Compromise and Corporatism in the Policies of the British State* (London: Humanities Press, 1977). See also Alwyn W. Turner, *Crisis? What Crisis? Britain in the 1970s* (London: Aurum Press, 2008).

8   See, for example, Lavaca Collective, *Sin Patrón: Stories from Argentina's Worker-Run Factories* (Chicago: Haymarket Books, 2007). The Call for Papers for a Special Interest Stream in "Alternative Work Organisations" at Rutgers University stated, "In the labour movement's history one of the forms in which the dominating system has been contested... has been through workers' run and controlled production. Defined as workers self-man-agement or *autogestión*, to use the more catchy Spanish definition, different forms of workers' empowerment at the level of production have been used in different geographi-cal contexts alongside the history of the capitalist system of production." 28th Annual International Labour Process Conference at Rutgers University, March 15–17, 2010, http://www.ilpc.org.uk/Portals/56/ilpc2010-docs/ilpc2010-callforpapers-altworkstream.pdf.

9   Steve Wright, "Mapping Pathways Within Italian Autonomist Marxism: A Preliminary Survey," *Historical Materialism* 16, no. 4, 2008, 113; Toni Negri and Others, "Do You Remember Revolution? A Proposal for an Interpretation of the Italian Movement in the 1970s" [1983], in Toni Negri, *Revolution Retrieved: Writings on Marx, Keynes, Capitalist Crisis and New Social Subjects (1967–83)* (Red Notes, London, 1988), 236–37.

10 *Australian*, April 2 1972.

11 Joe Owens, Interview with Meredith Burgmann, January 24, 1978, transcript in possession of authors.

12 John Wallace and Joe Owens, *Workers Call the Tune at Opera House*, booklet produced by National Workers Control Conference, Sydney, 1973, 24 pp.

13 Ibid., 3.

14 Ibid., 5.

15 Antonio Negri, "Keynes and the Capitalist Theory of the State Post-1929" [1968], in Negri, *Revolution Retrieved*, 13.

16 Wallace and Owens, *Workers Call the Tune at Opera House*, 5.

17 Ibid., 8.

18 Ibid., 5.

19 *Sydney Morning Herald*, April 24, 1972, 3.

20 Wallace and Owens, *Workers Call the Tune at Opera House*, 5

21 Ibid., 6.

22 Ibid., 10.

23 Ibid., 17–18

24 Ibid., 5.

25 Ibid., 8–9.

26 Ibid., 20.

27 Ibid., 18.

28 Ibid., 17–18.

29 *Sydney Morning Herald*, April 24, 1972, 3; May 1, 1972, 8.

30 Wallace and Owens, *Workers Call the Tune at Opera House*, 12.

31 Ibid., 13.

32 *Sydney Morning Herald*, April 21, 1972, 3; April 24, 1972, 3.

33 *Sydney Morning Herald*, April 26, 1972, 3; Wallace and Owens, *Workers Call the Tune at Opera House*, 13.

34 Wallace and Owens, *Workers Call the Tune at Opera House*, 14; *Sydney Morning Herald*, April 24, 1972, 3; April 26, 1972, 3; May 1, 1972, 8; May 6, 1972, 2.

35 Wallace and Owens, *Workers Call the Tune at Opera House*, 17.

36 *Sydney Morning Herald*, April 24, 1972, 3; May 1, 1972, 8; May 2, 1972, 2; Wallace and Owens, *Workers Call the Tune at Opera House*, 15.

37 Wallace and Owens, *Workers Call the Tune at Opera House*, 17.

38 Ibid., 2, 20.

39 *Sydney Morning Herald*, May 6, 1972, 2.

40 Barry Cavanagh, Interviews with Ray Jureidini, February 22, 1979, March 27, 1979, June 13, 1979.

41 Hansard, South Australia: House of Assembly, June 25, 1973, 41.

42 Barry Cavanagh, Interviews with Ray Jureidini, February 22, 1979, March 27, 1979, June 13, 1979.

43 Ibid.

44 Ibid.

45 Ibid.

46 Frank Blevins, Interview with Ray Jureidini, July 13, 1978.

47 *Advertiser*, November 21, 1972.

48 *Whyalla News*, Editorial, November 22, 1972.

49 Jim Gettings, Interviews with Ray Jureidini, February 10, 1979, March 21, 1979, April 21, 1979; Stan Aungles and Ivan Szelenyi, "Structural Conflicts between the State, Local Government and Monopoly Capital—the Case of Whyalla in South Australia," *Australian New Zealand Journal of Sociology* 15, no. 1 (March 1979): 33.

50 Jacqui Blakeley, Interviews with Ray Jureidini, July 20, 1978, February 10, 1979, March 21, 1979, April 20, 1979.

51 In February 1972, about forty-five women, employed making leather uppers for shoes at a factory in Fakenham in East Anglia, had declared the factory under workers' control in response to its impending closure due to the employer's bankruptcy. With machinery and scraps of leather to hand, they began producing leather items such as bags for sale locally under the label of "Fakenham Occupation Workers." However, the unions concerned were unsupportive: one official even told the Fakenham women they were "silly girls." See Judy Wacjman, *Women in Control: Dilemmas of a Worker's Co-operative* (Milton Keynes: Open University Press, 1983), 48–49.

52 The group certificates issued show the average total earnings of the women during the nine-month life of the cooperative was $681 whereas the total earnings of Gettings was $3,249.00.

53 Nancy Baines, Interviews with Ray Jureidini, August 5, 1978, May 22, 1979, September 10, 1979; Jacqui Blakeley, Interviews with Ray Jureidini, July 20, 1978, February 10, 1979, March 21, 1979, April 20, 1979; Heather Hudson, Interviews with Ray Jureidini, March 22, 1979, April 23, 1979; Margaret Myers, Interview with Ray Jureidini, April 25, 1979.

54 Nancy Baines, Interviews with Ray Jureidini, August 5, 1978, May 22, 1979, September 10, 1979.

55 Nancy Baines, Interviews with Ray Jureidini, August 5, 1978, May 22, 1979, September 10, 1979; Jacqui Blakeley, Interviews with Ray Jureidini, July 20, 1978, February 10, 1979, March 21, 1979, April 20, 1979; Heather Hudson, Interviews with Ray Jureidini, March 22, 1979, April 23, 1979; Margaret Myers, Interview with Ray Jureidini, April 25, 1979.

56 Nancy Baines, Interviews with Ray Jureidini, August 5, 1978, May 22, 1979, September 10, 1979.

57 Jacqui Blakeley, Interviews with Ray Jureidini, July 20, 1978, February 10, 1979, March 21, 1979, April 20, 1979.

58 Jim Gettings, Interviews with Ray Jureidini, February 10, 1979, March 21, 1979, April 21, 1979.

59 Nancy Baines, Interviews with Ray Jureidini, August 5, 1978, May 22, 1979, September 10, 1979; Jacqui Blakeley, Interviews with Ray Jureidini, July 20, 1978, February 10, 1979, March 21, 1979, April 20, 1979; Heather Hudson, Interviews with Ray Jureidini, March 22, 1979, April 23, 1979; Margaret Myers, Interview with Ray Jureidini, April 25, 1979.

60 Nancy Baines, Interviews with Ray Jureidini, August 5, 1978, May 22, 1979, September 10, 1979.

61 Ibid.

62 Heather Hudson, Interviews with Ray Jureidini, March 22, 1979, April 23, 1979.

63 Jacqui Blakeley, Interviews with Ray Jureidini, July 20, 1978, February 10, 1979, March 21, 1979, April 20, 1979,

64 Thomas, *The Mine the Workers Ran*, 6, 36. See also Pete Thomas, *The Nymboida Story. The Work-Ins that Saved a Coalmine*, Australian Coal & Shale Employees Federation, Sydney, 1975.

65 *Common Cause*, February 10, 1975, 1, 4.

66 Thomas, *The Mine the Workers Ran*, 2–9.

67 *Common Cause*, February 17, 1975, 1.

68 ABC documentary, May 1976, quoted in Thomas, *The Mine the Workers Ran*, 47.

69 *Common Cause*, February 24, 1975, 1.

70 *Common Cause*, March 3, 1975, 1, 4.

71 *Common Cause*, March 10, 1975, 1.

72 *Common Cause*, March 17, 1975, 4.

73 *Common Cause*, March 21, 1975, 2.

74 Thomas, *The Mine the Workers Ran*, 2–9. 27, 41.

75 Quoted in Thomas, *The Mine the Workers Ran*, p.56.

76 *Common Cause*, February 14, 1978, 2.

77 Quoted in Thomas, *The Mine the Workers Ran*, 64.

78 *Common Cause*, September 5, 1979, 3.

79 Thomas, *The Mine the Workers Ran*, 49; *Common Cause*, March 21, 1975, 1; April 21, 1975, 1.

80 *Common Cause*, October 10, 1975, 3.

81 *Common Cause*, February 14, 1978, 2.

82 *Common Cause*, March 21, 1975, p.1.

83 *Common Cause*, June 23, 1975, 4.

84 Quoted in Thomas, *The Mine the Workers Ran*, 49.

85 Thomas, *The Mine the Workers Ran*, 40.

86 Waterfront & Industrial Pioneer, quoted in Thomas, *The Mine the Workers Ran*, 43.

87 Quoted in Thomas, *The Mine the Workers Ran*, 64.

88 *Common Cause*, February 14, 1978, 2.

89 Quoted in Thomas, *The Mine the Workers Ran*, 35.

90 Thomas, Ibid., 69–70.

91 Waterfront & Industrial Pioneer, quoted in Thomas, *The Mine the Workers Ran*, 43.

92 *Common Cause*, March 10, 1975, 1.

93 *Common Cause*, March 17, 1975, 8.

94 *Common Cause*, April 21, 1975, 1.

95 *Common Cause*, June 9, 1975, 2.

96 Quoted in Thomas, *The Mine the Workers Ran*, 29.

97 *Common Cause*, October 10, 1975, 3.

98 Quoted in Thomas, *The Mine the Workers Ran*, 51.

99 Quoted in ibid., 56.

100 Quoted in ibid., 56–57.

101 Steve Wright, *Storming Heaven. Class Composition and Struggle in Italian Autonomist Marxism* (London: Pluto Press, 2002), 1–4.

102 Antonio Negri, "Archaeology and Project: The Mass Worker and the Social Worker" [1982], in Negri, *Revolution Retrieved*, 209.

103 Nick Dyer-Witheford, *Cyber-Marx: Cycles and Circuits of Struggle in High-Technology Capitalism* (Urbana and Chicago: University of Illinois Press, 1999), 65.

104 Negri, "Archaeology and Project," 226.

105 Timothy S. Murphy, "Editor's Introduction," in Antonio Negri, *Books for Burning: Between Civil War and Democracy in 1970s Italy*, Arianna Bove, Ed Emery, Timothy S. Murph, and Francesca Novello trans. (London: Verso, 2005), x; Wright, *Storming Heaven*, 1–4.

106 Glossary, in Negri, *Books for Burning*, xxxiv–xxxv.

107 Antonio Negri, "Preface to the Italian Edition: 1997—Twenty Years Later," Francesca Novello and Timothy S. Murphy trans. [May 1997], in Negri, *Books for Burning*, xlii.

108 Drew Cottle and Angela Keys, "The 1971 Harco 'Stay-Put': Workers' Control in One Factory?," *The Hummer* 4, no. 1 (Summer 2003–2004): 40–47. See also Lloyd Caldwell and Mick Tubbs, *The Harco Work-In... an Experience of Workers' Control*, A National Workers' Control Conference Publication (roneod), Sydney, February 1973, 24 pp.

109 *Sydney Morning Herald*, May 6, 1972, 2; May 12, 1972, 1.

110 *Wyong News*, May 8, May 15, May 29, June 5, June 26, August 28, 1974; *Newcastle Morning Herald*, May 3–18, 1974; *Wyong Advocate*, May 15, June 26, 1974; *Gosford Star*, May 22, May 29; *Gosford Central Coast Express*, May 8, May 15, May 29, 1974; "Building Workers Demand the Right to Work," Leaflet, n.d. [ca. May 1974], 2 pp., authorised by the

locked-out workers from Miruzzi South Seas; "Why Wyong Workers Work-In," poster authorised by Joe Owens and Bob Pringle on behalf of the NSWBLF, FEDFA, Central Coast Labor Council; *Scrounge*, May 31–June 14, 1974, 9–12; *FED News*, Supplement May 17, 1974, 1 p., authorised by Jack Cambourn, Secretary FEDFA; Meredith Burgmann and Verity Burgmann, *Green Bans, Red Union. Environmental Activism and the New South Wales Builders Labourers' Federation*, UNSW Press, Sydney, 101–2.

111 *Common Cause*, September 15, 1975, 3.

112 *Common Cause*, September 1, 1975, 1, 4.

113 Anonymous, "The Sanyo Work In," *Australian Left Review*, no. 66 (September 1978): 26–30; J.A. Dalton, "The Work-in/Sit-in: the Occupation as a Form of Industrial Protest in Australia," Unpublished paper presented to Industrial Relations Post-Graduates' Conference, University of Melbourne, November 12, 1980, in possession of the authors, 15–27.

114 Dalton, "The Work-in/Sit-in," 28–29.

115 Steve Prytz, unpublished manuscript in possession of the authors; Gary Nicholls, unpublished manuscript in possession of the authors; *Grey Collar. Bulletin of the Public Servants' Action Group* vol. 2, no. 2, August–September 1981; vol. 2, no. 5, June 1982; Jim Peace, "Social Security: Some Bad, Some Not So Bad," *ACOA*, January–February 1982, 3–4; ACOA, *Bulletins*, various dates 1981; Grey Collar, *The Fight for Jobs. Social Security 1981*, Public Servants Action Group, Sydney, n.d. [ca. 1982].

116 Dalton, "The Work-in/Sit-in," i.

117 Ibid., 28–29.

118 *Direct Action*, October 25, 1979, quoted in ibid., 29.

119 In possession of the authors.

120 Mario Tronti, "Lenin in England [1964]," in Red Notes (ed.), *Working Class Autonomy and the Crisis* (London: Red Notes), 1979, 1; Antonio Negri, "Marx on Cycle and Crisis" [1968], in Negri, *Revolution Retrieved*, 78; Antonio Negri, *The Politics of Subversion. A Manifesto for the Twenty-First Century*, James Newell trans., Polity Press, Cambridge, 1989, 64–65.

121 Negri, 'Keynes and the Capitalist Theory of the State', 15.

122 Ibid., 12–13.

123 Ibid., 29.

124 Ibid., 30.

125 Ibid., 35–36; Negri, *The Politics of Subversion*, 68.

126 Antonio Negri., 'Crisis of the Planner State: Communism and Revolutionary Organization' [1971], in Negri. *Books for Burning*, 34, 41.

127 Negri, "Keynes and the Capitalist Theory of the State," 35.

128 Antonio Negri, 'Crisis of the Crisis-State' [1980], in Negri, *Revolution Retrieved*, 185.

129 Negri, "Crisis of the Crisis-State," 185–86.

130 Negri, "Archaeology and Project," 211.

131 Negri, "Crisis of the Planner State," 41.

132 *Sydney Morning Herald*, April 13, 1972, 10.

133 *Sydney Morning Herald*, May 8, 1972, 2.

134 *Sydney Morning Herald*, April 28, 1972, 4.

135 Editorial, *Employers' Review*, April 1972, quoted in *Sydney Morning Herald*, April 29, 1972, 3.

136 Quoted in Thomas, *The Mine the Workers Ran*, 14.

137 Joe Owens, Interview with Meredith Burgmann, January 24, 1978.

Chapter 11

1 Daniel Gross, "Ray Kroc, McDonald's, and the Fast Food Industry," in *Forbes Greatest Business Stories of All Time* (Hoboken: Wiley, 1997).

2 Steve Babson, *Detroit: the Making of a Union Town* (New York: Adama Books, 1984).

3   NBC 5 Chicago News broadcast, January 19, 2011, http://www.nbcchicago.com/news/business/Gourmet-Sandwiches-on-the-Go-114236994.html.
4   "JimmyJohnIsaBigMan,withthePhotostoProveIt."*SmilePolitely*,June10,2011,http://www.smilepolitely.com/splog/jimmy_john_is_a_big_man._with_the_photos_to_prove_it/.
5   Paul Merrion, "Subs Served from the Right Wing," *Crain's Chicago Business*, 34, 1-1, June 20, 2011, http://www.chicagobusiness.com/article/20110618/ISSUE01/306189979.
6   Interview with JJWU Organizer, November 17, 2012.
7   Don Dodson, "Jimmy John's Founder Contemplates Moving Headquarters Out of Illinois." *The News Gazette*, Champaign, IL, January 19, 2011.
8   Fox News Broadcast, October 15, 2012, http://video.foxnews.com/v/1902585887001/jimmy-johns-founder-business-owners-unsure-of-the-future/.
9   Alexis Buss, *Minority Report*, Industrial Worker, December 2002.
10 Dues check-off, a hallmark of the bureaucratization of the labor movement, is the automatic collection of dues by the employer, rather than voluntary monthly contributions by the members.
11 Martin Glaberman, *Punching Out and Other Writings* (Chicago: Charles H. Kerr, 2002).
12 Kate Bronfenbrenner, *No Holds Barred: The Intensification of Employer Resistance to Organizing* (Washington: Economic Policy Institute, 2009).
13 Ibid.
14 Staughton Lynd and Daniel Gross, *Solidarity Unionism at Starbucks* (Oakland: PM Press, 2011).
15 City-Data, http://www.city-data.com/city/Minnetrista-Minnesota.html.
16 Mike Puddn'head, *Wages So Low You'll Freak: The Story of the Jimmy John's Workers Union* (unpublished, 2012).
17 Ibid.
18 Staughton Lynd, *We Are All Leaders: The Alternative Unionism of the Early 1930s* (Champaign: University of Illinois Press, 1996).

Chapter 12
1   UNISON is the second largest public sector trade unions in the United Kingdom, representing primarily public service and health care employees.
2   Howard Zinn, *A People's History of the United States* (New York: HarperCollins, 2009), 329–30.
3   Elizabeth Gurley Flynn was quoted in a speech on feminism and the IWW in 1912: "The IWW has been accused of pushing the women to the front. This is not true. Rather, the women have not been kept in back, and so they have naturally moved to the front." See: http://www.spunk.org/texts/groups/iww/sp000475.txt.
4   Howard Zinn, *A People's History of the United States* (New York: HarperCollins, 2009), 337–39.
5   Melanie Simms, Jane Holgate, and Edmund Heery, *Union Voices: Tactics and Tensions in UK Organizing* (Ithaca, NY: Cornell University Press, 2013).
6   Jane Wills, "Mapping Low Pay in East London: Telco Living Wage Campaign," Department of Geography, Queen Mary, University of London, September 2001, http://www.york.ac.uk/res/fbu/documents/mlpinel_sep2001.pdf.
7   Jane Wills, "Low-Pay-No-Way," *Red Pepper* (August, 2007), http://www.redpepper.org.uk/low-pay-no-way/.
8   National Union of Rail, Maritime, and Transport Workers.
9   An IWW Organiser,"Bravery and Creativity in the Crisis," *Workers Liberty*, November 22, 2012, http://www.workersliberty.org/story/2012/11/22/bravery-and-creativity-crisis.

Chapter 13
1   James R. Barrett, "The History of American Communism and Our Understanding of Stalinism," *American Communist History* 2, vol. 2 (2003): 175–82. While Communist CIO

leaders were complicit in the passage of the NLRA this critique is not intended to discredit their significant role in community organizing and fighting racism. In doing so, as James Barrett asserts, "we run the risk of equating the lives and activities of thousands of militants with national and international Communist bureaucracies, and missing entirely the experience of Communist activism, the vital role of Communists in local labor and community movements, and the meaning of Communism in the broader context of working-class everyday life" (178).

2 Staughton Lynd, *"We Are All Leaders": The Alternative Unionism of the Early 1930s* (Urbana: University of Illinois Press, 1996); Jennifer Luff, *Commonsense Anticommunism: Labor and Civil Liberties between the World Wars* (Chapel Hill: University of North Carolina Press, 2012); and Bryan J. Palmer, *James P. Cannon and the Origins of the American Revolutionary Left, 1890–1928* (Urbana: University of Illinois Press, 2006), 55–57.

3 Melvyn Dubofsky, *We Shall Be All: A History of the Industrial Workers of the World* (Chicago: Quadrangle Books, 1969); John H.M. Laslett and Seymour M. Lipset, eds., *Failure of a Dream? Essays in the History of American Socialism* (Berkeley: University of California Press, 1984.

4 Nelson Lichtenstein, *Labor's War at Home: The CIO in World War II* (Philadelphia: Temple University Press, 2003), 136–56. Lichtenstein shows that from 1935 to 1945, communist and CIO leaders "differed little" in a commitment to mainstream unionism, supporting the Roosevelt administration, wartime mobilization, and restriction of member self-activity. While communist local leaders in the United Auto Workers assented to the National War Labor Board, Lichtenstein demonstrates that they backed plant level rank and file mobilization against the no-strike pledge and incentive pay in response to shop-floor opposition.

5 Christopher Phelps, "Socialist Theories of Strikes" in Aaron Brenner, Benjamin Day, and Immanuel Ness, eds., *Encyclopedia of Strikes in American History* (Armonk, NY: M.E. Sharpe Publisher, 2009), 39.

6 For World War I strikes in the United States, see Cecilia Bucki, "World War I Era Strikes," in Brenner et al., *Encyclopedia of Strikes*, 191–203.

7 Werner Sombart, *Why Is There No Socialism in the United States?*, trans. Patricia M. Hocking and C.T. Husbands (White Plains, NY: International Arts and Sciences Press, 1976 [1906]).

8 In 1936, the CPUSA endorsed the reelection of FDR. All in all, under the leadership of Earl Browder, the party subordinated its apparatus to the state-capitalist order. The CPUSA's Trade Union Unity League was transformed to advance CIO unionization drives and the party's structure was directed at advancing the Democratic Party.

9 Stanley Aronowitz, *False Promises: The Shaping of American Working Class Consciousness* (Durham, NC: Duke University Press, 1992), 239–43.

10 Seymour M. Lipset and Noah M. Meltz, *The Paradox of American Unionism: Why Americans Like Unions More Than Canadians Do but Join Much Less* (Ithaca: Cornell University Press, 2004).

11 Dark, *The Unions and the Democrats*.

12 Paul Johnston, *Success While Others Fail: Social Movement Unionism and the Public Workplace* (Ithaca: Cornell ILR Press, 1994). Although Johnston optimistically believes that traditional unions can be transformed into socially inclusive activist labor organizations, most traditional unions have insisted on preserving bureaucratic, moderate forms of unionism that would continue to suffer long-term decline.

13 Kate Bronfenbrenner et al., *Organizing to Win: New Research on Union Strategies* (Ithaca: Cornell University Press, 1998).

14 Steve Early, *The Civil Wars in U.S. Labor: Birth of a New Workers Movement or Death Throes of the Old* (Chicago: Haymarket Books, 2011).

15 Peter L. Francia, *The Future of Organized Labor in American Politics* (New York: Columbia University Press, 2006).

16 Leo Troy, *The Twilight of the Old Unionism* (Armonk, NY: M.E. Sharpe).

17 In 2011 and 2012, to satisfy his business supporters, Cuomo sought to exact concessions beyond collective bargaining. In an effort to eliminate and reduce pensions for public employees, Cuomo insisted that if the Democrat-dominated State Assembly did not support pension concessions, he would force the shutdown of state government. At both the bargaining table and in the legislature, Cuomo threatened to lay off union workers if his plan was not enacted. Even in this hostile environment, union leaders claimed credit for averting layoffs, and many Democratic legislators did not have to vote in support of the action since Cuomo could count on votes from Republicans and his Democratic loyalists.

18 Marc Dixon, "Limiting Labor: Business Political Mobilization and Union Setback in the States," *Journal of Policy History* 19, no. 3 (2007): 313–44.

19 David Plotke, *Building a Democratic Political Order: Reshaping American Liberalism in the 1930s and 1940s* (Cambridge: Cambridge University Press, 1996).

20 Sidney Fine, *Sit-down: The General Motors Strike of 1936–1937* (Ann Arbor: University of Michigan Press, 1969), 321.

21 Immanuel Ness, "Workers' Direct Action and Factory Control in the United States," in *Ours to Master and to Own: Workers' Control from the Commune to the Present*, Immanuel Ness and Dario Azzellini eds. (Chicago: Haymarket Books, 2011), 302–21.

22 Michael Goldfield, *The Decline of Organized Labor in the United States* (Chicago: University of Chicago Press, 1989).

23 Michael Goldfield, "Race and the CIO: The Possibilities for Racial Egalitarianism during the 1930s and 1940s," *ILWCH* 44 (1993): 13–14.

24 Peter Cole, *Wobblies on the Waterfront: Interracial Unionism in Progressive-Era Philadelphia* (Chicago: University of Illinois Press, 2007).

25 Goldfield, "Race and the CIO."

26 Alain Badiou, *The Rebirth of History: Times of Riots and Uprisings* (London: Verso, 2012), 60.

27 David Brody, *Labor Embattled: History, Power, Rights* (Urbana: University of Illinois Press, 2005), vii.

28 Art Pries, *Labor's Giant Step: The First Twenty Years of the CIO* (New York: Pathfinder Press, 1964).

29 Jeremy Brecher, *Strike!* (Oakland: PM Press, 2014), 212. According to Brecher, under the War Labor Board's union security provision and the self-imposed no-strike pledge, the authority of labor unions over their members increased appreciably as workers were forced to remain within their union and required to pay dues. As a consequence, unions acquiesced to low wages and repressed rank-and-file autonomy, dissent, and activism. The no-strike pledge thereby expanded the power and political influence of union leaders as the intermediaries between labor, industry, and government at the expense of membership. Workers had virtually no recourse to improving poor wages, poor conditions, or employer intrusion on their rights.

30 Ibid., 211.

31 Ibid., 212.

Index

"Passim" (literally "scattered") indicates intermittent discussion of a topic over a cluster of pages.

Abrahamsson, Jan, 173–75
Abramovich, Roman, 80
absenteeism, 187, 196
accidents. *See* workplace accidents
ACFTU. *See* All-China Federation of Trade Unions (ACFTU)
ACORN, 237, 239
AFL. *See* American Federation of Labor (AFL)
AFL-CIO. *See* American Federation of Labor–Congress of Industrial Organizations (AFL-CIO)
African American workers, 206, 207, 223, 236–37, 263, 271–74 passim
African National Congress (ANC), 108, 111
agricultural workers. *See* farm workers
AGTSyP. *See* Delegados del Subte (Argentina)
air traffic controllers, 261, 293n17
Alabama, 273
Alfonsin, Raúl, 157
All-China Federation of Trade Unions (ACFTU), 14, 47–60 passim
aluminum industry, 78
AMCU. *See* Association of Mineworkers Union (AMCU) (South Africa)
Amendola, Giorgio, 23
American Federation of Labor (AFL), 2, 17, 235, 236, 259–63 passim, 272–77 passim
American Federation of Labor–Congress of Industrial Organizations (AFL-CIO), 238, 267

anarchists and anarchism, 6–7, 110, 111–12; Argentina, 147, 148; Sweden, 168, 169; UK, 244, 246, 247
ANC. *See* African National Congress (ANC)
ANGAP (Association Nationale pour la Gestion des Aires Protégées) (Madagascar), 121, 122, 123, 127
Anglo American, 131, 139
anticommunism, 265, 273, 274
antiprivatization, 47, 49
apprentices, 27, 44, 85, 86, 92
Arbetaren, 169, 170, 172, 182
Argentina, 15–16, 147–66, 179, 185
Arias, José, 132, 136, 137
Aronowitz, Stanley, 264
Arregocés, Eder, 139, 142, 143
arrest of protesters, 80, 177, 213
arrest of workers and organizers, 243; Argentina, 148; India, 15, 90, 91, 92; South Africa, 15, 101, 103–4, 106; UK, 243; United States, 237
Asociación Gremial de Trabajadores del Subte y Premetro. *See* Delegados del Subte (Argentina)
Association Nationale pour la Gestion des Aires Protégées. *See* ANGAP (Association Nationale pour la Gestion des Aires Protégées)
Association of Mineworkers Union (AMCU) (South Africa), 102, 103, 104, 108
Australia, 16, 141, 184–204
Australia Platinum, 103–4

"autogestion," 185, 301n8
automation, 151, 159
automobile industry: China, 49–59 passim; Germany, 151; India, 84–96; Italy, 26–30 passim; Russia, 63, 66, 74–76, 81, 293n17; United States, 270, 307n4
Autonomia Operaia (AO), 27, 28
autonomism, 8–10, 185, 198–200, 202; Italy, 8–19, 20–38
Autunno Caldo. See Hot Autumn, 1969 (Italy)
Azimut, 36

Badiou, Alain, 274
Baines, Nancy, 193
Bakunin, Mikhail, 98, 111
Baldwin, Roger, v
banks, 31, 240, 251
Barrett, James R., 307n1
barricading of roads. See blockades of roads and railroads
BBC, 242, 252
Berlinguer, Enrico, 27, 28
Berlusconi, Silvio, 32
Bernocchi, Piero, 30–37 passim, 288n57
Betsimisaraka people, 116, 118, 119, 125, 126
BHP Billiton, 131, 139, 142
blacklisting, 177, 243, 301n4
blockades of roads and railroads, 63, 69, 70, 78, 79, 80, 104, 105
Bloomberg, Michael, 269
bonuses, 25, 75, 102, 109, 160, 189
Boss, Emil, 180
bouncers, 91
boycotts, 90, 178, 220, 225, 236
Brahma Kumaris, 90
Brandworkers, 17, 273
Bravo, Luciano Ferrari, 28
breaks. See lunch breaks, rest breaks, etc.
Brecher, Jeremy, 276, 308n29
Brigate Rosse. See Red Brigades (Italy)
British Medical Association, 255
Brock, Joe, 222, 223
Brody, David, 275
Bronstein, Arturo, 292n13
Browder, Earl, 307n8
Brundtland Commission, 117
Buenos Aires, 147–48, 152–66 passim
Buhle, Paul, 6
builders, 185–89, 199, 200, 203, 221
bullying by management, 245–51, 255, 256
Bultitude, Cliff, 196, 197

bus drivers, 30, 153, 156, 161, 249, 252, 255–56

Canada as coal importer, 131, 132, 141
Capital (Marx), 24, 95
capitalism, second contradiction of. See "second contradiction of capitalism"
Cavanagh, Barry, 190
Central Organization of Swedish Workers (SAC). See Sveriges Arbetares Centralorganisation (SAC)
Central Unitaria de Trabajadores de Colombia (CUT), 138
Cerrejón, 131–46
CGIL. See Confederazione Generale Italiana del Lavoro (GGIL)
CGT. See Confédération Générale du Travail (CGT) (France)
Chapman, Bill, 194, 197
Cheng Guangshen, 290n17
Chile, 28, 175, 179, 241
China, 14, 39–61, 123
China Labour Bulletin (CLB), 58–59, 60
Chinese Communist Party. See Communist Party of China
Ching Quan Lee, 46
Chomsky, Noam, 286n1
Christian Democratic Party of Italy. See Democrazia Cristiana (DC)
cinema workers, 244
CIO. See Congress of Industrial Organizations (CIO)
CISL. See Confederazione Italiana dei Sindicati dei Lavoratori (CISL) (Italy)
Citizens UK, 237–38, 243
Clarke, Dennis, 197
class consciousness, 10, 37, 39, 42, 47, 48
class struggle, 7–9 passim, 185, 202, 203; Argentina, 149–52 passim; Italy, 38; Sweden, 172; United States, 211, 259, 265, 270–72 passim
Clayton Antitrust Act of 1914, 262–63
cleaners, 173, 177, 181, 233–34, 238–39, 243–57 passim
Cleaners Branch, IWW. See London IU640 Cleaning and Allied Industries Branch, IWW (Cleaners Branch)
Cleaver, Harry, 185
Clegg, Nick, 251
clerical workers, 201
CNT. See Confederación Nacional del Trabajo (CNT) (Spain)

coal industry, 15, 79, 108, 131–46, 194–98, 201

Cobas. *See* Confederazione dei Comitati di Base (Cobas) (Italy)

Cobas del Latte, 30

Cobas Scuola, 29, 31

coercion, 199, 203; Argentina, 161–62; China, 42, 48; India, 95; South Africa, 110

Cold War, 22, 277

Cole, Peter, 273

collaborationism, 5, 260, 265, 266

collective bargaining, 10, 52, 151, 239, 273, 277; opposition to (and elimination of), 264, 268

collective bargaining agreements (CBAs), 6, 142–43, 144, 170, 261, 273, 278; alternatives to, 176; IWW opposition to, 263

collectively owned enterprises (COEs), 43, 47

collectives and cooperatives, workers'. *See* workers' cooperatives

Colombia, 15, 131–46

Comintern, 264

Comitato Unitario di Base (CUB), 26, 31

communism, vi, 40, 271. *See also* anticommunism; council communism

Communist International. *See* Comintern

Communist Manifesto, The (Marx and Engels), 288n58;

Communist Party of Argentina, 156

Communist Party of China, 14, 41, 46, 55, 56

Communist Party of India (CPI), 94

Communist Party of South Africa, 113

Communist Party of Sweden, 170

Communist Party of the Russian Federation, 74

Communist Party of the United States (CPUSA), vi, 258, 264, 265, 271–77 passim, 307n1, 307n8

commuter transit workers. *See* public transit workers

company lockouts. *See* lockouts

company unions, 89, 90

Confederación General del Trabajo (CGT) (Argentina), 160, 162

Confederación Nacional del Trabajo (CNT) (Spain), 171

Confédération Générale du Travail (CGT) (France), 16, 169, 175

Confederazione dei Comitati di Base (Cobas) (Italy), 9, 13–14, 20–38 passim

Confederazione Generale Italiana del Lavoro (GGIL), 21, 22, 25–26, 29, 34, 37

Confederazione Italiana dei Sindicati dei Lavoratori (CISL) (Italy), 21, 34, 37

Congress of Industrial Organizations (CIO), v, vi, 2, 17, 232, 237, 259–65 passim, 271–77 passim, 307n8. *See also* American Federation of Labor–Congress of Industrial Organizations (AFL-CIO)

Congress of South African Trade Unions (COSATU), 104

consensus decision-making, 36

conservation work, 15, 115–30 passim

construction workers. *See* builders

cooperatives, workers'. *See* workers' cooperatives

Coordinadora Interlíneas (Argentina), 156

COSATU. *See* Congress of South African Trade Unions (COSATU)

council communism, 6, 7, 8, 9

court cases, 230–31

CUB. *See* Comitato Unitario di Base (CUB)

Cuerpo de Delegados del Subte. *See* Delegados del Subte (Argentina)

Cultural Revolution, China, 44, 45

Cuomo, Andrew, 269, 308n17

CUT. *See* Central Unitaria de Trabajadores de Colombia (CUT)

Dalton, John, 201

Daniels, Mitch, 268–69

day labor and day laborers, 85, 131

debt, international, 152

decision-making, consensus. *See* consensus decision-making

Delegados del Subte (Argentina), 15–16, 150–66 passim

DeLeon, Daniel, 252, 259

Delle Carbonara, Claudio, 155–66 passim

Delúquez Díaz, Jaime, 132–33, 141, 142, 143

Democratic Party, vi, 258–78 passim, 307n8

Democrazia Cristiana (DC), 21–23 passim, 27–29 passim

demonstrations. *See* protests and demonstrations

Deng Xiaoping, 42, 45

deportation, 175, 176, 264

Deripaska, Oleg, 79

deskilling, 92

detention center workers, 181–82
dictatorship, 42, 156, 157, 175
direct-debit dues payment, 248
direct deposit of pay, 228
dismissal of workers. *See* firing of workers; layoffs
Dixon, Marc, 269
dockers, 29, 190, 236, 237, 240, 293n17
downsizing. *See* layoffs
Dubofsky, Melvyn, 260
Duncan, Peter, 190
Durango, Alberto, 243–53 passim

Early, Steve, 267
Early Day Motions (UK Parliament), 247, 250, 251
East London Citizens Organization. *See* TELCO
Economic Stabilization Act of 1942. *See* Stabilization Act of 1942
ecotourism, 116, 117, 121
Effertz, Jason, 223
elections, NLRB, 213, 221, 225–28 passim
electoral politics (national), 3, 6, 98, 264, 265
Employee Free Choice Act (EFCA) (proposed), 277–78
Engels, Friedrich, 288n58
Environmental Action Plan of Madagascar. *See* National Environmental Action Plan (NEAP) (Madagascar)
Ericson, Wil, 214
Espionage Act, 264
European Union, 31, 171

factory and mine occupations. *See* takeovers
factory councils, 95–96
Fair Wine Trade (Sweden), 179–80
Fakenham Occupation Workers, 303n51
Fanfani, Amintore, 22
farm workers, 238, 260, 263
fast food workers, 205–32 passim, 256
Federation of Independent Trade Unions (FNPR) (Russia), 65, 76
FIAT, 26–32 passim
firing of workers: Australia, 188, 201; Madagascar, 123; South Africa, 100, 103, 109–10; UK, 244, 246, 247, 255–56; United States, 206, 212, 215, 216, 230–32 passim, 273. *See also* layoffs
Fletcher, Bill, Jr., 285n2

Flint, Michigan, sit-down strike, 1936–1937, 270
Flynn, Elizabeth Gurley, 306n3
FNPR. *See* Federation of Independent Trade Unions (FNPR) (Russia)
food service workers, 177, 178, 205–32 passim, 256, 260
Ford, Chris, 243–53 passim
Ford Motor Company: Argentina, 155; Russia, 63, 66, 74–76, 81
foreign debt. *See* debt, international
forest conservation, 115–30 passim
Forman, Erik, 205–9 passim, 217, 218, 222, 226
France, 16, 26, 152, 169, 184; Madagascar relations, 118–19
Francia, Peter, 267
Frankfurt School, 287n27
freedom of assembly, 107

Gapasin, Fernando, 285n2
Gelmini, Mariastella, 31
general strikes, 2, 212, 236, 260, 270, 274
Genoa, 22, 29, 30
Germany, 7, 8, 22, 76, 151, 170; compared to Italy, 25, 33. *See also* Frankfurt School
Gettings, Jim, 192
Giua, Nicola, 31
globalization, 65–66, 277
glovers, 189–94
GMB union (UK), 244, 247
Goldfield, Michael, 271–72, 273
Goldman, Emma, 5
Gompers, Samuel, 263
government workers. *See* public workers
Graeber, David, 3, 285n3
Gramsci, Antonio, 23, 28, 84, 95, 96, 154–56 passim, 289n73
gratuities. *See* tips and tipping
grievances: Argentina, 154; India, 89; Italy, 30; South Africa, 98, 99, 103; UK, 246, 250, 255; United States, 208, 211, 231, 232, 270, 275, 276
Gross, Daniel, 4
Group of the Undocumented (Sweden). *See* Papperslösasgruppen
Grundrisse (Marx), 23–24
Guajira, Colombia, 131–46 passim
Guangdong, China, 49, 51, 55, 59
Guevara, Che, 135
Guildhall, London, 245–47 passim

Hägglund, Joel. *See* Hill, Joe

Han Dongfang, 56, 58, 59
Hayes, Jim, 195–96
Haywood, Bill, 236, 237
health, 137, 149. *See also* working while
  sick; workplace health and safety
healthcare workers, 181, 250
health insurance, 206, 210, 269
Hedley, Steve, 247, 251
Hill, Joe, 183
holidays, vacation, etc., 93–94, 206, 208
Holmberg, Lotta, 175–76, 179
Honda, 49–59 passim, 85
Hong Kong, 55, 56, 181
Horkheimer, Max, 287n27
hospital workers, 181, 250
Hot Autumn, 1969 (Italy), 8, 21, 25, 27, 32
housing: China, 48, 60–61; India, 86, 87;
  Russia, 76, 77
Huang Qiaoyan, 55
Hughes, Davis, 189, 203
hunger strikes, 63, 69, 70
Huxley, Pat, 196, 197

IAM. *See* International Association of
  Machinists (IAM)
Illinois, 210
ILO. *See* International Labour
  Organization (ILO)
immigrant workers. *See* migrant workers
Impala Platinum, 100, 102, 104
India, 14–15, 84–96
Indiana, 268–69
Industrial Workers of Great Britain
  (IWGB), 252
Industrial Workers of the World (IWW),
  5, 6, 16–17, 213, 256–64 passim, 273–74,
  278; Bus Workers Branch, 249; early
  history, 233–35; influence in Sweden,
  169, 170, 183; Print and Creative
  Workers Branch, 249; Starbucks
  campaign, 17, 212–13, 217; UK, 17,
  174, 233–34, 243–57 passim; women
  in 236, 306n3. *See also* Jimmy John's
  Workers Union (JJWU); Lawrence,
  Massachusetts, textile strike, 1912;
  London IU640 Cleaning and Allied
  Industries Branch, IWW (Cleaners
  Branch)
inequality: China, 43, 50; Russia, 76, 77;
  South Africa, 110; United States, 224.
  See also racism
informal sector, 12
Ingrao, Pietro, 23

integrated conservation and development
  projects (ICDPs), 116–29, 299n18
International Association of Machinists
  (IAM), 262
international debt. *See* debt, international
internationalism, 174–75, 179. *See also*
  Comintern; solidarity, international
International Labour Organization (ILO),
  57, 64, 139, 142
International Union of Food, Agricultural,
  Hotel, Restaurant, Catering, Tobacco
  and Allied Workers' Associations, 57
International Workers' Association (IWA),
  169, 170–71, 174
interns and internships, 51, 52
Interregional Labor Union of the Workers
  of the Automobile Industry (Russia).
  See MPRA (Interregional Labor Union
  of the Workers of the Automobile
  Industry) (Russia)
Italy, 8–9, 20–38, 184, 185; emigrants, 147,
  148
IWA. *See* International Workers'
  Association (IWA)
IWW. *See* Industrial Workers of the World
  (IWW)

Jaime, Ricardo, 162
James North Glove Factory, 191, 192, 193
Jimmy John's Workers Union (JJWU), 17,
  205–32 passim, 273
job security and insecurity, 10, 29, 42, 129,
  176, 235
Joe Hill House, Gävle, Sweden, 183
Johansson, Per, 181
John Lewis and Company, 234, 251–53
  passim
Johnston, Paul, 267, 307n12
Johnstone, Pike, 197
Jones, Elwyn, 195, 196
Justice for Cleaners campaign (UK),
  239–46 passim
Justice for Janitors campaign (United
  States), 238

Karen, Igor, 145–46
Keynes, John Maynard, 202
Kirchner, Cristina, 161
Kirkland, Lane, 267
Kroondal Mine, 100–101, 105
Kumar, Shiv, 89, 90, 94

labor laws, 9; Argentina, 159, 160; China, 54, 61; India, 89; Russia, 63–75 passim, 81, 292n12–13; South Africa, 99, 108–9; UK, 247, 251; United States, 17, 262–63, 269, 271, 275. *See also* National Labor Relations Act (NLRA)

Labor-Management Relations Act of 1947. *See* Taft-Hartley Act

Landsorganisationen (LO) (Sweden), 16, 168, 170, 173, 176, 179, 181

land takeaways, 86, 127, 134

Larven, J. E., 190

Latin American Workers Association (LAWAS), 240–49 passim

Lawrence, Massachusetts, textile strike, 1912, 237, 238, 245

layoffs: China, 45, 50; Italy, 28; Russia, 70, 71, 72, 78; UK, 242. *See also* severance pay

leave time, 189, 208. *See also* holidays, vacation, etc.; sick leave (and lack of sick leave)

Lega Nord, 30

Lewis, John L., v, vi

Lewis and Company. *See* John Lewis and Company

Liao Yang Alloy, 47

Liautaud, Jimmy John, 210

Lichtenstein, Nelson, 260, 307n4

Lin Biao, 45

living wage, 33, 239–55 passim

lockouts, 88–92 passim, 110, 168

Lombardi, Riccardo, 22

London, England, 234, 237, 239–57 passim

London Citizens, 237, 239, 245

London IU640 Cleaning and Allied Industries Branch, IWW (Cleaners Branch), 17, 234, 245–55 passim

London School of Economics, 240, 251

longshore workers. *See* dockers

Lonmin, 98, 103, 106–7, 111

Lozano, Freddy Villarreal, 133, 136–37, 140, 142

Lukács, Georg, 287n23; *History and Class Consciousness*, 24

lumber workers, 236–37

lunch breaks, rest breaks, etc., 87, 206

Lynch, Phillip, 203

Lynd, Staughton, 4

Madagascar, 15, 115–30, 299n15

Malagasy people, 116–29 passim

management bullying. *See* bullying by management

Mao Zedong, 39–45 passim, 61

Marcuse, Herbert: *One-Dimensional Man*, 23, 287n16

Marikana, South Africa, 98, 105–112 passim

maritime workers, 249, 273

Maruti Suzuki Employees Union (MSEU), 88–95 passim

Maruti Suzuki Indian Limited (MSIL), 74–96

Marx, Karl, 95, 198–99; *Capital*, 24, 95; *The Communist Manifesto*, 288n58; eleventh thesis on Feuerbach, 23; *Grundrisse*, 23–24

Marxism, 117–18, 151. *See also* autonomism

massacres: South Africa, 105–6

mass transit workers, 15–16, 150–66 passim, 173–75, 180–81

Mastandrea, Ariel, 153, 155, 158, 159, 161, 164

McCarthyism, 272, 277

McDonald's, 109

McDonnell, John, 247, 248

McGrath, Rex, 197

McIntosh, Merv, 195

media, 154; Argentina, 155, 156, 159–64 passim; Australia, 203; India, 85; Italy, 32; Russia, 80; Sweden, 169–72 passim, 177, 182; UK, 252; United States, 218, 220, 225

Menem, Carlos, 149, 154, 157

Merina people, 119–25 passim

Metrovías, 154, 157–62 passim

Mexican workers in the United States, 263

Mezhdurechensk, Kemerovo, Russia, 79–81

migrant workers: Argentina, 147; China, 43, 47–49 passim, 53; India, 86; Russia, 76; Sweden, 16, 175–79 passim; UK, 17, 242–4, 239–55 passim; United States, 245, 263, 271–73 passim. *See also* nativism; undocumented workers

MikLin Enterprises, 214, 225

Milan, 26, 32

miners and mining, v; Australia, 184, 185, 194–203 passim; Colombia, 15; Madagascar, 117, 120; Russia, 63, 79–80, 292n17; South Africa, 97–114; Sweden, 169; United States, 236, 263, 264

Mingqi Li, 290n17

minimum wage: China, 55; UK, 235, 245, 247, 251, 253; United States, 206, 224
Minneapolis-St. Paul Metropolitan Area, 205–32 passim
Monti, Mario, 21, 31–32
morale, 187–88, 193, 194, 197–200 passim
Moro, Aldo, 22, 28
movie theater workers. *See* cinema workers
Movimento Sociale Italiano (MSI), 22
Moyano, Hugo, 162
MPRA (Interregional Labor Union of the Workers of the Automobile Industry) (Russia), 74
Mulligan, Linda, 214, 218, 221, 225, 227, 230
Mulligan, Mike, 207, 214, 218–30 passim
Mulligan, Rob, 207, 214, 218–30 passim

Napolitano, Giorgio, 23
National Environmental Action Plan (NEAP) (Madagascar), 115
nationalized enterprises. *See* state-owned enterprises (SOEs)
National Labor Relations Act (NLRA), v, vi, 208–12 passim, 227, 258–78 passim, 307n1
National Labor Relations Bureau (NLRB), 211–13 passim, 217–31 passim. *See also* elections, NLRB
national parks: Madagascar, 115, 118, 124–29
National Union of Journalists (UK), 248–49
National Union of Mineworkers (NUM) (South Africa), 99–109 passim
National Union of Rail, Maritime and Transport Workers (RMT) (UK), 247, 249
National Union of Workers in the Coal Industry) (Colombia). *See* Sintracarbón (National Union of Workers in the Coal Industry) (Colombia)
National War Labor Board (NWLB), 263, 276, 277, 308n29
nativism, 263–64
NEAP. *See* National Environmental Action Plan (NEAP) (Madagascar)
negotiations, 4, 29, 72, 272
Negri, Antonio, 23–28 passim, 33, 185, 186, 198–99, 202, 289n76
Nenni, Pietro, 22
New Deal, 202, 260, 264–75 passim
New York State, 269, 308n17
night work, 122, 160, 207

NLRA. *See* National Labor Relations Act (NLRA)
NLRB. *See* National Labor Relations Bureau (NLRB)
nonpayment and late payment of wages and salaries: Australia, 194; Russia, 62–63, 67, 68, 70, 79; South Africa, 98, 102; Sweden, 177; UK, 245, 256
no-strike clauses and pledges, 211, 220, 261, 275–76, 307n4, 308n29
NTT Communications, 247
Nymboida Mine takeover, 1975–1979, 184, 185, 194–203 passim

Obama, Barack, 286n1
occupations and takeovers. *See* takeovers
office workers, 201
Ohlsen, Les, 197
oil industry, 63, 76–79
One-Dimensional Man (Marcuse), 23, 287n16
Onganía, Juan Carlos, 157
operaismo, 8–9, 20–38
Operation Gladio, 9
outsourcing, 72, 76, 103, 111, 212; international, 267–68, 277
overtime, 74, 75, 102, 201, 206, 208
Owens, Joe, 184, 186–89 passim, 204

painters, 190, 191
Panzieri, Raniero, 23
Papperslösasgruppen, 175–79
Partito Comunista Italiano (PCI), 21, 22–23, 25, 27–28, 29
Partito Socialista Italiano (PSI), 21, 23, 28
paternalism and patriarchy, 98, 192, 241
pay. *See* bonuses; severance pay; wages, salaries, etc.; tips and tipping
Peralta, Pablo, 154, 155, 158, 165
Pérez, Carlos, 158
Perón, Isabel, 156
Perón, Juan, 148, 157
Peter Jones (UK department store), 253
petitions, 69, 217, 228
petroleum industry. *See* oil industry
Phillips, Evan, 194
Pianelli, Roberto, 160, 161, 164–65
pickets and picketing, 25, 26; Australia, 186; Russia, 68, 69, 75, 76; South Africa, 99; Sweden, 177, 178; UK, 251; United States, 218–19, 220, 230
Pikalevo, Russia, 78–79
Pirelli, 26, 31

Pizza Hut, 256
platinum mining, 100–105 passim, 109, 111
Plotke, David, 270
Plumbers and Gasfitters Employees Union of Australia, 201–2
police, 111; Argentina, 148; India, 90–91; Madagascar, 127; Russia, 80; South Africa, 101, 102, 104, 109; Sweden, 178
Pollock, Friedrich, 289n71
posters, 220, 224, 229, 230
Potere Operaio (PO), 27, 28
Potere Operaio vento-emiliano (POv-e), 25
precariousness of jobs. See job security and insecurity
privatization: Argentina, 149; Australia, 193; China, 46, 47, 49, 50
productivity, 42, 150–51, 193, 196, 203
Profsvoboda, 77
Progressive Miners of America, v
protests and demonstrations: China, 42, 44–45, 46, 50, 55; Italy, 26–27, 31; Russia, 62–82 passim, 293n22; UK, 243, 246, 247, 250, 251, 255; United States, 213, 217, 220. See also arrest of protesters; pickets and picketing; sit-ins
public transit workers, 15–16, 150–66 passim, 173–75, 180–81
public workers, 29, 234, 268, 269, 306n1
punitive firing of workers. See firing of workers
Putin, Vladimir, 78–79, 80

Quaderni Rossi, 23, 25
Queen Mary University, 239, 240
Quiroz Delgado, Jairo, 133, 135–36, 139–40, 143–44, 145

racism: South Africa, 97–102 passim, 110; UK, 246, 250, 251; United States, 206, 236, 263, 274
Rail, Maritime and Transport Workers (RMT) (UK). See National Union of Rail, Maritime and Transport Workers (RMT) (UK)
railway workers, 15–16, 150–66 passim, 173–75, 180–81, 263, 293n17
rainforest conservation, 115–30 passim
Ramaphosa, Cyril, 111
Ranchería River, Colombia, 145–46
Ratsiraka, Didier, 115, 123, 124, 299n15
Read, Jason, 24
Reagan, Ronald, 261
Rebirth of History, The (Badiou), 274

RECLAME (Red Colombiana Frente a la Gran Minería Transnacional), 145
Red and Black Coordination, 174
red-baiting, 222
Red Brigades (Italy), 27, 28
redundancy. See layoffs
rent strikes, 27
replacement workers, 104, 201, 221, 253
repression: Argentina, 148, 159; China, 45–48 passim; India, 89–92 passim; Russia, 76, 77, 80; South Africa, 101–9 passim; Sweden, 178
Republican Party, 268, 272, 278
restaurant workers, 177, 178, 260. See also fast food workers
rest breaks. See lunch breaks, rest breaks, etc.
right to organize, 3, 57, 208, 231
right to strike, 4, 45, 63, 64, 260, 261
"right-to-work" legislation, 269
right-wing extremism, Swedish, 171–72
RMT. See National Union of Rail, Maritime and Transport Workers (RMT) (UK)
road and railroad blockades. See blockades of roads and railroads
Rönnbäck, Klas, 182
Roosevelt, Franklin D., 260, 261, 276, 307n4, 307n8
Ross, Vane, 198
Rüdiger, Helmut, 170
Russia, 62–82, 292nn12–13, 292–93n17, 293n22

sabotage, 223, 236, 260
SAC. See Sveriges Arbetares Centralorganisation (SAC)
SAF. See Syndikalistiska Arbetarfederationen (SAF) (Sweden)
safety. See workplace health and safety
St George's Hospital, London, England, 250
salaries. See wages, salaries, etc.
Sanyo, 201
scabs. See replacement workers
Schäfer, Daniel, 151
Schlesinger, Arthur, 286–87n10
Schulman, Nicole, 6
"second contradiction of capitalism," 117–18
security surveillance, screening, etc. See surveillance, screening, etc.
Sedition Act, 264

self-management, 11, 112–14 passim, 188, 200, 301n8. *See also* workers' cooperatives
"self-valorization," 199–200
Service Employees International Union (SEIU), 238, 239, 267
Sesley, Monica, 206–8, 222
severance pay, 94, 189, 194
sexual harassment, 206, 216
shoemakers, 303n51
sick leave (and lack of sick leave), 196, 215, 222, 228–30 passim
sick workers. *See* working while sick
Sidicato Lavoratori Autorganizzati Intercategoriale (Slai) Cobas, 30, 35
Sintracarbón (National Union of Workers in the Coal Industry) (Colombia), 15, 131–46
sit-down strikes, 16, 212, 220, 260, 261, 270, 274
sit-ins: Australia, 185, 189–94 passim, 201; South Africa, 100–102 passim, 107, 110; UK, 247
slowdowns, 44, 45, 87. *See also* work-to-rule
Smale, Bill, 195
Smidt, Frank, 198
Smith, Rebecca, 221–22, 223
Social Democratic Party of Germany (SPD), 22
"socialism from above," 42–43, 61
social media, 257
social welfare, 42, 60, 273. *See also* welfare state
Söderberg, Björn, 171, 172
Sodikoff, Genese Marie, 116–25 passim
solidarity, 66, 212–13, 241; Australia, 190; class solidarity, 2; India, 88, 91; international, 131–46 passim; Madagascar, 126, 129; Russia, 80–81; South Africa, 104; UK, 233–34, 254; United States, 224, 231
Sombart, Werner, 264
South Africa, 14–15, 97–114, 179
South African Communist Party. *See* Communist Party of South Africa
Soviet Union, 13, 40, 62, 65, 148, 149, 265, 277; African American relations, 273; Haywood in, 237; Madagascar relations, 115, 123
Spanish Civil War, 170, 172
Spanish emigrants, 147, 148

SPD. *See* Social Democratic Party of Germany (SPD)
squatting, 27
Stabilization Act of 1942, 276
Starbucks, 17, 212–13, 217
state: anarchist views, 111–12
state-owned enterprises (SOEs): China, 39, 43–53 passim, 57
steelworkers, 49–51, 200
"stop-actions." *See* work stoppages
Strangers into Citizens campaign (UK), 243
strikebreakers, 67, 75, 93, 95
strikes: Argentina, 15, 159, 160–61; Australia, 189, 190; China, 44, 45, 51–53, 55, 59; Colombia, 139, 140; desired by management, 200; India, 86, 88, 90, 94–95; Italy, 25–32 passim; Madagascar, 121–24; Russia, 62–82 passim; South Africa, 100, 105; Sweden, 168, 170, 181–82; UK, 234, 251–52; United States, 220, 260, 261, 263, 270–76 passim, 308n29. *See also* general strikes; hunger strikes; no-strike clauses and pledges; right to strike; sit-down strikes; strikebreakers; sympathy strikes; wildcat strikes
student movements: Colombia, 138; Italy, 21, 25–28 passim, 31; UK, 255
subcontracting and subcontractors, 84, 103, 105, 149, 188; UK, 235, 245, 251
Subte union. *See* Delgados del Subte (Argentina)
subway workers, 15–16, 150–66 passim, 173–75, 180–81
SUF. *See* Syndikalistiska ungdomsförbundet (SUF) (Sweden)
suicide, 63
Sullivan, Sian, 118
SuperValu, 214
surveillance, screening, etc., 97–98
Suzuki, 84–96 passim
Suzuki Powertrain India Employees Union (SPIEU), 95
Svahn, Birger, 170
Sveriges Arbetares Centralorganisation (SAC), 16, 168–83, 301n2, 301n4
Sweden, 8, 16, 168–83
Swedish Trade Union Confederation. *See* Landsorganisationen (LO) (Sweden)
Sweeney, John, 267
Switzerland, 8, 141

Sydney Opera House work-in, 1972, 185–89, 199, 200, 203
sympathy strikes, 190
Syndikalistiska Arbetarfederationen (SAF) (Sweden), 169–70
Syndikalistiska ungdomsförbundet (SUF) (Sweden), 183
Systembolaget (Sweden), 179–80
Szabo, Louis, 198

Taft-Hartley Act, 269, 275
takeovers, 16; Australia, 184–86 passim, 190–97 passim, 200–203 passim; France, 184; India, 88, 89, 93, 94–95; Russia, 70; South Africa, 99–103 passim, 107, 112, 113; UK, 303n51
Tambroni, Fernando, 22
Tapp, Jack, 195, 196, 197
Tastas Duque, Ruben, 178
taxation: Argentina, 149; Illinois, 210; Italy, 32, 33, 36
taxi drivers, 209, 273
teachers, 181–82
Teamsters for a Democratic Voice, 241
TELCO, 237–40 passim
telephone workers, 153
temporary workers: China, 43; Colombia, 137, 139, 143; India, 85–93 passim
Third International. See Comintern
Thomas, Pete, 184, 194, 197, 203
Thomson Reuters, 247, 248
Tianenman Incident, 1976, 44–45
timber workers. See lumber workers
tips and tipping, 224
Togliatti, Palmiro, 23
Topalov, Christian, 152
Torme, Mauricio, 159
torture, 92
tourism: Madagascar, 116, 117, 120, 121, 126, 129
Trades Union Congress (UK), 238–39, 244
Trade Union Unity League, 307n8
Transport and General Workers Union (T&G) (UK), 240, 242
transportation, 126, 152, 201, 207, 228
transportation workers. See bus drivers; subway workers; taxi drivers
Tronti, Mario, 23, 24, 25, 38
Troy, Leo, 267–68
Truman, Harry, 275
TUC. See Trades Union Congress (UK)
Tuleev, Aman, 80
Two Rivers Mine, South Africa, 101–2

UAW. See United Auto Workers (UAW)
UFW. See United Farm Workers (UFW)
UMW. See United Mine Workers (UMW)
undocumented workers: Sweden, 175–79; UK, 242–43
unemployment funds, 101, 171
UNESCO, 124–25, 127
unfair labor practices charges, 225, 230
Uniden, 48, 290n19
union-busting, 212, 221–27 passim, 232
Union Carbide, 201
union democracy, 57–58, 112, 241, 248
union elections, 225–27 passim
union organizing: China, 48, 54; United States, 205–32 passim. See also right to organize
Unión Tranviarios Automotor (UTA), 153, 154–63 passim
UNISON, 235, 239–40, 250, 306n1
Unite (UK), 242–45 passim, 249
United Auto Workers (UAW), 270, 307n4
United Farm Workers (UFW), 238
United Kingdom, 17, 184, 185, 233–57 passim, 303n51; Argentina relations, 147; Parliament, 247–51 passim
United Mine Workers (UMW), v
United Nations, 117, 134. See also UNESCO
United States, v–vi, 4, 17–18, 205–45 passim, 258–78, 285n1, 306–8; Chamber of Commerce, 54; as coal importer, 131, 132, 133
unpaid wages. See nonpayment and late payment of wages and salaries
urbanization, 152, 174
USSR. See Soviet Union

vacations. See holidays, vacation, etc.
Venezuela, 185
Videla, Jorge Rafaela, 157
Virilio, Paul, 300n4
Vital Center, The (Schlesinger), 286–87n10
Volkswagen, 151

wages, salaries, etc., 151, 199, 202; Argentina, 149, 151, 154, 156, 158, 160; Australia, 195; China, 46–55 passim, 59, 61; Colombia, 137; direct deposit of, 228; Italy, 27, 29; Madagascar, 123; in Marxist theory, 117; Russia, 71–80 passim; South Africa, 98, 104–5, 107, 109; Sweden, 168, 176; UK, 239, 252, 254; United States, 206, 208, 222, 228, 260, 276. See also living wage; minimum

wage; nonpayment and late payment of wages and salaries
Wagner Act. *See* National Labor Relations Act
Walker, Scott, 268
Wallace, John, 186–89 passim
War Labor Board. *See* National War Labor Board (NWLB)
Wayuu people, 131, 134
welfare state: China, 60–61
Welinder, P.J., 170
West, Vic, 198
Western Federation of Miners, 236
white-collar workers. *See* clerical workers
Whyalla Glove Factory sit-in, 1972–1973, 189–94, 199
wildcat strikes: China, 45; Italy, 29; South Africa; 98–113 passim; Sweden, 181; UK, 245, 255, 257; UK, 255; United States, 258, 260
Wills, Jane, 239, 240–41
Wilson, Woodrow, 262, 263, 276
wine industry, 179–80
Wisconsin, 268
Witness for Peace, 131
women machinists, 189–94
women shoemakers, 303n51
women Wobblies, 236, 306n3
workday, 148, 150, 157–59 passim, 189, 237, 262
worker blacklisting. *See* blacklisting
worker firing. *See* firing of workers
worker layoffs. *See* layoffs
worker leave. *See* leave time
worker morale. *See* morale
worker occupations and takeovers. *See* takeovers
Workers Call the Tune at Opera House (Owens and Wallace), 186
workers' cooperatives, 185, 191–94, 199
workers' councils, 95–96, 184, 259
worker self-management. *See* self-management
Workers' International Industrial Union, 252
work hours, 246. *See also* lunch breaks, rest breaks, etc.; workday; workweek
working while sick, 222, 229–30
work-ins, 184, 185–89, 194–203 passim
workload, 87, 224, 250, 251, 253
workplace accidents, 87, 98

workplace health and safety, 98, 99, 102, 120, 156–60 passim, 181, 228–30, 256. *See also* sick leave (and lack of sick leave)
workplace surveillance, screening, etc. *See* surveillance, screening, etc.
workplace takeovers. *See* takeovers
work slowdowns. *See* slowdowns
work stoppages: Italy, 25; Russia, 66–67, 68, 74, 81; United States, 261, 262, 263, 275. *See also* strikes
work-to-rule, 74, 220; managers' version of, 222
workweek, 27, 186–89 passim, 201, 210, 245
World War I, 237, 262–63, 276
World War II, 170, 260–61, 264–65, 275–76

Xstrata, 131, 139, 142

youth organizations, 168, 183
Yu Jianrong, 45, 290n17

Zanini, Adelino, 24
Zhou Enlai, 44, 45

ABOUT PM PRESS

PM Press was founded at the end of 2007 by a small
collection of folks with decades of publishing, media, and
organizing experience. PM Press co-conspirators have
published and distributed hundreds of books, pamphlets,
CDs, and DVDs. Members of PM have founded enduring
book fairs, spearheaded victorious tenant organizing campaigns, and worked
closely with bookstores, academic conferences, and even rock bands to deliver
political and challenging ideas to all walks of life. We're old enough to know what
we're doing and young enough to know what's at stake.

We seek to create radical and stimulating fiction and non-fiction books, pamphlets,
T-shirts, visual and audio materials to entertain, educate and inspire you. We
aim to distribute these through every available channel with every available
technology—whether that means you are seeing anarchist classics at our bookfair
stalls; reading our latest vegan cookbook at the café; downloading geeky fiction
e-books; or digging new music and timely videos from our website.

PM Press is always on the lookout for talented and skilled volunteers, artists,
activists and writers to work with. If you have a great idea for a project or can
contribute in some way, please get in touch.

PM Press
PO Box 23912
Oakland, CA 94623
www.pmpress.org

FRIENDS OF PM PRESS

These are indisputably momentous times—the financial system is melting down globally and the Empire is stumbling. Now more than ever there is a vital need for radical ideas.

In the six years since its founding—and on a mere shoestring—PM Press has risen to the formidable challenge of publishing and distributing knowledge and entertainment for the struggles ahead. With over 250 releases to date, we have published an impressive and stimulating array of literature, art, music, politics, and culture. Using every available medium, we've succeeded in connecting those hungry for ideas and information to those putting them into practice.

Friends of PM allows you to directly help impact, amplify, and revitalize the discourse and actions of radical writers, filmmakers, and artists. It provides us with a stable foundation from which we can build upon our early successes and provides a much-needed subsidy for the materials that can't necessarily pay their own way. You can help make that happen—and receive every new title automatically delivered to your door once a month—by joining as a Friend of PM Press. And, we'll throw in a free T-shirt when you sign up.

Here are your options:

- **$30 a month** Get all books and pamphlets plus 50% discount on all webstore purchases

- **$40 a month** Get all PM Press releases (including CDs and DVDs) plus 50% discount on all webstore purchases

- **$100 a month** Superstar—Everything plus PM merchandise, free downloads, and 50% discount on all webstore purchases

For those who can't afford $30 or more a month, we're introducing **Sustainer Rates** at $15, $10 and $5. Sustainers get a free PM Press T-shirt and a 50% discount on all purchases from our website.

Your Visa or Mastercard will be billed once a month, until you tell us to stop. Or until our efforts succeed in bringing the revolution around. Or the financial meltdown of Capital makes plastic redundant. Whichever comes first.

From Here to There:
The Staughton Lynd Reader

Edited with an Introduction
by Andrej Grubačić

ISBN: 978-1-60486-215-7
$22.00   320 pages

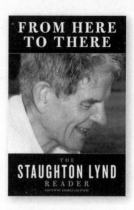

From Here to There collects unpublished talks and hard-to-find essays from legendary activist historian Staughton Lynd.

The first section of the Reader collects reminiscences and analyses of the 1960s. A second section offers a vision of how historians might immerse themselves in popular movements while maintaining their obligation to tell the truth. In the last section Lynd explores what nonviolence, resistance to empire as a way of life, and working class self-activity might mean in the 21st century. Together, they provide a sweeping overview of the life, and work—to date—of Staughton Lynd.

Both a definitive introduction and further exploration, it is bound to educate, enlighten, and inspire those new to his work and those who have been following it for decades. In a wide-ranging Introduction, anarchist scholar Andrej Grubačić considers how Lynd's persistent concerns relate to traditional anarchism.

"I met Staughton and Alice Lynd nearly fifty years ago in Atlanta. Staughton's reflective and restless life has never ceased in its exploring. This book is his great gift to the next generations."
—Tom Hayden

"Staughton Lynd's work is essential reading for anyone dedicated to implementing social justice. The essays collected in this book provide unique wisdom and insights into United States history and possibilities for change, summed up in two tenets: leading from below and solidarity."
—Roxanne Dunbar-Ortiz

"This remarkable collection demonstrates the compassion and intelligence of one of America's greatest public intellectuals. To his explorations of everything from Freedom Schools to the Battle of Seattle, Staughton Lynd brings lyricism, rigour, a historian's eye for irony, and an unshakable commitment to social transformation. In this time of economic crisis, when the air is filled with ideas of 'hope' and 'change,' Lynd guides us to understanding what, very concretely, those words might mean and how we might get there. These essays are as vital and relevant now as the day they were written, and a source of inspiration for activists young and old."
—Raj Patel

Labor Law for the Rank and Filer: Building Solidarity While Staying Clear of the Law (2nd Edition)

Staughton Lynd and Daniel Gross

ISBN: 978-1-60486-419-9
$12.00   120 pages

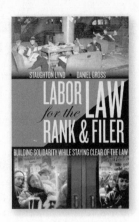

Have you ever felt your blood boil at work but lacked the tools to fight back and win? Or have you acted together with your co-workers, made progress, but wondered what to do next? If you are in a union, do you find that the union operates top-down just like the boss and ignores the will of its members?

Labor Law for the Rank and Filer: Building Solidarity While Staying Clear of the Law is a guerrilla legal handbook for workers in a precarious global economy. Blending cutting-edge legal strategies for winning justice at work with a theory of dramatic social change from below, Staughton Lynd and Daniel Gross deliver a practical guide for making work better while re-invigorating the labor movement.

Labor Law for the Rank and Filer demonstrates how a powerful model of organizing called "Solidarity Unionism" can help workers avoid the pitfalls of the legal system and utilize direct action to win. This new revised and expanded edition includes new cases governing fundamental labor rights as well as an added section on Practicing Solidarity Unionism. This new section includes chapters discussing the hard-hitting tactic of working to rule; organizing under the principle that no one is illegal; and building grassroots solidarity across borders to challenge neoliberalism, among several other new topics. Illustrative stories of workers' struggles make the legal principles come alive.

"Workers' rights are under attack on every front. Bosses break the law every day. For 30 years Labor Law for the Rank and Filer *has been arming workers with an introduction to their legal rights (and the limited means to enforce them) while reminding everyone that real power comes from workers' solidarity."*
—Alexis Buss, former General Secretary-Treasurer of the IWW

"As valuable to working persons as any hammer, drill, stapler, or copy machine, Labor Law for the Rank and Filer *is a damn fine tool empowering workers who struggle to realize their basic dignity in the workplace while living through an era of unchecked corporate greed. Smart, tough, and optimistic, Staughton Lynd and Daniel Gross provide nuts and bolts information to realize on-the-job rights while showing us that another world is not only possible but inevitable."*
—John Philo, Legal Director, Maurice and Jane Sugar Law Center for Economic and Social Justice

Organize! Building from the Local for Global Justice

Edited by Aziz Choudry, Jill Hanley &
Eric Shragge

ISBN: 978-1-60486-433-5
$24.95   352 pages

What are the ways forward for organizing for
progressive social change in an era of unprecedented
economic, social and ecological crises? How do political
activists build power and critical analysis in their daily
work for change?

Grounded in struggles in Canada, the USA, Aotearoa/New Zealand, as well as
transnational activist networks, *Organize!: Building from the Local for Global Justice*
links local organizing with global struggles to make a better world. In over twenty
chapters written by a diverse range of organizers, activists, academics, lawyers,
artists and researchers, this book weaves a rich and varied tapestry of dynamic
strategies for struggle. From community-based labor organizing strategies among
immigrant workers to mobilizing psychiatric survivors, from arts and activism
for Palestine to organizing in support of Indigenous Peoples, the authors reflect
critically on the tensions, problems, limits and gains inherent in a diverse range
of organizing contexts and practices. The book also places these processes in
historical perspective, encouraging us to use history to shed light on contemporary
injustices and how they can be overcome. Written in accessible language,
Organize! will appeal to college and university students, activists, organizers and
the wider public.

Contributors include: Aziz Choudry, Jill Hanley, Eric Shragge, Devlin Kuyek, Kezia
Speirs, Evelyn Calugay, Anne Petermann, Alex Law, Jared Will, Radha D'Souza,
Edward Ou Jin Lee, Norman Nawrocki, Rafeef Ziadah, Maria Bargh, Dave
Bleakney, Abdi Hagi Yusef, Mostafa Henaway, Emilie Breton, Sandra Jeppesen,
Anna Kruzynski, Rachel Sarrasin, Dolores Chew, David Reville, Kathryn Church,
Brian Aboud, Joey Calugay, Gada Mahrouse, Harsha Walia, Mary Foster, Martha
Stiegman, Robert Fisher, Yuseph Katiya, and Christopher Reid.

*"This superb collection needs to find its way into the hands of every activist and
organizer for social justice. In a series of dazzling essays, an amazing group of radical
organizers reflect on what it means to build movements in which people extend control
over their lives. These analyses are jam-packed with insights about anti-racist, anti-
colonial, working-class, and anti-capitalist organizing. Perhaps most crucially, the
authors lay down a key challenge for all activists for social justice: to take seriously
the need to build mass movements for social change. Don't just read this exceptionally
timely and important work—use it too."*
—David McNally, author of *Global Slump: The Economics and Politics of Crisis and
Resistance*